BOUNCERS

CLARENDON STUDIES IN CRIMINOLOGY
Published under the auspices of the Institute of Criminology,
University of Cambridge, the Mannheim Centre, London School
of Economics, and the Centre for Criminological Research, University
of Oxford.

GENERAL EDITOR: PER-OLOF WIKSTRÖM (*University of Cambridge*)

EDITORS: ALISON LIEBLING AND MANUEL EISNER
(*University of Cambridge*)

DAVID DOWNES, PAUL ROCK, AND JILL PEAY
(*London School of Economics*)

ROGER HOOD, LUCIA ZEDNER, AND RICHARD YOUNG
(*University of Oxford*)

Recent titles in this series:

Crime and Markets: Essays in Anti-criminology
Ruggiero

Parliamentary Imprisonment in Northern Ireland:
Resistance, Management, and Release
McEvoy

Repair or Revenge: Victims and Restorative Justice
Strang

Policing World Society:
Historical Foundations of International Police Cooperation
Deflem

Investigating Murder:
Detective Work and the Police Response to Criminal Homicide
Innes

Accountability in Restorative Justice
Roche

Universal Jurisdiction: International and Municipal Legal Perspectives
Reydams

Bouncers

Violence and Governance in the
Night-time Economy

DICK HOBBS
PHILIP HADFIELD
STUART LISTER
SIMON WINLOW

OXFORD
UNIVERSITY PRESS

*This book has been printed digitally and produced in a standard specification
in order to ensure its continuing availability*

OXFORD
UNIVERSITY PRESS

Great Clarendon Street, Oxford OX2 6DP

Oxford University Press is a department of the University of Oxford.
It furthers the University's objective of excellence in research, scholarship,
and education by publishing worldwide in

Oxford New York

Auckland Cape Town Dar es Salaam Hong Kong Karachi
Kuala Lumpur Madrid Melbourne Mexico City Nairobi
New Delhi Shanghai Taipei Toronto
With offices in
Argentina Austria Brazil Chile Czech Republic France Greece
Guatemala Hungary Italy Japan South Korea Poland Portugal
Singapore Switzerland Thailand Turkey Ukraine Vietnam

Oxford is a registered trade mark of Oxford University Press
in the UK and in certain other countries

Published in the United States
by Oxford University Press Inc., New York

© D. Hobbs, S. Winlow, S. Lister, and P. Hadfield 2003

The moral rights of the author have been asserted

Database right Oxford University Press (maker)

Reprinted 2008

ISBN 978-0-19-928800-7

General Editor's Introduction

The *Clarendon Studies in Criminology* was inaugurated in 1994 under the auspices of the centres of criminology at the Universities of Cambridge and Oxford, and the London School of Economics. It was the successor to the *Cambridge Studies in Criminology*, founded by Sir Leon Radzinowicz and J.W.C Turner almost sixty years ago.

Criminology is a field of study that covers everything from research into the causes of crime to the politics of the operations of the criminal justice system. Researchers in different social and behavioural sciences, criminal justice and law, all make important contributions to our understanding of the phenomena of crime. The *Clarendon Studies in Criminology* aims at reflecting this diversity by publishing high-quality theory and research monographs by established scholars as well as by young scholars of great promise from all different kinds of academic backgrounds.

In their conceptually rich, protean odyssey into the 'political economy of violence' *Hobbs, Hadfield, Lister, and Winlow* give an essentially ethnographic account of the 'night-time economy' as 'the context in which bouncers ply their trade'. They reveal that 'bouncers are complex human beings working in an often stressful environment' and argue that 'the quasi-liminal zones that have developed in our urban centres are essentially non-conducive to normative comportment'. *Bouncers: Violence and Governance in the Night-time Economy* is a challenging narrative and political analysis of a central problem of order in contemporary urban areas. It includes expressive descriptions and insights into the inner workings of city-centre nightlife and its management of disorder. It also raises important questions about social control. The book is likely to attract a wide readership among those that are interested in the politics and governance of crime and disorder.

Per-Olof H Wikström,
University of Cambridge
February 2003

Contents

Yes all human life is inevitably here

In a midnight circus
And I must make it clear
That the beer is pricey, the music pulsating
The atmosphere is intoxicating
We four will try to illustrate the sort of things that happen late
At night in every town
When the pubs are shut and the beer's been downed . . .

Now down at the disco is the place to be
The lights are so bright
Like a colour TV
The music is loud And the beer flows free
It's a disco place for you and me
Now on the door, you pay your money
The place is packed, the place is funny
. . .

. . .

Come to the place
Where the beat pulsates
In the heat of the night
The walls gyrate
In the bowels of hell
The scent is strong
There's sex in the air
And the hunt is on
And the children of England
Sing their song

John Godber, *Bouncers*

Introduction

Russ'z Bar

This city was once the epitome of British prosperity, its skyline dominated by heavy industry. Now waves of de-industrialization and the expansion of consumer capitalism have changed the place almost beyond recognition. Most of its buildings were created during the false dawn of the 1960s boom years, when 'jobs for all' in the local factories, machine shops, and engineering works forged the optimism of its once-gleaming modernist brutality. The remnants of this urban dream now merge with Victorian debris to form a jumble of bricks and mortar that is part threat, part promise. Approaching Russ'z Bar you hear the dull thud of bass-heavy dance music, blending with a cacophony of indistinct sounds emitted from the other nearby venues. Nothing much happens in or around Russ'z during the day; draymen deliver and cleaners clean, but little else besides. The streets are full of the unemployed killing time window-shopping, and wan-faced wage slaves grabbing a sandwich and a fag before the afternoon grind begins in earnest. But Russ'z is a night place.

Down the stairs to the basement bar, past a print of an old Chicago newspaper proclaiming the St. Valentine's Day Massacre, a photograph of a dead film star, another of a suited 'Rat Pack' looking smart and smoking cigarettes in 1960s Vegas. There are other more local images, an old industrial scene with men staring unsmiling at the camera with their sleeves rolled up, arms folded, and a photograph of a busy pre-war street vaguely identifiable as an area just around the corner. Perhaps the licensee has a casual day-job as a sociologist with a deep-seated sense of post-modern irony.

The carpets, a heavily soiled shade of dark blue, waft beer into the stale atmosphere with every step. I greet my colleagues, talk bollocks

for twenty minutes, and then, by 8.30, the punters start arriving. They are out for a good time and it is my job to watch over them.
The lighting is low and customers navigate the rooms with the aid of neon and whirling spotlights. The DJ controls the lighting system from a raised booth. He decides how fast and in which order the lights will change, move, and flash, creating different moods to match the music. For the most part it is light enough to make out the features of customers, their comportment, and the odd designer label or logo. For brighter light to see and be seen, head for the bar; it is bright enough there to count out your money. Three huge refrigerators emitting a powerful glow like walk-in tanning booths, display chilled and premium packaged hangovers at three quid a bottle.
The bar's clientele resemble a football crowd, or customers in a particularly crowded street market, out in their best clothes. Clusters of drinkers form protective enclaves as shuffling trade routes to the bar and toilet form and dissolve around them. The DJ plays mainly pop and commercial dance music, with a sprinkling of more nostalgic sounds. Occasionally he will begrudgingly play a request and give a brief spiel over the microphone to a group out on a stag or hen night, or a 'dedication' for an eighteenth birthday or an office night out. Getting the beers in, drinking and leering, laughing, shouting to be heard, singing, showing off, and checking out the 'talent' are the main activities now. No one's dancing yet—too early, but the symptoms of night fever are multiplying rapidly. The sickly sweet smell of dry ice emanates from smoke machines hanging from the ceiling, creating a distinctive lingering odour as it mixes with perfume and aftershave, the smell of stale beer, cigarette smoke, sweat, and if you are standing adjacent to the men's toilets, those blue tablets that they put in the urinals. Russ'z is known as a good spot for unwinding with friends. Alcohol, sex, drugs: on a night like this everyone's on a promise. As the advert in the local paper enquires, 'why go anywhere else?'

This is a book about the political economy of violence. The project started life in 1998 as ' "Bouncers: The art and economics of intimidation".[1] ESRC project number L133251050'. Initially our central

---

[1] Throughout our research we use the terms 'bouncers', 'doorstaff', 'door security', 'door supervisors', etc. interchangeably—the former being the more historically grounded UK and international colloquialism.

concern was to understand the dynamics of interpersonal violence and explore any relationships between the occupation of 'bouncing,' de-industrialization, and the transformation of masculine identities. However, soon after the project commenced our concerns broadened to encompass the context within which bouncers ply their trade. We began to explore the money behind the muscle, and the political and economic forces that shaped the contemporary nighttime economy. The fieldwork and writing continued for two and a half years after the money from the ESRC grant ran out.[2]

We are fully in accord with Courtwright's contention that 'A grant, a computer, and six variables spanning the last decade are not enough to comprehend... violence and disorder' (1996:7), and from the outset we sought to adopt an appreciative stance to an occupational group whose physicality and demeanour all too easily invoke dismissive sneers from behind the protective shadow of broadsheet sensibilities. We met bouncers who risked their bodies every time they went to work, and who carried out their jobs responsibly, treating customers with respect. We also met bouncers who were violent, enjoyed confrontation, and showed little respect for anyone. One night during our fieldwork at an English seaside resort, a bouncer working at a large nightclub at the end of the town's pier had jumped, in total darkness, into icy water 250 metres out to sea to save the life of a reveller who had fallen from the pier. On the same night we observed a bouncer at one of the town's other nightspots grab a man half his size by the throat and smash him against a parked car. Bully, hero, villain, gentleman, street-corner politician, as this book will show, bouncers are complex human beings working in an often stressful environment; as such we should not be surprised to find that in the course of their work they display a range of emotions and personality traits.

When the media first discovered that two academics had been awarded public money to research the world of bouncers, we found our fledgling project filling up pages and airtime that would otherwise be dominated by the weather and the New Year sales. The wave of attention that the project generated was not always of a positive nature. A Sunday tabloid printed a cartoon of a gorilla

[2] Earlier versions of some of the material appearing in this book has appeared in a number of journal articles: Hadfield et al., 2001; Hadfield et al., 2002; Hobbs et al., 2000; Hobbs et al., 2002; Lister et al., 2000; Winlow et al., 2001.

wearing a dinner jacket and a mortar board: a local radio station suggested that public money would be spent on drinking in night-clubs, and provincial hacks insisted on associating the project with various atrocities linked to pubs and nightclubs in their own back-woods Gomorrah. But we also received dozens of phone calls, letters and emails, from doorstaff, police, local government officers, victims of violence, and their parents. Letters came from people serving prison sentences, phone calls came from doctors treating the casual-ties. All had been touched personally or professionally by violence in the night-time economy and they all had stories to tell. Some warned us not to get involved, many offered information and assistance, others pleaded for help, but cumulatively this deluge of responses convinced us that we were on to something and enabled us to hit the ground running.

One of the authors had worked as a bouncer whilst conducting postgraduate research, and for this project he carried out a covert ethnography of bouncing far away from his home turf in a Midlands city. One author had worked as a DJ and club promoter and used this insider knowledge to interview stakeholders and players in the night-time economy, while another of the authors came to the project with a specialism in socio-legal issues which he applied while investigat-ing aspects of control and regulation. The fourth author had an interest in violence, organized crime, and the political economy. All of the authors enjoy drinking alcohol, a point worth making considering the misconceptions of certain sections of the alcohol and leisure industries who appear to regard our work as being linked to the temperance movement. We have received outraged letters, cheap jibes and insults, and on one occasion a cartoon Wanted poster of one of the authors was published in a trade paper in an attempt to discredit our project (it was not even a good likeness). We would like to thank all those with a vested interest in suppressing the 'bad news' for keeping us on our toes.

The authors, who are listed in no particular order, fully acknow-ledge the contribution of Steve Hall who, with Dick Hobbs, was the co-grant holder on the original ESRC project that ran from 1998–2000. The authors would also like to thank Betsy Stanko, Director of the ESRC Violence Research Programme who provided valuable contacts, as well as a forum to present early versions of our work. Betsy was never less than helpful and supportive at all times. We are also grateful to Alan Houghton, then of Lifeline, for his advice and wisdom during the process of formulating the project, to Andy Walker for his insider knowledge, to Lee Monaghan for his insight, and to Tony Leonard for the extraordinary access that he offered the research team.

Initially, with the notable exception of Tony Leonard, we received little support from the police, who seemed so tied up by the political restraints of inter-agency co-operation that they were unable to publicly acknowledge the blindingly obvious problems being generated in British streets every Friday and Saturday night. They seemed to fear casting an investment blight upon their town or city, and consequently we were accused by the police of exaggerating, and in one case of 'scaremongering': the latter from a police force who, within a year, were employing us as consultants into what had suddenly become a 'problem'. The official recognition by the police of this problem came in the summer of 2000 with the publication of detrimental crime figures, an acknowledgement of the relationship between alcohol and violence, and the commencement of the Labour Party's re-election campaign. From that time on we have been afforded a great deal of co-operation from police officers around the country.

During the course of the research, data was collected from the following UK towns and cities: Birmingham, Birstall, Blackpool, Bradford, Bridlington, Cambridge, Cardiff, Crawley, Doncaster, Driffield, Durham, Hereford, Hull, Leeds, Leicester, Lincoln, Liverpool, London, Macclesfield, Manchester, Mansfield, Middlesbrough, Newcastle-under-Lyme, Newcastle, Nottingham, Oswestry, Penrith, Pontefract, Preston, Salford, Scarborough, Solihull, Southport, Stamford, Stockport, Stoke, Truro, Watford, Wolverhampton, Worthing, and York.[3]

Our focus is the night-time economy and the dilemmas of control that this new economy poses. Consequently, the punters, those who spend their hard-earned cash in this economy, along with the barstaff, cleaners, taxi-drivers, and all of the other non-coercive nighttime workers have not received the acknowledgment that they undoubtedly deserve. Their stories will have to wait for another time. However, although they do not receive top billing, we have not disregarded them entirely. Indeed, the very nature of this study

---

[3] One of the above fieldwork locations is referred to in the text as 'Eastville' in order to honour a promise of anonymity to all those who assisted us.

6 Violence and Governance in the Night-time Economy

involved immersion in the night, and it would have been impossible to ignore the workers or revellers who constitute the majority of the night-time population, and provide both a context and a human backdrop for the problems of control in the night-time economy.

Dick Hobbs would like to thank Rob Hornsby, Louise Westmarland, Laurie Taylor, Terry Morris, Mickey (the gout) Childs, Geoff (the editor) Pearson, Richard Wright, Bob Lilly, Greg Condry, Grace Zaffutto, Patricia Rawlinson, Paul Crace, Tony Coutures, Steve Wraith, Graham Hurley, and Tiny the Dog for various, occasionally work-related, acts of friendship. Thanks to John Louth of OUP for his support of our work, to Nigel South for timing his suggestions so well, and to Nigel Fielding for the time and effort that he gave up in reading part of the manuscript. His suggestions and comments were always enlightening and insightful. David Downes was fully behind this project from the off. Always encouraging, his gentle cajoling and prompting was crucial in getting this project started as well as finished.

Back at 'work,' the late Ian Taylor was relentless in insisting that academic work should be fun. Ian was totally supportive of this project, and always generous in sharing his priceless time. Dave Chaney retired 32 not out, but not before he fired some good ideas our way, and Ian Roberts made some excellent comments on an early draft of one of the chapters. John 'I'll phone for a cab' Tierney read various parts of this book and was always generous with his wine, his time, and his knowledge of criminal justice politics. Robin Williams read several chapters of the book and commented with characteristic precision. He also taught DH the value of a long walk. With the management of British universities increasingly resembling a Marx Brothers movie, DH is particularly grateful to both Tierney and Williams for persisting in defying its boneheaded managerialism by laughing at it. Finally Dick Hobbs would like to acknowledge the usual suspects, in particular Mary and Jack Hobbs, Pat, who despite his discovery of the night-time economy has grown up nicely, Nik who is smart enough as it is, and Sue without whom . . .

Phil Hadfield would like to thank everyone who helped him to turn a good idea into a major life project. Vicky Battell, Liza Dixon, Martin Elvins, Rob Hornsby, Kate O'Brien, Andrew Smith, and Emma Uprichard continue to inject fresh supplies of life and laughter into that project. PH remains indebted to the staff and students of Keele's Criminology and Philosophy departments 1995–1999 for permitting him the indulgence of a second adolescence whilst getting his act together and turning his vices into virtues. PH was born three times in Stoke-on-Trent, once in North Staffs Royal Infirmary, once again on the dancefloor of Shelley's and thirdly in S and Q Blocks Horwood (solemn respect is due to all (pri)mates). PH still owes much to the support and inspiration of Evi Girling, Barry Godfrey, Ruth Jamieson, Tony Jefferson, Ian Loader, Brian Smart, and Richard Sparks. PH's first-year tutor Lyn Hancock deserves a special mention for her encouragement and for giving him his first academic kick up the backside. Ann Musgrave and Kath Pye went some way beyond the call of duty in sympathetically fielding his constant enquiries. More recently, Anthony Bottoms and Loraine Gelsthorpe indulged PH greatly in his efforts to produce a 30,000-word thesis in nine months. Barry Godfrey and Bronwyn Morrison gave freely of their time and insight in reading Chapter 2 of this book. Beyond institutional walls, a number of police officers have helped and inspired PH, in particular this list must include Jan Brown, Paul Dubberley, Mike Schofield, Laz Szomoru, and Steve Thomas. Elsewhere in the moon-washed field, PH's journey was illuminated by Dave Haslam, C.P. Lee, Andy Lovatt, Ken Mackie, and Pete Walsh. The necessary nocturnal habits for researching this book were nurtured from infancy by Sam (oldest roadie in the business) and Una Hadfield. Their attempts to instil common sense remain futile. For PH, this book is dedicated to Lily whose arrival was the best bit of all.

Stuart Lister wishes to acknowledge his co-authors, Dick Hobbs, for opening the iron doors of academia, Phil Hadfield, for academic solidarity, and Simon Winlow, for not taking up the offer of a bare knuckle dust-up to determine authorship order. Many thanks to the officers of Queen's Garden Police Station (formerly D-Division), Humberside Police for co-operating with (i.e. tolerating) yet another 'bloody researcher' at what was an acutely sensitive time for all concerned at the division. In particular, Sergeant John Blanchard, Inspector Ian Fleming, PC Taj Krawczyk, former Chief Constable Tony Leonard, and Sergeant John Savage should each be singled out for praise.

Colleagues at the Centre for Criminal Justice Studies, University of Leeds merit great credit for producing a non-coercive working atmosphere, as do the Estate lads for keeping the bushes of the paths and the cleaners for keeping the offices ... In particular, Adam Crawford provided intellectual acumen and continues to be a willing learning resource *par excellence*; Ben 'Kinkladzee' Fitzpatrick merrily tolerated the customary pre-football outbursts; Clive Walker, Head of Law Department, steadfastly and expertly held 'the collective' together; and Dave Wall, in unique fashion, mainlined venomous wit into the writing-up process.

Stalwart friends in the licensed trade have served SL well. Notably, Gerard Feltham, Nigel Long, and Nick Pring oversaw 'pleasures and wayward distractions' and instilled confidence that the project was running along the right lines. SL also wishes to thank other acquaintances less commercially indebted to the booze trade, for facilitating and enriching the research process. Jonathon Smith organized a particularly enjoyable whistle-stop tour of three UK police forces and never failed to see the ironies of police compliance. Neil 'Daily Mail' Sears kick-started a central aspect of the research and continues to exude infectious enthusiasm for the project even to this day. SL is most grateful to Anne Deehan, Jonathon Tuffin, and Rob Warm, for reading and commenting upon a part of the manuscript. Thanks also to Marc Cunliffe for endorsing this book's 'realistic' approach to sociology. Special thanks to Maria Humphrey for unswerving support throughout the life of the project.

Simon Winlow, persisting with an emerging theme in his research, cannot personally thank anybody for their support as the people who helped the most are happily destined to spend their lives free from the vague attractions of the academic spotlight. To most of them, academic enterprise is about as useful as a concrete parachute, and they can see no earthly reason in seeking to analyse the 'real' world. After surviving some of the more 'exciting' evenings afforded by this piece of research, SW was often inclined to agree. However, SW would like to thank all of those who helped with the ethnography, and those generous enough to grant an interview. SW would also like to mention some people who didn't help with the book in any way whatsoever, but were occasionally polite enough to ask how it was going and if it was finished yet. So, thanks to all my family, and Sara, for all the usual reasons, and thanks to all the criminology staff and students at the University of Teesside for keeping the nine-to-five interesting.

Communally we wish to thank all of the bouncers, planners, lawyers, licensing officers, magistrates, drug dealers, town centre managers, club promoters, bar staff, residents, venue managers, taxi-drivers, bodybuilders, noise experts, takeaway staff, surgeons, licensing and security consultants, street cleaners, crime prevention officers, hoteliers, sex workers, journalists, restaurateurs, licensing inspectors, ambulance crews, 'cultural industry facilitators,' property owners, DJs, hardnuts, posers, punters, blaggers, and loafers who made this book possible.

In Chapter 1 we describe some of the key characteristics of the night-time economy which provide a forum for our later discussions of consumption, urban regeneration, leisure, and pleasure. We also discuss those very special qualities of the night, which meld with commercial interests to produce opportunities for disorder and transgression. Chapter 2 presents a case history of Manchester, the world's first 'industrial' city, where, in the face of grinding poverty, the new urban poor sought solace in the beer house and singing saloon and the City's industrialists devised new levers of discipline in order to secure a docile workforce. We go on to trace the development and regulation of commercial night-time leisure in the twentieth century within the context of fundamental social and economic changes culminating in the demise of the industries upon which Manchester had been built.

In Chapter 3 we examine the ascendant political and economic project which sought to build a new post-industrial Manchester of service industries, high technology, sport and 'culture' via programmes of environmental regeneration and entrepreneurial governance. We describe how, as part of this project, Manchester's new entrepreneurial élite began to embrace, promote, and commodify the City's night-time leisure economy as a zone of liminality and transgression closely associated with hitherto marginal elements of popular culture and sexual identity. Criminal networks also sought lucrative new opportunities within this leisure economy, which prompted a series of violent struggles for control of the city centre's recreational drug and security markets.

Chapter 4 offers insight into the changes that have taken place after dark from the perspective of a veteran of the night-time economy. In particular, this chapter enables us to consider night-time leisure in terms of the shifts occurring within Britain's wider political economy. The chapter enables the reader to understand fluctuations in the leisure market and developing forms of youth culture through the eyes of someone who has experienced four decades in the shadow of bright neon lights.

In Chapter 5, bouncers speak for themselves about the subtle harshness of door work. Most were highly articulate in their ability to describe the lived experience of dealing with violence and of attempting to impose order in a chaotic and stressful environment, where customers are encouraged to cast aside day-time protocols and rules of restraint and embrace transgression. In this chapter we utilize classic sociological literature on the occupational culture of the public police in analysing the enacted realities of door work and the commonality of problems faced by purveyors of force, whether their mandate be provided by the state or by commercial interests.

Chapter 6 examines the local state's attempts to regulate the social action of bouncers through the introduction of licensing systems. We consider the politico-economic context out of which these 'registration schemes' emerged and, in so doing, implicitly draw reference to the outcomes of the regulatory process. We proceed to discuss the operational scope and haphazard implementation of licensing schemes, using an array of interview data from persons on either side of the regulatory divide. We engage with the literature on private security to discuss both the tensions of state-sponsored training regimes and the broader role of bouncers within the night-time economy. We conclude by locating the regulatory drive within attempts by the state and economy to 'professionalize' the trade through virtuous accommodation.

In Chapter 7 we consider some of the origins of bouncing as an occupation that utilizes fundamental essences of industrial masculinity and applies them to a post-industrial setting. We look at bouncing as class work and the links between bouncing and organized crime. Both dimensions, we argue, feature at their core violence as a personal and commercial resource. We proceed to suggest that it is in cases where doorwork is linked to organized crime that the weaknesses of the state become fully exposed and sinister practices emerge that threaten to spread beyond the shaded parameters of the night.

In Chapter 8 we argue that our study raises a number of important issues for public policy. We identify a series of profound and dynamic shifts in governmental arenas as diverse as alcohol licensing, planning law, public and private policing, and town centre management, all of which impact significantly upon the nature of the night-time urban environment. A number of normative issues are raised in relation to processes of de-regulation and marketization broadly identifiable across these arenas. In the light of this discussion, we offer a critique of recent crime prevention strategies for the night-time economy, pinpointing an apparent failure to adopt integrated and interventionist approaches to municipal control and the atrophy of local democratic accountability and individual and collective opportunity.

In our concluding chapter (Chapter 9), we argue that our study reveals much more than a chequered and apparently discordant history of hedonism, capitalism, politics, criminality, repression, pride, debauchery, machismo, and greed and suggest that urban leisure markets are intimately linked to the political economy of place. Indeed, we argue that attempts to manipulate the liminal (Turner, 1967; 1969) and transgressive aspects of city life now lie close to the heart of contemporary municipal governance. Further, we stress the historical role of the state in enabling new forms of social control to emerge in accord with the prerogatives of the market.

We finished this study with feelings of trepidation. We do not fear bouncers, as for all the problems that they pose, they perform an essential function in an environment that craves a very specific, malleable, and commercially functional form of social control. If their muscular presence were suddenly removed, the state police would not fill the void. But we do fear the anarchic and predatory marketplace that has been so irresponsibly embraced by politicians and regulators. If you cram tens of thousands of individuals together from the age group most prone to criminal behaviour and then fill them with alcohol, does anyone really believe that it won't occasionally 'go off'? This is a book about an environment where it regularly 'goes off'.

1

Let the Good Times Roll: Liminality and the Night-time Economy

Thus leisure enters into the division of social labour (Lefebvre, 1976:84).

It is almost nine and the bar is beginning to fill up. I take first shift at the door with a bouncer with years of thick-skinned experience, and make my way up to the top of the staircase and out onto the street. It is beginning to turn dark and now looks a lot different from when I entered the bar an hour ago. A large group of young women on a hen night pass by on the other side of the street fervently singing at the top of their voices. Some of them are in fancy dress. Several men pass on the other side of the street, and both groups shout abuse at each other, swearing loudly. Further down the street I can see a parked police van and some officers in shirtsleeves talking to a group of casually dressed young men. Three young women with blonde hair and colourful matching outfits are standing on the corner of the street giving out flyers advertising a nearby nightclub. Seasoned drinkers can't be bothered with being polite to the young women and merely wave them away, while others take the flyers only to discard them in the bin a couple of metres further on.

Couples flirt, groups have shouted discussions across the street, people run to catch up with friends, others wander aimlessly. The general flow of human traffic is moving from left to right along the street, from the quieter venues of the early bar route onto the disco bars further along. Later, between ten thirty and eleven thirty, the flow will change direction as many people head back towards the more popular nightclubs. The deluge is coming; the rush is about to begin.

'Let's go get stoned' *Ray Charles*

Venture into most British towns and city centres during the day and you might be hard pressed to notice any evidence that the night-time economy exists. The social world of daylight is almost completely divorced from the night at virtually every point of reference. Branches of the big leisure chains start the day as pseudo-café bars, gently mutating through coffees, bar snacks, and microwaved lunches, until the late afternoon when they raise the corporately controlled decibel levels of the sound system to cater for those shop and office workers with no taste for rush hour commuting. Night-time identities are tucked away in shadowed alcoves, and the true identity of the bars and clubs that dominate our city centres after dark are often hidden behind shutters during daylight hours, while there are many others with nothing more than a portal tendering the aromatic remnants of last night's burger and lager fest as evidence of nocturnal activity. Other economic staples of the night-time economy are also hard to detect; takeaways often remain closed during the day, the kebab vans are in lock-up garages, taxis are less common, drug dealers are in bed, and social comportment is, of course, very different.

When workers and shoppers evacuate our urban centres in the late afternoon and early evening, trains become engorged, queues for buses snake the pavements, and cars inch between traffic lights, all keen to join the journey back to the suburbs and the commuting karma of safe streets. It is not hard to imagine tumbleweed blowing down the subdued high streets of British towns and cities during this prelude to the 'change over'. Seven o'clock brings the arrival of a new clientele. The dull thud of bass heavy dance music reverberates through the now dark streets to welcome or ward off those racing to or fleeing from the urban night, with its pubs, bars, nightclubs, and associated industries of hedonistic enablement. What comes next is darkness, and a multitude of leisure and pleasure opportunities for those seduced by the night-time economy's excess of commodities, signs, and services.

Consumerism, carnival, and forms of incorporation and exclusion are increasingly played out in our after dark, city centre leisure environments, and it is here, amid the booming reverb and intoxication that the young, and sometimes the not-so-young, increasingly invest meaning. The night-time economy is also an environment diffuse with various forms of disorder, and its clientele, attracted as they are by the promise of pleasure, excitement, and excess, need to be controlled. This is why bouncers frame the doorways of the pubs, clubs, and bars that lie at the core of the night-time economy's cultural and commercial reality.

The employment by licensed premises of personnel to ensure a level of order acceptable to commercial prosperity is of course not new (see Chapter 4: Benney, 1981 [1936]:181–183, 186–187; Pearson, 1973; Chapter 3: Samuel, 1981:216–217). However, the past decade has seen an unprecedented expansion in the business of bouncing. At night normal rules of comportment become negotiated via the acceptability of varying levels of intoxication, of aggressive sexuality, and of a demeanour inappropriate to the concerns of daylight hours. The police enforce the law, but the bouncer operates according to a highly ambiguous cocktail of law, occupational codes, and personal discretion that is underpinned by an interpretation of what is good and what is bad for business.

This chapter will examine the development of the night-time economy in the context of historical and socio-legal sources. It will provide the empirical and theoretical base upon which the study will stand, and introduce the reader to what we argue are new strategies of the forces of capital that have evolved in response to de-industrialization and subsequent economic restructuring. In essence, we argue that these strategies, which involve the promotion and commodification of the night-time economy as a zone of liminality and transgression, closely associated with previously marginal elements of popular culture and gendered identity, should be regarded as a paradigmatic form of post-industrial entrepreneurial governance.

Crawling from the wreckage: cultural industries and urban regeneration

The cheapest and easiest way to become an influential man and be looked up to by the community at large was to stand behind a bar, wear a cluster-diamond pin, and sell whiskey (Mark Twain).

Since the early 1970s, significant transformations have occurred within Western cities. These changes involve two key interrelated processes: first, a shift in economic development from the industrial to the post-industrial; and second, a significant reorientation of urban governance, involving a move away from the managerial functions of local service provision, toward an entrepreneurial stance primarily focused upon the facilitation of economic growth (Davies, 1988; Hall and Hubbard, 1996; 1998; Harvey, 1989a; Randall, 1995). In many British towns and cities these processes have been intimately connected with the development of night-time leisure economies (Bianchini, 1995; Jones, 1999; Jowit, 1999; Lovatt and O'Connor, 1995; Lovatt, 1999; Montgomery, 1994). In the following paragraphs we will initially describe the nature and constitution of such economies, before proceeding to emphasize their contemporary significance within the political and economic context of the post-industrial city and shifting paradigms of urban governance.

A number of scholars have linked changes in the political economy of place to the decline of industrialism and 'Fordism', and the emergence of post-industrial, and 'Post-Fordist' modes of economic organization and forms of work (Amin, 1994; Esser and Hirsch, 1989; Lash and Urry, 1987; Martin, 1988). As the resilient flame of the post-war economic boom was finally extinguished during the early 1970s, many British cities entered a new era of significant post-industrial re-structuring (Healey et al., 1992; Martin, 1999; Pacione, 1997). Economic redevelopment in these 'rustbelt' cities often involved shifts from manufacturing to the provision of services, and shifts in the labour process from lifetime employment to flexible and temporary forms of working, frequently involving fixed-term contracts and seasonal, casual, or part-time employment, which necessitated new forms of mobility and adaptability within a workforce previously defined by its largely static and regimented structure (Jessop, 1994; Mingione, 1991). Within the 'Post-Fordist' context, work is often conducted at times, and in locations, which in the industrial era would have been regarded as 'unsociable' or atypical (Gregson et al., 1999; Kreitzman, 1999).

Furthermore, as Scott has argued, within contemporary post-industrial cities, we are witnessing 'a very marked convergence between the spheres of cultural and economic development' (1997:323). Others, such as Zukin, point to the increasing importance of 'symbolic economies based on such abstract products as financial instruments, information, and "culture"—i.e. art, food, fashion, music and tourism' (1998:826). More generally, it has been argued that the products of economic activity are becoming increasingly semiotic and aesthetic, rather than simply 'utilitarian' in value and form (Baudrillard, 1968; Lash and Urry, 1994; Scott, 1997) as part of a process referred to by Featherstone (1991) as the 'aestheticization of everyday life'. Within this context, some commentators argue that many Western cities are reinventing themselves as sites of consumption and leisure (Hannighan, 1998; Zukin, 1991), with leisure being narrowly conflated with spending, becoming 'yet another economic sector' (Worpole, 1991:138).

Moreover, as the 'urban fortunes' (Logan and Molotch, 1987) of many post-industrial towns and cities become tied to the vicissitudes of local and global markets in consumption, leisure, and tourism (Urry, 1990), it has become increasingly important to attract investment from external and 'mobile' sources. Thus cities are forced to compete, and as Begg (1999:805) notes, 'the competitive ethos is increasingly affecting cities, obliging them to be more active in marketing themselves and in trying to identify and reinforce their assets'.

Whilst the economic and cultural life of cities has also become increasingly infused with 'global' influences, far from undermining the importance of locality, processes of globalization involve the 'new dynamics of re-localization ... the achievement of a new global-local nexus' (Robins, 1991:34–35). Concomitantly, 'the free flow of capital across the surface of the globe ... places strong emphasis upon the particular', producing 'a heightened sense of awareness of what makes a place special' (Harvey, 1989b:271). As Robertson argues, 'globalization ... involves the linking of localities' but also involves the intensification or '"invention" of locality ... an ideology of home' (1995:35). In the national and global marketplace competitive advantage is enhanced by producing and consolidating difference and variety (Robertson, 1992:173) via economic agglomeration and specialization (Porter, 1996). According to some commentators the advantages of 'clustering', are especially salient for the 'cultural/leisure' industries, especially when their products draw upon specifically local or regional cultural assets or traditions, becoming infused with 'peculiar imageries and sensibilities' (Scott, 1997:333), which connect product image to place (Molotoch, 1996).

A major problem for many British cities is that the modernist planning policies of the post-war years destroyed many unique features of the urban landscape and segregated and homogenized urban spaces and activities in ways which 'contributed significantly to the demise of the public realm' (Punter, 1990:9). As a result, British cities became ' ... impoverished aesthetically, socially and culturally ... increasingly distinguished from their European [sic] counterparts by their design mediocrity, deadness and public squalor' (Punter, ibid.).

During the late 1980s, in response to de-industrialization and the loss of traditional sources of (typically male) employment, local government administrations in Europe and North America began to acknowledge the potentially important role that 'cultural/leisure' activities could play in urban regeneration (Bassett, 1993; Bianchini and Parkinson, 1993; Dziembowska-Kowalska and Funck, 1999). In Britain, this realization was informed by a small, but significant, body of research exploring the links between urban life, cultural activities, and the reinvigoration of city centres via novel planning initiatives (see Bianchini et al., 1988; Comedia, 1991; Montgomery, 1990; Worpole, 1992). Rather than focusing exclusively on the traditionally narrow conceptions of 'culture' employed in British urban policy, which had been restricted to 'the arts,' these studies assumed a wider definition of culture, one encompassing popular cultural and leisure-based commercial activities (Bianchini, 1993). Furthermore, a number of consultants and academics suggested that such activities had the potential to reanimate and revitalize public space in British towns and cities. As Montgomery (1995b:143) argued: 'Central to this approach is the view that cultural activities can . . . provide the catalyst for physical and environmental renewal, attract spending and capital investment to an area, generate new economic activity and jobs and change or enhance an area's image'.

Whilst acknowledging that urban public spaces seem especially vulnerable to problems such as crime and anti-social behaviour, the pessimistic analyses of urban life found in the work of classical sociologists such as Park (1916), Simmel (1995), and Wirth (1938) were implicitly rejected. Rather than seeing the urban public realm as a site of personal estrangement, these commentators followed Jane Jacobs (1961) in their criticism of modernist urban planning, and their embrace of Southern European notions of public sociability, based upon face-to-face interaction and the animation of public space.

By the early 1990s, many British towns and cities, notably Manchester, Leeds, Liverpool, and Wolverhampton, were pursuing city centre regeneration initiatives in which popular cultural activities integral to the night-time economy were playing a leading role (O'Connor, 1998; O'Connor and Wynne, 1992). In such places, the night-time economy, that 'previously marginal zone of space and time', was 'being promoted as central to the image of a modern "European" city' (O'Connor and Wynne, 1996a:9). Such changes have involved nothing less than a 'process of restructuring in which many of those activities deemed peripheral to the activity of the "productive" or "Fordist" city have now moved centre stage' (ibid.:4).

The business of pleasure: communities of consumption in every-night-life

...the more ritualized the occasion, the more it has to be presented as an autonomous set of events, in which the backstage props are kept entirely out of view of audiences or observers (Giddens, 1984:127).

The construction of centres of leisure consumption to physically replace nineteenth-century centres of production and their commercial and bureaucratic infrastructures, is a marked characteristic of late twentieth-century and early twenty-first century British cities. Manchester is the most visible of these new cities, with Leeds, Newcastle, Glasgow, and others following closely behind. As industrial capitalism created the industrial city, so consumer capitalism has created quite distinct night-time leisure arenas such as contemporary Soho in London, Newcastle's Quayside, and Manchester's Gay Village, as well as a multitude of less-celebrated provincial High Street locations. The velocity of the capital hitting these old industrial and commercial centres has been quite remarkable, and its trajectory ricochets around cities built on the rhythms of industrial production as the configuration of the night-time economy continues to evolve. As Mike Payne of nightclub giants First Leisure, a company which at the time operated over forty venues throughout the UK explained, 'There has been a change in the city centre environment. Councils encouraged bars and they have become important again. Now the nightstrip scene is where the future is' (Finch, 1999:3).

In the opening words of his classic essay 'The Metropolis and Mental Life', George Simmel asserts that 'the deepest problems of modern life flow from the attempt of the individual to maintain the independence and individuality of his existence against the sovereign powers of society, against the weight of the historical heritage and the external culture and techniques of life' (Simmel, 1995 [1903]:30). Simmel's famous reflections on the dynamic estrangement, blasé indifference, and calculative instrumentality of metropolitan social interaction accord with his earlier work on modern experience (1900), in which he argues that individuals increasingly attach importance to a vacuous 'money economy', and construct a sham individualism which finds expression in the pursuit of social distinction and group status. For Simmel, the anonymity and experiential pressures of the urban condition foster an 'external culture' within which individuals adopt various 'techniques of life' in their perpetual struggle for self-assertion and a sense of distinction from the masses, sometimes developing:

...the strangest eccentricities...extravagances of self-distanciation, of caprice, of fastidiousness, the meaning of which is no longer to be found in the content of such activity itself but rather in its being a form of 'being different'—of making oneself noticeable (1995:42).

Simmel was of course writing about developing forms of urbanism brought about by the entrenchment of industrial capitalism, but his analysis of the metropolis has now taken on a new resonance as industrial capitalism dies and consumer capitalism emerges to dominate our economic and cultural life.

Within the contemporary context of de-industrialized urban space, the leisure zones that house, foster, and lend a basic organizational and product-based identity to the night-time economy, are one of many sites of consumption (Gottdiener, 2000:265–285). It is within such a socio-economic context that, 'shopping is elided with leisure, it becomes a hobby, it becomes a way of enacting an identity' (Chaney, 1994:177). This pressure to consume is most keenly felt by youth (Presdee, 2000), and the power of consumerism to create and modify self-identity is increasingly apparent in evolving youth cultures (Miles, 1998) which constitute, we suggest, the dominant cultural form within the enacted environment of the night (McCracken, 1990:xi). Further, within these cultures the pressure to engage with the commodified hyper-reality of the night-time economy, to consume and consume correctly, to be culturally knowing, is increasingly intense (Winlow, forthcoming).

Leisure has become progressively more important to youth (Griffin, 1993; Widdicombe and Wooffitt, 1995), particularly in ex-industrial cultures where previously dominant methods of

forging identity have faded with other Fordist certainties. De-industrialization, and the consequent fragmentation of traditional communities, has led to the erosion of clearly structured, class, and
work-based life patterns (Beck, 1992; Pakulski and Waters, 1992).
Individual lives are now increasingly exposed to processes of dis-
juncture, and the overlapping of shared experiences and attitudes
with, for instance, colleagues or neighbours, is becoming less and
less apparent (Bauman, 2001:160–165). Young people who 'go out'
together, may know relatively little about the lives of other members
of their group. Knowledge of where they work, what they do at
work, of family relationships, and schooling increasingly appear
limited as a range of new concerns assume dominance. Increasingly
what they do know, and know in detail, are the consumption characteristics and patterns of those they share social intimacy with in the
night-time leisure zone, as consumer-led individualization and instrumentality force adaptation within existing patterns of self-identity and social and cultural engagement (see Winlow, forthcoming).

However, we also need to consider ' . . . the shifting societal contexts in which identities are located, as well as the changes in the
social resources on which identity formation seems to depend' (Williams, 2000:32). For those who for geographical, class, or ethnic
reasons possess biographies that exclude them from adopting the
latent assumptions of Fordism, the hedonistic allure of night-life
offers alternative or supplementary means of forging identity,
which due to the sheer weight of capital impacting on the night-
time economy, are overwhelmingly more influential and prominent
than the paltry leisure economies accessed by previous generations.
It is within these contexts that an individual's relationship to the
means of consumption becomes crucial, as it is increasingly on
Friday and Saturday nights that a sense of self is formed, and cama-
raderie is moulded (see Armstrong, 1998). As Malbon argues in his
excellent ethnography of 'clubbing,' the appeal of contemporary
nightlife lies most centrally in its ability to offer a form of 'experiential consuming', that is, 'a form of consuming in which nothing
material is "taken home", but which can nevertheless produce
important memories, emotional experiences and imaginaries (remem-
bered imaginations) that can be sources of identification and thus of
vitality' (1999:183). As regular users of the night-time economy,
groups of young people form loose 'communities' based around
the consumption of a particular set of quasi-liminal experiences in

which the repeated practice of communal rituals offers an important rite of passage to peer approval and group status.

Consumer culture needs to be in constant motion to prevent stultification (Veblen, 1994 [1899]), and the social pressures placed upon young people are considerable. Consequently in order to retain commercial viability, the night-time experience must continually reinvent itself as a potentially liberating respite from work, and at no point be exposed as a packaged, marketed interlude, which is as restrictive in terms of social differentiation as any other aspect of consumption (Rojek, 2000). This is, after all, where the best of *life*, in all its heightened vitality, is lived, the social arena that matters most, a place where culture, consumption, and capital embrace most passionately. The form that this contemporaneous British carnival takes, the night-time economy, offers us an evidentiary snapshot of our economic, social, and cultural life at a particular point in history.

Pivotal to any analysis of this carnivalesque world is consumer capitalism, 'where the pursuit of happiness becomes the only bench mark of value' (Chaney, 1998:541). Situated at the very core of the night-time economy, consumer capitalism drives consumption and offers itself as the resource with which the individual consumer must negotiate in order to receive a direct affirmation of accomplished (bought) identity (Lunt and Livingstone, 1992: 24–25). However, although consumption *à la mode* is manifested in every facet of this economy, it is profoundly susceptible to 'the pure play of signs' (Slater, 1997:11) and engagement with this economy is necessarily transitory. For many it constitutes little more than a compensatory drift coinciding neatly with the transition to full adulthood, at which point other arenas of consumer capitalism such as the do-it-yourself store, the fitness centre, or the out-of-town shopping mall emerge as more appropriate temples of identification and self-actualization.

Central to consumption in the night-time economy are mechanisms of self-affirmation: designer fashions, body language and attitude, which circle of friends you associate with, and which bars or clubs you hold dear. As one of Malbon's informants states when describing his own nights out, 'we don't just go out for a good time, nor even the best of times—we go out to put on a show. Tonight, just like every Saturday night, the curtain was set to go up on another superb performance' (1999:69). Such 'supra-individuality' (Frisby, 1985:98) is driven forward by the foibles of the market; wearing the wrong designer label in the wrong bar can generate sly mocking

(Malbon, 1999), the wrong haircut and you may not make it into your nightclub of choice (Chatterton and Hollands, 2001). The key to achieving and maintaining cultural acceptance, whilst correspondingly displaying some degree of individuality, lies in the ability to consume regularly and knowledgeably. Yet, the pleasure experienced in affirmation and acceptance is crucially both encouraging and fleeting, as the vagaries of market-led fashion are consistent only in their ability to continually mutate (Simmel, 1900).

Good time working

The increasing centrality of leisure identities to a sense of self (Rojek, 1993) is a reaction to changing local and global economic conditions, which have in turn spawned a variety of night-time leisure options through which flow employment as well as commercial opportunities. For, 'one person's leisure is for many others low-paid, part-time and casual work' (Worpole, 1991:138), and as Montgomery (1994:303) notes, a significant part of the evening economy is a cash economy whose labour market:

... is to a large extent flexible and casual: jobs are often part-time, temporary or even supplementary to a day job. For these reasons it is very difficult to gauge the amounts of money which circulate in the evening economy in relation to the goods and services sold and the labour bought...this informal dimension is one of the defining features of an evening economy.[1]

Night-time economic activity in Britain has traditionally been dominated by the licensed trade, in public houses, bars, restaurants, nightclubs, theatres, and music venues, and by gambling establishments such as casinos and bingo halls. However, bar and club economies have also developed ancillary industries to capitalize on the influx of money and market opportunities now flourishing on the crowded streets of our towns and cities. For instance, the hunger that alcohol often inspires has led to the proliferation of fast-food outlets

---

[1] This informal dimension can include undeclared profits and earnings from both legal and illegal transactions. Studies (Beattie, 1986; Winlow, 2001) suggest that the flexible, irregular, and casual nature of much employment in the night-time economy can provide numerous opportunities to earn money whilst remaining 'officially' unemployed. Since these activities are by definition 'hidden', they remain extremely difficult to quantify.

in and around city centres, usually within close proximity to popular bars and clubs. Other trades and services have also recognized the market opportunities offered by the developing night-time economy, 'after midnight on a weekend, the streets are awash with taxis speeding between fares' (Winlow, 2001:120), their drivers favouring night-time working hours over scrambling for fares during the day. Some hotels will rent rooms by the hour, late opening restaurants 'staffed by abuse-resistant waiters' (ibid.), gear both their fare and service delivery to a drunken clientele, and street traders stress the aphrodisiac qualities of plastic roses to drunken and hormonally-charged young men.

The bulk of investment in the night-time economy is centred on the 'business of pleasure' (Bailey, 1986), and is characterized by a flow of capital aimed at the development of licensed premises. That the focus of this capital investment is predominantly upon city centre sites is, we found, typically lamented by the police, yet largely welcomed by the town planners, whose primary aim is to regenerate and preserve the city centre as a focus for public usage. As one town planner in 'Eastville' suggested:

the office market is dead, the residential sector is dead and the retail sector patchy...the leisure sector is so strong that it is just about the only sector where we are seeing new planning applications...licensed premises can generate investment that other usage types can't.

However, the 'problem' with this commercial reality, as identified by police and commentators alike, is that the development of licensed premises can quickly saturate an area (Hadfield et al., 2001; 2002). What Jacobs (1961:256) labels 'the economic equivalent of a fad' occurs because low-risk investments are made in areas 'where success is already a well-established fact' (see Chapter 8). The resultant clustering of licensed premises has well-documented implications for crime and disorder (Hope 1985; Tuck, 1989) as alluded to over forty years ago by Jacobs:

Night spots are today overwhelming the street, and are also overwhelming the very life of the area. Into a district excellent at handling and protecting strangers they have concentrated too many strangers, all in too irresponsible a mood, for any conceivable city society to handle naturally. This duplication of the most profitable use is undermining the base of it's own attraction, as disproportionate duplication and exaggeration of some single use always does in cities (Jacobs, 1961:259).

The night-time economy

The liquor licensing statistics for England and Wales demonstrate a significant and consistent rise in the number of on-licensed premises over the last twenty-five years. For instance, recent figures show that there are presently over 110,000 on-licensed premises, an increase of 30% during this period. This figure is comprised of 78,500 pubs and bars, 28,000 restaurants and hotels, and 3,800 licensed clubs (2,000 of which are 300-plus capacity venues), a respective increase of 20%, 68%, and 28% over the last twenty-five years (Home Office, 2002). Nationally, applications for new on-licences are currently running at over 5,000 a year, of which 3,072 were granted to pubs and bars in 2001–2002. This represents an increase of over 145% on the number of equivalent licences granted in 1980 (ibid.). Within these figures, the relatively recent phenomena of the city-centre-located 'branded high street' bar market has been particularly prominent. The number of such venues has increased by 23% in the last two years, and turnover risen by 22%, to £2.5 billion, over the last year alone (Mintel, 2002). The financial turnover for this market is forecast to rise to £4.4 billion by 2006 (ibid.).

These increases and their subsequent impact upon the urban landscape must be viewed within the context of falling numbers of rural pubs. Estimates suggest that a steady decline in the number of rural licensed premises has occurred over the last twenty years (DETR, 2000a) and that as many as six currently close per week (The Countryside Agency, 2001). It seems clear that over the course of the last two decades the licensed trade has undergone, and continues to undergo, both a sustained period of growth and a significant process of spatial restructuring.

Montgomery identifies the economic value of the sector, suggesting that 'the evening economy represents between 5% to 15% of a local GDP' (1995a:103), and at a national level, the on-licensed leisure trade is clearly making an increasingly significant financial contribution to the British economy. In England and Wales alone the licensed trade, which unlike modern automated production is body-intensive, now employs around one million people, and represents the 'biggest area of employment growth', creating '1 in 5 of all new jobs' (Home Office, 2000a:25). Each year, brewers, leisure companies, and entrepreneurs invest around £1 billion within the sector, which is currently growing at a rate of 10% per annum (ibid.). The pub and club industry presently turns over £23 billion, equal to 3% of the UK Gross Domestic Product. The average turnover of a pub is £329,000 (Mintel, 2001) although the busier, larger city centre unit can have a turnover, similar to a large nightclub, of £1–3 million (BLRA 1998).

This flourishing of city centre licensed premises is reflected by an increasingly diverse marketplace that offers a broad range of 'themed consumer space' (Gottdiener, 2000:270–285), from sports bars, gay bars, family pubs, retro-fun pubs, dance bars, and lap-dancing venues to pool bars, Irish bars, and student pubs. Although, importantly, within the night-time market at least, the extent to which this multitude of themes translates into any significant diversification of function and clientele remains highly questionable (see Chapter 8). Hidden from the licensing statistics is the increasing scale of many modern drinking establishments as venue size can range from the 'superpub' which can be anything up to twenty times the size of the traditional pub, to the café-bar where capacity can be less then one hundred (Jones, 1996). The former, an increasingly prevalent sight on the landscape of our city centres, can represent huge investment in local economies, the weight of which many councils, although already overloaded with licensed premises, find difficult to resist. One premises in central London, the first of a chain, recently opened at an outlay of £3 million; this single leisure complex has a capacity of over 2,000 and features seven different bars, a restaurant, a delicatessen, and a 4 a.m. entertainment licence.

Another significant contemporary feature of the city centre drinking environment is the growth of so called 'chameleon bars' that function as pubs or café-bars during the day and dance-bars by night. As one operator suggests, 'During the day we offer a comfortable, pubby environment for shoppers and people wanting lunch or a drink after work. Later, the music is turned up and the lights turned down to attract a younger crowd. The day-time customers wouldn't recognize it by late evening' (Jeremy Blood, Marketing Director, Rat and Parrot Group, in Fenn, 1999). This development is the response of leisure operators seeking to exploit a niche in the market by offering a cheaper late-night drinking facility than that previously found within the conventional nightclub scene, a scene that in recent years has consequently experienced a dip in its commercial fortunes.

For instance, in 1996 revenues from nightclubs and discos were £1,808 million, yet by 1998 this figure had dropped to £1,784 million (Mintel, 1998). This drop in revenue seems likely to have been fuelled by the emergence of 'dance bars', newly equipped with late-night drink licences, and open to two and three in the morning, often with no or merely nominal admission fees. Wary of this threat, the nightclub leisure corporations have responded by introducing their own 'themed' late-night bars and so the significance of the late-night market has escalated. This process is complemented by a more flexible approach to regulation by licensing authorities whose officials, acting at a local level, perceive considerable benefit in promoting a city that appears more in tune with its Continental European neighbours. The outcome has been to expand both the size and the scope of the night-time economy as indicated by the granting of an increased number of ordinary and late-night licence applications.

In 'Eastville' city centre, as well as an increase in the number of licensed premises there is a detectable change in the nature of existing venues. This change involves a move away from 'traditional' public houses catering for a wide range of customers, toward the targeting of a loosely defined youth market based around 'dance bars'. Within such establishments, in order to access the high disposable income of the upper echelons of the youth market, entertainment provisions are installed, stone floors are replaced by wooden dance floors, and a cross-section of quality bitters is replaced by a narrow selection of strong lagers. For those who don't enjoy their 'volumes', a range of exotic vodkas and Premium Packaged alcoholic 'energy' drinks are made available to keep the punters, and in turn the accountants, happy. Those premises that fail to adapt are in danger of going under. For instance, over the last decade, of the fifteen traditional pubs in 'Eastville' city centre only four are now left. In their place have stepped the large impersonal (quasi) disco-bars that feature an imposing lighting rig, a booming sound-system, and always the necessary cast of bouncers on the door.

Youth dominates both the private and the public spaces of the night-time economy, and the notion of a mixed nocturnal economy within which the youth market is a mere segment is the product of an unlikely alliance of self-styled *flâneurs* and metropolitan 'boosters'. The result is 'city councillors and city businessmen, buying old warehouses, planning new lives for their town, dreaming of a city reborn' (Wilson, 2002:165). For the night-time economy not only floats on alcohol, but it is a largely unregulated zone of venture capitalism whose relentless logic excludes from its ever-expanding portfolio any innovation that is not oozing with profit-able potential. For instance the booming night-time town centre of Wolverhampton has had to resort to seeking development funds from non-commercial sources such as the Lottery and the European Regional Development Fund to finance an artists' quarter in a bid to broaden the appeal of its 'cultural' economy.

This is not to deny the existence of various audiences and con-sumers of city centre leisure. Indeed part of the 'multiplication of urban spaces' (Graham and Clarke, 1996:172) that typifies late modernity is the emergence of leisure enclaves based upon market differentiation, and as Ian Taylor (1999:103) has noted, larger cities at least, permit the constitution of a '... configuration of distinctive "social areas", each characterized by discrete social functions...'. However, few British cities have serious aspirations of mimicking the 'gay villages' of Manchester and London's Soho, or the chic cosmo-politan sensibilities of Barcelona, or Amsterdam, and given the meteorological realities of British summers, a version of café society is unlikely to last longer than a couple of weeks a year. Whilst 'a much more sophisticated and mixed economy [featuring] more ele-gance, variety and refinement' (Montgomery, 1998:7) may consti-tute the planning professional's ideal, the reality is that the night-time economy is largely an unregulated zone of quasi-liminality awash on a sea of alcohol (Hadfield et al., 2001).

However, even if the licensed sector is considered in isolation, a simple quantification of turnover and jobs at the 'point of delivery' ignores the income and employment generated in supply and sup-port industries, for example construction, graphic design, catering services, and sound and lighting technology. Thus, what is beyond dispute is that local night-time economies have become an increas-ingly important part of the social, economic, and cultural fabric of many British towns and cities, constituting a process of change that has necessarily incorporated shifts in regulatory policy.

Regulation of the night-time economy

We are currently witnessing the rapid development of differentiated centres of economic power in the form of leisure outlets catering to a range of audiences, but with a hard core of alcohol-based dance music bars and clubs designed predominantly for young hetero-sexuals. What constitutes 'young' is, of course, negotiable at every point, as is assumptive sexuality, but the nightstrip scene, built around circuit drinking, or pub crawling, often situated in dilapi-dated Victorian sites that have been subjected to a late twentieth-century makeover, dominates the night-time economy.

Each economic era has made demands upon agents of social control to impose systems of discipline and regulation that maximize the opportunity for profit and attract investment, and these systems are tailor-made to suit particular sites and specific situations (see Chapter 6). For instance, the imposition of industrial discipline in the mid-nineteenth century included not only the rigid routines of factory labour, but also the maintenance of pre-industrial militias to police disorder, political protest, and industrial unrest (Silver, 1967). However, this combination of economic discipline complemented by military force was not regarded as universally appropriate. In urban settings devoid of industrialism, combinations of private and public policing were combined with policies designed to divide and separate disruptive segments of the population to maintain a semblance of order commensurate with the new commercial order (Bowden, 1978; Hobbs, 1988; Manning, 1977; Miller, 1977; Rubinstein, 1973:6–7).

Incorporation into various capitalist forms of production was achieved by the combined ingenuity of the state and private enter-prise. These essentially industrial forms of discipline, designed to maintain a workforce appropriate to the various forms of mass production whose disciplines and cultures remained relatively con-sistent (Thompson, 1963; see Chapter 2), achieved a substantial measure of success in the USA and Northern Europe until the late 1950s. This process of pacification, central to the success of market capitalism (Hall, 1997; Horne and Hall, 1995), was hugely stabiliz-ing and an essential ingredient of the 'civilizing process', based around the maintenance of socio-economic interdependencies, the internalization of behavioural codes, and the state's apparent mon-opolization of physical violence (Elias, 1994). These behavioural codes and their manifest demeanours were enforced by '[increas-ingly] stringent and widely approved urban policing ... brought to bear upon the drunken and disorderly individuals whose rhythms were out of tune with industrial society' (Brown, 1991:131).

De-industrialization has created a breakdown in those taken for granted codes and cultures of restraint that during the industrial era kept violent crime down (Currie, 1997a; Hall, 2000) This is not to suggest that industrial communities were ever crime free, indeed dissent, criminality, and various forms of deviance have always formed part of their cultural infrastructure (Hobbs 1988; Samuel, 1981; White, 1980). However, the harnessing of aggression, and the practical qualities of resilience and physical strength (Hall, 1997), along with the containment of crime and deviance via, for instance, municipal housing policy (Damer, 1976; Stedman-Jones, 1971) and aggressive, highly selective policing (Cohen, 1979), were all vital in suppressing any activity contrary to the well-being of the industrial project.

The clear compartmentalization of work and leisure that was such a distinctive feature of early capitalism has been rapidly eroded, and we are now witnessing the extinction of those industrial modes of production that this compartmentalization was designed to protect and enhance (Taylor and Jamieson, 1997). The end of much meaningful labour, and the engagement of large swathes of the workforce in occupations that no longer abide by the rhythms and routines of industrialism, has impacted on our perceptions of the differentiation between day-time and night-time economies. However, it must be stressed that the expansion of the night-time economy has its roots not in the loosening of industrial shackles, resulting in the freedom of individuals to select from a cornucopia of economic options, identities, and destinations, but upon the ability of late-twentieth century capitalism to adapt and mutate according to opportunities thrown up by the detritus of industrialism. Central to this process of adaptation is the fact that the post-industrial leisure sector is not as dependent as its predecessor upon inflexible and oppressive forms of regulation and policing. In the contemporary context, the dominant forms of control are now essentially pragmatic systems of restraint that are manifested as market-orientated protocols featuring a multiplicity of sensual enticements, and cultivating an ethic of 'aggressive hedonism' (Gurr, 1989:369).[2]

In the industrial city of the late nineteenth and early twentieth centuries, working-class leisure activities were strictly regulated and contained to ensure that they did not threaten the interests of capital,

[2] The consumption of alcohol is often aggressively encouraged by means of discounting ('drinks promotions' and 'happy hours') and the marketing of many 'designer drinks' and of events promotions within venues can often utilize explicit references to drug culture in an attempt to attract and retain clientele (Brain, 2000; Collin, 1997).

or the sensibilities of the 'respectable classes' (Bailey, 1978; Cunningham, 1980; Thompson, 1967). However, in the post-industrial city, such constraints have fallen increasingly out of step with market forces and the political and economic imperatives of urban governance. The discourses of repression now appear archaic. For example, with regard to alcohol consumption, the moral entrepreneurship of the nineteenth- and early twentieth-century temperance movements (see Harrison, 1967, 1994) has largely been replaced by the discourses of medical and criminal risk (New Scientist, 1999; Thom, 1999; Valverde, 1998). Current licensing laws are widely regarded as out of step with contemporary trends in consumer demand (Holgate, 1999; Kreitzman, 1999), a view recently endorsed by the Home Office (see Home Office, 2000a). On 5 May 1998, Home Office Minister George Howarth told the British Institute of Innkeeping that 'the time is right to blow away the cobwebs in British life by modernizing the liquor licensing system' (cited in Holgate, 1999:117). Likewise, in their report of July 1998, the Better Regulation Taskforce (a commission appointed in 1997 to advise government on the effectiveness and legitimacy of regulatory policy) concluded that:

The law appears to bear little relationship to present day social reality; a strong movement toward the pub as a centre for the community, new leisure activities, family use of licensed premises, eating out, tourism and, above all, consumer choice (Better Regulation Taskforce, 1998a:10).

Many of the Better Regulation Taskforce's recommendations were later incorporated in the White Paper, *Time for Reform: Proposals for the Modernization of our Licensing Laws* (Home Office, 2000a), a document that recommends the replacement of statutory licensing hours with a flexible and discretionary system based upon the individual decisions of new local government licensing committees (see our discussion in Chapter 8).

Within this new political discourse it is assumed that when combined with carefully targeted 'multi-agency' crime prevention strategies, the de-regulation of licensing hours will assist many local governments in their mission to create harmonious and cosmopolitan urban leisure spaces. However, as well as being sites of public sociability, city centres are also 'worlds of strangers' (Lofland, 1973), environments in which, especially at night, forms of informal social control are often weak. As Stenson and Watt (1998) have pointed out, town centres are contested places, and the realities of socio-spacial borderlines are not eradicated with the onset of darkness. Further, the gathering together in one place of individuals and groups who embody antagonisms that may be rooted in ethnic, racial, class, or territorial motives, quite apart from random or alcohol-inspired aggression, suggests that the city centre at night is no free-floating post-modern nirvana, overflowing with subversive and emancipatory potential (see O'Connor and Wynne, 1996a; Wilson, 1991:7–8) no true sanctuary from the tensions, rigours, and inequalities that infest the daylight hours (Savage and Warde, 1993:118).

Many existing night-time leisure economies have already followed an established path of competitive advantage which leads away from restraint and control, toward de-regulation and an 'invitation to transgression' (Lovatt, 1996:162). Such problems are compounded by the fact that market forces have encouraged the development of mono-cultural drinking circuits, which market a similarly transgressive ambience (Hobbs et. al., 2002). Although there are signs of change, particularly in large cosmopolitan cities where market diversification may be a sustainable and potentially profitable option (see Chapter 8), the general lack of diversity in night-time economic development has a tendency to exacerbate problems of crime and disorder, significantly reducing the appeal of such areas at night for many (especially older) people. Nonetheless, full economic exploitation of the temporal 'frontier' (Melbin, 1978) requires strategies that are underpinned not only by structural and economic demands, but also by a fundamental shift in the political-ideological paradigm of local government.

The new urban governance

Local governments are increasingly involved in partnerships with the private sector, and have become 'imbued with characteristics once distinctive to businesses—risk taking, inventiveness, promotion, and profit motivation' (Hall and Hubbard, 1996:2). Some authors suggest that we have entered a new era of urban politics, in which the ideological rationale of local government has shifted away from a 'municipal socialist' stance, whose central axiom was the provision of local welfare services, toward a 'municipal capitalism' which seeks primarily to facilitate local economic growth and development (Davies, 1988; DiGaento and Klemanski, 1993; Hall and Hubbard, 1996, 1998; Harvey, 1989a; Osborne and Gaebler, 1992). As Cochrane (1995:268) argues: 'localities are both increasingly able and increasingly required to operate in an entrepreneurial fashion, to market themselves in ways which will enable them to provide economic growth and employment opportunities for their residents'.

Civic entrepreneurship is premissed on two key assumptions: first, that public–private sector partnership is the most efficient and effective way to achieve economic growth and prosperity, and secondly, that the extra wealth generated will 'trickle down', thus improving social and economic conditions for the poor, without burdening the 'wealth creators' with higher rates of taxation. The private sector 'partners' are typically members of a ' . . . business élite that collectively wields power over the pattern of urban development by virtue of its control over substantial material and intellectual resources and its ability to smooth access to external investment' (Harding, 1995:43).

The term local 'governance', as opposed to local 'government', is used by some commentators (e.g. Goodwin and Painter, 1996 and Tickell and Peck, 1996) to indicate that the direction of urban policy is no longer determined solely by the local state. Within the entrepreneurial discourse of the new 'urban growth coalitions' local economic development is 'apolitical' and 'pragmatic', being 'concerned only to bring the benefits of economic growth to the whole community' (Bassett, 1996:542). Yet, the emergence of such partnerships has involved a radical restructuring of the local political arena, effectively reducing the power of 'elected local governments' whilst enhancing 'local private sector interests' (Geddes, 1994:158).

This realignment of urban politics can 'create strong pressures for the (re)orientation of local public expenditure and services towards the needs and priorities of business' (ibid.), rather than the interests of the wider community. Thus, whilst partnerships between the public and private sector can enhance the power of local business élites, affording them entry into urban politics and policy-making, they can also mark a 'retreat from the politics of community development and a shift away from a concern with the political process in favour of . . . top-down managerial prerogatives' (Quilley, 1999:203). Thus, not only can 'growth coalitions' (Molotch, 1976) undermine local democratic processes and the public accountability of local government, they can also, by eschewing social goals, have a detrimental effect upon the welfare of relatively powerless local inhabitants (Randall, 1995), for example, those who find themselves attempting to reside among the night-life.

Whilst civic entrepreneurship has a long history, especially in the United States (Elkin, 1987; Ward, 1998), the novelty of recent developments lies in the way that the approach appears to have become central to the rationale of local government. Quilley (1999:189–190) suggests that 'British models of urban regeneration have been highly influenced in a very direct way by the U.S. experience, especially in cities such as Boston, New York and Baltimore', British councillors having 'made the pilgrimage to garner inspiration from the Baltimore model' (ibid.). However, as Harvey notes, 'what is remarkable' about the contemporary context is that the 'entrepreneurial ... consensus seems to hold across national boundaries and even across political parties and ideologies' (Harvey, 1989a:4).

Scholars have offered a number of explanations for the increasing importance of civic entrepreneurship: the demands of market forces in an era of globalization, and the resultant loss of local economic sovereignty (Quilley, 1999); the political dominance of neo-liberalism at national and international levels, and concomitant demise of 'Keynesian interventionism' (Jessop, 1998, Randall, 1995), and the discursive hegemony of 'enterprise culture' (Keat, 1991). Within the entrepreneurial discourse, all places are 'forced to play the same game', yet not all places can 'be equally successful' (Cochrane, 1995:269), for there will always be both 'losers' and 'winners'. Thus, if cities are to compete in an 'increasingly unpredictable and globalized economy' they must pursue 'proactive strategies designed to secure competitive advantage over their perceived rivals' (Hall and Hubbard, 1998:2).

As mentioned, such 'proactive strategies' usually involve a number of high-profile 're-imaging' and 'place-marketing' initiatives designed to secure investment from external and 'mobile' capital, to attract an influx of skilled and professional residents, and to boost the local tourism, leisure, and retail sectors. Such 'beauty contests' (Jessop, 1998) often centre around 'flagship' projects such as waterfront developments, heritage and theme parks, concert halls, shopping centres, prestigious office and leisure complexes, and the hosting of major cultural and sporting events (Healey et al., 1992; Kearns and Philo, 1993; Loftman and Nevin, 1996; Ward, 1998).

As part of these processes, the development of the night-time economy is often encouraged by the provision of relevant support structures, and by forms of deregulation and financial inducement. Support structures can include the provision of appropriate parking, traffic and public transport regimes, city-centre street lighting and CCTV systems, 'door supervisor' registration schemes, and high-profile public policing patrols. Regulatory facilitation often involves a liberal approach to both alcohol and entertainment licensing and to planning applications. It can also involve more direct financial inducements in the form of grants and loans. Such initiatives are designed to encourage investment from breweries, entrepreneurs, and leisure corporations, and to attract a sufficient number of customers to animate both business premises and the streets.

The growth of the night-time economy has refocused concentrations of power away from the temples of industrial authority such as factories, mines, docks, and shipyards, and from symbols of local political power such as the town hall. The balance of repression has swung away from these workplaces and their corresponding civil institutions, in favour of a commercial ethic based upon a hedonistic dynamic. Within the zones of liminality of the post-industrial city, regional power is now located by asking 'how many late-night bars?' and whether the city has a J. D. Wetherspoons, Pitcher and Piano, or All Bar One, all of whom are national enterprises currently investing in the expanding night-time economy. These sites of consumption constitute highly visible examples of new concentrations of demonstrable economic power, a power based, like industrial society, upon huge capital investment.

The highly visible investments made by major leisure corporations into the night-time economy constitute the symbolic and operational foci of post-industrial economic power. Along with the shopping mall (Kowinski, 1985), the existence of a thriving night-time economy is now taken as a prerequisite for any city hoping to make a claim upon progressive profitability. However, the post-industrial response by cities forged in nineteenth-century assumptions of what constitutes the fundamental project of the metropolis vary considerably. Cities 'demonstrat(ing) very different capacities, institutionally and strategically, for responding to the challenges of a post-Fordist world' (I. Taylor, 1999:131), and exhibiting few elements of blanket co-ordination, although some common themes have emerged. Under the gloriously hyped term, 'the 24-hour city', local politicians are now able to claim for cities with a common industrial heritage, a phoenix-like rise from the ashes, not only of Victorian laid bricks and mortar, but also of systems of traditional bourgeois control over urban leisure, which also has its foundations deep in the Victorian era (Holt, 1989; Rojek, 1993:31–45).

This massive switch in temporal economic and social life stands in stark, but lucrative contrast to our traditional perception of the night, and this contrast creates a conflict that is integral to our understanding of the essential ambiguity that is the very essence of night-life. Yet by the dawn of a new millennium, town planners and city managers were beginning to admit to the harsh reality that lies beyond the glossy rhetoric of the 24-hour city: that the night-time economy is as dependent upon hedonistic drives cultivated in the alcohol/youth nexus, as industrial society was on the motive power of coal and steam (see Walsh, 1998). As Osborne and Rose note 'urban governmentality uses the insidious ungovernability of the city as a resource and an inspiration' (1999:759).

Booze, the urban night, and the human ecology of violence

Truth be told, the drug that really did the business was *Stella Artois* (Wilson, 2002:179).

Alcohol is the vital lubricant that aids the propulsion of young people into this carnivalesque and consumer-orientated world. It also frames the 'grounded aesthetic' (Willis, 1990:102) of possibilities that languish in young peoples' passionate embrace of risk. In purely commercial terms, alcohol is the commodity that draws people into our city centres after dark, and in addition, sustains associated, complementary markets. In cultural terms it provides an accepted means of altering the mundane, pressurized, regimented, and unattractive world of daylight comportment, realigning meaning and understanding to fit a more seductive and alluring world of hedonism and carnival.

Rather than alcohol consumption revealing a culture-free 'natural' self, the social element of drunkenness is learned behaviour like any other (MacAndrew and Edgerton, 1969), and the cultural expectation of alcohol's 'disinhibitor effect' (Room and Collins, 1983) aids consumers in abandoning their regulated and constrained daylight personas and immersing themselves in the comparatively ambiguous and chaotic culture of the night. Alcohol consumption provides both a culturally and legally sanctioned way of altering behaviour, and it is this opportunity to enjoy legitimized 'time out' in the form of hedonistic forms of experiential consumption and identification, that renders the night-time economy so alluring to young people. Indeed, without the acceptance of certain night-time forms of disorderly intoxicated behaviour, the night-time economy would be less attractive to contemporary youth; for it provides an excuse to 'start breaking down', loosen sensibilities, and abandon oneself to behaviour which would otherwise be contained.

The switch from industrial to post-industrial, from an emphasis on production to consumption, also marks a shift from the problematic producer to the problematic consumer (Ritzer, 2001:233–235). There is a wealth of evidence to suggest that violence is a major by-product of this mass transgression in the form of 'cultural understandings of the connections between rowdy and violent group drinking, the construction and projection of empowered masculine identity, and the symbolic rejection of respectable social values' (Tomsen, 1997:100), which lie at the core of the enacted, as opposed to marketed night-time economy. Yet, this by-product is, in itself, far from a homogeneous phenomena, and any simplistic conception of 'alcohol-related violence' should be prefaced by a rider differentiating between context and pharmacology (Tierney and Hobbs, 2003).

However, evidence compiled from a huge sample of Accident and Emergency departments around the country (Hutchinson et al., 1998), indicates that 24% of facial injuries were caused by assault, and that 90% of facial injuries in bars, and 45% of facial injuries in the street were associated with alcohol consumption. The busiest period for alcohol-related injuries was found to be between 21.00 hours to 03.00 hours. The 15–25 age group suffered the greatest number of assaults, and 79% of patients assaulted were male, although where injuries involving bottles or glasses had occurred, 83% of the victims were male. Most of the assaults took place in the street (43%), and pubs and bars were the sites of 21%. The peak times for assaults coincided with the closing times of licensed premises, with Friday and Saturday the busiest days. Assault with a blunt instrument (including parts of the body) was the most common form of interpersonal violence (89%), bottles or glasses were used in 8%

of cases, and knives in 2%. Just over half of the assaults with bottles or glasses occurred in bars.

Much male violence is associated with drinking in bars (Homel et al., 1991), and those most likely to become the victims of bar-related violence are also young males (Langley et al., 1996). In addition to these contextual relationships between alcohol and violence, an association has been established between alcohol and violent crime (Graham and West, 2001). For example, alcohol has been causally implicated in aggression (Bushman, 1997; Lipsey et al., 1997), and the level of male intoxication has been associated with frequency of aggression (Homel and Clarke, 1994).

Crowded and smoky environments (Graham et al., 1980; Homel and Clark, 1994), where large intoxicated groups mingle (ibid., 1994), are venues for displays of aggression (Lang et al., 1995; Martin et al., 1998), and in terms of the compulsive dramas (Willis, 1990:105) ritually played out in the local night-time economy, alcohol inspires the drinker to focus upon the present (Graham et al., 2000), to become impulsive (Berkowitz, 1986), and to overestimate personal power (Gibbs, 1986; Pernanem, 1976), while crucially eroding the ability to contrive non-violent resolutions to perceived provocations (Sayette et al., 1993). Further, research indicates that some males have concerns with their personal power when they drink (McClelland et al., 1972), are easily provoked (Guftanson, 1993), and become sensitive to the behaviour of third parties (Wells and Graham, 1999). Researchers have also found that retaliatory aggression often constitutes a means to settle grievances (Felson, 1982; Tedeschi and Felson, 1994) and is often linked to going to the aid of a friend (Archer et al., 1995; Berkowitz, 1986).

The alcohol-fuelled night-time economy also provides an ideal environment for those who regard fighting as an expressive hobby (Burns, 1980; Dyck, 1980; Tomsen, 1997), providing a common thread linking current generations of drinkers to the hard case cobblestone fighters of yesteryear (Morton, 1993: Chapter 1; Pearson, 1973: Chapter 1; Samuel, 1981; Winlow, 2001). However, the key difference between these muscular urban legends of the past and the current crop of 'weekend warriors' (Marshall, 1979) is the scale, sheer power and pre-eminence in political and economic terms, that their arena, the night-time economy, has attained in contemporary Britain.

Drawing upon the concept of 'routine activities' (Cohen and Felson, 1979), quantitative research within the ecological tradition has long demonstrated the way in which various forms of crime have a tendency to be highly concentrated in space and time (Bottoms, 1994; Hope, 1985; Sherman et al., 1989). Such studies have identified urban centres with a high density of licensed premises as the 'hot spots', and weekend evenings as the 'hot times' for incidents of assault and disorder (Felson, 1997; McClintock and Wikström, 1992; Phillips and Smith, 2000; Roncek and Maier, 1991). Clearly, the links between alcohol consumption and various forms of crime and disorder have long been acknowledged. However recent research has uncovered more about how, why, when, and where alcohol-related incidents in public places occur. In England and Wales, approximately 70% of crime audits published in 1998 and 1999 identified 'alcohol as an issue, particularly in relation to public order' (Home Office, 2001a:1). The majority of hot-spots for violence and disorder (in public) were located in areas containing high concentrations of licensed premises with the number of incidents peaking between 9 p.m. and 3 a.m. on Friday nights/Saturday mornings and Saturday nights/Sunday mornings.

Of course, whilst simple correlations do not explain causation, and the relationship between venue density/proliferation and associated violence and disorder is complex, evidence from deregulated city centre night-time economies such as Manchester, Hull, and the West End of London, many smaller English towns such as Oswestry, Worthing, Macclesfield, and Newcastle under Lyme, and also from Scotland would suggest that increases in the number of licensed premises and in their total capacities and terminal trading hours, are often accompanied by rises in assaults and public order offences, particularly in areas which have a high density of licensed premises.

In Manchester City Centre for example, the capacity of licensed premises increased by 240% between 1998 and 2001, whilst the number of assaults reported to the police increased by 225% between 1997 and 2001 (Home Office, 2001b:57). Manchester's 2001 crime audit recorded 1,277 assaults in and around the Gay Village (an area with a particularly high density of licensed premises); this figure was more than double the number recorded in any other part of the city centre (MCC, 2001). The same audit identified the Peter Street/Quay Street area as a hotspot for 'assault and wounding'. This area had not appeared in the two previous Manchester audits, however, during 2000 a large multi-leisure complex and a number of licensed premises opened in the vicinity, transforming a comparatively quiet street into an extremely busy drinking circuit (see Chapter 3). Similarly, the total number of recorded incidents of violence and disorder in Newcastle upon Tyne city centre fell between 1997 and 2001, however significant rises were recorded in the Quayside area which corresponded with the redevelopment of this area as the North East's most popular nightlife destination. Between 1997 and 2001 there was a 19% increase in the total capacity of Quayside licensed premises, a 38% increase in drunk and disorderly offences, a 38% increase in assaults and an 18% increase in criminal damage (McWilliams, 2002). Further, an 18-month survey of patients attending the Accident and Emergency department of Hereford General Hospital found that 44% of alcohol-related night-time assault victims received from the county of Herefordshire as a whole, were assaulted in just one street, known locally as 'alcohol alley' (Commercial Road, Hereford) which contains a small, but densely concentrated, number of licensed premises (Ballham, 2002). Evidence from the evaluation of a Home Office-funded Targeted Policing Initiative to reduce alcohol-related violence and disorder in Cardiff found that during the period July 1999 to June 2001, virtually all the rise in disorder 'was accounted for by one street (St Mary's Street) which contained the densest concentration of pubs and clubs and where a number of new premises opened over a short period' (Maguire and Nettleton, 2003:52). The evaluators note that:

Where *violent* incidents were concerned, St Mary's Street showed a rise of 42 per cent, compared with a fall elsewhere of 15 per cent. And for incidents of *disorder*, St Mary's Street showed a rise of 99 per cent compared with a rise elsewhere of 38 per cent. Moreover, the increases were seen in all locations in this area—incidents inside premises here rose by 66 per cent, incidents outside named premises more than doubled (a rise of 151%), and incidents elsewhere in the street rose by 46 per cent. It is almost certainly relevant that the southern end of the street has seen the greatest growth and concentration of new licensed premises over the past few years (Maguire and Nettleton, 2003:45).

The evaluators of a concurrent inter-agency initiative providing data to the project regarding the circumstances of violence obtained from assault patients attending the Accident and Emergency department University Hospital of Wales concluded that:

There was a statistically significant, positively correlated, relationship between city centre licensed premise capacity and street assault...An increase in the number and particularly capacity of licensed premises on a particular street was associated with a disproportionate increase in the number of assaults in that street...There was a highly significant increase in assault in St Mary's Street, despite a well-funded targeted policing project, which focussed on alcohol-related violence during the study period...city centre violence prevention should be highly responsive to drinks licence applications, new licensed premises, levels of street violence and changes in character of existing licensed premises (Warburton and Shepherd, 2002:27).

Our analysis of violent crime data recorded by the police in 'Eastville' (see Hobbs et al., 2000) reveals a distinctly similar pattern. For example, one particular road in Eastville, 'Lager Street', had developed between 1996 and 1999 into an archetypal 'nightstrip'. Within a stretch of two hundred yards there were two licensed nightclubs, one 'superpub' with a special hours licence, a further six pubs and a restaurant-bar, and also a further three applications pending for special hours certificates. Over this period, Lager Street witnessed an increase in recorded violent crime of 106% with 79% of recorded violence occurring between the hours 21.00 and 03.00.

Analysis of the above trends is hardly a matter of 'rocket science', the most obvious and simple explanation being that *when the activity levels of an intoxicated night-time consumer base increase, then, as one might expect, more crime and disorder will be generated* in the streets and public spaces of our night-time leisure zones. However, once a large intoxicated consumer base is formed, such problems do not remain restricted to these distinct leisure locales, but also impact upon late-night pedestrian and vehicular exit routes throughout the area, which become, in the early hours of the morning, the sites of further violence, disorder, anti-social behaviour, criminal damage, vandalism, and noise (Bromley and Nelson, 2002; Hadfield, forthcoming a; Nelson et al., 2001). Further, as the tracing of such incident patterns is based primarily upon police-recorded crime statistics it will undoubtedly underestimate the total number of incidents that actually occur (Tierney and Hobbs, 2003).

Our research (interviews with doorstaff, observational fieldwork with police public order patrols, and examination of 'Eastville' Accident and Emergency records) indicates that recorded crimes represent only a fraction of the problem (see Lister et al., 2000).

However, as others have demonstrated (Cuthbert, 1990; Shepherd, 1990; Shepherd et al., 1989; Shepherd and Lisles, 1998), medical data can reveal additional portions of the 'dark figure' of unrecorded violence and its relationship to alcohol consumption. Such statistics highlight the potential for violence that has long existed within our night-time leisure zones (Hope, 1985; Tuck, 1989). Nonetheless, they reveal little about the enacted environment of the night-time economy and its decidedly criminogenic situational and experiential dynamics. Whilst a small number of ethnographic accounts have served to highlight the 'recreational' or carnivalesque dimensions of alcohol-fuelled, night-time disorder (Dyck, 1980; Gofton, 1990; Tomsen, 1997), we would suggest that the problems of 'friction producing encounters between intoxicated strangers *and* acquaintances' often cited as central to the aetiology of alcohol-related violence (Homel et al., 1992; Wikström, 1995), are being exacerbated within the contemporary night-time economy as the leisure industry targets a mainstream audience of young high-spending consumers.

A variety of promotional tools and marketing strategies are being employed which invite experiential transgression and are shrouded in promises of quasi-liminality (Hobbs et al., 2000). The breakdown of old rules has been hastened by the marketing strategies of entrepreneurs who put together special offers and packages aimed at both attracting customers to their premises and keeping them there. Scantily-clad bar staff, striptease artistes, organized drinking games, hen nights, stag nights, and special nights for nurses, students, and even police officers (the wonderfully entitled '999 Disco') are offered, together with '£10-in—and-all-your-drinks-free' nights, and the inevitable three shots of whatever is not selling well for a pound.

Cheap drink and other bait are usually offered on mid-week evenings to maximize profits outside of the weekend deluge that signifies peak business, when drink prices can remain high without fear of dissuading custom. During the week custom must be attracted, and it is here that drinks' promotions work their charms. The promise of half-priced bottles of lager, or two or three shots of spirit for the price of one, a free Tequila with every pint, or a free cocktail upon admittance to a nightclub is often enough to seduce custom away from the television and mid-week hibernation, and back to the city centre to spend money. Bars often offer cheap drinks on the same night as their competitors, not as a form of direct competition, but to create a varied and cheap drinking environment, multiplying custom rather than competing for it, thus acknowledging the culturally informed attractions of circuit drinking. While selling drinks for half of their weekend price may seem like bad business, bars are boosting custom to premises which would in all likelihood remain relatively empty were it not for these marketing strategies.

Thus, consumers of the night-time leisure experience are encouraged to regard our urban centres as liminal zones: spatial and temporal locations within which the familiar protocols and bonds of restraint which structure routine social life loosen and are replaced by conditions of excitement, uncertainty, and pleasure (Turner, 1967, 1969). Within such milieux, interpersonal tensions and conflicts emerge (Arantes, 1996), aggressive hedonism and disorder is normalized (Gofton, 1990; Tomsen, 1997), and violence and intimidation become the blunt instruments of social control.

Public police: the night-time omission

Across Britain, the police are forced increasingly to juggle operational resources in an attempt to cope with the disorder that has frequently accompanied the expansion of these night-time leisure zones. For example, the number of licensed premises in Manchester City Centre has increased from approximately 200 in 1993 to a current level of over 500, whilst incidents of street violence within the City Centre at night have increased dramatically since the early 1990s (see Chapter 3).

Following a decade of rapid expansion within its leisure infrastructure, as we will discuss in Chapter 3, Manchester City Centre now attracts crowds of up to 100,000 people on Friday and Saturday evenings. A liberal estimate is that approximately thirty to forty officers are engaged on public order duty at these times, whilst the crowds are simultaneously controlled by an estimated 1,000 bouncers working per night. Similar comparisons can be drawn in towns and cities throughout the UK. For example, Nottingham City Centre, which regularly attracts 50,000 weekend night-time visitors, is 'policed' by over 400 bouncers, but only twenty to twenty-five police officers. In 'Eastville' a similar number of officers support 250 bouncers as they oversee the conduct of up to 20,000 revellers. And then there is the West End of London which the Metropolitan Police anecdotally suggest regularly attracts somewhere in the region of 500,000 weekend drinkers. Although estimations vary, these locally derived figures are broadly illustrative of the scale of the night-time policing task that now faces numerous city centre commanders, every weekend. Moreover, these figures should be interpreted within the context of the range of diverse demands currently being placed upon the police in city centre divisions, for example, the high level of inner-city burglaries and incidents of domestic violence. Potentially, violent public order situations require a swift, labour intensive response which, as we have witnessed, frequently leads to the 'swarming' of units (see Ekblom and Heal, 1982). Furthermore, pressure upon resources is intensified by the highly skewed temporal concentration of violent incidents (Hope, 1985).

Receiving shadows

We improve our grasp of the ecology of a region by recognizing the night-time activity of raccoons, owls, and rats, as well as by knowing the spatial dispersion of these and other animals. The same area of a forest or meadow or coral reef is used incessantly, with diurnal and nocturnal creatures taking their active turns (Melbin, 1978:5).

The distinction between day and night is commonly regarded as:

the most fundamental zoning demarcation between the intensity of social life and its relaxation... Night-time was a 'frontier' of social activity as marked as any spatial frontiers have ever been. It remains a frontier, as it were, that is only sparsely settled (Giddens, 1984:119).

We traditionally approach the night as a time zone that is riddled with ambiguity. Perceptions of the 'hours of darkness' as a time of danger, fear, crime, and sin seem to be persistent and deeply embedded components of British culture. As Thomas Burke (cited in Bianchini, 1995:122) noted:

Night-life... nightclub... nightbird. There is something about the word Night, as about the word Paris, that sends through some Englishmen (sic) a shiver of misgiving, and through another type a current of undue delight...a club they can tolerate. Call it a night-club, and they see it as the ante-room to Hell.

Nonetheless at night men and women seek out times and spaces that are demarcated for leisure (Sennett, 1990), it is a time of release from civilizing influences or 'ceremonial codes' (Goffman, 1967:55) of both occupational and domestic labour inherent to the '... temporal regulation of the day...' (Giddens, 1984:144). However, apart from a release from the rigours and restraints of the daylight hours, the night also inspires fear and apprehension. It is:

...a place associated with death and the grave, (and) is opposed to the day...The link between night and death, which is underscored by nocturnal sounds like the howling of dogs and the grating of the sleepers' teeth, similar to that of the dying, is marked in all the taboos of the evening:... bathing...looking in mirrors, anointing the hair, touching ashes—have the effect of, in a sense doubling, the malignancy of the nocturnal darkness...(Bourdieu, 1977:148).

The dualism of the night that celebrates a relaxation of the restraints associated with the workplace and the home, acknowledges and utilizes the night's association with decline via a celebration of dissolution and degradation that constitutes a recoding of agency in the wake of decline.

The decline of the sun...is in a sense the paradigm of all forms of decline, in particular old age and all kinds of political decadence (...his sun has fallen) or physical decay...to go westwards, towards the setting sun...is to go towards darkness, night, death, like a house whose westward-facing door can only receive shadows (op. cit.:153).

Consequently 'going out' at night is something of an adventure (Simmel, 1950:243–6), for it is beyond the parameters of routine time and place, and is experienced in isolation from the mundane circumstances generated by the responsibilities of work and family. 'In its periodicity and episodes, the adventure gives zest and meaning to life' (Lyman and Scott, 1970:18). The episodic loosening of the bonds of restraint imposed by paid employment and domestic labour, when repeated as an eternal recurrence in the same space by successive generations, leads to the emergence of '... the zoning of time-space in relation to routinized social practices' (Giddens, 1984:119).

The routinization of liminal practices requires designated spaces, and these city centre pleasure zones are entertainment quarters that function as zones of patterned liminality which must create the impression of being set aside and secluded from the principal arenas of normative, non-liminal social life (Turner, 1974:232). This stress upon the deliberate creation of a liminal impression is crucial, for central to our thesis is the opposition to strict culturalist interpretations of social phenomena. The night-time economy commodifies space and establishes created environments. The bulk of liminal arenas cater to a youth-orientated market grounded upon the consumption of alcohol, and in many smaller towns, this appears to be the only commercially viable option.

Increasingly public culture has become keenly aware of the seductions of transgression and nowhere is this more clearly seen than in the carnivalesque world of the night-time economy. Not only is this a world in which the black and grey economies thrive, but a powerful atmosphere of dangerous adventure exists, diffuse with suggestions of the illicit. As we have discussed, violence and disorder are regular fixtures in our night-time economy, and it is increasingly the amphitheatre of drug, alcohol, and sexual experimentation. Carnival revels in abuse, violence, sex, and carnality (Bakhtin, 1984) and it is here that the promissory note of a 'time out of time' (Presdee, 2000:33) is proffered, a break from all that disappoints and frustrates in the slate grey glare of daylight, a special place and time where, 'the artificial stimulation and amusement of consumption' (Frisby, 1985:94) rules.

The symbolic domain (Turner, 1969:80) of the night, harbouring for consumers at least, none of the attributes of either paid work or domesticity, is made concrete by the construction of profit seeking venues, and the aim of many night-time entrepreneurs is to create a sense of communitas within the festival built around weekend rituals of liminality. Communitas is highly valued commercially for, when associated with a particular venue, it is converted into customer loyalty around the notion of an unstructured community of equal individuals who submit together to the general authority of hedonism fronted by the ritual elders: promoters, DJs and, ideally, the true custodians of the liminal zone, bouncers (Malbon, 1998:273).

We became aware during the course of our research of venues that had managed to harness this spontaneity, and by implementing various practices, most importantly non-intimidatory door strategies, communitas became a genuine characteristic of the venue. This was particularly noticeable in a few independent venues with their origins in late 1980s/early 1990s dance culture. As Malbon cogently notes, 'This communal ethic, the pleasure of being with others, is born both from the sharing of space (a territory) and the proximity of that act of sharing, and from the establishment and maintenance of some sense of unity or membership' (1998:273).

However, such successes are few and far between and, for the most part, liminal zones thrive on the promise rather than the deliverance of communitas. Further, far from being a zone of infinite possibilities, where individuals are free to explore a multiplicity of masked identities, the thread of structure through ritualized communitas within liminality is '... highly characteristic of long established and stable cultural systems, in which ... communitas has been thoroughly domesticated, even corralled' (Turner, 1974: 254). The night-time economy provides structured provision for liminality (op. cit.: 260), via stratified consumer choices, and with a choice of venues ranging from maverick independents to corporate chains.

The social structure does not disappear within zones of liminality, but is simplified, generalized (op. cit.: 262), and glossed by commercial forces with an innate understanding of the lure of liminality and the desire of individuals to envelop themselves in a sense of communitas lacking from the alienating humdrum rhythms of everyday life. The repertoire of liminal symbols employed by commercial forces includes imagery relating to overt sexuality, inebriation, and egoism. References to affluence and exotic locations confirm that liminal festivals, particularly those that thrive upon fixed locations regularized by the establishment of entertainment quarters are sites for '... the circulation of wealth, of the most important trading, of prestige gained through the distribution of accumulated reserves' (Caillois, 1959:123–6).

The glaring neon of consumption that lies at the core of the night-time economy, should not blind us to the temporary make-believe nature of the identities constructed within this 'liminal masquerade' (Turner, 1974:243), that denies the routine existence of the material world, and creates via communitas a festival whose function is to be spontaneous, self-generating, potentially dangerous, and revitalizing. Sometimes the night-time economy is situated in traditional environments, marking the site of liminal locations for generations of night-time customers, and the identity of such locales is reinforced (sometimes to the extent of parody) as a result of heavy investment by commercial and municipal forces. Consequently, the night-time economy harnesses a liminal tradition in order to establish the routinized festival of Friday and Saturday nights out. This process becomes essential to the institutionalized order as seemingly 'spontaneous forms of communitas are converted into institutionalized structure' (Turner, 1974:248).

This routinization of communitas via the establishment of the commercial exploitation of traditional forms of liminal expression into part of the bedrock of the local political economy constitutes, 'not inversions of the social order but mirrors of it' (Schechner, 1993:48). The transformation of economic activity within cities such as Manchester from industrial to post-industrial systems of accumulation, emphasizes the nature of the tensions apparent in these spatially ordered liminal rituals. This tension stems from the fact that although these ritualized inversions of the social order are tolerated, in the form of drunkenness, rowdy behaviour, etc., this is merely a 'temporary respite from the conventional social order to which it will return' (Jackson, 1989:80). As Osbourne and Rose explain, 'transgression itself is . . . brought back into line and offered up as a package of commodified contentment. The city of plea-sure . . . has itself been fed into the programmatic imagination, in an alliance between city politics and commercial imperatives, (1999:757).

In the light of this brief discussion of liminality we are obviously in conflict with those writers who have adopted a somewhat romantic view that emphasizes the maverick nature of night-time dwellers and the essential dislocation of nightlife from the organizational and disciplinary restraints of the day-time. Our discussion of the training and registration of bouncers (Chapter 6) clearly shows the inability of the local and central state either to enforce and administrate existing laws or to create appropriate legal edicts. With the exception of a small embattled shift of police officers, and the occasional environmental health or licensing officer, the socio-legal and administrative framework of our cities work hours ideally suited to day-time industrial production: the very foundation of many of our great cities. Yet, the night-time economy comes into its own as city managers, administrators, and senior police officers are taking to their beds for the night.

Lawlessness and violence in the night-time economy are of course concentrated in certain places and at certain times. Consequently, the traditional Chicagoan concern with the evolution of a 'natural' deviant area (Shaw and McKay, 1942) becomes problematic when applied to those towns and cities which have developed a night-time economy based around space originally designated as industrial or commercial. These liminal spaces come alive at night, and are stra-tegically situated as integral to modern city centres that also incorporate elements of retail shopping, and commercial and administrative office space:

In the day-time the areas are part of business districts. Many people shop at department stores nearby, or otherwise pass through and patronize eating places and businesses there. So the combat zone designation refers to these places only at certain hours, and is not true for all the city all night (Melbin, 1978:12).

And one more for the road

All it actually confirms is that the real point will never be reached, that the diner must be satisfied with the menu (Horkheimer and Adorno, 1973: 139).

Post-industrial cities have invested heavily in developing 24-hour economies that require codes and protocols unique to a populace who in previous generations were subjected to rigid laws constructed to limit pleasure and leisure to forms commensurate with industrial production. As we will stress, ambiguity dominates formal attempts to regulate the night-time economy, and efforts to enforce protocols and ensure the incorporation of the night-time population take place via the explicit expression of intimidatory devices that are embodied by commercial security staff in the form of bouncers or doormen. The utility of these devices provides an essential co-ordinating element that sometimes blends and sometimes conflicts with the co-ordinating devices of the state as represented by what is normally a small police presence. Yet, while the police are mere gatekeepers of the criminal justice system (Reiss, 1971), bouncers are gatekeepers of the liminal zone.

The rules, codes, and protocols of the night-time economy are essentially ambiguous, yet distinct from those applied to the same physical settings during the day-time. For although the projected impression of a hedonistic environment devoid of restraint is central to the allure of night-time leisure, this impression is illusory. For when viewed from within, it is apparent that there are distinct boundaries maintained by commercial imperatives every bit as pragmatic as those employed during the traditional working day. The marketing of liminal licence, which is crucial to the appeal of the night-time economy, is the key to the sector's ambiguity, and vital to any understanding of the inevitability of violence and disorder in a new economic era where 'all is life, avarice, lust, deviltry, and enter-prise...abounding in strange exhibitions and startling combin-ations of the human passions' (Browne, 1871:348).

A Case Study of Manchester

The city of Manchester in the north-west of England is internation-
ally renowned as both the cradle of eighteenth- and early nineteenth-
century urban industrialism and late twentieth- and early twenty-
first-century de-industrialization and post-industrial restructuring
(see Taylor, Evans and Fraser, 1996). The following two-chapter
case study pursues a narrative of the relationship between the political economy of this city and the development, regulation, and
policing of its night-time leisure economy. Manchester is a particularly appropriate setting for such a study since it is known throughout the world as the 'leisure/cultural' capital of the North of England
with a rich heritage of successes in popular music, media, and football and (by English standards) a particularly 'vibrant' nightlife (see
Haslam, 1999). Contemporary Manchester is widely regarded as a
British pioneer of the '24-Hour City' concept (see Heath and Stickland, 1997), wherein commercial night-time leisure pursuits are
actively facilitated by local government. In the popular imagination,
this 'glamorous' Manchester is often juxtaposed against other
potent images: the 'gloom' of the 'Rainy City', and the risk posed
by high levels of crime.[1]

Our case study will reveal how commercial night-time leisure and
its associated problems of crime and disorder have played a key role
in the creation, maintenance, and reproduction of these Mancunian
mythologies. It will be argued that this 'business of pleasure' has
had a significant impact upon the projects and strategies of urban

[1] In recent years, official crime statistics have consistently shown Greater Manchester to have particularly high levels of recorded crime. In figures released by the Home
Office in July 2000, the conurbation had the highest overall crime rate in England and
Wales with 14,630 crimes per 100,000 of population, whilst the rate for violence
against the person was the highest outside London with 27.3 offences per 1,000
population (Home Office, 2000b).

governance and has led variously to the repression or incorporation of night-time leisure within the City's political and economic 'landscapes of power' (Zukin, 1991). The need to balance economic growth against more 'democratic' goals such as political legitimacy, public accountability, social inclusion, public order, and community safety has been a recurrent dilemma for Manchester's political and business élite. The following case study aims to present a politically and historically informed analysis of these issues.

2

After-dark 'Fun' and its Control in the Industrial City

The industrial city

Look up and all around this place and you will see the huge palaces of industry. You will hear the noise of furnaces, the whistle of steam. These vast structures keep air and light out of the human habitations which they dominate; they envelop them in perpetual fog...From this foul drain the greatest steam of human industry flows out to fertilize the whole world. From this filthy sewer pure gold flows. Here humanity attains its most complete development and its most brutish (exterior appearance of Manchester 2 July 1835, de Tocqueville, 1958:107–108).

Until the Industrial Revolution Manchester was a small, unremarkable market town with an economic basis in the wool trade. Between 1650 and 1750 its population grew from approximately 4–5,000 to 17,000 as the town became a regional manufacturing and distribution centre for the growing cotton industry (Tupling, 1934). However, Manchester's growth was at its most rapid between 1780 and 1850. The 1801 census recorded its population as 70,000, fifty years later it was 303,000 and by 1901 it had reached a staggering 544,000! (Shercliff, 1983). According to Jones (1982:144), the City's population growth was a mixture of 'natural increase, migration and immigration'.

It was Manchester's burgeoning textile industry that was responsible for the City's economic growth. Cotton was central to Britain's early industrial development: it was 'the pacemaker of industrial change' (Hobsbawm, 1969:56) and a commodity of vital importance to Britain's export trade (Singleton, 1991). Due to a number of geographical advantages (such as the damp climate and lime-free water) and a tradition of textile manufacture, 'cotton meant Manchester and its region' (Kidd, 1993:21). By the mid-nineteenth century Manchester and its environs had become the 'largest manufacturing centre in the world' (Bee, 1984:2). However, it would be a mistake to assume that Manchester was ever simply a cotton mill town, since its true economic character has always been mixed: in addition to cotton weaving, Manchester has also been an important site for engineering, warehousing, marketing, and distribution expertise. Indeed, the multiple origins of Manchester's economic pre-eminence during the Industrial Revolution of 1780–1840 include: locational advantages, a ready supply of labour, technological innovation and novel forms of transportation via canals, and later, the rail network. Manchester's trading links with the rest of Britain and indeed, the World and the diverse origins of its population meant that, unlike many of its provincial contemporaries, Manchester was a truly cosmopolitan city.

By the 1830s, Manchester had become known as 'Cottonopolis', the 'shock city' of nineteenth-century British society (Briggs, 1996:60), a city which heralded the new industrial age and its unprecedented social and economic changes (Hobsbawm, 1969; Wirth, 1978). Within nineteenth-century Manchester's specific social, historical, and cultural context, a local 'enterprise culture' developed within which 'Manchester men', especially the self-made captains of industry, were ascribed distinctive traits of diligence, ambition and business acumen (Messinger, 1985; Shapely, 1988; Taylor et. al., 1996). Yet, although Manchester represented progress in terms of being the 'first industrial city' (Kidd, 1993; Messinger, 1985; Wirth, 1978), it also came to epitomize the social *problems* of the new urban order, notably poverty, criminality, and vice.

In the early decades of the nineteenth century a residential separation of the classes had occurred. The 'mill owners' and emergent middle classes had largely abandoned the city centre for the rarefied environment of the suburbs and a number of notorious working-class 'slums' such as Little Ireland and Angel Meadow had developed (Jones, 1982; Kidd, 1993; Thompson, 1963). This darker side of Manchester's new industrial urbanism is immortalized in the contemporary writings of local novelist Elizabeth Gaskell (1970) and of two foreign visitors: de Tocqueville (1958) and Engels (1987). Written in 1845, Engels' *The Condition of the Working Class in England* is arguably the first ethnography of an industrial city. Engels describes in intimate detail his first hand observations of the social horrors of Manchester's labyrinth of working-class slums. He also describes how, in order to escape the grim reality of their living and working conditions, Manchester's new urban population had developed their own alcohol-centred popular culture.

Leisure in the industrial city

As much of the history of England has been brought about in public-houses as in the House of Commons (Sir William Harcourt, 1872).

By the mid-nineteenth century, leisure activities in the new industrial city had come to reflect the deep divisions of its class structure. Concert halls, theatres, and fine art facilities catered for the demands of the middle classes (Burton, 1987), whilst working-class leisure was 'for the most part public and gregarious, and...its principal setting was that of the public house' (Bailey, 1978:9; Cunningham, 1980). As Bailey explains, 'in an age of social dislocation the pub remained a centre of warmth, light and sociability for the urban poor, a haven from the filth and meanness of inadequate and congested housing' (1978:10). A large infrastructure of licensed premises emerged in the mid-nineteenth century as brewers and publicans began to exploit lucrative commercial opportunities to service the 'social needs' of the Mancunian worker. This prototypic night-time economy was facilitated by the free-trade principles embodied in the Licensing Act of 1828 and the Beer Act of 1830.

The Licensing Act placed no statutory restrictions on drinking hours except to recommend that drinking establishments should close during Sunday morning service (Harrison, 1994). The Beer Act permitted any ratepayer to brew and sell beer on payment of a nominal annual fee of two guineas. Unlike the traditional variants of the public house which continued to be licensed by the magistracy, the new 'beershops' drew their licences direct from the Excise, making them effectively exempt from the justices' control (Baggott, 1986; Harrison, 1994; Wilson, 1940). Beershops proliferated in Manchester, often operating from the front of terraced houses. According to Kidd, 'by 1843 the *Manchester Directory* recorded 920 beershops, 624 taverns and pubs and 31 inns and hotels: a total of 1, 575 liquor establishments, or one for every 154 inhabitants' (1993:52).

In the years following the Beer Act, public drunkenness in the new industrial centres became widespread and the free-trade approach became the subject of sustained criticism. Although the legislation made beer more readily available and appeared to encourage its consumption, there was a lack of corresponding regulatory provision (Baggott, 1986). Engels, like many of his middle-class contemporaries, was appalled by the extent of drunkenness, disorder, and vice in 1840s Manchester. He offers the following description of nightlife on a typical weekend:

On Saturday evenings, especially when wages are paid and work stops somewhat earlier than usual, when the whole working class pours from its own poor quarters into the main thoroughfares, intemperance may be seen in all its brutality. I have rarely come out of Manchester on such an evening without meeting numbers of people staggering and seeing others lying in the gutter. On Sunday evening the same scene is usually repeated, only less noisily (Engels, 1987:152).

Engels' description implies that the working-class population had an almost universal propensity for public drunkenness and disorder.[1] However in reality, these informal street gatherings were predominately *youthful*, and although public spaces were regularly colonized by young women as well as young men (A. Davies, 1999), those arrested for drink-related violence were predominately lower-working-class males. When females were arrested it was typically for drunkenness, disorderly conduct, prostitution, and petty theft (Jones, 1982). Public violence and disorder in Manchester was frequently fuelled by religious and ethnic tensions, especially within the Irish community who inhabited the poorest districts, and between the Irish and the City's other inhabitants. As Jones notes:

The police statistics suggest that in the mid century between a third and a half of those arrested were Irish . . . about a third were females, and a third of these and up to half the males were under the age of thirty. Typical female drunkards were prostitutes and servants . . . those males arrested were poorly educated, and gave their occupations as labourers, unemployed, factory hands, hawkers, joiners, sawyers, tailors, clerks and agents (Jones, 1982:164).

In the 1829–1880 period there was considerable anxiety within 'respectable society' about the behaviour and mores of the urban working classes. According to Jones, 'Manchester became a focal

---

[1] This book focuses on *public* violence, however we also acknowledge the high level of (often alcohol-related) domestic violence. According to Jones 'the most dangerous place in nineteenth century Manchester was the home' (1982:152).

point of the well-publicized debate over the morality and effects of industrial capitalism' (1982:145). Manchester's propertied classes had a 'profound fear of the poor' due to the perceived threats of violent insurrection and moral decay' (Davies, 1985:30). Within the discourses of the middle-class orthodoxy, the inhabitants of the City's 'rookeries' were cast as the 'mob', a seething mass of intemperance, irreligion, immorality, and crime. These views found classic expression in J.P. Kay's *The Moral and Physical Condition of the Working Classes Employed in the Cotton Manufacture in Manchester*, published in 1832. By the 1830s, several alliances of industrialists and predominately lower middle-class moral entrepreneurs (such as the Manchester and Salford Temperance Society) were attempting to reform and regulate popular alcohol-based recreations in Northern English towns and cities (Bailey, 1978; Gutzke, 1989; Harrison, 1967, 1994; Thompson, 1967). By serving a stiff cocktail of persuasion and legislation, the reformers aimed to wean the workers away from the 'evils' of drink, toward the more sober and 'rational' leisure pursuits to be found in the public parks, libraries, and church halls. However, regardless of their evangelical tone, the temperance campaigns were sometimes informed as much by economic imperative as by moral indignation. As Harrison explains:

The change in methods of production . . . created an employing class with a direct interest in curbing drunkenness . . . Because drink and customary recreations were inseparable, it was difficult to obtain precise and regular workmanship—qualities which were precisely what the factory system required. Protest against drunkenness became frequent in the early nineteenth century as much because it was no longer convenient to unite work with recreation as because drunkenness had become more prevalent (Harrison, 1994:41).

In 1839 Edwin Chadwick was to use the 'Manchester problem' as evidence in support of his campaign for a national preventative police force (Davies, 1985; Jones, 1982) and attempts to impose social discipline on the working-class city were eventually assisted by the introduction of the 'New Police' in 1842. One of the main duties of the early Manchester constabulary was to monitor and suppress popular leisure activities considered by the City's élite to be 'conducive to immorality, disorder, or crime' (Storch, 1976:483; see also Davies, 1985; and Jones, 1982). As Kidd (1993:59) argues, the '"carrot" of rational recreation was accompanied by the "stick" of police action'. In 1843, for example, the police made a total of 12,147 arrests, 4,198 of which were for drunkenness (Chief Constable's Report for 1843, cited in Hewitt, 1979:62). S.J. Davies argues that from about 1855 there were increasing demands for more forceful police action against 'drunkards, brawlers and prostitutes often linked to strong anti-Irish feelings' (1985:36). The vigorous policing strategies led to:

… an explosive growth in the number of arrests and cases proceeded with. Between 1860 and 1869, the number of cases proceeded with rose from 9,877 to 28,229. There was an increase in prosecution and arrest in every area of crime but the largest increase by far was in charges of drunkenness which went up from 2,329 cases in 1860 to 11,461 in 1869 or put another way, from 23% of the total to 40% (Davies, 1985:36).

Although 'between a third and a half of arrests were for drunkenness and disorderly conduct' (Jones, 1982:150), such statistics give the impression that Manchester was experiencing a more general crime wave. Manchester became famous not only for its enterprise and innovation, but also for its crime. As W.B. Neale wrote in 1840, 'if you say in any other part of England that you are from Manchester you are at once supposed to be a thief' (ibid.:58). Later commentators such as Alfred Aspland (1868) claimed that the Manchester 'crime wave' was the result of inadequate policing.

The Manchester policing initiatives of the late 1860s and early 1870s coincided with national temperance campaigns demanding more stringent licensing laws (Jones, 1982). Partially as a result of such campaigns, licensing laws in nineteenth-century England gradually shifted from the laissez-faire to the interventionist. The Wine and Beerhouses Act of 1869 brought all licences back under the control of the magistracy, thus in effect repealing the free-trade legislation of 1830 (Baggott, 1986). Moreover, the Licensing Acts of 1872 and 1874 made drinking hours subject to statutory control: pubs and beershops in provincial towns and cities were now required to close at 11 p.m. Monday–Saturday and 10 p.m. on Sundays (see Harrison, 1994:315–317).

Temperance campaigners became particularly concerned with the corrupting influence of 'singing saloons', pub function rooms in which informal 'tavern concerts' took place. By the 1860s, Manchester's more enterprizing publicans were seeking to develop this remunerative market formula and the singing saloons became more professionally managed, heavily promoted, and commercially successful (Bailey, 1978; Poole, 1982). Pubs and singing saloons such as Ben Lang's near Victoria Bridge (see Haslam, 1999) were 'big business' providing the licensed trade with an even greater economic stake in the new popular culture. Throughout the nineteenth century 'the trade' offered powerful and firmly entrenched opposition to the reforming zeal of the temperance movements (Gutzke, 1989; Wilson, 1940).

The singing saloon developed into the music hall and variety theatre of later decades (Bailey, 1978; Burton, 1987). Kidd notes how 'music hall entrepreneurs like Edward Moss built "empires" literally and commercially... In 1899, *Moss Empires Ltd.* was formed with share capital of around £1m' (Kidd, 1993:129). For Kidd, the importance of the music hall cannot be underestimated as it was to form the 'prototype of the modern entertainment industry' (Kidd, 1993:129).

By the late nineteenth century, sobriety and decorum had become powerful indices of social mobility in Northern England and alcohol consumption declined from the mid-1870s through to the early 1930s (Weir, 1984) as the skilled and semi-skilled manual workers and their families who made up the 'respectable' working classes, began to consume less alcohol. Although recorded levels of non-indictable 'drunk and disorderly' offences for England did not peak until 1876, they were to drop sharply in the 1880s and 1890s (Gutzke, 1989), with official statistics for public violence of all kinds showing a similar pattern of decline (Gatrell, 1980). Yet, the Criminal Statistics for this period cannot be regarded as simply revealing the 'facts' about patterns of drink-related crime and disorder (H. Taylor, 1999:113), nor should they be naively interpreted as evidence of any concordant 'civilizing process' (Elias, 1994). Like its contemporary-focused counterpart, historical criminology remains 'haunted by the dark figure of hidden crime and offenders' (Coleman and Moynihan, 1996:1), its statistical indices charting not only substantive patterns of deviant and transgressive behaviour, but also the shifting sands of political discourse, police recording practices and cultural and legislative change. Howard Taylor (1998; 1999) for example, notes how in the late nineteenth and early twentieth century, traditional preventative policing strategies which sought primarily to maintain *public order* via an emphasis on non-indictable prosecutions, fell out of step with the increasingly managerial imperatives of central government. Howard Taylor argues that between 1900 and 1939, shifts in the political economy of crime control had a profound effect upon street-level policing with officers encouraged to switch their attention away from 'drunks and vagrants to motorists and indictable offenders' ('real criminals') (1999:113).

This shift can also be understood within the context of what Garland (1985) has termed the 'penal-welfare complex', a political, discursive and substantive policy development which gained prominence in the 1880–1920 period. Penal-welfare strategies prioritized the assessment and classification *of offenders* and the establishment of new agencies and institutions to administer a more specialized and differentiated range of sanctions (see Garland, 1985:22–24). As Garland notes, 'many of the new sanctions directed attention towards the type of character and antecedents of the offender, rather than the gravity of the offence' (p.24), seeking to reform and to 'cure', as much as to discipline and punish. During this period, low-level drink-related disorder temporarily moved off the criminal justice agenda being regarded as a symptom of 'the disease of inebriety' (Valverde, 1998), a problem requiring medico-social, rather than purely punitive intervention. Thus, the Inebriates Act of 1898 established new ways of dealing with 'habitual drunkards' and other drink-related offenders by placing them, not within the 'general mixed prison' (Garland, 1985:22), but within the distinctly curative regime of the inebriate reformatory (Hunt et al., 1989; Johnstone, 1996). Agencies such as the National Society for the Prevention of Cruelty to Children (NSPCC) and the Salvation Army were particularly instrumental in placing the drink-related diseases/vices of the 'dangerous classes' within the realm of disciplinary-rehabilitation/ penal-welfare policy (see Valverde, 1998, Chapter 3). Female inebriates, especially neglectful working-class mothers were of particular concern to the penal-welfare agencies, whilst the police and the courts continued to target their 'usual suspects', young male delinquents (typically unskilled labourers) and vagrants, described by magistrates as being of 'amongst the lowest class' (Gutze, 1989:33; Harrison, 1994:397).

Legislative shifts were also beginning to have an impact upon the availability of alcohol by reducing the number of licensed premises:

As magistrates regained authority and greater power over licensing in the the years 1869–72, three developments ensued: approval of new licences virtually ceased; many beerhouses closed, unable to meet higher rating qualifications or comply with harsher laws; and licence prices correspondingly rose (Gutze, 1989:50).

Yet, despite the decline of the 'beer house' and the strong social pressures, placed especially upon women (Godfrey, 2002), to conform to the ascendant codes of asceticism and respectability, attempts to impose new disciplines of 'play' to mirror those of the workplace, continued to face resistance. In Manchester and Salford, 'fights outside public houses at closing-time at weekends assumed the status of a spectator sport in working-class districts' (Davies, 1998:354). Violent gangs of young men, known locally as 'scuttlers' (Davies, 1998; Humphries, 1981; Pearson, 1983) and associated 'rough girls' (A. Davies, 1999; Godfrey, 2002) would converge on the streets of the night-time city. As Davies explains:

On Friday and Saturday nights, the city centre formed a contested terrain, as gangs drawn from as far apart as Salford and Bradford confronted each other in music-halls, nearby beer houses and the surrounding streets. In these conflicts, the reputations of the leading figures were constantly adjusted, whether enhanced or undermined. Moreover, scuttlers who were worsted in an affray frequently appear to have launched revenge attacks in attempts to salvage their reputation and honour (Davies, 1998:362).

The Scuttling gangs were staunchly parochial, taking their names from the street or area from which membership was drawn (Humphries, 1981) and they displayed a fervent dedication to the defence of 'turf' and neighbourhood reputation.

With the onset of the Great War in 1914, the alcohol problem became an issue of national security, giving the temperance movement an unexpected boost. The government believed that the war effort was being severely undermined by excessive alcohol consumption:

Low productivity in the munitions factories and the shipyards was blamed on excessive drinking by the workers...The Defence of the Realm (Amendment) Act of 1915 introduced a number of emergency measures which reflected this concern including a drastic reduction in the permitted hours of licensed premises (Baggott, 1986:11).

During the War years there was a dramatic fall in levels of alcohol use (Williams and Brake, 1980; Wilson, 1940), a factor which persuaded the post-war government to incorporate many of the war-time restrictions into the Licensing Act of 1921. This legislation has now formed the basis of licensing control for over eighty years (Baggott, 1986, 1990).

After a brief upsurge following the end of the War, alcohol consumption continued to fall. A Home Office statement of 1924 attributed this to 'the high price and diluted strength of intoxicating liquors, to restricted hours of sale, to unemployment, to the increased cost of living, and, last but not least, to a gradual change of habit and opinion' (British Parliamentary Papers, 1926:8, cited in H. Taylor, 1999:119–120). By 1931 the Royal Commission on Licensing felt it could justifiably claim that 'the drink problem had ceased to be a "gigantic evil"' (Weir, 1984). In the inter-war years, financial hardship caused by economic depression coupled with the emergence of new leisure pursuits such as the 'pictures', the 'wireless', the growth of professional football and the rise of the commercial dance hall all served to challenge the dominance of pub-centred working-class culture (Kidd, 1993; Weir, 1984; Williams and Brake, 1979).

The 'dance craze'

Dance halls had emerged in the early years of the twentieth century, yet reached their peak of popularity in the 1920s and 1930s. The growth of the dance hall after the Great War seemed to symbolize a new freedom amongst working-class youth as old social mores and barriers gradually began to break down (Davies, 1992; Haslam, 1999). In *The Classic Slum*, an autobiographical account of his youth in Salford, Robert Roberts recalls that 'there was no going back for the young . . . they turned their faces to the twentieth century and went dancing . . .' (1971:219). Manchester's most famous dance halls were the Ritz on Whitworth Street and the Plaza on Oxford Street (Burton, 1987; Kidd, 1993). These halls were large and glamorous, yet admission prices remained modest as dance hall entrepreneurs sought to fill their venues almost every night of the week. Roberts' evocative description of the dance halls invokes intriguing semantic parallels with the clubland argot of the early 1990s:

. . . the band struck up, the great hall dimmed and a searchlight hit a huge ball of coloured mirrors turning at the ceiling, setting a myriad bright dabs of spectrum gambolling along the walls . . . the young sons and daughters of the common herd danced night after night, bodies close in an ecstasy of rhythm (Roberts, 1971:233–236).

Access to the 'dance craze' was often strictly differentiated by gender; 'dance enthusiasts, especially girls' remained the subjects of parental discipline (Davies, 1992:89) and might be forbidden to attend. For young men, dance halls could sometimes be dangerous places, particularly if some of their peers had violence, rather than 'dancing or courtship in mind' (Davies, 1992:92). Like the pubs and music halls of the nineteenth century, dance halls were sometimes the sites of 'confrontations between rival street gangs' (ibid.). The dance hall entrepreneur shared with the publican and the music hall proprietor a determination to maintain levels of decorum and respectability conducive to the dual imperatives of security and profitability (Bailey, 1978). Strict controls over dance hall proceedings were imposed by 'MCs', whose authority was maintained by the presence of 'large chuckers out' (Roberts, 1971:234). A local man interviewed by Davies recalls that the Mancunian dance halls of the 1930s would often employ local boxers and 'hardmen' on their doors (Davies, 1992).

The popularity of the dance halls continued until the 1950s when a period of relative affluence and the corresponding emergence of what Abrams (1959) has called *The Teenage Consumer*, brought new forms of night-time leisure consumption to the city centre. According to Abrams' survey, by the late 1950s almost full employment and a general rise in living standards had permitted young people to enjoy unprecedented levels of disposable income. In response, a new market sector had been developed to supply the increasing demands for youth-oriented products such as rock 'n' roll records, clothes, films, magazines, and cosmetics. The 'newly affluent' young also sought their own spaces within which to socialize and consume: coffee bars, milk bars, and 'record hops'.

In his book on the early Manchester 'pop' scene Alan Lawson argues that, 'for many teenagers in the mid-fifties the coffee bar performed a crucial social function particularly when they began to introduce that great American institution, the juke box' (1992:8). The generally raucous ambience of the coffee bars served (sometimes intentionally) to alienate older generations, thus providing young people with exclusive 'ownership' of these new commercially organized spaces. At this time, Manchester coffee bars were rarely licensed to sell alcohol. The bars were essentially a place for the young to meet, listen to popular music and dance. Haslam describes the famous Oasis Coffee Bar, opened in 1961:

... styling itself 'Manchester's Most Fab Club for Young People,' the *Oasis* opened at 10am for coffee and snacks, closed at 2pm and then reopened from 6pm until 2am with live music and DJs, maintaining a no-alcohol policy throughout the day and night (1999:91).

Record-hops often took place in dance halls and youth clubs with the live dance band now replaced by a disc jockey playing beat-heavy American rock 'n' roll records. Increasingly, from the early 1960s, such entertainment could also be found in purpose-built 'disco-theques' (see Jones and Kantonen, 1999; Thornton, 1995).

Coffee clubs and licensed nightclubs attracting a young clientele proliferated during the North West's 'Beat Boom' of the early 1960s; Lawson (1992:136–139) lists over 200 such venues in the Manchester conurbation. According to many commentators (for example, Haslam, 1999; Lawson, 1992; Lee, 1996; Lovatt, 1999), Manchester's nightlife flourished during this period. As Lovatt states:

...there are many who remember cities like Manchester in the '60s as exploding with clubs, pubs and cafes... this night-time activity was rooted in the lives and works of large, wealthy industrial cities which had nothing to prove to anybody, and were out having fun (Lovatt, 1999:18).

This expansion of night-time leisure was facilitated by a relaxation of the licensing laws. The Licensing Act of 1961 reduced the power of the Justices to refuse a new licence by giving the applicant a right of appeal. There was also a generally low level of enforcement of the licensing laws during this period (Baggott, 1986), allowing a number of Manchester city centre venues to gain reputations for serving 'after hours'. The coffee clubs, however, were alcohol-free private members clubs and therefore, unlike *licensed* premises they were not subject to strict regulatory control. Unlicensed coffee clubs were in effect 'free of direct police supervision' since 'a warrant had to be obtained before any member of the Constabulary could gain access if the owner had originally refused them admission' (Lee, 1996:101). This regulatory void generated considerable consternation within local government and the Manchester police.

Chief Constable J.A. McKay's Annual Report of 1964 included a sensational exposé entitled 'Coffee Beat Clubs' prepared by Chief Superintendent Dingwall which was based on intelligence gathered by teenage cadets, 'The Mod Squad', (as they were known by local clubbers) (Lee, 1996). Dingwall denounced coffee club proprietors as 'unscrupulous' characters, condemned their premises as 'dimly lit' and 'insanitary', and their patrons as, at best, naïve and vulnerable, and at worst, unsavoury and criminal. Particular reference was made to the consumption of amphetamines and cannabis, the 'sinister' presence of 'men of colour' and the corruption of (white female) innocence (Lee, 1996). According to the local musician turned academic, C.P. Lee:

So concerned was the Chief Constable that by August 1965 he had almost singlehandedly generated a moral panic sufficiently large to warrant the passing of a special Act of Parliament allowing the police sweeping, some would say draconian, powers to deal with the problem created by the coffee clubs (1995:7).

The Manchester Corporation Act of 1965, a private Act of Parliament, was 'an astonishing piece of legislation...an Act of Parliament to close down the clubs in Manchester, just in Manchester' (C.P. Lee interviewed by Haslam, 1999:101). The Act, which came into force on 1 January 1966, gave Manchester police extended powers of regulation and control. Henceforth, 'no-one could own, operate or run a club without explicit police permission' (Lee, 1996:113). All premises were to be:

'properly registered' by a person deemed 'fit and proper' to run such a club. The police would have the power to veto any application to open such premises ... would decide if health and safety standards had been breached and would have powers to enter the premises without recourse to an official warrant (Lovatt, 1999:16)

The implementation of the Act was swift: clubs in Manchester were subjected to frequent raids by the police and City council inspectors and many premises were closed down. According to Haslam:

Some closed even during 1965 when the owners realized that they would never be able to meet the fire, safety and sanitation standards, nor control the clientele in the draconian manner the Act required (club owners, for instance, were liable to have their licences revoked if any illegal drugs were consumed on the premises, whether they were aware of such activity or not) (Haslam, 1999:102).

In order to remain financially viable, the clubs that did survive were forced to obtain alcohol licences and to become more adult-orientated. According to C.P. Lee, 'by 1968 there were only two city centre venues catering exclusively for young people: the *Magic Village* and the Twisted Wheel' (1996:115).

In the early 1970s, the Twisted Wheel was to become the first 'Northern Soul' venue (Milestone, 1998), a dance music genre which attracted a dedicated, predominant white, working-class following throughout Lancashire, Cheshire, West Yorkshire, and North Staffordshire. Northern Soul sessions were characterized by their duration, the notorious 8 p.m. to 8 a.m. 'all-nighters', and by the acrobatic dancing of many devotees.[2] Unlike mainstream 'discos', whose audiences primarily sought alcohol and sex, Soul nights were 'dance-orientated' and often amphetamine-fuelled, thus having 'clear parallels with the Rave events of 1988 and beyond' (Haslam, 1999: 146). Moreover, like the temples of the later dance scene, Soul venues such as the Twisted Wheel were heavily policed, being 'frequently raided by drug squad and fire officers' (Milestone, 1998:136).

Despite its important place within the chronology of Mancunian nightlife, Northern Soul was only ever the passion of a minority. By the early 1970s, social and economic factors such as industrial recession, suburbanization, and the decentralization of businesses and entertainment facilities (Burton, 1987; Law, 1986), together with strict regulation and repressive policing (Lee, 1995, 1996; Lovatt, 1999; Milestone, 1998), had all contributed to the decline of city centre nightlife.

Manchester and the mill towns of Lancashire were some of the first areas in Britain to suffer the effects of wholesale de-industrialization, the cotton industry's decline preceding the 'crises in steel, shipbuilding, and coal by several decades' (Singleton, 1991:1). Due to the manufacture of artificial fibres, the oil crises of the mid-1970s and the impact of increasing overseas competition:

Employment in the cotton industry halved between 1963 and 1974. Famous firms, which had employed hundreds for over a century, were forced to close. Hundreds of workers were made redundant as factories closed. The industry which had created Manchester was dying; Cottonopolis no longer existed (Branigan, 1999:10).

Manchester's de-industrialization was not restricted to its cotton industry. According to Lloyd and Mason (1978), between 1966

---

[2] For an exhilarating autobiographical account of the Northern Soul scene see McKenna, 1996.

and 1972 the inner core of the conurbation lost one in three of its manufacturing jobs and one quarter of its factories and workshops closed. Summarizing the work of Peck and Emmerich (1992a, 1992b), Taylor et al. reveal that:

The best estimates we have suggest that at least 207,000 manufacturing jobs were lost in Greater Manchester between 1972 and 1984, with about three-quarters of these losses occurring in the period after 1978. In the last thirty years, more than half of Manchester's industrial jobs have disappeared...changes in the pattern of employment are clear. By far the largest absolute increase in jobs has been in the banking, insurance and building service sectors, with the second most significant area of increase being in hotel and catering (Taylor et al., 1996:61).

According to Kidd (1993:189), since the 1950s the shift towards service employment in north-west England 'has been particularly marked in Manchester'. By 1985 only '23% of the workforce in the Manchester metropolitan district were employed in manufacturing' (ibid.). However, Peck and Emmerich, (1992b:19) argue that it is mistaken to assume that Manchester has made a smooth evolutionary 'transition from a manufacturing-dominated past to a services dominated future'. Writing in the early 1990s, Peck and Emmerich (1992a, 1992b) suggested that Greater Manchester's economy remained structurally weak, the growth in service sector employment having proved insufficient to compensate for the losses sustained in manufacturing. Whatever the economic facts, a number of commentators (for example, Lovatt, 1999 and Milestone, 1996) suggest that with the demise of the manufacturing sector and subsequent increases in unemployment, Manchester was effectively stripped of much of its identity and purpose, creating a mood of crisis and melancholia which was to have a profound effect upon leisure life in the city centre.

At this time the physical signs of economic collapse—deserted and decaying mills and warehouses, derelict land and silent machinery—were clearly visible in many parts of the city. As W.S. Sebald describes:

I would go out...and walk amidst the City's immense and time-blackened 19th Century buildings...On those wonderings...I never ceased to be amazed by the completeness with which anthracite-coloured Manchester, the city from which industrialisation had spread across the entire world, displayed the clearly chronic process of its impoverishment and degradation to anyone who cared to see. Even the grandest buildings, such as the *Royal Exchange*, the *Refuge Assurance Company*, the *Grosvenor Picture Palace*, and indeed *Piccadilly Plaza*, which had been built only a few years before, seemed so empty and abandoned that one might have supposed oneself surrounded by mysterious facades or theatrical backdrops (Sebald, 1993:156–7).

In Moss Side, an inner-city area just two miles South of the city centre, long-standing tensions between local youths and the police erupted into riot in July 1981. Yet, Manchester's social and economic problems were not unique, indeed they appeared to reflect a national urban crisis. In the early 1980s, public and political concerns regarding young people's drinking habits were also being voiced following the apparent (re)emergence of a weekend 'binge-drinking' culture (Dorn, 1983; Gofton, 1990; Hope, 1985). These anxieties were later fuelled by serious incidents of alcohol-related violence in 'non-metropolitan' areas occurring in the summer of 1988 (McMurran and Hollin, 1989; Tuck, 1989) and by subsequent media representations of the 'lager lout' (Ramsay, 1989, 1990). Within this context, the Chief Constable of Greater Manchester Police (GMP), James Anderton, launched a timely campaign to control and repress Mancunian nightlife.

Anderton was renowned for voicing his own controversial opinions. At a seminar on AIDS in December 1986, he told delegates that homosexuals, prostitutes, and drug-addicts were 'swirling around in a cesspit of their own making' (Prince, 1988:97). Anderton's religious asceticism was reflected in GMP strategy. As Quilley (1997:283) notes: 'the police took a meticulous and highly obstructive interest in licensing applications', particularly those of gay venues. Gay clubs such as the 'men only' Napoleon's 'became a particular target during the late 1970s and the early 1980s' (Whittle, 1994:34). Following a raid in 1978, GMP unsuccessfully attempted to bring a prosecution against Napoleon's under a nineteenth-century by-law forbidding 'licentious dancing'. During a raid on the same venue in 1984, 'customers were asked to provide their names and addresses and the club membership list was seized' (Whittle, 1994:34). However, economic collapse and repressive policing were not the only factors contributing to the decline of the city centre's night-time economy.

Central Manchester's economic problems were accompanied by huge population losses. Between 1951 and 1981 the population of the City's inner core fell by 52.1% (Law, 1986). In the mid-1980s, after decades of suburbanization, only about 200 of Manchester's city-wide population of over 400,000 people lived in the city centre (Lovatt, 1997). The twentieth century saw the city centre become encircled with deprived inner-city estates. Kidd (1993:213) notes how 'the outflow to the suburbs left behind generation after generation of poor inner-city inhabitants, ill-housed and poorly supplied with amenities'.

Decentralization intensified in the 1970s and 1980s with the growth of shopping facilities and offices in the outer conurbation (Law, 1986). Manchester was rapidly becoming what Joel Garreau (1991) has termed an 'Edge City', a declining urban core surrounded by a functionally independent residential, industrial, and commercial hinterland (Oc and Tiesdell, 1997). Although central Manchester did remain important for service sector employment, entertainment, and leisure activities, many social groups came to regard the night-time city as a place of fear and desolation. The economic crises and street violence merely fuelled deeply embedded cultural discourses of 'anti-urbanism' within which cities have long been associated with 'poverty, disease and dirt, crime and disorder' (Bianchini, 1990:4). Manchester City Centre, like the core of many British cities during this period, became a location that had 'acquired purely negative connotations' (Lovatt, 1999:10). Thus, for the suburbanite having perhaps already commuted to the city in the day, 'the thought of a return to "enjoy" what the city centre had to offer (at night) was seldom agreeable' (Williams and Brake, 1980:271).

3
Post-industrial Manchester: From Cotton to Carlsberg

In this, the second chapter of our case study, we describe how in the globalized post-industrial context of contemporary Manchester, pressure from political and economic forces largely external to the local state has encouraged the deregulation of many arenas of economic activity. At the same time, many policing and crime prevention duties which were traditionally the responsibility of the central state are now being performed by local private sector interests who 'police for profit' (Spitzer and Scull, 1977). These changes have had a number of disturbing and troublesome consequences for Manchester's night-time economy, specifically in relation to problems of public violence and the activities of (dis)organized criminal networks.

The phoenix and the night-owl

Although in many ways, the late 1970s and early 1980s were possibly Manchester city centre's darkest hour, it was during this period that the seeds of its public–private sector partnership funded, property-led, and leisure-based regeneration of the 1990s were sown (Law, 1992). In the mid-1980s environmental and accessibility improvements such as pedestrianization and the cleaning of buildings were backed by the 'City Centre Promotional Campaign', a policy initiative jointly funded by the public and private sectors which was designed to rejuvenate the retail sector (Law, 1986). There were also efforts to develop 'heritage' and 'cultural' tourism (Law, 1993a; McIntosh and Prentice, 1999; Urry, 1990). In 1982, the derelict Castlefield basin (site of the Roman fort of Mamucium and Manchester's earliest canal and rail terminals) was designated as Britain's first 'urban heritage park' (Brumhead, 1988). Granada Television opened their gates to the public in 1988 and the 'Granada Studios Tour' soon became Manchester's most popular tourist attraction, in particular because of the opportunity it offered to walk around the *Coronation Street* set (Law, 1993b). In the same year, the Thatcher government set up Britain's first Urban Development Corporation (UDC), the Central Manchester Development Corporation (CMDC), a centrally designated planning, development, and marketing initiative which subsequently played an important role in the early property-based regeneration of the city centre. However, the efforts of the CMDC were predated by a number of other initiatives.

In order to retain the Victorian character of the city centre, redundant buildings from Manchester's industrial and commercial past were converted rather than demolished to accommodate new retail and leisure facilities. Amongst the most successful of these early transformations were: the conversion of Central Station into G-Mex—the Greater Manchester Exhibition Centre (opened 1986)—the conversion of the former Affleck and Brown store on Oldham Street into Affleck's Palace, small units for fashion, music, and art retailers (which opened in 1984, and was the first development by local entrepreneur Tom Bloxham, who went on to establish the highly acclaimed property development company Urban Splash), and the transformation of a disused yacht warehouse on Whitworth Street into the world famous Hacienda nightclub (opened in 1982).

The city centre regeneration initiatives of the early 1980s were informed by a 'sense of urgency in the areas of planning and policy' (Law, 1986:37) and as such were a direct response to the social and economic impact of de-industrialization and processes of decentralization. However, it was not until later in that decade, following a fundamental shift in the politico-ideological rationale of local government, that the pursuit of economic growth through 'hallmark' events and 'prestige' developments would come to *dominate* the agenda of Manchester City Council (MCC).

In 1987, a significant policy shift occurred within Manchester's Labour-controlled city council under the leadership of Graham Stringer. Quilley argues that this shift involved:

...two radically different political and economic projects: municipal socialist resistance to Thatcherism in the period preceding 1987, and (following Labour's defeat at the 1987 general election) a subsequent ... accommodation with central government, active partnership with the local private sector, and the development of a new entrepreneurial model of development (1999:187).

MCC embraced the same free market agenda that had previously served to undermine its own (local) interventionist project. The change within Manchester's 'Municipal Left' was a response to the policies of successive Tory governments. As Stoker (1988:142) notes, the first two Thatcher administrations passed over forty major Acts of Parliament with 'significant implications for local government', usually of an adverse character. This flurry of legislation reflected the New Right's political commitment to bring the disciplines of the free market and competitive tendering to bear on Labour-controlled local authorities and their 'inefficient' public service deliveries (Gurr and King, 1987; Stoker, 1988). The Tories succeeded in restricting the power of local authorities at a time when processes of de-industrialization had already undermined the economic base of many provincial cities. As Gurr and King (1987:71) argue, whilst many local governments were becoming 'increasingly dependent fiscally on the central state', key economic decisions were simultaneously being placed outside of the local state's jurisdiction.

Quilley (1999:187) claims that councillors in Manchester were well aware of the limits that both national government and economic globalization had imposed on their own 'local economic sovereignty', and therefore made a 'calculated decision' to embrace the entrepreneurial agenda. The City Council justified its new style of local governance as a pragmatic response to the pressures and demands from political and economic forces at regional, national and global level and as an attempt to 'get the best for Manchester'. The new strategies involved co-operating with central government's property-led regeneration initiatives such as City Challenge and the CMDC and also with Manchester's local business élite (Peck, 1995; Tickell and Peck, 1996). As Loftman and Nevin note:

Although Manchester City Council was originally hostile to the imposition of an Urban Development Corporation, the CMDC . . . became a crucial and integral part of the public-private sector coalition in the City, committed to a pro-growth local economic strategy (1996:1008).

Manchester's regeneration initiatives were also galvanized by bids to host the 1996 and 2000 Olympic Games. In the run-up to the second bid in 1993, Graham Stringer told a local newspaper:

Cities, like sprinters, can't stand still. They have to make progress or go into decline. The great days of heavy industry won't return. We have to find new ways forward, and that is where the Olympic Games come in. Our bid for the 2000 games is no town hall fantasy. It is a calculated move capable of transforming Manchester (*Manchester Evening News*, 17 February 1993:2).

Although both campaigns were unsuccessful, the *Manchester 2000* bid committee were able to secure 'infrastructure spending to the tune of £200 m' (Cochrane et al., 1995:1322), including a significant amount of central government grant aid. Moreover, the bid 'brought marked increases in international business awareness of the city' (Ward, 1998:207). Crucially, the bidding campaign also helped to consolidate the new spirit of co-operation and partnership between MCC and the local business community (Cochrane et al., 1995; Quilley, 1999).

The new corporate slogan: 'Manchester City Council: making things happen' emphasized the new entrepreneurial discourse, replacing the old 'defending jobs, improving services' of 'municipal socialism'. For the most part, 'making things happen' has involved facilitating economic growth and attracting investment from the EU, from central government and from private corporations (Peck and Tickell, 1995; Quilley, 1995). It has also involved attempts to attract people to the city, as visitors, workers, and residents via sustained place-marketing campaigns.

During the 1990s, the regeneration of the built environment and other 'symbolically important' (Peck and Tickell, 1995:56) civic achievements continued apace. Manchester Airport became '*the* major international airport outside south east England, (Law, 1993a:39), handling over 17 million passengers per annum. Other developments since the early 1990s include: the opening of the Metrolink light railway system, the Lowry Centre at Salford Quays, the regeneration of Ancoats 'the world's first industrial suburb' (King, 1999a) and the opening of the largest Marks & Spencer store in the world, following the terrorist bombing of June 1996. The city centre continues to change rapidly as a result of a sustained and radical programme of property development (Webster, 1999a, 1999b), with developers such as Urban Splash driving a renaissance in city centre living (Dunkerley, 2001). 'Hallmark' events have included Manchester's nomination as City of Drama for 1994, victory in the City Challenge competition for the regeneration of the inner city area of Hulme, and selection as host city to the 2002 Commonwealth Games.

With the aid of the local business élite, MCC have forged a new urban politics of 'strategic consensus' (Quilley, 1999:203) based on a policy of civic 'boosterism'. This boosterism involves promoting what are seen as Manchester's service, information, cultural, arts, and leisure-based strengths (for example, financial services, industrial heritage, football, youth culture, pop music, nightlife, and general cosmopolitanism), whilst ignoring or downplaying its weaknesses (the loss of manufacturing jobs, inner-city poverty, crime, and wet climate). As Quilley notes:

According to the *Manchester script*, the city has been reborn as a post-modern, post-industrial, and cosmopolitan city, standing in Europe's 'premier league'. New Manchester is a vibrant and culturally diverse place to live, and well-connected to take advantage of the emerging information economy (1999:190–191).

There are, however, good reasons to be sceptical about a place-marketing campaign which, by continually reciting words and phrases such as 'vibrant', 'cosmopolitan', 'European', 'creative', and '24-hour city' seeks to depict Manchester's economic development from an industrial to a post-industrial city, as linear, evolutionary, and unitary (Mole, 1996).

The City Council's private sector partners have sometimes sought to remind councillors that, despite the ravages of the 1970s and 1980s, Manchester still has a manufacturing base (Quilley, 1999). Indeed, as recently as 1997, Urban Geographers Peck and Tickell estimated that a quarter of Greater Manchester's workforce were still employed in manufacturing (Peck and Tickell, 1997). As Quilley argues:

In some senses references to post-industrial Manchester are the product of . . . high-octane boosterism . . . the modus operandi of these regeneration mechanisms is to disseminate positive imagery, they tend to reduce complex economic processes to one-dimensional and highly optimistic formulations that characterize change in terms of painless but fundamental transition (1999:192).

As an MCC marketing officer commented, 'a lot of it is to do with shedding Manchester's old image. I don't think we are brave enough to say "manufacturing and it rains a lot"' (cited in Quilley, 1999:193).

Despite these concerns, spectacular growth *has* occurred within at least one sector of the Council's vision for economic regeneration: the *night-time* economy. In the following paragraphs we examine the ways in which previously marginal elements of local youth culture and sexual identities have been acknowledged and commodified by the local state as municipal assets. These transgressive aspects of the 'post-industrial script' have become central to the 're-imaging' and marketing of Manchester as a '24-Hour City' and the exotic possibilities and temptations of a cosmopolitan and hedonistic Mancunian lifestyle.

Madchester

The recent resurgence of Manchester city centre's night-time economy began in the City's rave revolution of 1988–1991 and so-called 'Madchester' years of 1989 and 1990 (see Champion, 1990; Collin, 1997; Garratt, 1998; Haslam, 1999; Redhead, 1990, 1993; Wilson, 2002). It was during this period that Manchester acquired its reputation as an innovative 'music city', a city at the 'cutting edge' of Britain's popular culture. Manchester had an established reputation for popular music prior to 1988, having produced 10cc, Herman's Hermits, The Hollies, Joy Division, The Buzzcocks, The Fall, The Smiths and Simply Red amongst others. However, the Manchester legend was created in the late 1980s by the *dance* music explosion and the bands influenced by it, most prominently: 808 State, James, New Order, The Happy Mondays, The Inspiral Carpets and The Stone Roses.

In an age of global media and commercial flows, cultural forms and practices inevitably become 'hybrid', rather than locally authentic or 'pure' (Reeves, 1993). However, such forms and practices also 'originate within, interact with, and are inevitably affected by, the physical, social, political and economic factors which surround them' (Cohen, 1991:342). As Cohen argues, with respect to the 'Liverpool sound' 'pop musicians can invoke local sensibilities and influences in their music, which in turn help to "construct" particular places and the ways in which "people conceptualize them"' (1994:117). Thus, the heady mix of guitar pop, combined with the electronic pulse of acid house and the streetwise swagger of the white male working-class 'Manc', became the 'Manchester sound' and its peculiar set of 'imageries and sensibilities rooted in place' (Scott,

1997:333).[1] Furthermore, the emergence of the 'Madchester' scene enabled the city to establish its own, specifically local commercial leisure milieu within the national and international marketplace. Through the notoriety of their key players, Shaun Ryder, Bez (The Happy Mondays) and Ian Brown (The Stone Roses), the 'Madchester' bands sold the image of the Mancunian 'scally', and the accompanying sensibilities of the City's dance scene to the world. A distinctively Mancunian brand of popular cultural product became 'appropriatable' by local musicians, clubland, and fashion entrepreneurs as 'competitive advantage' (Scott, ibid. and see Brown et al., 2000). The 'clued-up' urban lad, the 'blagger', the small-time drug dealer, the DJ, and the dance entrepreneur were all potent icons of the Manchester music scene, becoming role models for a generation of young men (and to a lesser extent young women) and establishing a stylistic template which was to evolve throughout the 1990s and beyond (see Redhead et al., 1998; Robb, 1997, 1999).

The Madchester bands of the late 1980s drew much of their inspiration from the ecstasy-fuelled 'playground' atmosphere then to be found in a handful of city centre House clubs including Konspiracy, The Venue and most famously of them all, The Hacienda.[2] In 1988 and 1989 House nights at The Hacienda achieved that elusive state of 'communitas' (Turner, 1969) or 'unicity' (Maffesoli, 1995), often promised, but rarely delivered in British clubland. A surge of frenzied, but on the whole good-natured hedonism had been harnessed, manifested in 'new revivals of contact (hugging, kissing and massaging) and exchange (drinks, joints, cigarettes and poppers)' (Redhead, 1993:36). This 'sense of unity or membership' (Malbon, 1998:273) was established and maintained via an intricate interweaving of the 'dynamics of commercial manipulation and spontaneous creativity' (Negus, 1996:22).

The growth of Manchester's dance scene was inextricably linked to the 'normalization of recreational drug use' (Measham, Newcombe and Parker, 1994) amongst young people. It heralded the cultural and economic ascendance of north-west England's

---

[1] The rise and fall of the Manchester music scene is charted in the film *24 Hour Party People* (released February 2002), by Liverpudlian director Michael Winterbottom. See also the recent semi-fictional account by Factory Records owner and television presenter, Tony Wilson (Wilson, 2002).

[2] For a frank and amusing autobiographical account see Bez (1998).

'chemical generation'. As the author and former Hacienda DJ, Dave Haslam notes:

The ultimate agent of synthesis was chemical. There is no doubt that the entry of ecstasy into dance clubs gave the scene a huge boost; it opened minds, loosened the crowds, fed the atmosphere, and undoubtedly contributed to the staggering rise of house music (1999:169).

Both the music press (especially the two national weeklies *Melody Maker* and the *New Musical Express*) and the tabloids took a close interest in the early 'Rave' scene (Thornton, 1994) and in particular the links between House music, Mancunian clubland, the Madchester bands, and the 'dance drug' Ecstasy. However, celebration of 'Madchester' was not restricted to British niche media such as the *NME*; Manchester was also touted as the new capital of British youth culture by mainstream publications worldwide, including front-page coverage in U.S. magazines *Newsweek* (Foote, 1990) and *Time*. As O'Connor notes:

Manchester was briefly thrust into the very centre of the global information flow... journalists, commentators and consumers headed for the city. They pored over its spaces as a new pop vernacular exploded... (cited in Lovatt, 1996:154–155).

The publicity surrounding 'Madchester' had a direct social and economic impact on the city, attracting an influx of young 'pop' tourists, a huge increase in student applications to the city's three universities and capital investment from music and fashion entrepreneurs and the licensed trade. As Tim Booth, lead singer of local band James, told the *New Musical Express* in August 1990, The Hacienda had become 'Manchester's Eiffel Tower' (cited in Redhead, 1993:14), 'the most important Northern English venue since The Cavern in Liverpool in the era of Beatlemania' (Redhead: ibid.). However, it was a local landmark that was soon to be threatened with closure.

The Licensing Act of 1988 was widely regarded as a step toward the liberalization of alcohol licensing (Coulson, 1994) due to its removal of afternoon drinking restrictions. However, it also gave the police extended powers to monitor licensed premises and to raise objections to licence applications and renewals. Furthermore, the Act increased the number of licensing sessions from one per annum to seven, affording magistrates many more opportunities to revoke licences. These new powers were soon applied to police Manchester's clubscene. In February 1990, after a sixteen-month surveillance operation, Greater Manchester Police (GMP) urged local magistrates to close The Hacienda on the grounds that it attracted people who were blatantly trading and consuming drugs (see Collin, 1997; Redhead, 1993; Wilson, 2002).

However, somewhat belatedly, the city's nightlife and popular music scene had begun to attract the attention of the local state who were beginning to regard such activity as a potential catalyst of city centre regeneration (Frith, 1993; Wilson, 2002). In an unprecedented display of commitment to the night-time economy, both the Lord Mayor and Council Leader Graham Stringer pledged their support for The Hacienda. Stringer argued that 'The Hacienda is to Manchester what Michaelangelo's David is to Florence' (Brown et al., 2000: 446) an attraction which drew in visitors, made 'a significant contribution to active use of the City core' and helped to raise Manchester's international profile (cited in Redhead, 1993:16). By the summer of 1991, GMP had decided to drop the case and The Hacienda, after a brief period of voluntary closure, continued to trade until June 1997.

The defence of The Hacienda's licence was the first in a series of moves by MCC in its assistance to night-time leisure businesses in the city centre. As the 1990s progressed, Council initiatives became increasingly purposeful. In documenting these strategies we will draw extensively upon the work of Andrew Lovatt of the Manchester Cultural Industries Development Service (formerly a researcher at the Manchester Institute for Popular Culture) who has been directly involved in the monitoring and analysis of these issues since the early 1990s. In an interview with Lovatt in June 1993, Pat Karney, then MCC's Chair of Arts and Leisure stated:

The City's cultural and entertainment industry will not only provide new jobs but also make Manchester a better place to live, work and play. Expansion of this sector will allow us to compete for inward investment on a global stage ... it is the future of this city (cited in Lovatt, 1996:159).

In order to facilitate the development of the night-time economy, MCC began to establish a dialogue with the City's leisure industry 'producers'. A number of key figures in the night-time economy expressed the view that existing licensing laws and entertainment regulations were anachronistic and impeding the development and potential profitability of their businesses (Lovatt, 1999; Redhead,

1997). In a display of their new commitment to the night-time economy, MCC responded by co-ordinating the 'Manchester: More Hours in the Day' initiative, an 'experiment' in extended city centre licensing hours (Heath and Stickland, 1997; Lovatt, 1994a). This initiative, which ran throughout September 1993, allowed licensed premises to remain open until midnight and clubs until 4 a.m., and was timed to coincide with the Boddington's Manchester Festival and the run-up to the second Olympic bid decision. 'More Hours in the Day' was therefore able to exploit a loophole in existing legislation permitting magistrates to extend licensing hours on 'special' occasions.

An MCC-funded evaluation of the initiative found that although more people had used the city centre at night and bar and door takings had increased, there had been a substantial fall in both the number of arrests (−43%) and the number of alcohol-related 'incidents' (−14%) reported in comparison with the previous month (Lovatt, 1994a). Thus, the 'More Hours in the Day' experiment appeared to lend support to the view that a more liberal licensing regime, in which permitted hours are extended but 'staggered', could not only generate additional revenue for the late-night leisure sector, but also lead to a reduction in public disorder. Civic entrepreneurs and licensing applicants used such findings to discredit police objections to new licensed premises developments and to cast GMP as 'killjoys' who were needlessly obstructing city centre regeneration by adhering to a 'dated' and 'puritanical' control mandate.

In pursuit of their new goal, the development of a 'vibrant' night-time economy, MCC developed a number of strategies which sought to 'creatively' interpret or circumvent traditional late-night trading restrictions. In a forthcoming article, Lovatt (p.12) lists a number of important initiatives undertaken by MCC between 1992 and 1994 including:

(i)   Through negotiation with magistrates and the police, MCC led the way to remove the prerequisite to demonstrate 'need' before being granted a new liquor licence.[3]

(ii) Removal of the 'time limit' on PELs (Public Entertainment Licences). This meant that venues holding a PEL could in principle remain open for twenty-four hours a day, seven days a week.

[3] This shift was later reflected at a national level following the publication of revised policy guidance notes from the Justices' Clerks Society in 1999. See Chapter 8.

(iii) The formation of new partnerships with 'cultural entrepreneurs' (including the licensed trade)—particularly the Pub and Club Watch a forum intended to permit Police, licensees, Magistrates and Council to discuss issues of mutual concern.

(iv) The introduction of Doorsafe, a local 'door supervisor' registration scheme.[4]

By emphasizing the economic and social importance of night-time leisure, MCC succeeded in persuading both the local justices and GMP to adopt a more 'positive' and liberal approach to city centre licensing applications. This resulted in a sharp increase in Special Hours Certificate allocations for venues fulfilling the local PEL criterion (providing music, dancing and food, employing registered door staff, and meeting requisite health and safety standards).

Until recently, premises holding both the annually allocated PELs and Special Hours Certificates might typically have been classified as 'nightclubs' or 'discotheques'. However, in Manchester and many other cities, a more liberal allocation of this licence 'pairing' has permitted the once stark divide between 'pubs', 'restaurants', 'discotheques', and 'live music' venues to break down. Manchester's nightlife is now dominated by what are often referred to as 'chameleon bars,' operating as fashionable 'café bars' in the day and boisterous 'dance bars' in the evening (Haslam, 1999; Naylor and Morrison, 1998). Such venues typically offer extensive food and drinks menus and music and dancing until late (usually 1 a.m.).

Urban 'Éxotica'

Facilitation and promotion of the night-time economy now forms an integral part of MCC's campaign to actively reinvent Manchester as a 'progressive European city...cosmopolitan and culturally rich' (MCC, 1994:2). This strategy also involves commodification of the City's social and ethnic diversity. Within the entrepreneurial discourse, the culture and 'lifestyle' of minority groups has been harnessed as 'exotic proof of Manchester's cosmopolitan and progressive credentials' (Quilley, 1995:44), each group being assigned their own market niche and spatial enclave. As Quilley explains:

[4] These schemes are described in detail in Chapter 6.

The Asian communities have been given a place in the new economic project by virtue of their association with Rusholme's 'curry mile,' and the Chinese and other southeast Asian communities with the restaurants in China Town. A similar logic has led to the tentative embrace of the gay community and the burgeoning clubs and cafes in the Gay Village (1999: 196–197).

The role played by gay communities in urban regeneration is increasingly acknowledged in literature on the late-modern city (Castells, 1983; Ingram et al., 1997; Lauria and Knopp, 1985) and has typically raised issues of gentrification and the economic importance of the 'pink' pound. In Manchester, the meteoric rise of the Gay Village has been a key component of night-time economic development. In the following paragraphs we will briefly trace the history of the Village, focusing on the enabling and facilitating role played by MCC.

Gaychester

According to Skeggs (1999:218), 'known gay spaces have existed in Manchester since the early 1900s'. However, prior to the 1967 Sexual Offences Act, which de-criminalized sex between consenting adult males over the age of 21, these meeting places were necessarily informal, secretive and thus, largely 'invisible' to the members of Manchester's straight communities. Although The Rembrandt is commonly cited as Manchester's first gay pub with a history reaching back to the 1930s (Hindle, 1994; Waller, 1999), it was not possible to establish an openly gay venue before the 1967 law reforms. A number of gay pubs and clubs were established in the 1970s close to popular 'cruising' areas (Whittle, 1994). These included The Union, New York New York, and Napoleon's, the latter venue, as described in Chapter 2, attracting considerable police attention during the Anderton years. By 1984, a fledgling scene catering primarily for gay men, was emerging in the Bloom Street, Sackville Street, and Canal Street area, a compact, low-rent textile warehouse district adjacent to the Rochdale Canal.

Consolidation of this area as a 'gay developed space' (Evans and Fraser, 1993:12) was assisted by the concurrent ascendance of the radical urban left within local government. Following Graham Stringer's appointment as council leader in 1984, MCC began to take an active interest in gay issues and provided financial and ideological support for gay community initiatives in the city centre (Quilley, 1995, 1997; Whittle, 1994). By 1990, the 'commercial leisure scene' in what became known as the Gay Village, had not only forged intimate connections with the 'Madchester' phenomena, but was also being allocated its own particular niche within MCC's political and economic project of 'entrepreneurial' governance.

In 1991–2 the Central Manchester Development Corporation renovated the city centre's derelict Rochdale Canal, encouraging businesses to open along Canal Street. This canal-side commercial development was anticipated by the opening of Manto in 1990, 'a stunningly modernist bar with 30 foot glass windows', which epitomized the new 'visibility' of Manchester's gay leisure market (Skeggs, 1999:218). In 1991, the area was also acknowledged as a planning entity, a specifically gay place with 'a spatial coherence . . . significantly absent in other comparable urban areas' (Quilley, 1997:275). The success of Manto encouraged the development of the many other fashionable café-bars now clustered within the quarter-square-mile area of the Village. The media coined a new label for Manchester: 'Gaychester', the 'Gay Capital of the North' (Collin, 1997; Ryan and Fitzpatrick, 1996), the City with the 'largest single concentration of gay businesses and interests in the country . . . vocal, visible and never shy of flamboyance' (City Life, 2000:189).

Within this newly 'visible' leisure space, gay identities have become aestheticized and commodified in ways which appeal to fashionable heterosexuals (Skeggs, 1999; Whittle, 1994). Skeggs argues that the Village has had a particular allure for straight working-class women as it offers a 'trendy, aesthetically pleasing, modernist . . . space' which provides 'legitimation of their cultural capital, alongside the potential for fun and greater safety' (Skeggs, 1999:224). Thus, in 1990s Manchester, the gay leisure market became incorporated into the fashionable leisure market (Ryan and Fitzpatrick, 1996) and the occupation of gay space became a marker of mainstream (i.e., straight) social and cultural distinction (Bourdieu, 1984). Due to its reputation for both 'style' and 'safety', by the mid-1990s the Village had come to occupy a position of both economic and symbolic importance to the City's night-time leisure economy.

MCC continued to assist the development of the Village throughout the 1990s (see Waller, 1999). Council initiatives involved not only licensing and planning deregulation and environmental improvements such as the pedestrianization of Canal Street and brighter street lighting, but also *active* involvement in gay community affairs. In 1998 and 1999 following the dissolution of promoters, the 'Village Charity', MCC helped to co-ordinate the annual August bank holiday 'Mardi Gras' festival, an event which typically features a gay 'pride' parade through the city centre and major night-time clubbing and live-music fixtures. By 1998 the Mardi Gras, originally a small-scale Village-centred charity carnival, had risen to become not only Manchester's largest public event, but also the largest gay and lesbian festival in Britain, attracting hundreds of thousands of visitors from all over the world, including many straight 'voyeurs'. During the festival rainbow flags were flown from the roof of the Town Hall as a symbol of solidarity and the Hall itself has played host to the 'Lavender Ball', one of the event's largest parties. MCC and the festival's other organizers bore the brunt of major criticism in 1999, when despite attracting huge crowds, entertainment attractions at the event cost so much to stage that very little money was raised for the HIV and Aids charities who were its supposed beneficiaries. As a result of these problems Mardi Gras was re-launched in 2000 as 'GayFest', a scaled-down event, largely confined to the gay community in the Village, however GayFest 2001 saw a return to more ambitious city-wide celebrations.

MCC estimated that over the four-day period of the huge 1998 event, revellers spent in excess of £20m on goods and services (Sitford, 1999). As well as providing a significant annual boost to the city centre's licensed trade, Mardi Gras/GayFest has also helped to promote the long-term economic interests of Manchester's leisure industry by raising the City's profile as a 'gay destination'. As Quilley notes:

The success and increasing importance of Mardi Gras in the civic calendar is the most visible aspect of a new symbiotic relationship...between the increasingly commercialized gay scene and the City's new entrepreneurial economic project. The extent to which the Village is becoming increasingly mainstream is evident in the gay-club-scene references that now appear in tourist brochures and press commentaries. For instance, in a 1995 special issue on Manchester, British Rail's *Inter-City Xcursions* refers to the *Paradise Factory* as 'situated on the edge of the Gay Village, club nights here can be camp and colourful' (1997:288).

It is in such ways that the discursive and aesthetic attractions of the Madchester/Gaychester nexus become 'spatialized' or 'situated'

(Shields, 1991), within the night-time economy. The city centre at night becomes a zone of permitted and legitimated pleasure (Rojek, 1985, 2000; Shields, 1992), where Manchester's particular 'brand' of popular cultural product can be sought, found, purchased, and consumed. Moreover, the creation and maintenance of this liminal impression (Hobbs et al., 2000) is of crucial importance to the continuing development and prosperity of Manchester's night-time economy and to its marketing as a tourist attraction (R.R. Currie, 1997).

In a bid to boost tourism, Marketing Manchester, an MCC funded agency responsible for promoting the City, recently launched a campaign seeking to package Manchester as one of the 'gay capitals of the world'. Partially funded by a number of city centre bars, hotels, and nightclubs, the campaign aims to attract affluent American gay and lesbian visitors. The campaign's advertisements, which have been placed in American magazines and on the Internet, focus upon the 'vibrancy' of the Village and the GayFest, or what Clift and Forrest describe as the 'gay social life and sex' dimension of gay men's tourist motivations (1999:615). In a *Manchester Evening News* interview, Andrew Stokes of Marketing Manchester was forthright: 'we have a really marketable gay product and it's good business sense . . . it's a valuable niche market and we are building on what we have' (cited in Meakin, 1999:4). The gay leisure market and the wider night-time economy now play leading roles in the MCC place-marketing script, and as we shall see, the economic importance of such activities for the regeneration of central Manchester should not be underestimated.

In order to catch a glimpse of the reality that lies behind the place-marketing façade, we need to examine the scale and economic importance of the night-time economy and its impact upon the urban environment. The following paragraphs will trace four important themes: the growth in the number of licensed premises, the growth in the number of consumers, the economic importance of the night-time economy and its actual and potential effects upon urban life in Manchester city centre.

The number of licensed premises

During the 1990s there was an explosive growth in the number of licensed premises in Manchester City Centre, a trend which, as we have seen, was encouraged and facilitated by local government policies of strategic deregulation. According to information supplied by GMP licensing division, in September 1993 there were 225 licensed premises in the city centre. By September 1998 this figure had risen to 430, and by January 2002 to over 540. In May 2001, 166 venues held PELs with a total capacity of 113,250 persons. Twenty-six city centre premises were issued with new PELs in 2000–2001 alone. Following the relaxation of Public Entertainment Licensing in 1994 an increasingly large proportion of licensed premises are now granted Special Hours Certificates. Whilst traditional high-capacity night-club developments have been conspicuously absent from the City, growth within the late-night entertainment market has involved a proliferation of the aforementioned 'chameleon bars'. Moreover, expansion of the licensed infrastructure has involved significant capital investment by major brewers and leisure corporations seeking to emulate the success of the independent 'pioneers' of the early 1990s (principally Dry Bar, Manto, and Atlas), rather than any significant increase in local entrepreneurial activity.

Home Office liquor licensing statistics (by petty sessional division) show that by 1998, Manchester had the third largest number of 'public houses' in England and Wales (Allen, 1998).[5] In June 1998, the City as a whole had 863 such non-restaurant 'on-licence' premises, a figure topped only by North and South Westminster and Liverpool with 1,318 and 874 respectively. The expansion continues with a number of major new leisure developments including The Printworks at Shudehill, Oxford Circus on Oxford Road, and the Great Northern Warehouse on Peter Street. GMP estimate that these and other projects will soon bring the total number of licensed premises in the city centre to over 550.

The number of consumers

There are seasonal fluctuations in the use of the city centre at night, related to such issues as the timing of the student academic year, bank holidays, events such as Mardi Gras, major football matches, and of course the weather! However, night-time activity generally

[5] As petty sessional divisions vary enormously in the size of area they cover, it is not strictly possible to assume that the number of licensed premises in each city division is an accurate reflection of the comparative size of the licensed infrastructure in each city. However, Manchester's prominent position in this 'league table' does serve to illustrate the extent of licensed trade investment.

follows a predictable pattern with peaks at the weekend. In 1992, GMP estimated that on an 'average' Friday or Saturday night there would be an influx of 30,000 (mostly young) people. By 1998, the number of licensed premises had almost doubled and the average number of 'peak' night visitors had reached 65,000–85,000. At the time of writing (September, 2002), GMP estimate that the city centre attracts up to 100,000 visitors on Friday and Saturday nights.

The economic value of the night-time economy

As noted in Chapter 1, due to the fluid and informal nature of night-time economies, it is very difficult to quantify their contribution to local GDP. However, a 1994 economic survey conducted by the Manchester Institute for Popular Culture (MIPC) did focus on the licensed trade. This research (see Lovatt, 1994b) indicated that approximately 4,500 people were employed in over 200 (non-restaurant) licensed premises then trading in the city centre. The jobs were mostly part-time, although 40% were full-time positions. MIPC estimated that over £86m per annum, or £1.65m per week was being spent in these licensed premises alone. The survey did not include money spent in restaurants, theatres, cinemas, or takeaways, nor did it include taxi or public transport fares, etc.

Although no subsequent surveys have been conducted, given the significant growth in both infrastructure and volume of consumers, the MIPC findings must now be regarded as considerable underestimates of the current levels of activity in terms of both employment and revenue. More recently, it has been suggested that Manchester city centre's night-time economy as a whole, including hotel takings, is worth over £300m per year (Bolton Town Centre Partnership, 1998). A local economic assessment of *Greater* Manchester has estimated that 20% of the workforce are now employed in 'Distribution, Hotels and Restaurants' (Manchester TEC, 1998) and clearly a large proportion of this employment will be generated in the city centre.

A new urbanity?

By promoting the night-time economy alongside extensive re-development of the built environment, an improved transport infra-structure and a strong portfolio of public events, Manchester's public/private sector entrepreneurial partnerships have succeeded in re-inventing the 'prestige of centrality' (Lovatt, 1999:10). More specifically, nightlife areas such as Canal Street, Quay Street, the Castlefield basin and Deansgate Locks have re-kindled some sense of sociability and animation in public space not seen in Manchester since at least the mid-1960s (Russell, 1999; Spinoza, 1999). For MCC, promotion of the night-time economy has formed part of a strategy which seeks primarily to attract new investment and jobs, but also to regenerate the built environment, (re)populate the city centre (Wynne and O'Connor, 1998) and animate the streets at night. Night-time activity is seen to underwrite the image of a 'European' and 'cosmopolitan' city centre which functions as 'a catalyst for civic identity and public sociability' (Bianchini, 1993:10). This image has been reasserted by promoting a previously suppressed night-time economy as a 'quasi-liminal' (Hobbs et al., 2000) 'realm of play... encounter, and of the carnivalesque' (Lovatt: 1996:150) as encapsulated in the Village-based Channel 4 drama series *Queer As Folk* (see S.J. Davies, 1999). However, we have told only half our story, for all is not well in Manchester's night-time leisure spaces.

Dodgin' the rain and bullets

The rapid growth in Manchester's night-time economy has stimulated a concomitant increase in the demand for 'guardian forces' (Bottoms and Wiles, 1996): policing and security services capable of establishing and maintaining an environment conducive to the extraction of profit from (alcohol and illegal drug enhanced) pleasure. This demand has outstripped the available resources of the public police and the politico-regulatory regimes of market society now dictate that 'security' (in the form of technologies of formal social control) must be 'bought and sold in the marketplace like any other commodity' (Johnston, 1996:56). Within the night-time economy, as in many other commercial spheres, the public police are no longer the sole, or even the key providers of this elusive commodity (Jones and Newburn, 1998; Loader, 1999, 2000; Spitzer, 1987). Whilst the police retain sole responsibility and authority for patrolling public space, licensed premises are primarily 'policed for profit' (Spitzer and Scull, 1977) by private firms and agencies specializing in door supervision. The principal training officer for Greater Manchester's Doorsafe registration scheme told us that approximately 4,500 people are currently (September, 2002) licensed to work on the doors of central Manchester. This figure compares with only 1,000 in 1995 and reflects a surge in demand as not only city centre pubs and clubs, but also other businesses such as restaurants, takeaways, and hotels now employ door staff.

Regulatory intervention at both a national and local level is increasingly requiring the licensed trade to 'police their own premises'. Whilst initially, the training and registration of door staff was mandatory only for PEL holders, Manchester licensing justices later extended this regulation, requiring (as a condition of the liquor licence) that *all* new on-licence premises employ only trained and registered security staff. The demand for door staff has also been fuelled by recent legislation. The Public Entertainment Licences (Drug Misuse) Act 1997 has permitted police to seek the immediate closure of any licensed premises should they consider that a 'serious problem related to the supply or use of a controlled drug' (paragraph 6A-(1)) exists.

Yet, despite the veneer of 'professionalism' and 'accountability' which surrounds door registration schemes (see Chapter 6), the policing of late-night youth-orientated entertainment venues at least, can only be effective when firmly rooted in the creation and maintenance of a credible threat of violence (Hobbs, 1995, 1998). As a consequence, door security firms and agencies of 'reputation' have competitive advantage over those who are merely 'reputable'. The premium placed upon local infamy can however have inherently paradoxical consequences for venue management. For example, several Mancunian providers, through their links with local networks of (dis)organized crime, have amplified many of the problems within licensed premises which door staff are nominally employed to prevent.

Gangchester

Night-time leisure has long held an allure for 'glamorous gangsters' who seek to display their power and notoriety before a clubland audience. Yet, before the arrival of the 'Acid House' scene in 1988 and its attendant drug market, the professional criminal had little reason to mix pleasure with the business of venue security. More recently in a number of British towns and cities, (dis)organized criminal networks have become inextricably linked with the role of door supervision. This trend has been acknowledged in both journalistic (Barnes, 2000; Collin, 1997; Morton, 1994; Thompson, 1995) and anecdotal (Anthony, 1998; Haslam, 1999; O'Mahoney, 1997) accounts and has also attracted the attention of academic (Hobbs, 1995, 1998) and Home Office (Jacobson, 1999; Morris, 1998a) researchers. This literature documents how in some areas, locally-based criminal networks have sought to control the lucrative trade in 'recreational' drugs such as amphetamines and Ecstasy by infiltrating the 'security' market 'in and around the point of consumption; youth orientated pubs and clubs' (Hobbs, 1998:410).

A variety of strategies can be used when seeking to control the drug market within a venue. Although door staff will sometimes sell drugs directly to the consumer, in Manchester it is more common for them to work with floor dealers ('authorized salespersons'). In such operations, the doorstaff may act either as 'wholesalers' (selling drugs to the salesperson, or supplying them on a 'sale or return' basis) or simply as 'security providers'. A cut of the floor dealer's takings are then demanded as a protection payment, or alternatively in the 'sale or return' operation, the door staff will seize all the proceeds and simply pay the salesperson a commission. Door staff and dealers will often employ a combination of these methods, however regardless of which strategy is used, dealing by 'unauthorized' persons (competitors) is almost always strictly controlled, drugs being confiscated and then resold or occasionally handed to the police as a token gesture! In Manchester, such activities have been linked (especially in the late 1980s and early 1990s) to incidents of extreme violence and (especially since the early 1990s) to protection racketeering and the intimidation of licensees and clubland entrepreneurs.

Such problems have had an acute and enduring impact on Manchester's *clubscene* (if not its wider night-time economy) and, perhaps uniquely amongst British cities, have also received national media exposure and been the subject of local political debate. In the following paragraphs we explore the emergence and entrenchment of this market-led and criminally orchestrated violence and intimidation and GMP's and the local state's various and ambivalent responses to it.

Most credible commentaries on Mancunian nightlife (for example, Collin, 1997; Haslam, 1999; and Swanton, 1998) cite mid-1989 as the time when the local criminal fraternity began to impose their own form of order on the City's burgeoning dance scene. In retro-spect it now seems inevitable that the lucrative financial opportun-ities created by a surge in demand for illegal drugs, which had hitherto been met by a band of small-time user-dealers supplying their own network of friends and associates, would attract the attention of more 'serious' and intimidating characters.[6] It should be stressed that such problems were (and are) not unique to Man-chester: they feature in the night-time leisure development of other British cities such as Liverpool and Newcastle (see Morris, 1998a, 1998b). What made Manchester *appear* exceptional was not the presence of such activity *per se*, but rather a series of newsworthy incidents, and a salience within local political discourse which was missing in cities which (in the early/mid-1990s) lacked such carefully cultivated reputations as 'party capitals'.

During the 1980s a more visible, violent, and unpredictable form of *dis*-organized criminal activity began to develop in Manchester's inner-city housing estates as a new generation of villains began to exploit the financial opportunities of a burgeoning illegal drug market. Like the scuttling gangs of the nineteenth century, these criminal groupings emerged as loose, but coherent fraternities rooted in parochial affiliation and notions of spatial dominance. These new 'gangs' adopted the names of their immediate locality: Salford, Cheetham Hill (an area of North Manchester), Gooch (Gooch Close in the Moss Side area of South Manchester) and Doddington (Doddington Close also in Moss Side). By the late 1980s, two of these groups: Salford (a predominantly white network) and Cheetham Hill (a mainly black and mixed-race network) began to take an interest in door security and the control of drug markets in Manchester clubs. Competition within this marketplace became distinctly unhealthy as violent struggles to monopolize the sale of drugs within prime targets such as The Hacienda, Konspiracy, and The Thunderdome began to escalate.

Gunchester

It is very difficult to use legitimate doormen in a place like Manchester. If you wanted to employ five or six strong, hefty, fit guys who maybe do

---

[6] For a poignant account of this transition including a Mancunian user-dealer's first encounter with organized crime, see Garratt (1998:231–233).

martial arts, people without criminal records—straight members of society...if you put them on a door in Manchester that is going to be frequented by people with guns and knives, it is an unequal contest, there is nothing they can do about it—muscle cannot win—Steve (a local journalist).

Let's face it, you've got to have people like that (with criminal connections), think about it—you're stood at the door and a group of blokes comes up and one pulls a pistol out, one pulls a machete out, one pulls a baseball bat out...you're put on the spot...the police aren't there...what are you gonna do?, say 'sorry mate you've got trainers on, you're not comin' in?—Darren (a local doorman).

In the absence of a strong (i.e. armed) and visible (i.e. uniformed) police presence on their doors, it was impossible for clubs to deny entry to what were some of the City's most notorious and dangerous criminals. The gangs began to put licensees and their staff under increasing pressure and to take control of the doors. As the former Hacienda disc jockey, Dave Haslam (1999:196) recalls:

The Manchester gangs developed a strategy: destabilize a club by sending in young wannabes to instigate brawls and cause mayhem, and then point out to the licensee that your firm is the only one capable of controlling the situation...control of the door not only gives you control of the drugs trade, but also puts the club owner in your pocket.

In his highly acclaimed history of 'Ecstasy Culture and Acid House', Matthew Collin describes events in greater detail. In The Hacienda 'the staff were scared...the gangs would demand champagne and sandwiches; no one dared refuse' (1997:163) and in Konspiracy, 'they'd want their people at the door, all their people in for free, to order drinks and not pay for them, and to openly sell drugs' (ibid.: 164). The gangs started to regard certain venues as their own territory; territories to be ruthlessly guarded against the infiltration of their rivals. For those venues attempting to hire bouncers from out-of-town, revenge was swift: in June 1990 The Thunderdome was forced to close after masked men brandishing shotguns knee-capped three of the Club's doorstaff in full view of more than 300 people (Morton, 1994).

By early 1990 GMP had responded to these problems by launching a plain-clothes, intelligence-led operation known as Operation Clubwatch, using powers bestowed by the Licensing Act 1988. Several venues had their licenses revoked as a result of this initiative including Konspiracy (in December 1990) and Precinct 13 (in January 1991). In July 1989 drug dealing at The Hacienda was linked to the 'first known fatality... as a result of Ecstasy use in Britain' (Redhead, 1993:14): sixteen-year-old Claire Leighton. At the end of 1990 a number of smaller venues such as The Thunderdome, Konspiracy, and The Gallery were closed down thereby denying the gangs access to some of the City's most lucrative recreational drug markets. The Hacienda then came under yet greater pressure as the rival factions converged upon it (Wilson, 2002).

Although also threatened with closure, The Hacienda gained a reprieve from the licensing magistrates at a second hearing in January 1991 following the intervention of MCC leader Graham Stringer. However, within weeks the club was to close voluntarily for several months following a number of violent incidents involving the Salford and Cheetham Hill gangs including a gun threat against the door manager. In a statement to the press regarding the closure of The Hacienda, owner Anthony H. Wilson said, 'we are forced into this drastic action to protect our employees, our members and all our clients... we are simply sick and tired of dealing with instances of personal violence' (cited in Collin, 1997:173). When it reopened on 10 May 1991, The Hacienda had increased security measures including a metal detector and in-house CCTV. Despite the murder in the interim of 'White' Tony Johnson, one of the most dangerous of the Cheetham Hill fraternity, the violence did not go away: within weeks of reopening, six Hacienda bouncers were stabbed in an attack by a group of Salford men.

The culture of clubland violence that bedevilled the early Rave scene was to continue almost relentlessly throughout the 1990s. The following are just a few of the most infamous incidents, all of which have been reported in the press (for example, Swanton, 1997, 1998) and were confirmed by our Manchester informants:

June 1992   Having been denied access to the Wiggly Worm, a group of Salford men return in a stolen car and ram the vehicle into the Club's entrance.

April 1995   A doorman from The Hacienda is shot dead near his home in Swinton, Greater Manchester.

Summer 1995   At Drum 'n' Bass events at the PSV, members of the crowd regularly express their musical appreciation by firing guns at the ceiling.

	Three girls are injured by ricochet bullets and future events are cancelled.
Autumn 1995	The Home nightclub closes after a series of drive-by shootings and a terrifying battle between police and over twenty balaclava-clad Salford men within the club.
May 1997	Three youths attempt to murder nightclub door staff in a drive-by shooting incident.
June 1997	The Hacienda finally loses its licence when on a routine visit, licensing magistrates and police witness an attempted murder outside the club.
July 1997	A Manchester doorman is followed home after work and shot in the leg as he fills up his car at a 24-hour garage.
October 1997	The dance promoters Fantazia hold a 12,000-capacity event at the G-Mex arena. The Birmingham-based security team attempt to impose a strict door policy, however, local gangsters succeed in entering the venue by force, simply walking up to the main entrance, telling the bouncers which gang they come from and threatening to shoot anyone who gets in their way (Swanton, 1998).
July 1998	AVP Films begin filming a television documentary about Manchester's gang culture for the BBC *Modern Times* series. The film crew follow a notorious local villain around the City's nightspots. The gangster stabs a man in the groin outside the Beat'n Track nightclub and the film company's tapes are seized by the police.
October 1998	A nightclub manager is stabbed to death outside the Niche Club in Sheffield. Police link the murder to a Salford gang.

September 1999   A doorman from the Epic nightclub is battered to death by a gang of four men near his home in Salford. Police link the murder to a previous incident in the club.

It would clearly be mistaken to link *all* of the above events to 'door wars' concerning the control of drug markets, however, such a chronology does illustrate the levels of violence involved in the local context of lawlessness which the media has termed 'Gunchester'. In the early 1990s, the local casualwear company Gio Goi attempted to capture the mood on a T-shirt design emblazoned with the words: 'Dodgin the rain and bullets' (Collin, 1997).

Despite the highly publicized problems, most consumers of the night-time economy remain oblivious to the power and influence local criminals can exercise over the venues they visit, however, 'behind the scenes' security issues are at the very top of many a licensee's list of concerns. Indeed, 'security' in Manchester clubland has long been a very expensive and elusive 'commodity' (Loader, 1999). During the 1990s clubs such as Sankey's Soap, Holy City Zoo, and Club Havana spent huge sums of money on 'target hardening' initiatives such as airport-style metal detection and CCTV. With respect to door staff, a local club promoter told us that his security bills for dance events in Manchester city centre were over three times larger than in neighbouring cities. Whilst door staff in many areas are paid approximately £50 per night, in Manchester the rate for club security is often £200 per night, with some 'Security Consultants' charging 'retainers' of £1,000 per week. One promoter said that he was told: 'Manchester is a very dangerous city... if you want to work here you have to have the best security and the best security doesn't come cheap'. As he explained, the 'best' security teams must include at least one person who is member of (or at least, known and respected by) the local criminal fraternity. The promoter went on to suggest that the 'excessive' security bills themselves amounted to protection payments.

Promoting events can be a risky business for the naïve and those who fail to go through the 'right channels'. In May 1994 a young man was shot dead in the early hours of the morning whilst sticking fly-posters to the walls of Sackville Street. A subsequent report in the *Manchester Evening News* claimed that 'control over fly-posting operations was worth over £200,000 a year and was a business

fiercely contested by rival gangs' (Barnes, 2000:211). Our informants told us that in Manchester the music policy of a venue must
always be chosen with security in mind—'black' sounds such as
RN'B, Garage, and the hard and fast dance music favoured by
(white) gang members and other 'roughnecks' being avoided in
favour of commercial dance and 'party' music, student-friendly
'indie', and more 'underground' or esoteric sounds. In addition, it
can be difficult to raise the profile of new events as many 'big name'
disc jockeys refuse to play in Manchester because they have concerns
with regard to their personal safety.

As a result of the propensity amongst local gangsters to carry,
threaten to use, and when 'necessary' actually use, firearms and
other weapons, even with the 'best' people on the door there can
be no guarantee of security: some people remain 'untouchable'. In
his recent book, Dave Haslam neatly summarizes the enduring
problem of club security in Manchester:

… in the era of guns, the threat of armed retaliation has made the policing
of nightlife almost impossible. On many occasions I've heard lads who
have been denied entry to a club drop gang leaders' names and threaten to
come back later with guns. Occasionally they have done (1999:195–196).

As one nightclub manager put it: 'you can't stop them on the door—
the doormen are powerless, you either have to go to war with these
people, or let them in'. Indeed, even the City's civic leaders are not
immune from threats and intimidation. In 1998, after calling for a
police crackdown on criminal activity in Clubland, Councillor Pat
Karney, the outspoken chairman of MCC's City Centre Committee
received a sinister 'we know where you live' message from an underworld figure. In a statement to the *Manchester Evening News*
(1998b:2) the Councillor said, 'I am putting my safety in the hands
of the Chief Constable. This is a threat by one person very well
known to the police and I am taking it very seriously'. Councillor
Karney linked his experience to that of others: 'this is an example of
how much this cancer of fear has spread through the City and has
made club owners feel similarly intimidated' (ibid.).

Door teams who are not 'connected' stand little chance of denying
entry to local gangsters. When Applejacks on Portland Street sacked
their Manchester door team, replacing them with a security firm
from the South of England, trouble ensued. The old door team
arrived at the club one night and caused havoc, fighting a vicious

battle with their successors. The incident was captured on the Club's CCTV system and several of the Manchester men were arrested. In such a context, if they are to stay in business, licensees and venue-owners are sometimes compelled to use security firms that are affiliated to a local crime network. As Haslam explains with regard to The Hacienda:

> The management employed a door firm controlled from Salford, some of whose employees were alleged to have taken part in the (previous) violence, and charged, though cleared, with matters relating to the killing of Tony Johnson, Wilson reasoning that the only effective security firm was one unafraid of anybody or anything (Haslam, 1999:203).

Indeed, Tony Wilson has never sought to deny such rumours. In a published interview he states:

> ... in one 12-month period, *The Hacienda* spent £374,000 on 'protection.' Forget drug dealing, that's what the gangs were *really* doing. Running protection rackets, taxing us—which would have been fine if they actually *had* protected us, instead of using our club as a shooting gallery! (Push and Silcott, 2000:66).

In a controversial article on Manchester's problems by journalist Oliver Swanton (1998), a GMP Inspector commented that if The Hacienda were ever to reopen a security team from out of town *must* be found:

> Otherwise they're going to come with the baggage of all the local villains and gangsters, whoever you pick. You can fly them in from Brussels for all I care, just as long as they're from outside Manchester (Swanton, 1998:76).

Such sentiments are a revealing indictment of Doorsafe, as it appears that, in the opinion of some police officers, the scheme has done little to free the local door security market from the influence of (dis) organized crime.[7]

Both GMP and the 'Manchester Pub and Club Watch' told us that they routinely advise new licensees to avoid certain 'disreputable' security firms in favour of other, more 'professional' providers (often from outside the City). Such advice is based upon police intelligence regarding the activities of local doorstaff and their associates. This form of 'informal' intelligence-led regulation is clearly controversial

---

[7] A detailed discussion of such schemes and their shortcomings can be found in Chapter 6.

as it is premissed upon police prediction of *likely offenders* and their *future crimes* (Baldwin and Kinsey, 1982), rather than simply focusing (as the Doorsafe scheme does) on the previous crimes of convicted criminals. Thus, a 'quiet word' with the licensee is often seen as an effective way to cut through the 'red tape' of due process, whilst achieving the primary goal of crime prevention.

Yet, in addition to the violent feuding that has often followed attempts to introduce out-of-town firms or agencies, there are obvious logistical problems associated with bringing staff in and out of the city each night. Door staff from outside Greater Manchester are still required to register with Doorsafe and may also be required to complete the Manchester training course. Such training can bring them into contact with hostile or corrupt local doorstaff. Furthermore, if local staff are employed on a sub-contractual basis by an out-of-town agency they can become especially vulnerable to intimidation from the gangs or they may themselves be affiliated to a local crime network and thus simply reintroduce the original problems. Although GMP have been advising licensees to employ doorstaff from outside the City for several years, the door security market in Manchester is still largely monopolized by local providers. In answer to questions regarding the existence of 'legitimate' local providers, a Manchester-based crime journalist replied 'who *are* the legitimate door firms? . . . I certainly can't think of any'.

In view of such comments, we would suggest that Doorsafe should essentially be understood as an occupational licensing scheme designed to focus narrowly on improving the quality of interpersonal interaction between the 4,500 individuals it currently licenses and consumers of Manchester's night-time economy. Bluntly stated, the scheme may well encourage a number of doorstaff to be more 'tactful' in their dealings with the public, however, it is a wholly inadequate tool with which to tackle the problem of (dis)organized criminal activity. Since 1997 the criminal activities of the City's bouncers have been less visible and spectacular as the established 'security providers' have become firmly entrenched and a number of the key protagonists serve lengthy prison sentences. Whilst doorstaff in the City had occasionally faced bouts of extreme and unpredictable violence at the hands of young 'wannabe-gangsters' (see Swanton, 1997, 1998) and intoxicated customers, it had seemed for a number of years that the door wars had ceased. However, in the spring of 2001 a new spate of incidents, coinciding with a number of notable prison releases, was to again cast shadows over the future of the Manchester door trade.

To conclude, despite over a decade of violence and intimidation on the city's doors, and a series of regulatory and policing responses, it seems that the links between door supervision, gangland, and an ever-expanding night-time economy remain strong. Notwithstanding the paradoxical attractions of this 'dark' side of the night-time economy, (inadequate) regulatory initiatives such as Doorsafe have been integrated into MCC's promotional 'script' in the name of public safety. As in other towns and cities, the regulation of bouncers is now a component of what local 'crime and disorder reduction partnerships' present to the public as an integrated managerial strategy for the city at night (Hadfield et al., 2001). Such initiatives provide 'good press', an image of order, control, and responsibility with which to counter the sometimes tragic local media reports and allow urban centres to be marketed as 'Fun cities': exciting but 'safe' places in which to 'play'. What the Manchester script fails to mention is that in recent years, whilst 'bar culture' has boomed, the city's nightlife has lost many of its larger 'flagship' attractions, due in no small part to the activities of criminal doorstaff. One of the City's night-time 'flagships' is now the Gay Village, a late-night entertainment zone which, as we shall see, has not escaped the problems of crime and disorder which continue to bedevil the Mancunian night.

Street violence, alcohol, and young men: an old problem for the 'new' city

In the words of one local: 'It's certainly very continental out there, but less like Paris, more like the Somme' (Haslam, 1999:265).

Although the upsurge in demand for *illicit* drugs in 'post-Acid House' Manchester has created a new set of crime and disorder issues for the city's night-time economy, a historically familiar set of problems has (re-)emerged from the archaic mixture of young men, nightlife, and alcohol. The problems of street violence and disorder which plague the night-time economy have been illustrated in recorded crime figures published in accordance with the Crime and Disorder Act 1998. Manchester's first three local crime audits (MCC, 1998; MCC, 2000; MCC, 2001) have shown that recorded crime and disorder incidents are unevenly distributed across the

City: some spatial and temporal 'hotspots' have highly concentrated problems. The audit data for one category of crime, 'assaults and woundings' has highlighted violence as a major issue within the night-time leisure milieu.

GMP figures suggest that although inner-city areas of South Manchester, such as Moss Side, Longsight, and Hulme, have long been 'symbolic locations' for the city's (more racialized) crime problems; in terms of recorded incidents at least, they are not the most violent areas of the city. Moss Side in particular has achieved an 'iconic status as the epitome of "Dangerous Britain"'[8] (Fraser, 1996:55). Yet despite this, the levels of recorded street violence in Moss Side are considerably lower than in many parts of the city centre. Indeed, recorded crime data indicates that the central entertainment zones which form the cornerstone of the MCC-sponsored 'vibrant cosmopolitan café culture' are, at least at night, significantly more 'violent' than almost any location to be found within the 'inner-city'.

Summarizing patterns of recorded crime between April 1998 and December 2000, the 2001 audit (MCC, 2001) identifies five police beats as 'hotspots' for 'assaults and woundings'. Four of these hotspots are areas of the city centre which have a high concentration of licensed premises and very small (but increasing) residential populations. The audits show that most incidents happen on the streets (rather than within licensed premises) and occur between the hours of 6 p.m. and 3 a.m. The victims are predominately white males in employment and under 30 years of age. By far the most violent Manchester police beat is in and around the Gay Village and along Portland Street and Whitworth Street (see MCC, 1998:31). As noted in Chapter 1, 1,277 woundings were recorded within this beat between April 1998 and December 2000, over twice as many as were recorded in any of the city centre's other hotspots during the same period (MCC, 2001). There were 501 woundings recorded within this beat in December 1999–December 2000 alone (ibid). GMP officers told us that the true extent of assault in this area is likely to be much greater as the beat includes Minshull Street, a 'red light' area with drug problems. Prostitutes, pimps, and dealers working in this area are particularly susceptible to attack, yet often fail to report their victimization experiences to the police.

---

[8] A racially-charged stereotype stemming largely from the riots of the early 1980s and isolated firearms incidents associated with the local drug market.

Returning to the first audit (MCC, 1998), we find that having identified the Village as Manchester's key hotspot for 'assaults and woundings', the authors go on to explain such violence in the context of a wider prevalence of 'homophobia' and 'hate crime' (p.31). However, there are reasons to be sceptical about this explanation. First, without wishing to deny that Manchester's 'gay community' face high levels of victimization, the audit provides no data in support of this claim, for example it does not state the proportion of those victimized in and around the Village who were gay or lesbian.[9] Secondly, as previously suggested, the Village, especially on weekend evenings (when most violence occurs), has gained a mass appeal; it is no longer essentially 'gay' (see Corner, 2000). As Tracy Walsh, for 10 years the licensee of New York New York (one of the Village's oldest venues) told the *Manchester Evening News*:

When I came here it was a totally different place. I was one of the very few straight people in the area . . . it was very gay, very outrageous, very camp and very safe. The Village has become more and more straight; it's losing its identity (MEN, 1998a:21).

Another Village licensee told us that a lot of gay people were now boycotting the area because it is 'getting over-run by straight people acting in an unacceptable way'. A doorman at the New Union recently told *The Independent* journalist, Lena Corner: 'it's like a cabaret . . . people are coming here to have a look at the people they used to poke fun of at school. I've had more trouble here in the last twelve months than in 15 years of doing doors' (Corner: 2000: 7). A bar-owner quoted in the same report said 'I see ambulances on Canal Street virtually every weekend' (ibid.).

Following the demise of The Hacienda-era clubscene, the Village became the 'flagship' of Manchester's night-time economy. However, given the problems of violence and disorder, it would appear that, like its predecessor the Village has become a victim of its own success. In response to the vocal concerns of those within Manchester's gay community who feel that the Village has now irretrievably lost its former utility as a (comparatively) 'safe gay space', a number of prominent gay entrepreneurs are now seeking to develop a 'New

---

[9] Indeed, the authors of the 1998 audit admitted that they did not have access to a reliable data set for homophobic assault (p.30).

Gay Quarter'. To this end, several businesses aiming to attract a 'strictly' gay clientele have opened in the vicinity of London Road, near Piccadilly station, an area somewhat removed from the former Canal Street-focused circuit. In a recent *Manchester Evening News* interview, Julia Grant, a hotel-owner and prominent figure in the City's gay community commented:

> You can call it a [gay] ghetto if you like, but I'm trying to create an area where gay men and women can walk safely on the street... the punters are sick of being ripped off for years, and there will be people who will point their finger and say, how can that area be called the New Gay Quarter? But really, this gay quarter would not be being built if Canal Street had kept its strength (MEN, 2001).

Such sentiments appear to suggest that, for at least some within the gay community, the market-led integration of the Village within the City's wider aspirations for a new cosmopolitan, mixed-sexuality nightlife have now failed. Within such a crowded city centre leisure market, the willingness and indeed economic necessity of Village café-bars to sell alcohol to consumers of all sexual orientations has perhaps unavoidably served to destroy the basis of the area's initial attraction (Jacobs, 1961). Such market forces have turned what was the *Gay* Village into what is now perhaps more accurately described as the *Late-Night Entertainment* Village. Thus, rather than a surge of violent homophobia, perhaps what the Manchester crime audits indicate is something rather more pedestrian: that 'assaults and woundings' are concentrated in areas where people congregate at night and consume intoxicants, principally alcohol. The text of the 2001 audit would suggest that MCC may have somewhat belatedly begun to acknowledge the importance of such 'contextual factors' (MCC, 2001:46). Having noted the high levels of assault within city centre police beats, the authors make reference to the 'effect of the evening economy... the "24-hour city and the increasing number of alcohol outlets"' (ibid.).

Manchester's hotspots display many of the classic characteristics of 'clustering' and 'congestion' identified by Tuck in her Home Office study of *Drinking and Disorder* (1989). For Tuck, a 'congestion point' is 'a thoroughfare where large groups of people are likely to be moving from one area to another and where they might collide' (p.52), whilst a 'cluster point' is a 'location where people are likely to gather and remain for a period of time' (ibid.). Portland Street can thus be understood as an area of 'congestion', whilst, due to the high concentration of licensed premises in the Village, the pedestrianized Canal Street can be identified as a site of both 'clustering' *and* 'congestion'.

Another hotspot, incorporating areas of Portland Street, Moseley Street, and Piccadilly is a 'cluster point' for people leaving the city centre late at night, with large queues forming as people wait for buses and taxis. Manchester's Crime and Disorder Strategy Co-ordinator told us that at around 2.15 a.m. on Saturdays and Sundays there are usually around 300 people queuing at the taxi ranks in this area. Taxis are often the only late-night transport option as the trains and the Metrolink trams finish at around midnight. Buses do run late at night on the main arterial routes, particularly to the south, however, until recently there were no late-night services at all to the east and north of the City. The Portland Street-Moseley Street-Piccadilly beat also contains hotels, bars, nightclubs, and fast-food outlets, thus attracting a considerable amount of night-time 'congestion' and 'clustering', factors which, as we have seen, can contribute to friction between intoxicated strangers (Wikström, 1995).

Some of the violence within the city centre at night has been of a very serious nature. Between October 1996 and May 1998 there were six murders on the City's streets. The victims were all young men. Labelled the 'Good Samaritan' murders by the local press (Nott and Taylor, 1997), four of the victims (Andrew Poynton aged 21; Simon Speakman, 27; Steven Hughes, 22 and Nick Centi, 27) were killed when intervening in street incidents in an attempt to assist other victims of assault. All of these incidents occurred late at night or in the early hours of the morning, in areas of close proximity to high densities of licensed premises (such as Princess Street, Oxford Street, and Whitworth Street).

These highly publicized murders (which attracted national media attention, for example, Jenkins, 1997) indicated the tensions between a prosperous alcohol-fuelled night-time economy, efficiently creating jobs and profits, and the demand for order. On 12 March 1998 the front cover of the *Manchester Evening News* carried details of a strongly worded letter sent by the Leader of MCC, Richard Leese, to the then Chief Constable of GMP, David Wilmot. The grim tone of the letter stood in stark contrast to the Council's usual '24-hour city' marketing rhetoric. Leese described a state of 'rampant lawlessness' in which problems of both street violence and the intimidation of licensees had reached 'critical' proportions. It was 'a crisis' Leese claimed that GMP appeared 'either unable or unwilling to address' (Panter and Watson, 1998:1). Calls for police action began to intensify when, less than a month later, local bank clerk Nick Centi was kicked and stabbed to death by a group of men on Whitworth Street West in the early hours of Sunday 5 April. Colin Sinclair, a spokesman for the Manchester Pub and Club Watch called on consumers in all city centre licensed premises to sign a petition demanding 'greater police resources, zero tolerance by courts and the immediate implementation of the city centre CCTV scheme' (Panter and King, 1998:1).

Whilst there are now over 500 licensed premises in the city centre and over 4,000 door supervisors registered to work on their doors, on a typical Friday and Saturday night there are only approximately forty police officers on duty. An Inspector at GMP Central Licensing provided the following approximations for the numbers of officers involved in weekend evening and night operations: Plain Clothes Licensing officers (seven), street patrols, in vehicles and on foot (twenty), Special Constabulary officers (two–twelve). These officers can request back-up from the Tactical Crime Unit which deals with serious public order incidents (fifteen officers) and the Tactical Aid Team (four-thirty officers based at GMP headquarters). On Friday and Saturday evenings, the uniformed street patrols work two over-lapping shifts. Officers on the 9 p.m.–7 a.m. 'nightshift' are supplemented by others who began their shift in the late afternoon and who work until approximately 3 a.m. This system, as Tuck (1989) suggests, allows GMP to optimize their resources during the 'peak' period for public disorder: 10.00 p.m.–3.00 p.m. However, we found that in Manchester, as in many other British towns and cities, the resources available for policing the night-time economy were being stretched to unprecedented levels. As a GMP Superintendent commented:

At one time we would have been able to concentrate resources largely around what was the busy part of town—Piccadilly. Resources, which have not been increased of course, are now being stretched right across the City and the implications of that, if we have serious incidents, are quite plain to see.

Following local press claims (for example, King, 1999b; Narain and Scheerhout, 1998) that policing strategies for the City at night were insufficiently 'visible' to have a deterrent effect (specifically that

GMP relied too heavily upon 'reactive' methods and upon intelligence-led, plain-clothes offender targeting), a number of high-profile operations were launched, starting in May 1998 with the three-month Operation Suli. On Friday and Saturday nights and occasionally mid-week, road blocks were established on key access roads to the city centre (using powers conferred in Section 60 of the Police and Criminal Evidence Act 1984). 'Spotchecks' involving car and body searches were conducted on vehicles entering the city. At the same time GMP also increased the number of unannounced uniformed visits to licensed premises. Suli resulted in over 200 arrests and similar operations have since been conducted sporadically, employing extra officers from the Tactical Aid Group and horse patrols.

The political and media pressures being placed upon GMP to 'do something about violent crime' in the City reached a peak in the summer of 2000. In recent years, official crime statistics have consistently shown Greater Manchester to have particularly high levels of recorded crime. In figures released by the Home Office in July 2000, the conurbation had the highest overall crime rate in England and Wales with 14,630 crimes per 100,000 of population, whilst the rate for violence against the person was the highest outside London with 27.3 offences per 1,000 population (Home Office, 2000). In addition to this 'bad news', the aforementioned findings of the local crime audits appeared to merely confirm local media perceptions that violent crime in Manchester was on the increase, especially in the city centre at night. In September 2000, Channel 4 broadcast a TV documentary on the night-time economy in Manchester which, in following a group of girls on their night out, showed them consuming alco-pop 'buzz' drinks containing the recommended units of alcohol for an entire fortnight in just three hours. In a memorable and hard-hitting commentary, the CH4 reporter described what was being filmed as 'drinking to get drunk, rather than to oil the wheels of sociability'. GMP's 'nightmare' came to a head when the *Manchester Evening News* published a further front-page article showing the serious facial injuries sustained by 'the young mother' Rachel Franks in a city centre 'glassing' attack (Dillon, 2000). The newspaper began their own campaign entitled '*Safe Glass, Safe City*' calling for the use of safety glass in licensed premises.

Such events, images, and reputations clearly held the danger of impacting significantly and detrimentally upon the prosperity and reputation of Manchester and were certainly not the kind of imagery that the City's entrepreneurial élites wanted to show to the world in the run-up to the 2002 Commonwealth Games. Something had to be done.

The Manchester Citycentresafe Initiative

In September 2000, a wide-ranging programme of police-led multi-agency interventions were marshalled and branded to the public under the banner of the Manchester Citycentresafe Initiative. This strategy (still ongoing at the time of writing) combines situational crime prevention (such as on-street CCTV, the promotion of safety glass and plastic alternatives, and 'Night Net', a radio-link scheme), with regulatory interventions (such as a by-law forbidding on-street drinking (introduced 3 August 2000), a revised Doorsafe scheme, and exclusion orders for persistent offenders) and public health campaigns highlighting the dangers of 'binge' drinking. The Programme's more innovative and controversial proposals include the introduction of Public Help Points. Piloted in Burnley town centre and also in London, these on-street points comprise a yellow metal board marked 'SOS' and a distinctive red button illuminated at night with a blue light (DETR, 1999:9). People seeking assistance are put in direct contact with a central CCTV control room. Other pilot initiatives have included the collective funding of an extra police officer by a number of licensed premises.[10] GMP have matched this private finance thus enabling two dedicated officers to provide a level of late-night weekend service to the Peter Street area of the city centre that could not otherwise be guaranteed. This development is significant as it implies that certain sections of Manchester's licensed trade are beginning to accept some degree of responsibility for the disorder that occurs upon the City's streets in association with the night-time economy, their widely-defined business environment. The campaign also incorporates a late-night bus service with various built-in security measures, the aim of which is to get people out of the city centre at night quickly and efficiently, thus avoiding the aforementioned problems of crowd convergence at transport termini.

GMP have reported small reductions in recorded levels of night-time violence and disorder in the city centre since the inception of

[10] Schemes of this nature are discussed in Chapter 8.

Citycentresafe and the campaign has received a high media profile, thus fulfilling its ancillary function of disseminating 'good news' about the night-time economy and enhancing the public 'feel good' factor. As in many other towns and cities, direct market intervention in the form of plans to regulate and restrict the number and density of licensed premises in key 'hot spot' locations via planning and licensing controls has remained largely absent from the campaign. However, despite this omission, Citycentresafe is undoubtedly a serious attempt to address the problems of the night-time economy in a more holistic manner and has facilitated a working partnership between control agencies, health professionals, and more progressively, the licensed trade. The strategy is however extremely resource intensive and many of the initiatives depend upon short-term sponsorship from the private sector, making the future of the current and envisaged strategy somewhat uncertain. It will prove interesting to discover whether the current level of resolve, funding, and strategic implementation can be maintained once the symbolic milestone of the Commonwealth Games 2002 has been passed.

Conclusion

As we have seen, the history of nightlife in Manchester is as long as that of the City itself. From the beer shops, singing saloons, and music halls of the early Industrial city, through to the dance halls of the 1920s, cinema revolution of the 1930s, record hops of the 1950s, coffee clubs of the 1960s and the discotheques of the 1970s and early 1980s, Mancunians have always wanted to have 'fun'. Fun has always been controlled and regulated in Manchester, if not formally by the police officer, the publican, and the magistrate, then informally by market forces, economic necessity, the bounds of respectability, the employer's clock, and the hooligan's fist. Throughout our case study, the night-time economy and its liminal attractions have been variously banished from, or incorporated within, the shifting political and economic imperatives of the urban polity. In times of social and economic crisis and transition (such as the 1830s and the 1970s), night-time leisure in the Industrial city was *suppressed*, whilst in times of relative prosperity (such as the late 1950s and early 1960s), a degree of incorporation occurred. Since the mid-1980s, this previously marginal commercial leisure market has become *central* to the economic fortunes of the post-industrial city.

Thus, despite being closely associated with a motley crew of unruly, even criminal attendants and the miscreant allure of licit and illicit intoxicants, the undeniably 'vibrant' night-time economy has assumed a key role in the political economy of contemporary Manchester and many similar projects of urban governance across Britain.

4

Tommy Smith's Story:
Four Decades On The Door

In the old days, everybody stepped back when a young man walked by
(Mose Allison).

This chapter is based upon a case study that will introduce the reader
to the world of 'bouncers'. As a veteran of four decades spent
working within the night-time economy, Tommy presents a not
unsurprisingly jaded view of the world. However, given the intensity
of his experience, it is our belief that his observations warrant the
same degree of respect that one might afford to, for instance, those of
a veteran police officer. Although our primary concern is to examine
the contemporary scene, given the lack of anything other than a
handful of autobiographies to flesh out the 'door trade's' recent
history, the following case study will serve as a scene setter for the
analysis that follows. Tommy's story highlights some of the fears and
concerns of a career bouncer who has personally experienced many
of the changes in the leisure industry discussed above. The chapter
charts a career that began as a local hard man employed to fight
other hard men, and finished as a club owner, among the drugs, guns,
and commercial violence of the contemporary marketplace.

Tommy has been a doorman in his hometown for over thirty years;
his CV is impressive, but not unusual for this job in this city. He has
the obligatory S-shaped nose, a map of scars is clearly visible through
his crew-cut, a chunk of his shin is missing thanks to a machete, a
triumvirate of stab wounds decorates his belly, and he's also been
shot. His entry into the trade was a simple choice requiring only one
qualification:

Basically all the doormen, myself included, were fighters, if you could have
a go, it was like end up in the boozers fighting, or go to get paid for
it . . . You've got to be a nutter to work the door, to actually stand there
and take the violence which is given out today. You've got to be a bit mad

anyway haven't you, you're not normal are you if you want to take a beating? I wouldn't class myself as normal, but because you need money you have to do it, but if I could pack it in tomorrow and get a job with the same pay and same enjoyment I get out of it, I would change me job tomorrow.

Tommy regards himself as a traditional doorman, hardworking and proud of his role in the local leisure industry. He speaks with lament about how the job and the industry have changed since he began working 'the doors' in 1965:

Years ago it used to be families that ran the doors, they all had their own little areas, so it was controlled by families in Portville, and the local hardcases. But you didn't get bullies on the door. If you saw someone bullying on the door we'd have a meeting and they were thrown off the door. Things were okay then due to respect, it was a case of pride, but the Government and the police decided this was a bad thing and started saying you've got to register as a security firm.

After so long on the doors Tommy mourns the gradual passing of the crucial and very basic indigenous informality that enabled him to ply his trade with a minimum of formal or institutional involvement. Although as we stress in Chapter 5, the importance of locality in defining legitimate control remains crucial, there should be little doubt that these previously *ad hoc* arrangements have undergone a process of commercial reconfiguration (see Chapter 6). Tommy recognizes the impact that security firms have had on the industry as he knew it, both in terms of new opportunities for organized criminal activity and the creation of local legal monopolies.

There's still good doormen, it's just that everyone's got a bad name. But because of a minority of doormen the other doormen are suffering. The firms are overpowering them through numbers. A security firm in Portville would say have three hundred men, that's a lot of men, it's like an army isn't it? So the little guy working his small pub, getting his forty pounds a night and not bothering no one, they walk in, it's just a week but it's if you've got a hundred, the money's in the volume. It's organized crime run by a minority of people because they've the power to do it. They're getting the power to do it from the police and the Government by them saying you've got to register as a firm. If they left it to individuals to each door they wouldn't have it, because if you're in a firm you've got to go along with what that firm says. But if you're individual like what it used to be years ago with families, you had your own door and no one would come near you 'cos you also had the backing of the police. The police used to be with you, they'd talk to you, nowadays they're against you right away, they're anti-doormen.

At the end of the day, the security firms aren't making all that much money by the time they've paid their VAT. They have what's called an administration charge and they might make five pound a man on a shift, but it doesn't work out a lot of money unless you've got volume. But the other way is they've got the power to control the doors, they can control who sells the drugs inside. If you've got control of the door you can sell your drugs, and this goes on everywhere. In Portville there is only two main firms 'cos it's not as big as London or wherever, and they've got a lot of men on doors so they can control it.

Tommy is anti-drugs, and this was not an entirely unusual stance within a profession that features a spectrum of commercial as well as attitudinal possibilities (see Chapter 7). Tommy does not like what drugs do to customers or to doormen. More generally however, he regards drugs as a corrupting influence upon his profession that have introduced a complex series of dilemmas and ambiguities into an occupation that, in his eyes, was simple but honourable.

These new doormen, they're not in it for the job, they're in it to sell drugs. I'm in it to get me thirty or forty pound a night to support me wife and kids, they do it to actually sell drugs. People know that wherever you go in any big city...Look at my house, I've got nothing, I can take you to houses of doormen who work in certain clubs and they've got marble fire places, tiled floors, fifty-inch screen TVs, BMW cars. You don't get that on fifty pounds a night. You have people coming in who want to sell and certain doormen let them sell and then tax them maybe forty or fifty pounds a night. So the taxing stops the doormen handling the drugs, and he's on a good earner if he gets fifty pound off the door and fifty pound off the people inside, and he might have five fellers selling inside. Basically, he's got a licence to let people sell. Most of the fellers in the clubs know who's dealing for who, so you're told anyway to lay off them. If you pull someone for selling, you're told leave him alone he's selling for Charlie or Joe or whoever. There's doormen now working, who are actually getting paid by the police as informers. They're actually selling drugs and they're police informers; so a lot of lads won't say nothing 'cos it will come back, they can find out who's talking in Portville. It gets complicated, they say it doesn't go on, but it does go on. A lad's just been shot in Portville five weeks ago. He was a police informer, [and] also a security guard for a company, plus he used to take drugs off people. He was like a mugger of drug dealers, but he worked both sides of the coin, he was a police informer and a gangster, so no one complained about him because it would get back who'd snitched.

Tommy suggests that drug use is not just prominent among club customers but also among the doormen. This he says can have particularly bad consequences for punters when trouble breaks out. He would like to see mandatory drug tests introduced for bouncers to weed out the guilty 'just like the train drivers'.

A good doorman who's a bit of a tasty lad, a good fighter, has that feeling of confidence, that if you're throwing someone out that you can have a go at them. But if you haven't got it in your heart then you tend to fall back on the pack. Nowadays, it's not even a case of carry him out, it's a case of do him in, that's what's happening . . . 'Cos a lot of doormen now, well fifty per cent of them are on steroids and cocaine, and it's a bad cocktail. So what happens is that they build their bodies up at the gym but they can't handle themselves, so they tend to look good, look the part, but when it comes down to fighting and throwing people out they can't, it's got to be a firm. And what happens is they get excited, go off their head and do them in.

Doormen used to be referees, just separating people and throwing them out. To be a good doorman you've got to be able to handle yourself and that gives you the confidence so as not to beat someone, but nowadays they tend to be in packs.

Tommy estimates that there's something of a fifty–fifty split between 'good and bad' doormen operating in the business. Many of the former practised door work as their secondary occupation because the hours of work accommodate for this opportunity. This notion flies in the face of much of the rhetoric emanating from the security industry that stress the desirability of 'professionalizing' door work (see Chapter 6), while serving to support other aspects of the same rhetoric that stress the alleged benign respectability of many door-men (see footnote 1, Chapter 7).

There's bent doormen and then there's lads who do the door as a bonus, i.e. to buy a car, maybe help out with the mortgage, I mean there's firemen work the doors, I know prison officers who work the doors . . . They're okay, they top their money up by doing the door. For one, they're getting a night out and they're getting paid for it, and they don't want fighting, a good doorman—the last thing we want is fighting. We just want to go in earn our money, be sociable and go home.

Tommy was particularly vociferous on the subject of why club managers don't specifically demand 'good' doormen, and the importance of understanding the relationship between managers and door security was stressed to us on countless occasions throughout our study.

Because they're fearful, they get intimidated. Not intimidated as in threats to kill or anything like that, it's a case of you've got a door security firm and they put whoever they like on to the club. They just put them there and the actual managers got no say in it. If I've got a security firm and put a big seven foot feller on the door that's up to me. The managers won't take it on their heads to speak up and knock them back. They will come along put someone there and you don't say boo, we're getting paid as security by your firm and it's none of your business. We order them round, we tell them what to do and it's nothing to do with you, you run your bars. But basically, it is something to do with the licensee because I've been a licensee myself and you're responsible for what happens in your club. But unfortunately they're losing contact with that, by just ignoring it. If he's getting the numbers, i.e. the big discos, through the door and he's getting two thousand people in at five pound or ten pound a go, he's not bothered 'cos he's keeping the bosses happy, so he thinks this is a good thing. But in the long term it will be closed. It'll be closed in a couple of years because there will be that much trouble.

Tommy is keen on doorstaff being accountable, which was for him an easier and more acceptable prospect in a previous era of relatively low key indigenous problematics that stressed solely the abilities of individual doormen. The contemporary scale of the industry makes this difficult, and for Tommy, the rise of security firms and the advent of 'superclubs' which may hold two or three thousand people, has also contributed to an increasing gang mentality among doormen.

I'm self-taught, you used to have to use your brain and your mouth because there might have been only two of you against ten fellers. Nowadays with bigger clubs there tends to be fifteen or twenty doormen on, so they all rely on each other, they're not individuals anymore, they're an army and they're there to do the business. They are there to fight aren't they? They're not individuals no more. I work on my own Friday and Saturday night getting three hundred people, but I'm responsible to me. If I want to kick off on someone then I will do. If I want to be nice I will be nice, but that's down to me. I'm accountable to myself, but when you're with a pack, i.e. twelve doormen on a door, you're not accountable to no one, you're just a pack, you don't have to fight on your own so you just rely on everyone else to help and that's where it gets a bit dangerous because it will go over the top. There's no control.

The huge growth of the leisure industry has resulted in increasingly large venues, along with an increasing edge of competition. The outcome in many cases has been a 'pack-them-wide-and-pile-them-high' mentality among proprietors, managers, and promoters. Tommy recognizes the detrimental effect this has had upon the role of doormen and his ability to control a crowd through traditional means.

> Clubs are not very selective no more, years ago you'd have your head doorman who vets people coming in, and three nice doormen on the door and a bouncer inside to bounce people out. Doormen don't study people any more, you're just cattle going right through, paying your tenner. Now you've got two thousand people in a club, there's nothing personal about it. You used to have little clubs with say one hundred members so you knew the person coming through the door. They used to come every Saturday night 'alright Tom, alright Mary' and it was personal. Now you've got two or three thousand people and you've got to get them in within an hour. So it's just cattle going through the till. No vetting goes on, you don't talk to them no more, it's just get them in and pay the tenner. You don't open the door for people now you just usher them in. At a little club you open the door for everyone and say 'good evenings' to everyone.

Tommy believes that this lack of personal contact is symptomatic of the changing role of the bouncer. Tommy's traditional role as a 'meeter and greeter' of valued clients developed a mutual respect which was an established means of control for doormen. And although as we will discuss in Chapter 5, diplomacy and verbal skills have far from disappeared from the bouncer's repertoire, Tommy believes that the changed environment in which doormen now operate has eroded the status of this crucial aspect of doorwork:

> The attitude has changed, there's no pride on the door any more. I used to wear a dickie bow, black suit, clean shoes, and be smart, same as the police or army, or any service, and that used to give you a bit of pride because you was a doorman. Now it's the old bomber jackets and loose-fitting tops, sweatshirts, it takes that pride out of it. The attitude goes along with the uniform doesn't it? Being smart and opening doors for people and saying good evening and getting to know the clients—that makes a difference. The attitude has definitely gone . . . I'll socialize with people and try to get to know people because a few times it's saved me life, because the people coming to the club know me first name and know I'm decent. So I've been working and been attacked by five fellers, and customers have jumped in to help me, 'cos they say, 'he's all right him', so the respect has got to go both ways.

As we discussed in Chapter 1, the new night-time economy is overwhelmingly youth orientated, and Tommy acknowledges that changes in the attitudes of bouncers are also a response to a change in the attitude of customers that inhabit the pub and club environment. It is on this point more than any other that Tommy echoes the pessimistic analysis of long-serving police officers.

Now the kids on the drugs are that cocky that they are turning on doormen, they've no respect anymore. I'd say eighty per cent of young lads going out now take cocaine at the weekend, so rather than spending twenty pound on ale, they're spending it on cocaine. That might sound like a high number, but that's what they're doing. If you open the door for them most people would respect that, but now you get the kids who think you're a divvy. They take nice for being stupid, they think well mannered is soft. If you're well mannered then they don't tend to have respect for you, or at least that's what's in the mind of the doormen. So the new bouncer is like big, angry, don't smile, don't talk to no one, don't show your weaknesses. Because they're fearful of showing their emotions or showing they're soft, because a lot of them are just on steroids, they're just big men they haven't got a brain and they just think they are there to do violence. I'm not just there to fight. I'm there to get them out the fire escape if there's a fire; if someone's getting attacked to help them; if someone's robbing, to stop handbag robbers, there's a lot to do if you're a good doorman. We're there to protect people. If someone's collapsed I give them first aid 'cos I'm self taught, if I see someone who can't breathe I'll help them out . . . I've known doormen to just drag people out with asthma attacks and throw them in the street.

Drunks [are] the same, nowadays it's just throw them out. I've seen people choke on vomit. I take them outside, give them a glass of water, sit them up and keep an eye on them. But that's me, and I class myself as a good doorman. There's no concern no more, I mean you ask them new bouncers where the fire escape is and they wouldn't know. The only reason they'd go to the fire escape is to take someone there to beat them up.

This is, as we maintain throughout the book, rather more than the golden age reminiscences of an aged door retainer, for as we will show, increases in violence have paralleled the growth of the night-time economy. Tommy maintains that the world of the bouncer is more violent today than it's ever been, yet unlike our analysis does not consider alcohol as significant in this change. The infiltration of the business (both in the club and on the door) by criminal networks, and the changing nature of drug use are blamed for this.

There's more fighting now, it's murder now. If there was a fight in a club years ago, people used to separate themselves from the fight, like form a circle so you could run right into the fight, so pick out the people fighting straight away. Now no one cares, [they] will just stand there drinking, they're not even concerned about it . . . Years ago if a lad came to the door and he was told to go, then he'd go. For one, he'd only be drunk, he wouldn't have no drugs down him . . . there was respect there so he used to go. Nowadays . . . if they get a beating with so many people being on cocaine, when they go down they keep getting back up, so they get worse injuries.

The stress by Tommy upon what he regards as the basic highly individualized foundations of doorwork have been further threatened by attempts to control the door trade (see Chapter 6). He replicated the stance of many of our informants, by highlighting the basic skills required of a bouncer, and the ease with which unscrupulous doorstaff can bypass efforts at control. As Tommy shows me a photograph of himself as a younger man, grinning with his knuckles upright posing with the fresh-faced world champion boxer Charlie Magri, I ask him about the proposed national registration scheme.

We're all employed by security firms because they wanted someone to be accountable for us, i.e. doormen. But what's happening now is, [or even in the future] when you register with the council, 'cause in Portville we're to register with the council and do a three day course, you've got to have no criminal record. You'll get people who've never been in trouble in their lives on the door. Say four on the door, and then there'll be eight others inside with tracksuits on who are fighters. So this will just push it under the mat, because with them having form they're not going to be able to front it with the uniform on so they will be in the background, so it's just going to be the same. There's people who've killed people working the doors in 'Grimtown', but they don't have a uniform on and they stand in the background with tracksuits on or jeans but they're on the payroll . . . I can see it working to an extent, but the police know who's who, they know who's selling, who's running doors, they know everything about them but they can't touch them. The police are turning a blind eye, I think to certain things, because it suits them, maybe their hands are tied, I don't know.

Tommy's jaundiced view of the world is based on hard shifts on the doors of a hard city. His scars bear witness to a world where the promises of pleasure meld all too seamlessly with the possibility of pain. In this world the competitive scuffle for profit that is integral to consumer capitalism is mirrored by the constant skirmishing for control of the constantly evolving, essentially transgressive protocols of the liminal night. Given that these skirmishes are played out within a minimalistic formal regulatory framework, it is unsurprising to find doorstaff so often replicating the often cynical, but essentially pragmatic informal strategies of the lower ranks of the police.

If the customers weren't naughty you wouldn't have us, you wouldn't have bouncers. If the customers were all lovely angels and nice people you wouldn't need bouncers would you?

5

A Word At The Door: Bouncers On Their Work

...what a lot of people fail to realize is that it is hard to politely escort somebody to the door seconds after they've punched you in the mouth. Roy

This chapter is based upon both interviews with bouncers, and our ethnography, and will attempt to describe and analyse the informal strategies upon which the job of 'bouncing' is based. Using the testimony of doorstaff, we will highlight the way that these strategies are created, not within the pedagogical frames of formal training, but as a result of both personal and vicarious experience, retrospective contemplation of performance, and enculturated transmission. We will look at the importance of bouncers as gatekeepers to the night-time economy, and stress the value placed upon local knowledge, and the strategies that are utilized in dealing with trouble, from verbal reprimand to violence. We also attempt to construct a model of informal commercial policing that has body type, demeanour, local knowledge, and gendered and class-specific habitus at its very foundation. The existing literature on the sub-culture of policing is examined and comparisons made between public and private policing, for both are grounded in the informal pragmatism of the enacted environment. We will theoretically explore the tenuous links between those that police in the name of the state, and those that police in the interests of commerce, and show how salient issues of control and accountability arise with respect to both agencies.

At night, new rules of comportment are negotiated via the acceptability of varying levels of intoxication, of aggressive sexuality, and of a spatial demeanour alien to the business of daylight hours (Hobbs et al., 2000). The police enforce the law, but the bouncer, although like any other citizen subject to the law, operates according to a highly ambiguous cocktail of extra-legal maxims, occupational codes, and personal discretions, underpinned by an interpretation of what is good and what is bad for business.

To him they are the public, an unpleasant job, a threat, the bad ones, unpleasant and whining, self-concerned, uncooperative, and unjust (Westley, 1953:49).

Access denied

You have to have a door mentality, a street mentality, you have to know how to read people, body language, facial expressions. You learn so much just by looking at people. Chris

Doorstaff have the responsibility for controlling who enters the premises, and control of the door is a vital first principle if the decorum of customers is to be influenced. For once customers enter the premises, policing them is far more difficult, and every effort is taken to exclude potential problems at the door. The devices and strategies utilized to control the door vary enormously from venue to venue. Formal door policies, where they exist, provide a framework of rules for bouncers to work within. Drugs and weapons are explicitly prohibited and in the case of the former, posters, often associated with police, local authority, or drug agencies, vie for customers' attention along with explicit warnings issued by the venue's management. However, bouncers themselves acknowledge the importance of controlling the door by devising informal strategies, strategies forged through experience and performance:

If they're aggressive with me at the door, then they'll be aggressive inside with either the punters or the barstaff...don't stop it at the door and you've no chance...the door is the only point of control, because if you've got a big gang of fifty lads you don't let them in because they can do whatever they want once they're inside. So don't let them in, that's the only option you've got. If it kicks off at the door, hopefully you can get the door shut before you get seriously hurt yourselves...If you stop it at the door you've stopped it, they're not in. Steve North

The process of selection that takes place at the door is crucial, it sets the tone for the ambience inside the venues, which is an environment that is considered relatively marginal, chaotic, and difficult to manage. The vetting of customers is a skilled process, and although the discretion utilized by individual bouncers is immense, certain themes emerged both from the interviews and from our observations, which overwhelmingly related to issues concerning the perceived threat of violence to doorstaff, barstaff, and customers. These issues take precedence, but must also be balanced against the commercial concerns engendered by a highly competitive marketplace. For instance, we were made aware that the commercial sustainability of 'protected' premises can become compromised by the 'safety-first' attitude of overly anxious doorstaff. Inevitably, this can raise tensions with the licensee, who, whilst not wanting, for instance an excessively boisterous crowd, will be committed to keep the tills ringing.

The door is where you start. To prevent trouble you have to make sure that the customers coming in are suitable . . . On the other hand, customers want to be relaxed, they don't want to see five scowling fellas at the door and be thinking 'oh no, I'm gonna get battered.' Paul

However, the door is not merely a site of inclusion or exclusion, it also offers opportunities for assessment and surveillance. For the environment in which bouncers make their crucial decisions can be chaotic, noisy, and confusing; skilled doorstaff such as Glen will opt for an approach that allows for a fusion of surveillance and negotiation:

You get a group of lads, they're regulars in the bars and they want to walk straight in 'cause they come here every week. Sometimes you've got to tell them, 'well listen can you line up please and wait your turn' . . . some of them take it personal 'cause there's nothing worse than rejection, I understand that. But when they start saying 'well why can't I go in?' That answer must be short and sweet, [but] if you go into it then you create yourself a situation. Like we had a load of Portville lads, seventeen of them . . . 'at the end of the day you know you can't come in like, that it's impossible', and they're like, 'why not? we've spent this and we've spent that, we've come all the way from Portville just to come to this club'. Well what I do when I work, and I have my guys do it as well, I have them standing out and keep them there just a few minutes, maybe ten minutes in some cases and then you can assess their temperament well before they even come in there. And if they're like 'uh, why can't I do this, why can't I do that?' . . . once they start with the bad language or anything, saying it's a shit club, or this is a load of shit what's going on, then automatically he's telling me he's not suitable . . . That's the trick with being a doorman is to keep the trouble at the door and not in the club, 'cause once they are in the club its much harder to sort it out. Glen

The 'attitude test' is clearly soaked in discretionary practice, yet the very application of the test, front stage at the door with an intense knowledgeable audience in the queue, enables the bouncer to act out a highly theatrical rendition of personal power within a highly charged environment. Strangers, particularly in large groups, are especially problematic.

Sometimes you get coachloads of lads from all over the place come into town for a night out... sometimes you can just tell. They might have different clothes and that, just a different look about them and they always come up to the door not saying anything and not talking like most people do if they're out. There can be like sixty of them, they split up into smaller groups so they can get in. Most times you can see it coming and turn them back. If you miss it you can have serious bother. You got sixty lads from out of town... All sorts of shit can happen, they might start singing fucking football songs, touching up peoples' girlfriends and that, and then you know the locals are going to get their boys together and you can have a fucking riot... Alan

However, in customer culture, the exclusion of large rowdy groups is an unwritten but well-understood part of the night-time code, and by attempting to negotiate the code at the door, customers can acquire status. There is unlikely to be any formal backing for banning large groups, no posters proclaiming prohibition that doorstaff could point to. As a tactic doorstaff can invoke either the 'rules of the house' ('You can't come in. It's not me, it's the rules of the house'), filtering his discretion through the frame of formal rules. However, if this is regarded as unnecessary or strategically inappropriate, he can choose to ban entrance to the venue in a manner that essentially defies the numerical odds, and places authority firmly upon his broad shoulders ('because I say so'). This use of discretion often appears so arbitrary and personal that doorstaff are vulnerable to attack, and as a consequence, an aura of potential violence is commonly utilized to discourage violent reactions from those denied access.

Common to all venues, and regardless of subtle or not so subtle dress codes, is the deliberate construction on the part of doorstaff of typologies of disrepute that refer to the types of individuals who will always be refused entry. Large groups of men are the most obvious, but there are also individuals whose appearance and demeanour suggest trouble, and trouble as we will go on to discuss, overwhelmingly means violence.

The barred

'assholes'—those who do not accept the police definition of the situation (Van Maanen, 1978a:223).

I got a list of arseholes I won't deal with: 1/ Lippy flash bastards. 2/More than three black men together at the Kings are a fucking race riot, plain and simple. I'm not racist but everybody else there is and somebody is going to lift off and start a ruck. I tell them its full up. 3/ Drunks. 4/ People who look like they got guns. 5/ People who look like they gonna be sick. If anybody's dealing don't let me see. Lay your hands on my body in any way and I will hurt you. Clear the fire doors and back up your mates . . . make sure that we run the gaff and not scum . . . By going in harder than the normal person is ever going to dream of. That means the level of pain I am going to put on the scum.
Q, Who are the scum?
People who are not willing to do what I tell them (Douglas, a 27 year old black bouncer).

The above descriptions refer to analytic categories, the bouncer's version of 'police property' (Reiner, 1985), 'shit lists' (Van Maanen, 1978a: 229) of individuals with whom bouncers regularly deal. From the bouncers' point of view, 'they and they alone are the most capable of sensing right from wrong; determining who is and who is not respectable; and most critically, deciding what is to be done about it' (Van Maanen, 1978a: 222). Moreover, as the status of customers declines in the eyes of doorstaff, so the level of deference displayed to customers equally declines (Sykes and Clark, 1975). By addressing the types of people barred from clubs and pubs, we can begin to understand the twin nexus of the bouncers' authority, which as we suggest above, constitutes a subtle blending of the commercial mandate afforded to doorstaff by an interpretation of the 'rules of the house', rules of entry that relate to the management's perception of the venue's market niche, with a categorization of the potential customer's violent capacity as 'symbolic assailants' (Monaghan, 2002a; Neiderhoffer, 1967; Skolnick, 1966). This, as we stress, is grounded in no small way within the bouncers' concerns for the maintenance of his own well-being (Rubenstein, 1973), and we found that most of the customers who were barred were excluded as a result of the bouncer's perception of them as violent or potentially violent. These are highly pragmatic decisions, as Mark explained: 'If they've been pissed on the Friday causing bother then you're not getting in on the Saturday are you?'

If entrance is denied, the barred customer may attempt to persuade the bouncers of their error of judgment. This is almost a matter of course, and for the most part, the bouncers take it in good humour, simply reiterating the reason the individual had been denied entry, but without being drawn into detailed justifications. However, if the individual persists beyond what was considered to be reasonable boundaries, in terms of the longevity of the protest, or the use of aggressive language, this would be taken as confirmation of flawed identity, and could provide a justification for a pre-emptive strike (Van Maanen, 1978a:224). However, doorstaff normally seek to indicate that the protestations had failed and would never succeed, and that it was time to give up and move on before something untoward occurred. This could be anything from 'Look, you're not getting in, it doesn't matter how long you fucking stand there', or a simple 'fuck off!'.

The onus is on the bouncer to control the situation, and it is not uncommon for the violence that is implicit in the language utilized as part of a control strategy to escalate into physical violence. Quantitative data emerging from a Home Office-funded project revealed doorstaff involvement in a range of violent incidents.

Most of these (at least 273 out of 392) entailed assaults *by* doorstaff rather than *on* them. Doorstaff were additionally involved in 95 assaults in the street or elsewhere, mainly outside the premises where they worked . . . and in 142 incidents of disorder (mainly 'altercations' over entry or ejection from premises). Overall they were involved in at least 16% of all known alcohol-related incidents of disorder in the central Cardiff police sectors (Maguire and Nettleton, 2002:29–30. See also Homel and Clarke, 1994; Tomsen et al., 1991).

In an arena that is geared towards the defining and refining of consumer identity, everyone is engaged in a voyeuristic quest to define fashionable and unfashionable, attractive and unattractive. Labels are worn with various degrees of deliberation, and exaggerated demeanours, with or without alcoholic or chemical assistance, are the norm. Even when there is a formal dress code in practice, the discretion of doorstaff is at the forefront of entrance policy. This can be problematic, particularly for older doorstaff who are of a different generation to the clientele:

... the different rules are deep nightmares for someone of my age. Like one [club] says no trainers, one next door no jeans. Gazza comes up in a pair of £120 trainers and a pair of Versace jeans and I have to say 'no you can't come in'... but he's worked all week, saved up for all the right gear and then an old man like me says 'no', and he's had a few beers and while he's arguing with me he has to watch some soapy fucker in a Woolworth's suit go in. 'Good evening sir, have a nice time'. Steve South

Despite such age related ambiguities relating to a venue's target clientele, bouncers regard themselves as expert at reading signs of trouble. With both their own safety and the interests of their clientele in mind, they are willing to make decisions that can banish certain individuals to forever wander the night-time streets as part of the legion of the banned.

What I won't have is visible tattoos, anything on their face or neck don't get in... arms ain't a problem, but all that weird Pikey stuff, spiders webs and tears, no they are trouble... usually got something else wrong with them so usually you don't tell them that it's the tattoos, you usually say 'not your night mate'... its my policy. With all my experience it's my decision to say no—to whoever. Steve South (see Black, 1968; Sacks, 1972)

Our ethnography suggested that seemingly arbitrary decisions on admittance were actually grounded in a fierce enacted logic stemming from the personal experiences that constitute the occupational culture. For instance, as indicated above, tattoos are often read as a primary indicator of potential threat and therefore unsuitability for admittance:

People who have visible tattoos tend to be of a certain type. Many of the people I've had bother with recently have tattoos. John

Similarly, indicators of trouble could take on distinctly temporal characteristics, and this was illustrated to us during our ethnography by the prohibition of 'Trainer Sundays'. Where our ethnography was located, it was common practice for men to go out all day drinking on Sundays. They'd start out in local pubs and then head into the city centre during the evening. The bouncers' use of trainers as signifiers of potential trouble was clear: crudely put, men in trainers on

Sundays had probably been out drinking for some time, and men who had been out drinking for some time were more likely to cause trouble. To the bouncers involved in our ethnography, this kind of discriminatory practice was obvious and clearly justifiable. Occupational culture and local knowledge provided the tools with which to unpack sartorial codes and create rational informal admittance policies.

If bouncers perceive that a potential customer, by virtue of their clothing, demeanour, or body type are likely to be involved with violence inside the premises they will be denied entrance. Similarly the barred include those who have already proved themselves disruptive, or those who bring with them a reputation:

If they've started real bother they might never get back in... but if he's saying sorry, I was pissed and all that you might just swallow it... you might think fuck it, he's alright, he was only pissed and he's normally no bother, or you might think, this bastard's working himself every week, so then he doesn't get back in. Mark

Doorstaff, by virtue of their prized gatekeeper role, are able to negotiate with the barred from a position of strength, and several explained that after a violent disturbance and a decent interval, a handshake and an apology could afford the barred re-entrance to the venue (see Van Maanen, 1978a:233).

But he would need to look at me first, show that he knows I am there and maybe... shake hands, whatever. Steve South

However, venue managers tended to take a harder, less 'local' line than doorstaff.

Anyone who is involved in any conflict in the venue is barred for life... irrespective of who started it we will use the ultimate sanction that we can use, which is a lifetime ban. Kevin

However, doorstaff were adamant that it was not violent people *per se*, but those deemed likely to be violent *within the premises* who were barred:

It's only a fucking pub, so if you do get gangsters in, they're only out for a drink. We always know who's who so you just treat them ok and there's no bother. Mark

Local knowledge

Working the same sector regularly, the patrolman develops a collection of impressions and facts about the people he deals with. These are what he uses in evaluating them (Rubinstein, 1973:184).

For all its aspirations as an outpost of a global culture whose attractions include anonymity, most night-time economies are controlled by 'locals' and populated by 'regulars'. Although some venues, particularly at the more high profile and prestigious end of the market, do have door strategies that involve bringing in staff from outside the immediate area, the overwhelming opinion was that local staff were by far preferable. Indeed, like the 'operational' public police officer, a detailed local knowledge is regarded as a crucial tool in carrying out the job (Rubinstein, 1973:129).

It's like Birmingham city centre, you won't get no Londoners down there doing security. They'll give it to Brum 'cause any excuse to kick off or wreck it; it'd be like 'Cockneys what are you doing down here, get back to your own city', any excuse sort of thing, and it'll go off, so you tend to keep it local. Alan

Some clubs have developed huge national and international client bases, and security at the venue takes on the characteristics of for instance, a festival, concert, or sporting event. At these venues security from outside can be brought in, often with a mix of local doorstaff. For example, one high profile south London nightclub successfully blended a Midlands doorteam with local security. Such a 'half-and-half' strategy provided the venue's management with valuable 'political' options in relation to how the security attempted to prevent local dealers from operating in their own backyard. However, the long-term costs of such an exercise are prohibitive to all but the most profitable, and the vast majority of venues rely solely upon security firms that combine local knowledge with a highly valued, locally forged reputation. Indeed, the local bouncer can, if perceived to be effective, command a high premium, and the local form of control imposed will comprise of a collage of formal and informal measures that combine to create an indigenous commercial mandate. 'From such knowledge of this social stage comes the corresponding evaluations of what particular conditions are to be considered safe or unsafe, troubled or calm, usual or unusual' (Van Maanen, 1978a:226).

It's better to have doormen that know people than strangers... I'm not saying that doormen should never work outside their own area, but pubs like to have people from the town who know the local idiots... if you get doormen from out of town who don't know anyone and a proper idiot comes up to the door, they will just let him in; because they don't know him. It's not their fault, but they are just causing trouble in the pub... The landlords get all the flak for it and people in the pub don't enjoy themselves because they know idiots are in. Darren

Definitions of what constitutes 'local' vary enormously, although typically place of residence is the defining variable that establishes the local nature of door security. Long term employment, for instance on a particular nightstrip, creates symbiotic familiarity between bouncers and their clientele. The latter enabled doorstaff to commute to work without being regarded as part of an invading force.

The ability to perceive and interpret threat is central to the bouncer's toolbox of competencies, and local knowledge is widely regarded by doorstaff and managers alike as vital in this process of interpretation. 'Such specialized knowledge is therefore crucial and provides an immensely detailed backdrop of rich, non-shared, and particularistic knowledge...' (Manning and Van Maanen, 1978: 217). The constitution of a specific competence is determined by the perspective of various audiences (Fielding, 1984), and the bouncer's enacted environment consists of a variety of audiences capable of testing the depth and voracity of the bouncer's knowledge by subjecting themselves to very public examination. This knowledge is gleaned from various sources, but it should be stressed that the world of bouncers is shot through with gossip, about who is working where, for whom and for how much, who is dealing, buying, and selling, and the nature of any feuds that are brewing. All of the above and much more are played out in an arena where senses are deliberately blurred, and where many of the participants are intoxicated, and it is part of the bouncer's business to posses this 'local intelligence', so that regular and impromptu threat assessments can be made:

The best [bouncers] know everyone as well. They know bouncers, they know tough lads who might come in, they know the form of the younger lads, they just know everything that's going on. They know who's been arguing with who, they know who's got out of prison, they know stuff about the women who are in. That's another part of the job, you have to know people. Trevor

Some sections of the bouncers' clientele have extremely violent reputations that are highly specialized and associated with professional, commodified, physical violence. Off duty bouncers fit into this category. They bring with them on a night out reputations that will vie with those of the home team.

It is another Friday evening in Russ'z bar. We haven't had anything to do all night, and it has been a quiet week. I had to turn three young women away two hours ago and that's it. My feet and legs are aching, and this is the fourth time I've heard this particular song tonight and about the fiftieth this week. An ex-doorman at Russ'z is in tonight with a group of local doormen and ex-bouncers. Dressed as they are they wouldn't normally get in, with jeans, baggy shirts, and trainers. They are celebrating a birthday, are loud, boisterous, obstructing ordinary punters' route to the bar. One of the regular female patrons has been groped, tensions rise and a glass smashes on the floor. When the group starts to do a strip, the team of bouncers move in and the strip stops. These are large, physically capable drunks with reputations for violence, and are irritated by the intrusion. Things are about to escalate when the head doorman intervenes to take the edge off, and with a deluge of tactical affability renegotiates the parameters of this particular 'boy's night out'. Any other group would have been out on their ear. The phrasing of the head doorman's request was crucial as the first bouncer on the scene had treated the men like ordinary punters, and was about to provoke violence. But the head doorman understood the need for mutual respect to be maintained. Nobody lost face, and the door team retained its professional integrity. The door team's sense of order had been maintained. Groping women and smashing the odd glass did not breach any rules, but doing a striptease was an indefensible breach of protocol.

Also within this problematic category will be well known professional criminals whose violence has a price, and are therefore unlikely to become involved in alcohol-related fights. However, when these customers do become violent, bouncers are forced to call upon highly refined and very special qualities of mediation. All of the impudent and oppositional aspects of nightlife find parallels with the mythical qualities that dominate the identities of professional criminals (Katz, 1988:230). They stand in opposition to the diligence and prudence of the equally mythic nine-to-five worker, and the casting aside of the cloak of economic rationality is one of the key motifs and allures integral to the night-time economy. Whilst the instrumental involvement of organized crime in this economy will be dealt with elsewhere (Chapter 7), it is the very presence of the gangster that is one of our key concerns here. For them, 'Life is lived without a safety net' (Pileggi, 1987:39), and they are prime examples of the night-time consumer par excellence, motivated by an explicitly hedonistic drive to live 'life as a party' (Shover and Honaker, 1991), by 'earning and burning money' (Katz, 1988:215) and with little thought for the mundane workaday travails of the morning.

Another Saturday, and the presence of a local gangster and his entourage has raised the temperature inside Russ'z Bar. The DJ puts on a remix of the old 'Kung Fu Fighting' song and the door team have to ask several groups of young men to cease their Bruce Lee impersonations. It started with a bump and a slightly spilt drink. One of the gangster's group grabs another man by the shirt and head-butts him, and the bouncers eject the victim for his own safety. The head doorman suggests that if the group want to go after the man then it would be quicker if they used the fire exit. This is not necessarily true, but it gives the impression that he is attempting to be helpful. He cautions the group on the prevalence of CCTV cameras in the city centre, and engages the gangster in conversation. They talk about whose fault the incident was, commiserating, placating, and generally slowing the group down as they are unlikely to leave in pursuit of the man without their leader.

The incident has not escalated, nobody has been seriously hurt, and Russ'z Bar carries on earning money. If the door team had attempted to move the aggressors we may not have succeeded, and there would have been serious repercussions. Throwing out the victim also meant that the person upon whom the violence was focused was no longer present, and so any opportunity for further violence was removed. The victim may not have appreciated the strategy adopted by the bouncers, but their response was based upon complex cultural, environmental, and occupational know-ledge, and was highly pragmatic. If the man had been allowed to stay on the premises in all likelihood he would have been seriously injured. In cases such as this, it becomes apparent that the bouncers in Russ'z Bar are far more than hired muscle whose sole purpose is to stand around and intimidate customers into observing the vague bar rules. They are also there because of who they are and what they know. Knowledge of the intricacies of their social environment and the appropriate forms of social interaction become a valued and extremely marketable commodity.

Nightlife creates various niches and enclaves within which committed, serious criminals ply their trade and spend their money, therefore gangsters are an integral part of the local night-time order. They offer a taste of local glamour and are intrinsically linked to the edgy ambiguity of the night-time economy. Further, leisure outlets such as pubs and clubs provide an ideal arena for the ritualized performances of exaggerated respect that are played out for eager audiences seeking a frisson of danger with which to spice a routine night out:

The local villains, I mean right villains, are never a problem. You are talking about people who we all know and can really have a war. Now, I'm not saying that when they was kids you wouldn't see them having a ruck, but that is just kids. The real hounds are people who have done their bit, earned their corn and when they come in you are pleased to see them, they are people to be respected, people you want in your place 'cos they are spending money like water. They always shake your hand, which goes down well if there is someone in who was thinking of having a pop. They sometimes come in with people off the box [TV] or a footballer, and if I was the manager I would be begging them to come in every night, cos the word gets out and then punters want to come in to be seen with one of the local Faces, or some sort [woman] off EastEnders. Steve South

In both doorwork and organized crime, geographical knowledge is linked to territorial jurisdiction (Rubinstein, 1973, 19:129). Bouncers, who are, ostensibly at least, non-aligned, but nonetheless familiar with local crime groups, their personnel, and histories, are especially useful in devising strategies that avoid trouble. For the bouncer can act as a mediator, not to solve local problems, for that is not his role, but to prevent those problems from manifesting themselves as violent acts in his pub or club:

The easiest places are where they know you and you know them. I can sort out if somebody from a rival firm is in and then I just take people aside and let them know the situation then let them decide whether they want to go in or not. Like in the case of working at *Martins*. The local firm are all in and they are as good as gold, we know them all and they know us. But three

guys turn up who were friendly with a mush who was stabbed over Wal-
worth way. Now that was over a year before, and we had a few 'he's got a
shooter' panics and a few threats, but it all went quiet. But this night
they've turned up and so I just let them know who is in and let them
make their minds up. As luck would have it they knew that if they went in
they would have to have a row, so this way they was able to walk away
without losing face. Plus I done a bit of good for myself, cos it was me that
blew in their ear. Charlie

Along with confrontations with 'dangerous faces', dealing with
women also calls for levels of discretion not usually required in the
control of ordinary male punters.

Other difficulties: disorderly women

If it wasn't a girl we would just thump her (Holdaway, 1983:122).

Women presented particular difficulties for bouncers (Thompson,
1994:141) and 'niceness' was often a tactic used by the bouncers in
order to solve incidents involving female customers. The bouncers
would listen to more 'troubles talk' than they would with men,
lending an ear to complicated explanations, justifications, and neu-
tralizations. Listening to the outpourings of drunken women was
'being nice', and the tactic was employed with the hope that the
problem could be resolved without having to confront the taboo of
laying their hands on a woman. Far better to play the understanding
listener and persuade the women that it would be in everyone's best
interests if they left. When women become involved in disturbances
in the night-time economy, they seldom reached the scale or severity
of male conflicts:

We do get lasses in here getting into fights and that. You should see some of
them. If we get there quick enough we'll stop it because women always
have a bit of shout and push and that before they kick off don't they?
Someone's usually fucking crying and that. Mark

However, they did pose a notably different set of obstacles for
bouncers to negotiate. In dealing with these obstacles, the aims of
doorstaff were much the same, to maintain commercial order, and if
necessary to remove those involved from the premises. However, not
only did bouncers clearly believe that it was necessary to deal with
female confrontations differently, but in most cases female reactions
to the presence of the bouncers was unlike that of most men. For

instance, for most men, the very presence of doorstaff served as a
disincentive to transgress:

> Lasses fucking shout at you, like, 'what do you think you're doing? Get
> your hands off me'... You've just got to grab an arm and say, you know,
> 'sorry but you'll have to go out'. You don't want to be grabbing them and
> that. Sometimes they'll say, 'I'll send my Billy round to see you', or
> something like that. You just laugh at them. One time this lass has a go
> at me, trying to slap me. The rest of the lads were just standing there pissing
> themselves. If a woman ever has a go at you all you've got to do is hold
> your hand above your head like that, lasses always punch downways. Paul

Although women understood the sign value and the cultural power
of these men, in most cases they disassociated themselves from
orthodox male protocols in their dealings with bouncers. As Mark
notes:

> You've got to throw them out, and usually they want to explain everything
> to you, as if you're going to understand and let them stay in the pub. That's
> all they're bothered about half the time, staying in the pub. If a lad has a
> fight he's worried about what's going to happen and if he's going to get
> jumped on the way home...

The following passage demonstrates some of the practical and social
concerns of bouncers in dealing with problems involving women.
Male doorstaff would normally espouse a traditional chivalry and
revulsion to using violence against women. If the situation
demanded it, women would be asked to leave. They would then be
asked to leave more forcibly. The bouncers may then appeal to third
parties to persuade the woman to leave, they may then take hold of
an arm, gently, and attempt to escort the woman to the door. Then
they will usually be grabbed by the arms and pushed towards the
door. These tactics are of course dependent on the situation. If the
woman or women have merely been disruptive, the act of ejecting
them from the premises may take some minutes. If the woman has
been involved in a physical fight, the bouncers are likely to skip the
verbal stages and move straight to her physical removal from the
premises, the style and urgency of which would relate to the severity
of the disturbance and level of violence. The following incident,
drawn from our ethnography, highlights the change in protocol.

*The young women are shouting at each other, with the two main
combatants being separated by a couple of aspiring peacekeepers.*

The group are in their late teens to early twenties, fashionably dressed for a warm night in Ibiza, and very drunk. Glenn is making his way towards the group now. He doesn't seem in too much of a hurry as he politely negotiates his way through the packed bar. The group of young women, only a short distance away from me, are now getting a little more vocal, and from where I am standing, it appears that one of the women who was attempting to keep her friends calm has given up and taken sides in the dispute. Glenn is talking to one of the young women not directly involved. Although I can't hear what is being said, from her frantic gesticulations it appears that the group are all out together as friends, and some kind of dispute has developed between two of the young women, who are still shouting at each other despite the presence of Glenn. The rest of the young women in the group have taken sides and all seem keen to offer their opinion on whatever the dispute is about. Glenn is nodding along as one of the young women talks into his ear and the others continue their discussions.

Glenn has now begun to directly mediate in the dispute. He has tapped one of the more animated women on the arm, and is carefully asking her to calm down. He is using deliberately neutral, non-partisan language, not threatening her. He has his head tilted to one side and is offering placating gestures, hands outstretched, palms exposed. She has now launched into a monologue, about the foundation of the dispute. The other main combatant has turned away and is talking to a smartly dressed man standing close by. This is not good. The last thing Glenn and the rest of us need is for boyfriends to become involved, bringing with them a set of fragile masculinities in a heroic defence of their womenfolk. Glenn is still talking to one of the more vocal women. He is telling her that whatever the dispute involves she must calm down or she will be asked to leave. Glenn has left it at that for the time being, but instead of returning to his position at the door, he has ascended a small set of steps to join me at my viewing post. I ask him what's happening and he says, 'Just the usual shit, she said this, she said that . . .' and trails off.

Back to work. I am surveying the room and Glenn is watching the group of young women who continue to argue. Suddenly one of the original combatants has attacked the other, grabbing at her hair, as her friends attempt to keep the two apart. Glenn whispers, 'Shit', and heads off to the scene once again. It is now apparent that the attacker is going to be asked to leave. A group of men standing close by are laughing and pointing at the fight, but by the time Glenn gets to the scene the attacker has withdrawn and is being calmed by friends. She is tearful: her victim is shouting at her while being held in check by two friends. Glenn taps the young woman who launched the attack on the arm, and says, 'Sorry, but you're going to have to leave'. Immediately she and her friends start to plead her case. Some of the young women are getting right in his face, pushing him to get his attention, to get Glenn to listen to them instead of the others. Glenn is now pushing away arms, and showing himself to be unwilling to negotiate: the young woman has to leave.

I catch the last part of a sentence: '... I don't care, she's got to go outside.' He pushes away a few arms and takes hold of the young woman's arm. The group of young women back off slightly, the young woman about to be ejected is now crying and is clearly unwilling to leave. Another young woman is now pushing me, telling me that it wasn't her fault, it was the other one, she didn't start anything, and so on. Glenn holds the young woman gently by the arm now, and is slowly leading her towards the door while attempting to placate her friends who continue to try and talk him out of this course of action, they follow behind in his wake and shout to make themselves heard. The head doorman is now being harangued, and one of the women knows his name, and is liberally sprinkling her dialogue with it with the hope of prompting some semblance of empathy.

The assailant is now being escorted up the stairs and at the door, one of her supporters proclaims 'He is a right wanker, she didn't do anything'. Pete and Chris are no longer understanding listeners. Their friend and colleague has been insulted for carrying out his job. The placating gestures evaporate. Chris has grabbed the young woman's arm and says loudly, 'Right, that's you out as well.' This young woman is not escorted to the exit, but roughly led to the door. More protestations come from the group of young women, who remain in the bar, while others follow their friends out onto the street. Glenn returns, proclaiming this trivial mundane incident, 'fucking unbelievable'. When I return to my position in the bar the ejected woman's original opponent and her two remaining friends are dancing and laughing.

Within the established configurations of gendered social interaction, women were treated differently from men. Bouncers often expressed disbelief at the behaviour of women involved in disturbances. *Why didn't they just leave? Didn't they understand what was being said to them? Did they think the bouncers were stupid?* Ejecting women from the bar was regarded as one of the most annoying aspects of the job. The prevailing logic seemed to be better to deal with a group of brawling men than a group of irate women.

In dealing with men, bouncers employ stronger language and a sterner demeanour is adopted much earlier, thus attempting to intimidate rather than placate. In most cases, the structure of acceptable forms of interaction with disruptive men was clearer, and far more likely to be acknowledged by the men in question. A violent male customer would be ejected by utilizing considerably more force, and at an earlier stage. Similarly, bouncers are less likely to be willing to listen to protestations by friends, which were far less likely to be offered by men.

Different doors

Niche marketing within the night-time economy often relies upon the creation of a highly distinctive ambience, and this can relate to a number of variables that function as clues to the potential customers' suitability to engage with a specific sector of the night-time economy. For instance, rules of the house at a venue designated exclusively for the gay market will frequently exclude straight men and women (see Chapter 3; Chatterton and Hollands, 2001; McVeigh, 1997). The interpretation of management rules always involves the filtering of such commercial edicts through the everyday codes that evolve from the bouncers' enacted environment. Managers of venues that employ their own in-house doorstaff offer less scope for interpretation, as there are fewer ambiguities than when agency or security firms provide door security (see Chapter 6). This is particularly apparent in highly specialized venues, where the management have a very clear idea of the market sector to which they seek to appeal. As the owner of an independent 'upmarket' bar and restaurant explains:

...the trendier ones will understand...we try to describe to them [the bouncers] the kind of customer we want, the attitude, you know we don't employ morons...we don't want drunks in, we don't want to have to refuse to serve them and then get a potential ejection problem. The new guys who come in, we train up...and we actually pay for them to be badged. They have only ever worked here, so they only know our way...I think a lot of venues they get a firm in and there is very much an us and them attitude as to how the business develops...the door is the door and what happens inside is something else...we try to avoid that...The first image that anybody gets of a premises is the first person that they meet... the person on the door. Now we have a quality restaurant so our age group can go anywhere from 21 to 55 or 60. I can't have bomber-clad, radio-controlled super-club doormen with attitude on. They have got to be suited up, respectable, able to escort somebody through to the restaurant...to understand the nature of the business...they have got to have a fair idea of what goes on and how the various audiences interconnect with each other.

This rather subtle blending of age and taste across a multi-functional venue obviously calls for a specialized security presence; although it should be stressed that here physical prowess has been refined rather than eliminated. Diversity and variation within this market also creates variations, or more accurately, flexibility within the occupational culture of doorstaff that we discuss in detail below. As with the public police, specific roles and tasks, particularly when they are perceived as professional specialisms (Hobbs, 1988), can create cultural variations. However, unlike the public police, who are tasked to perform a cornucopia of roles within the rubric of a bureaucratically-driven hierarchy, variations in the tasking of doormen are rather more subtle. Yet all feature, at their core, a notion of *real* doorwork that primarily stresses the role of the bouncer as the visible embodiment of social authority in the night-time economy.

The people who we badge up are not doormen, they are ex-army, keep-fit instructors, just people we know. Glen

Crucial to the establishment and exploitation of niche markets is the choice of music, and doorstaff are often left to interpret appropriate audiences for musical forms that may require significant unpacking. This unpacking is carried out by doorstaff with, or without, the assistance of management, and their aim is to avoid disorder, rather than to further the cause of any particular cultural niche. For instance, Jason's early experience on the door was at a club that was pioneering Jungle music, which was a distinctly 'black' musical form.

...that was in the early days of Jungle. It ain't called that now, its garage and speed garage, and you can hear it anywhere...what we did have was a group of white boys and white girls and they were all into Jungle...the girls are going to get pulled by the regulars, the boys will think they are gangsters, and people will get seriously hurt. The first time one of the... mob fired a gun. I was on the door at the time, it was pretty terrible...it was like an avalanche of people, [I was] shit scared, could have got trampled. The till got done and there was some cutting, a few old scores.

This was the first of two violent incidents resulting from doorstaff 'getting it wrong', on Jungle nights. The remedy was provided by the head doorman who ensured that the venue employed a white boun-cer with the explicit task of 'turning away white guys if he thought there might be a problem...he was very good'.

Although at many venues, managers will spend at least some of the night at the 'front of house' overseeing the selection process, door-staff will often seek to resist any attempts to limit their discretion, and sometimes, particularly where security agencies provide the staff, this stance may be presented as non-negotiable.

So when managers turn around and say let anyone in...if you can't control it at the door then you've no chance inside, you haven't got a hope in hell inside when they've had a few more drinks and they've got bottles in their hands. Steve North

Dealing with trouble: talking nicely

The bottom line is that we get our wages from the place we're minding. The idea is that we make sure everyone behaves so the property isn't damaged and ordinary blokes don't get hurt (McLean, 1998:174).

In dealing with trouble it is vital for the bouncer to establish inter-personal control (Cruse and Rubin, 1973:3), but unlike the police officer, for whom the authority of the state and his personal author-ity are indistinguishable, doorstaff are unable to muster and imple-ment state power (Manning, 1977). However, bouncer-to-customer exchanges are nonetheless 'moral contests' (Van Maanen, 1978a: 229) in which the authority of not the state, but the bouncer, is 'either confirmed, denied, or left in doubt' (ibid.).

Most of our interviewees stressed a variety of available strategies in dealing with trouble, and the ability of doorstaff to utilize verbal skills was well to the fore (Chatterton, 1983). However, we would argue that the ability to utilize physical force of varying degrees remains sovereign. As Trevor explained, an experienced bouncer will, 'talk to people when they need to and dig people when they need to'.

Even the most viscerally inclined doorman recognized the importance of using verbal skills:

The first technique is you talk to them, if they are reasonable people, not too drunk, they will be reasonable back, 'come on mate, you don't have to do that do you'. You don't want to be throwing people out right left and centre. You have to go up to them confidently and talk to them calmly and clearly—because they will be drunk. If they become aggressive you have to try to calm them down, but still not aggressively…It's best to have a quiet word with 'em, tell 'em they are being a bit of a cock, but if they behave themselves they can stay. Lenny (head doorman)

The ability of doorstaff to utilize a range of control methodologies (Southgate, 1986:34–37) is crucial, and these various techniques are designed to ensure that troublesome customers are in a no-win situation. Max described his security team in the following way:

they're non-aggressive people who can look after themselves and defuse situations the way a situation should be defused. If a fight is called for, a fight is what you'll get—and you'll lose. If diplomacy is called for, diplomacy is what you'll get—and you'll lose again.

Socially skilled doorstaff are highly regarded by head doormen and security managers, not only for their ability to avoid violence but also as vital agents of local intelligence:

They know the business, they know how to talk to people. It's communication…You try to get on first name terms with your regulars 'cos they tell you more information than anybody about drugs, troublemakers, whatever. The more communication you have with your punter, the more successful your club's going to be. Andy

However, verbal skills should also be regarded as part of the bouncers' aggressive armoury. It is a last resort before physical violence, and subterfuge is a crucial strategy used to avoid, or at least minimize violence:

It's really busy, the pub's packed…they start messing about, a bit of a scuffle starting, or they've thrown a glass over the bar or whatever. Now you've got two choices: you approach the person…say it's a male, now they are quite aggressive and basically want to fight. You speak to him and you say whatever you have to say to get him to the door, even if you have to tell a bit of a lie…'don't worry you're not getting barred, you're not getting thrown out' ... I would get 'im to the door on his own accord, like walk with him to the door "cos I want a word with you at the door,' ... because if I grab 'im at the bar and the place is packed, then just say a fight broke out, people could get hit with a glass, people could get hurt. If you've got the bloke to walk to the door with a bit of a lie ... then tell him he is barred, then you've got less chance of anyone getting hurt because he is at the door... If you speak to 'em at the door... then if they say they aren't going you've got to grab hold of 'em ... it is easier to put someone out of the door than it is to drag 'em across a pub ... that could escalate into a lot of people fighting. Darren

When potentially violent situations are about to kick off many of our informants were willing to use aggressive language as a last resort, an intimidatory device that falls short of laying hands on the customers. Swearing was even used in conjunction with tactics more associated with 'being nice'. For instance, a bouncer may swear to indicate that he wanted to be nice, and he recognized the established protocols, but that his patience was wearing thin.

Steve North explained the importance of controlled verbal aggression in dealing with problematic customers:

'Excuse me sir can you just behave yourself, we don't tolerate that sort of fucking business in here'. And you always put an F-word in or a strong language word in at the end. You're very polite, very direct and at the end you just throw it in, as if to say 'I'm not a fucking schmuck'. It's a trick of the trade. 'I'm basically being nice to you. Now if you don't want to be fucking nice I can be fucking nasty, so please yourself'.

The authority of the bouncer is maintained, and the responsibility for the possible escalation of the encounter is passed on to the customer. This is a version of the Police's 'Fuck off or you'll get nicked' (Holdaway, 1983:97). The preference for 'talkers' as opposed to 'hitters' is marked:

[A] Head doorman to me is someone that's put in ten years service and therefore he expects quality wages, not someone who's got a scar across his face, that's not a sort of criteria qualification in a sense, that maybe 'cause his nose is spread across his face. No, it's the one who's stood there who's still got his looks and has been there ten years, he's the one that's got sense, because he can probably talk himself out of a situation more so than, you know, ones that go to town. Marcus

It was clear throughout our study that some bouncers were more comfortable with 'being nice' than others, judging that their aims could best be served with tactical affability.

I'm just a polite person anyhow... I always say, 'can you see your drinks up please'. I think if you're polite to them they'll give it back to you... [but] after so many times and you know they're totally ignoring you, that's when you just totally change. Tracey

Variations in how individual doorstaff read and react to situations were often apparent. An entrance to a pub, bar or club, is symbolic of a venue's inclusive yet private open regions (Cavan, 1966: 49; Monaghan, forthcoming), but for excluded customers it is a yawning exit to the public sphere of the pavement. The ability to talk troublesome customers from the venue and into this public sphere was a significant test of a bouncer's competance.

... so that is my target. Get them onto the pavement. Not to hurt them, if you can help it. Just gentle on the pavement. Jason

In venues with a regular door team, bouncers would often develop tactical specialisms to cope with the maelstrom of demands made upon their professional, and therefore personal resources. For instance, from our ethnographic analysis of a three-handed door team, Laurie was inclined to mediate, and if he could get a message across with words, and perhaps a subtle undercurrent of threat, then he did not feel it necessary to become physical. Vincent and Jock on the other hand would often feel that 'being nice' wasted time and verbal energy. Why negotiate when you could simply achieve your ultimate goal with a well-aimed shove? But despite this, not uncommon predilection for non-verbal communication, the usefulness of 'being nice' as an individual and group tactic was readily acknowledged:

There is trouble, but you try and solve it with words first. It's not like I want trouble, I want an easy life, standing around having a laugh. So if you're not coming in, I'll tell you why, be polite about it. Even if they start talking shite you make allowances. You do everything you can to avoid it... Trevor

But the balance is a fine one, and violence is an option to be explored when the limits of verbal persuasion have been reached. When this boundary is reached, personal and professional spheres meet, forming a mixture that produces a controlled explosion, which can vary from a guiding hand on the elbow, to something more 'full on':

A good bouncer is someone who knows his job. He's doesn't go daft causing trouble, but if it goes off he's right in there. A bad bouncer is anyone who is too full on, getting in people's faces or fucks off when the trouble starts. Trevor

'Being nice' is a tactic employed by bouncers in order to get people to do what they want with the least amount of effort, while being constantly mindful of the need to maintain face and present a palpable physical threat. If it is possible to remove a drunken man from the premises by asking him to leave rather than wrestle him to the door, and if this can be done without compromising a delicate sense of self (Winlow, 2001:97–160) then 'being nice' can be a very useful tactic.

'Being nice' also offered a workable strategy to deal with customers whose status or gender necessitated a less robust approach to dealing with troublesome situations. For the most part 'being nice' as a tactic was employed with women, and men or groups of men considered as constituting 'touchy problems'. Here 'being nice' could reap benefits where 'being nasty' could create further problems, but the former always remained a tactic which could be immediately withdrawn. Whatever happened next was often considered to be beyond the bouncers' individual responsibility. If they didn't listen, didn't do as they were asked, then it was their own fault if they got hurt. They had dictated the nature and progress of the interaction by failing to capitulate to the bouncers' polite request.

Dealing with trouble: looking the part

You want people to say, 'look at the state of him,' so they don't fuck around with you. Darren

Bouncers perceive a fine line between verbal negotiation and intimidation, and despite the formal rhetoric of both the licensed trade and the security industry (see Chapter 6), physicality is of immense importance. Currently there is a commercial trend within the leisure industry to present a modern user-friendly image of bouncers that contradicts the traditional image of large violent masculinity (see Chapter 6). We will discuss some aspects of these attempts later, but in addressing the methods used to deal with trouble inside premises it is impossible to ignore the fact that most bouncers are big, and most are endowed with overt violent potential. This suggestion of violent capability is an embodiment of the deterrence function that serves to prevent trouble before it has begun:

I'm not saying that doormen should stand there eighteen stone, look like a big meathead and frighten 'em to death, but if you have got doormen on who look the part... Darren

If someone does not 'look the part', there is every chance that they may become the target of violence and intimidation themselves, which in turn could put the sovereignty of the door at risk. 'Maintaining the edge' (Van Maanen, 1978a:226–227), in the absence of any non-ambiguous legal mandate, prevents personal and professional embarrassment by sustaining levels of respect and fear among a volatile audience of punters and colleagues. Their physicality can be used as an intimidatory device in disparate ways, from a rhetorical device that pronounces potential violence as an integral part of door strategy, to a non-tactile alternative to violent action. As Mark shrewdly observes, 'Most of the time, again, it can be sorted out because overall, people just don't want to fight people like me, do they?'

The suggestion of violent potential is crucial to the maintenance of non-violent control strategies, and shrewd operatives are well aware of the potency of presenting modes of physicality on the door that are some way removed from the norm (Winlow, 2001:98–103):

If you go to a door and you see an average person, well if you've got a cocky head on... you see two nobodys on the door. You might see 'em on the way in... and some lad is there with your girlfriend, they've done the sly on you and you think 'right I'm gonna fill him in'... bang!, they're off with anyone in the pub... because they look at the doormen and think 'well what can they do... the worst thing that can happen is that someone might get thrown out'. Now, they look at doormen who are proper, handy blokes, they think twice when they go in... Appearance does make a lot of difference and if you know that the guys are capable, big, strong, powerful lads you think twice before you start anything in the pub. Darren

Dougie, who has worked as a bouncer for seven years, stands six feet seven inches tall, and currently weighs around nineteen stones. In addition to his reputation, he is an expert in a number of martial arts:

People get a drink in them and all the shit starts. A lot of the time when you get arseholes you can sort it out just by going over. If they're fucking about spilling drinks or I don't know, you can just go over. Let them have a look at you. Show them you're on the case. I go over and, well, you just stand next to them. They're like looking into the middle of my chest or something, and you can see the expression change. They start apologizing before you say a word most of the time. Sometimes you just go over, say, 'pack that in will you,' and give them a nasty look and that's enough. If you do that you're stopping trouble for later in the night because a lot of the time you get lads, if you let them get away with stuff, they're going to keep on doing it to see how far they can get. If you let them start dancing on the chairs and that, throwing drinks around, they're going to think they can do anything and it's best to stop it early, let them know you've got them, you know?

The authority of the vast majority of bouncers is embodied in their physicality (see Monaghan's excellent discussion, forthcoming). Some doorstaff, particularly those employed in the larger more progressive venues which have a large security team, featuring specialized roles, can operate efficiently without any overt or potentially oppressive physical presence. But for the majority who ply their trade in the night-time economy, authority is derived from local reputation and the potential physicality of their bodies. This potential can be suggested by bulk, in the case of body builders, evidence of engagement in combat, for instance a battered or scarred visage, or in the presence of highly specialized bodies which are suggestive of equally specialized skills and capabilities.

Glen is ex-services, and runs a boxing and fitness school as well as his own security firm. He is also a certified bailiff:

The reason most of my doormen are boxers is because there's a new age of doormen. Like all these restaurant bars that are opening... you can't have big thuggy bouncers stood out there 'cause it makes the club look like there is trouble in there and there has been trouble. My idea is smaller people who are just as good as a big body builder, but more flexible and looking more like the people around him. Okay he's a doorman stood at the door, but he's got to be smart and look like he's on a night out, not like a commando.

Glen associates body type, with specialist violence and the specific form of discipline that this violent potential literally embodies:

He has to be able to handle himself but when you have big massive doormen it puts out the wrong message. I train down here with my guys... I get to know their strengths and weaknesses. And also under pressure, 'cause boxing training is one of the most hardest types of training you can do, so I can see character here, who's got communication skills. If there's a guy who can't talk he won't work at the door, he'll work inside.

Experienced doorstaff recognized the limitations of huge doorstaff, for once situations develop rather less obvious qualities will be at a premium, qualities that are not restricted to the most muscular sector of the night-time economy:

You can be fucking enormous and be a shit doorman. There's some of that about, 'give him a job because he's a big cunt', and 'oh, he's a big cunt don't fuck around with him'. But one day someone's going to test it. It's just the way it is. Door work isn't just about being big and ugly, you've got to be able to do the job as well. Muscles is just something everyone expects from doormen. Roger

The most potent device is reputation, a reputation that is likely to encompass the above qualities while being forged, and constantly modified, in the enacted environment of the night-time economy. Appearance and demeanour do not forge reputation, nor does verbal dexterity. Reputation is forged through action.

Local bodies

...the form of gender identity in place in particular localities will be inflected not only by actually existing regimes of work but also by *nostalgic evocations* of such regimes (Taylor and Jamieson, 1997:153).

Many of our informants spoke admiringly and with awe of experienced bouncers: old hands, from whom, as fledgling bouncers, they had learnt their trade (Niederhoffer, 1967:52; Wilson, 1968:283). For instance, Steve South first worked in a pub with an experienced doorman Stan, whose brother had been convicted for murder. Soon after the conviction Stan, who was a talented amateur boxer, found himself in the ring fighting an opponent representing the local police force. From the first bell Stan's tactics were distinctly non-Marquis of Queensbury, he head butted the police officer and continued the assault while the man lay on the floor, prompting a ringside riot and a lengthy ban from boxing. His reputation was assured:

When you had like Stan on [the] inside, then the only fighting was mad bastards, not hard men, gangsters and all that, just mad people who didn't care anymore. I got a bit involved a few times early on, mainly 'cos I would stand and fight them. I was up for it and that was my job. But then people said 'get it on the pavement'...On the pavement you could have a stand up and there's no glass or civilians, your back is up against the pub and they ain't coming in. But if you was on with somebody like Stan the first thing you know about trouble they are on the pavement. No fighting or nothing. Just he used to put his arm in here [small of back] and you sort of floated across the room. He done it with me and you are going where he takes you. Steve South

As we discuss in Chapter 7, the continuity of powerful masculine histories via the often underrated ability of the working classes to constantly adapt to the harsh logics of the market, is a central theme in the narrative of pragmatic violence that bridges industrial and post-industrial societies. Stan was clearly more than a teacher and mentor. He represents a simpler set of priorities from those derived from the commercial exigencies of contemporary doorminding. Priorities derived from the resilient traditions of the industrial working class, and made bright, shiny, and fresh by their transformation into economic capital, via strategic engagement within the night-time economy, and the commodification of the brutalized practical experience (Horne and Hall, 1995) of a common cultural inheritance.

Full exploitation of the commodification of violent potential can only take place when a way has been found to establish a reputation. Even after successfully locating this deep and rich vein of violent tradition, rookie bouncers, lacking either the physical prowess of Dougie, or the cultural collateral of the kind accrued by Stan, must work at their craft—literally the hard way:

When I first started I only weighed about eleven and a half stone or something. I was in good shape because of the boxing... You get to work and you've got these big nasty looking fuckers all over the place, so you get there and you're on your toes. It's dodgy when you first start because you don't know how to go on and that. I was probably a bit over the top when I started because you want people to show you the respect because I was smaller than the other lads. You want to prove you're up to it. Trevor

The importance of a local reputation for violence cannot be over-emphasized. Yet neither reputation, nor awesome physicality is always sufficient to nip potential violence in the bud. Feats of vicious derring-do pack the portfolios of local celebrity bouncers, their reputations for taking and giving punishment, forming the cutting edge of their marketability:

One time a little fight happened right at the top of the stairs coming into the club. A little group was having a go at one of the other lads, I went over and one thing leads to another and off it goes. I got kicked in the bollocks, I remember that. Everything happens at a million miles an hour. Anyway, we're into it, and I get kicked in the nuts, and something like that happens you want to go down, but if you go down you know they're going to be hoofing your head all over the place, so I stay on my feet, and I just remember thinking you little bastard, I'm taking digs, but I just go for him pick him up and throw him down the stairs. I mean I'm fucking steaming here, and it's a fair distance, he goes down to the first landing without hitting a single step. Everything stopped for a split second, and a few of the other lads had got there, everything stopped, people were just staring, then it kicked back to life. The lads just ran at them fucking screaming and that and this other squad of lads just legged it. I was in fucking agony but everyone else is laughing their tits off. It sounds daft, but you had to be there, it was really funny like, you know? Dougie

On such nights reputations are made, and incomes assured. The combination of Dougie's physical presence, and his ability if called upon to use violence has made him extremely marketable all over his region. For despite the exhortations of the night-time marketeers, trainers, and local authorities, and regardless of the specific needs and requirements of venues, there remains a high value placed upon the ability of security staff to deal with violence. The enacted environment of the night-time economy, as we demonstrate above, does feature some negotiation, and the amount of negotiation will vary according to individuals, venues, and specific situations.

However, once the limits of negotiation have been reached, or violence has already commenced prior to the involvement of security personnel, then physical force of some kind will be required:

If they don't back down you have to physically remove them from the building. You can't back down because if you do their mates will think, 'they are wankers, they are chicken shits, why are they workin' the door?'. Paul

Dealing with trouble: rough and tumble

Idiots won't go in a pub where you've got proper, good doormen on because, one, they know they won't get in, and two, if they do get in and they start gettin' aggressive, they know they're gonna go out of the door head-first. Darren

The acceptance among denizens of the night-time economy of levels of violence that are unparalleled outside of military and penal institutions is astounding. Whilst we have made some attempt above to quantify the violence that is associated with this new economic era, it became obvious to us that very few of the violent incidents that occur are ever brought to the attention of the health or police authorities (Lister et al., 2000). Although different venues produced control regimes featuring varying degrees of violence among both customers and staff, the police were involved in remarkably few incidents. Apart from the problem of drawing police attention to the venue, and possibly threatening the future of its licence, there is a clear feeling among most doorstaff that problems should be dealt with informally (see Chapter 6).

The ambiguity of the bouncers' role in relation to the public police is discussed in our concluding chapter, but the following quotation highlights the likelihood of bouncers being the victims of violence as integral to the job. They are always likely to be required to retrieve control of the premises from the hands of 'the barbarian' (Muir, 1977:23). Customers are screened for violent potential, and the constant assessment and reassessment of customers serves as a safeguard for doorstaff and clients alike:

Well, if you're getting paid to do a job you've got to be willing and take a chance that you could get punched in the face because that's what can happen... you've gotta accept that, I mean you don't want that, but it could happen... I mean if you've got a guy and he jumps on a girl and he just decides to glass her, if you see that guy with a glass and you see that he is gonna glass that girl, you jump on him. Now if you jump on him and get that glass off him and then he hits you, punches you, well that's just part of the job... if you don't think like that it's no good being a doorman... I've seen it so many times where a doorman has been stabbed in the face with a bottle. Darren

Doorstaff often expressed their feeling of isolation, both from the normal assumptions of propriety that rule in the sober day-time domain, and from the back-up provided by the police:

People don't realize how fucking mean and nasty the world can get when it's got a drink inside him. We stand there and the dregs of the universe are out on the piss, now we are on our own and there is no way that anyone understands because it's a young peoples' world. The nice people, the quiet people, don't notice we are there. And the older people are at home in front of the telly. If they realized how bad it can be and that we were the only ones there they would be shocked. Steve South

You can go over, drag some people out, it seems like it's over and then another fight starts over the other side. It gets to be one thing after another and at the end of the night you might think, fuck this. You're tired, everyone treats you like a cunt, you can get your money and think it's not fucking worth it. Trevor (See Muir, 1977:22).

I've worked in places where you get spat at, where you wade through sick in the toilets to get a fall down drunk out. There can be a queue of drunk punters wanting to have a fight, and at the end of the night, you stink of smoke and sweat and sick and the manager says 'here's thirty quid'. Charlie

If you go to the police all they'll say is 'well we'll assist you'... if you're a policeman you've got a truncheon and they say to you if someone attacks you, you pull your baton out and you defend yourself. Well how you gonna determine how hard you hit someone if they come at you? If a policeman hits you and breaks your arm, well... at the end of the day if you run at him and you're a big lad he's gonna hit you, he's not going to determine how hard he's going to hit you with the stick. He's gonna defend himself because he's scared, and if he breaks your arm it's an accident... that's the same for doormen if someone throws a punch at you and it's not quite as hard as the one you throw back at him you're the one whose charged because you've gone too far. Marcus

Short, sharp applications of rough justice are often justified as a means of avoiding escalation, for to let situations escalate could prove dangerous:

If it looks like it's going to get rough I'll give them a clip. You've got to. I know it's a job, but if it's you standing there and you've got some cunt in front of you who's letting his mouth go, you know what is going to happen. It might be a job but it's me who's going to take the dig and job or no job you're not just going to stand there are you? Fucking right you're not. Mark

This is not fighting, but demonstrating physical control, and what may seem like callous violence on behalf of the doorstaff is often a carefully calculated limited physical engagement designed to affirm and reinforce the status quo. The following passage will highlight this, and also establish that the strategies of doorstaff, albeit learnt informally, without institutional back-up and in the light of a generally hostile public, are often highly sophisticated expressions of practices learnt in the enacted environment, and expressive of a powerful and complex occupational culture.

About one o'clock the alarm bell goes off... The music stops and the lights are half up. There's a lot of movement, people moving at different speeds and it takes a while... as people are getting out the way you work out who is where, who's doing what. There's three people, ordinary looking, nothing special, with one arm in and the other swinging, but you can't work out who is who, then there's two people on the floor with the inside person who is the supervisor hovering. So the student [bouncer] helps him to separate him. Now what I don't know is that two other inside people have been allowed to shoot off at midnight to another job so it's 3 on 1 for me. Steve South

At this point, the layperson's prediction will probably be that the bouncer will commence fighting. But Steve South is a highly experienced doorman, and uses his physical powers to control the situation without attempting to damage the fighters.

If I start digging people, it's a stand-up, 3 on 1, so I go gentle. I grab the nearest in a bear hug from behind 'accidentally' elbow another one while I do it, and hope the third one has had enough—which he had. But as I loosen on the first one, he takes a swing, catches me on the cheek. Now he's hit a bouncer. Sammy piss head, about 25–30, [I] don't recognize him. I drag him out to the reception and slap him, open handed slap. He don't want to fight me, he shit himself really, but he has stepped over the mark. See another night with everybody on, he could have ended up in hospital, 'cos for the younger ones, and that includes me when I started off, I am going to fucking punish you if you raise your hands...

As Van Maanen points out, 'The person must be taught a lesson. And whether the teaching occurs in public or in the back of an alley, the person must be shown the error of his ways' (1978:233). Only the 'guilty' (Reiss, 1965) are punished. The authority of the bouncer is 'profaned by the assault' (Holdaway, 1983:123), but unlike the public police, for whom the ability to utilize violence is but a part, albeit an essential part, of an armoury of pragmatic and symbolic power, the bouncer's role as a custodian of commercial, as opposed to state authority, lies solely in the individual's embodiment of violent potential. Therefore, personal retribution enfolded in the fist of commercial authority is inevitable. 'It reinforces the working solidarity...It weakens the threat to their occupational identity...the grievance is redressed by the use of force' (Holdaway op. cit.):

It's not about standing doing karate or boxing. You have to get in close and grab what you can. Anyone can push, swing their fist, get lucky, or kick you in the privates. But if I get right in on top, smother people, overpower them, then I will win 'cos I am used to it. Steve South

Dealing with trouble: fighting

It is closing time and a group of drinkers refuse to finish their drinks. The lights are up and they will not move. We go gently but firmly. They get abusive. It all goes off. Both sides are punching and kicking furiously in the narrow space of the stairway. Heavy blows to the head rain down on the late drinkers, feet lash out and the drinkers start to go down. Anyone attempting to placate gets the same treatment. A brief lull and it's all off again. Boots to the head, a straight knockout, and a doomed kamikaze charge from one of the drinkers. There is blood and screams and shouts and furious attempts at retribution from both sides.

They've gone now, and we are back in the bar. Ice is placed on bruises and swellings, and there is much red-faced seething and pacing up and down. Reinforcements arrive in the form of five bouncers who also work for our security company. The post mortem begins. I keep quiet. Very quiet.

'When appeasement fails and fists start flying' (Punch, 1979:116), the essential essence of the bouncer emerges quickly to the fore. Although a few doorstaff began their interviews with us attempting to play down fighting ability as a resource, once they relaxed, they became adamant that the ability to win a fight was a highly prized attribute.

Someone does it on the street you're not going to take it are you? When stuff like that happens you forget it's work, it's not work, it's you against some cunt who wants to do you over... What if he wants trouble? He might be standing with a squad behind him, I'm standing with a couple of mates. Everyone's watching. If he can't walk away after I've been polite, whatever happens [then] is his fault. This is where a lot of shit gets mixed up. Bouncers get in trouble for winning fights. Mark

In all honesty the vast majority, ninety-five per cent of people who will work as a doorman have been involved in fights and trouble, because really, they're the sorts of people who will do the door. I mean let's be honest you can't just put like, a pansy on the door because what use is he? And you can't put someone on who is frightened to death of a fight... suppose a lad is beating a girl up and you're on the door, the first time in your life and you've never really seen a fight, or you've never been in one—what are you gonna do when that guy starts beating his girlfriend up severe? Are you going to go 'ooh, ooh'; are you going to stand there? You can't have them type of people on the door. That girl could get killed while you're stood there. Darren

The ability to fight is the bottom line. Of all of the attributes we have afforded to bouncers, verbal skills, local knowledge, and physical presence, the one that is non-negotiable is fighting skill. If someone is not articulate or lacks crucial qualities as a negotiator, they can be taken from the front door and put inside the premises. Similarly, with a lack of either local knowledge or an imposing physical presence. But without violent ability whether or not it is restrained or controlled, doorstaff will not be able to respond to emergency situations, and it is this attribute above all others upon which their commercial value rests:

> I've had blokes that look as hard as nails but don't turn up if the trouble starts, they'll say they didn't see it but you know they did and just stood there. All that counts is you've got to get stuck in there, go in and watch each other's backs. The most experienced bouncers, the best bouncers, can tell when it's about to kick off, and they always do things the right way. Trevor

Whether this involves talking or hitting, these decisions then are far from arbitrary, but rather result from personal, commercial, and subculturally informed judgments made within the enacted environment and constituted via the bouncer's habitus. For it is this heightened sensitivity to class- and gender-bound social life, expressed in the form of cultural knowledge, that provides the rules and parameters of the bouncer's social understandings and interactions (see Chapter 7). Within academic studies of the public police there is an orthodoxy that identifies the subculture as, by definition, transgressive, working in opposition to both institutional rules, and crucially as the result of a diminished moral commitment to systemic legal conformity (Reiss, 1971:138). Bouncers, however, given the relative lack of formal governmental or bureaucratic frameworks to cradle their practice, have little choice but to rely heavily upon the constellation of informal practices that constitute their occupational culture, and enable the development of their 'working personality' (Skolnick, 1966:42–70). Crucial among these factors is that they are enabled to act upon interpretations of actions and situations that provoke moral and private indignation; in essence, the profaning of fragile, taken for granted, commercial, and personal sovereignty. These interpretations are neither right or wrong, just or unjust, for violent professionals are asked to perform in circumstances that demand the kind of instant settlement that may not stand up well to leisurely reflection:

When you're there doing the job, you haven't got time to think about it, it should be just automatic. You don't go 'should I do this, should I do that', you just fucking get on with it. It sounds daft but you just do things automatic. If you hit someone it's because you think you have to . . . you've just got to get on with it. Les

The night-time excuse me

As with any social control agency, teams of bouncers are engaged in the selective and systematic presentation of their activities, 'and take special care to manage and control access to and knowledge of back regions' (Manning 1977:32). As members of an interaction team (Goffman, 1959:85), bouncers when accounting for violent action against customers, utilize four modes of excuses: *Accidents, defeasibility, biological drives,* and *scapegoating* (Lyman and Scott, 1970). These four modes of appeal were apparent both within our ethnographic observations of the bouncers' enacted environment and as part of the interactions inspired by interviews. Further, the routine utility of such categorizations enabled doorstaff to assure social, professional, and legal approval for actions that frame bouncers personally as violence specialists, whilst implicating them professionally as purveyors of market security. The bouncers' expert status, 'bridges the gap between guarantees of being in the right (which can only be social) and making the choices that one wants (which can only be personal)' (Bauman, 1991:199).

Doorstaff do not have the luxury of *post hoc* neutralization, which serves as a temporary time-out from normative restraint (Sykes and Matza, 1962). Consequently, after the application of physical force, bouncers tended not to use techniques of neutralization or indeed justification, for to do so would constitute a recognition that the action was impermissible. Excuses, however, 'are accounts in which one accepts that the act is bad, wrong, or inappropriate, but denies full responsibility' (Lyman and Scott, 1970:114), and these four modes of excuse serve to placate the demands of personal honour, professional competency, and ultimately of commercial order. The non-bureaucratic nature of the bouncer's job places a huge emphasis upon post-event narratives of excuse (Lister et al., 2000), and rather than temporarily distancing themselves from normative restraint, the excuses offered serve to first establish the hyper-reality that dominates modes of perception in the night-time economy, making it a special place, creating circumstances that are parodies of environments created by day-time economies (Hobbs et al., 2000).

Our research indicated that both this environment and the intoxication of the licensed trade's customers, created 'new rules', for 'new problems', and the policing of liminality demanded a specialist knowledge by doorstaff that rendered conventional strategies of control irrelevant: a temporal demarcation of the monopoly of violence.

Excuses referring to these new rules are not therefore devices of temporaneous distancation, but expressions of methodologies of control grounded in an amalgam of situationally justified action (Manning, 1977:103) and rhetorical necessity inspired by an awareness of the legally tentative nature of the application of physical force (Westley, 1953, 1970). Indeed, the utilization of physical force in order to implement social control shifts attention away from both abstract legal values and social norms (Manning, 1977:32), and focuses instead upon the agents and agencies of violence.

Excuses offered to cultural compatriots in the business of bouncing acknowledge the primary role of violent ability in retaining personal integrity and professional viability, and rather than attempting to neutralize, can simplify, give form to, and most importantly individualize, complex violent engagement. These excuses will serve to valorize the actions of the bouncer. Excuses offered by doorstaff to police and other enforcement agents should also not be regarded as techniques of neutralization, but rather as attempts to negotiate and collude with legal forces whose historical origins share with bouncers the principal project of the protection and maintenance of commercial order (Steedman, 1984). Yet unlike private security, the public police also has a mandate for the provision of social order and public safety (see Johnston, 2000:129–130 for a discussion of the relationship between public and private policing in relation to public order). There are few suitable terrains upon which customers can demand excuses from doorstaff regarding their violence. From the point of view of bouncers, such an offering would be regarded as placing highly individualized practices, albeit cloaked in a corporate blazer or bomber jacket, upon a highly vulnerable platform of personal accountability. Consequently, demeanour will dominate post-violent engagement with customers, and serve to render pathological the violent practices of professionals working on behalf of commercial interests in the night-time economy.

Accident. In an environment where people fall down stairs, trip, and stumble, the projection of customer injury as accidental, is a powerful means of explanation that distances the bouncer from blame. Accident explications have considerable plausibility within a context of intoxication and release, where senses are blurred and voluntary risk-taking, bravado, and 'horse-play' are commonplace. Moral culpability and contributory negligence have long been the repugnant bedfellows of revelry.

Defeasibility refers to lack of intent, and again the social and environmental specificity of the night-time environment engenders complex conflictual situations with qualities that may deprive the bouncer of crucial information that may result in customer casualties. 'I thought he had a knife' or 'I thought he was one of the fighters' can be invoked as excuses for violent action by a bouncer. Deprived of the knowledge that a beer bottle, lighter, or similar hand-held accoutrement to a night out was not a knife, physical force is justified. Similarly, the voyeur of violence or the rapidly moving violence avoider may give the impression of being a participant and therefore liable to be on the receiving end of some level of physical force from a member of the door team arriving at the scene of a fight. In both of these types of incident the bouncer is compelled to act, free will gives way to a cocktail of personal and professional commitments that make physical force inevitable. The consequences of the application of physical force may also involve the bouncer utilizing his lack of knowledge, or distorted knowledge as a means of denial of the intention to injure, or to distance oneself from the degree of injury. It is here that bulk or sheer physicality can be cited as the primary cause of an accidental elbow in the face, or a collision with a bystander while en route to an incident, particularly if the 'incident' proves to be a false alarm or relatively minor.

Biological excuses relate to the commonly held perception among doorstaff (and others) that bouncers are a distinctive type, in possession of less self-control than other denizens of the night, and so are inherently violent. In such accounts psychobiological processes are deemed to take over in certain situations as bouncers meet their professional, and therefore commercial obligations. Obviously accounts orientate to their audiences, so perhaps 'biological' is particularly suited to speculative chat among colleagues on long dull shifts (Fielding, Personal Communication).

As can clearly be gleaned from issues raised earlier in this chapter, any one of a cornucopia of slights to personal honour or the integrity of the door team can trigger these apparently non-negotiable processes. Similarly, behaviour deemed inappropriate, threatening, or disruptive, can inspire a reaction that is often regarded as separate from the processes of free will, and inspired by a biologically determined compulsion to utilize physical force. In such circumstances, gravity disclaimers such as 'he was asking for it' and 'he gave me no choice', come into play, and the bouncer's body becomes unaccountable in the light of circumstances beyond the boundaries of normative restraint. Physical force here is regarded as a natural drive that is beyond the responsibility of the individual and is a particular characteristic of bouncers as a social group. The identification of a biologically-driven violent reaction to certain stimuli is closely associated with the usually mesomorphic body types common among doorstaff, and their relationship to the 'body projects' (Shilling, 1993:4–8) that forge them. So boxers and martial artists are not only well-equipped to respond, but are obligated to socially respond to an apparently biological compulsion. As an excuse, the biological is particularly relevant, as it locates violence in a seemingly inevitable frame (Rubinstein, 1973:267) by turning the body projects inherent into bodily capital (Waquant, 1992, 1995a; Winlow, 2001:101–103) which can then be transformed into economic capital within a labour market that clearly rewards violent potential. The biological excuse enables the door security labour market to proceed in its hypocritical utility of violence by affording its violent operatives few rational get-out clauses in terms of instrumental rhetorics, and citing predisposition rather than cultural or economic form rooted in material practice (Hall, 2000). As a form of physical capital, the biologically-driven, irrational, non-instrumental body can charge a particularly high premium. Further, in the night-time economy, violent reputation serves both organized crime and the new security industry, but the more irrational the level of violence that is utilized, the greater the transcendence of rationality and the more valuable the reputation.

As an excuse, *scapegoating* is extremely potent, and used in conjunction with all of the above categories of excuses provides the most commonly expressed mode of retrospective exoneration. As we have clearly shown, in our discussion of the banned, combinations of clothing, demeanour, degree of intoxication, age, gender, race, and above all explicit demonstrations of potential threat, enable the bouncer to scapegoat almost anyone should the need arise. It is the bouncer's version of the police's 'ways and means act', an all-purpose category in which to place 'situationally justified' action (Manning, 1977:103). When scapegoating, the responsibility for violent action lies with the victim, and this category of excuse can also be comprehended as a form of justificatory expression. For when considered in the context of a disruption of the smooth flow of the bouncer's performance, the very status of victimhood can be denied and the punishment construed as deserving; the 'condemnation of the condemners' (Lyman and Scott, 1970:122).

Violent night

It is Saturday evening, around ten o'clock. A glass collector draws my attention to a fight next to the main bar. The barmaids look on in horror, whilst most customers regard this as no more than free entertainment. I get there just as one man appears out on his feet and I grab the victor and drag him towards the door, when he stumbles and falls another customer kicks him in the face, and both men are ejected. The beaten fighter's face has opened up like a ripe melon. We throw him out for fighting. A large pool of blood has gathered on the tiled section immediately in front of the bar, and combined with the debris of a night in Russ'z, briefly constitutes a vile slurry of hate, hope, and attempted oblivion before customers put aside their horror and are blithely sliding across it in order to get served. Fifteen minutes later a glass collector arrives with a mop and bucket.

Beyond the 'new leisure' rhetoric of a few commercially sensitive security entrepreneurs, it was commonly accepted that violence was the main threat to a quiet night for doorstaff and customers alike. Bouncers were there, so most believed, to deal with violence (Maguire and Nettleton, 2003:29–30). As we have noted above, during the course of our research it was apparent that violence was ingrained into the fabric of the night-time economy, and it could take a multiplicity of forms. However, violent physical assault is the last resort after verbal and physical warnings have been given, it is the end game beyond the training, the tactics, the verbal sparring, and the warnings, and after physical restraint has failed:

A fight might start and you might take a bit of a dig. You get them outside but that's not the end of it. They've spoilt your night, you're fucking furious. Someone's actually hit you. You know, it's like, 'you fucking bastards!' You can have fights breaking out all over the place. They don't have to be nasty, but one after another, and you know, you're thinking fucking hell...of course that's not good, that's what we're there for so that's what you're thinking about and when it happens you're on your toes. Plenty of times you can sort it out easy enough because not too many people want to really get into it with a team of bouncers. Plus you're sober which is important. You can have the nastiest looking fucker in the world, but you're one up because you haven't had a drink. Trevor (see Monaghan, 2002a)

This is where all of the assessment and surveillance comes to fruition. The customer has become an opponent, and any advantage that can be gained over a combatant will be exploited to the full:

You have got a responsibility, a job to do, and you are being paid to do it. It is all about people watching...When you are sober and some guy who is drunk gets aggressive you have got the upper hand...because you are not drunk. I've had people try to hit me and it is just like a slow motion film...In some instances the only edge you're gonna have over a potential troublemaker is that they've had a drink and you haven't...so if you're stone cold sober, if the police are involved or whatever, it's better. I mean once you've had a drink your reactions aren't the same. Also your recall of the situation won't be the same, so if the police are asking you questions and you are stone cold sober and the guy that they are arresting is pissed as a fart who are they gonna believe?—they're gonna believe me...you can't afford to be slow in this job. Paul (see Lister et al., 2000)

In the chaos of a late-night bar or club, in an environment replete with potential weaponry, the realities of many bouncer–client encounters are bloody. Even for the most professional, the cost of local control can be high, and casualties are an undeniable fact. For instance, Marcus had 'something put in my head that could have killed me. It was a hammer. That hurt. They tried to take me out didn't they? They wanted to kill me'. While Steve South's decades on the front line have also left their mark. 'I have had my arms slashed with a knife and I can't straighten this finger. I've had stitches and somebody take a hammer out, have a go at my back and legs while I was held down on the pavement'.

We certainly would not wish to suggest that all doorstaff are violent, but without the ability to deal with violence, doorstaff can put themselves, their colleagues, and customers at risk, and when violence reaches a certain boundary there is no room for bargains or compromises. Ideally, the security team will be able to muster sufficiently overwhelming and disciplined force to cope physically with the situation without resorting to combat, but not every venue possesses these resources, and violent ability then comes to the fore. Then, 'He is honourably following the knowledge of his trade, which is rooted in the realities of city life' (Rubinstein, 1973:265–266):

If you have got people who don't know the score, who don't look the part and can't back it up with whatever is necessary, you might as well close down. Because there are people out there who will take liberties, and they will damage young kids, customers, doorstaff, barstaff. Everybody is on offer if the people on the door can't have a fight. It's fucking dangerous. Charlie

The notion of some omnipotent superman gently escorting to the door an adult who is intent on inflicting physical damage on staff or customers is a fantasy. The real violence that we encountered during our research was some way removed from adolescent martial arts fiction. It was intense, messy, and painful, and far removed from coded gladiatorial combat. A detailed analysis of the pragmatics of violence will take place in Chapter 7, but for now it should be stressed that the environment within which bouncers work is often saturated with violent potential:

The big thing was if you could turn the door staff over. Fucking squads of lads kicking off all over the place. You'd be standing at the door fucking punching away trying to keep the fuckers out. And because of course, when you're pissed and you see a fight, everyone wants a piece of it, people coming from all over, fucking hundreds of them. The street would be busy and people would come out of the fucking pizza shops and that to join in. Les

The combination of danger and authority that lies at the heart of bouncing is a powerful antidote to the adoption of purely legal remedies. As Skolnick has noted in his discussion of police patrol work, the presence of danger produces fear and anxiety promoting self-defensive behaviour. This in turn creates the context in which authority morphs into a tool to deal with perceived threat, and the law becomes a secondary fall-back resource (Skolnick, 1966:67). Violence can become normalized to the point that it is both a threat and a tool of the trade, serving as an expressive outlet for an occupation that thrives on being under siege from both the real and the imaginary 'night dogs' (Anderson, 1998) of urban Britain. Further the expectation of violence brings with it an awareness of its potential and a desensitizing effect that is justified in terms of the harsh pragmatics of the job, which demands that personal safety and honour are shrouded by the cloak of professionalism. Individual vomit-stained ceremonies of barbarity are therefore commonplace as the violent, drunk, and sometimes purely innocent customer becomes the reified other, and is sacrificed so that both interpersonal and commercial order might be re-established or confirmed.

Some 'conflict management' trainers spoke confidently about the benefits of various minimal forms of restraint involving the controlled laying on of hands (see Chapter 6 for a discussion). However, our interviews with doorstaff, our observations, and our ethnography, all indicated that the environment within which night-time violence takes place poses both threats, and personal challenges which away from the idealized scenarios manufactured in the lecture room demand a cruder form of physical engagement: fighting ability:

You see on the box the Ninja geezer with the ripped physique who touches somebody on the neck or gets them in a nice clean wrist lock. I have never seen it, people have got a glass or a bottle and they are intent on killing you. So the idea of minimum force, like just enough to escort the nice gentleman to the door, it's nonsense. Fucking people go mad when they have had a drink and short of putting Bruce Lee on the door, you are going to get old-style fighters dealing with old-style fights. Charlie (see Thompson, 1994:92–110, for a highly pragmatic consideration of street fighting and various martial arts).

If a fight breaks out, you go over and it's suddenly all on you, you've got people trying to fucking kick you to death and that, so what do you do? You fucking defend yourself. I mean fuck the job, you know what I'm saying? These bastards are doing you harm, you can't just be lying in a ball saying it's wrong to hit people. You just can't go in to work with that attitude. Les

We would argue most strongly that the notion of polite physical force is a fiction, and the ultimate product of this fictional zone of violence is that violent action is sanitized. The idolatry of mythic masculinity, from westerns to cop shows, simultaneously valorizes violence and takes the blood out of bleeding, and the pain out of punches. The rhetorics of the night-time marketeers and their commercial and municipal allies places the bouncer within this fictional zone as a new urban hero, as brave and individualistic as the gunslinger, but as highly trained and professional as the police officer. We are presented then with images of a professionalized and highly specialized strand of violent action that somehow bypasses the messy reality of the whole spectrum of force: from assisting a troublesome customer to peacefully leave the premises, at one end, to rolling round on the floor of a pub/club or going toe-to-toe on the pavement at the other.

For bouncers, entering a violent situation without aggression is like a footballer going into a tackle half-heartedly: it is dangerous. Violence in the night-time economy is a tool of incorporation, and the various tactics and strategies that are put in play by doorstaff all have violence, either its potential as suggested by body shape, demeanour, and verbal style, or its actuality, at its root. Aspects of honour and personal integrity appear in all of the strategies discussed by bouncers (Neff et al., 1991; Winlow, 2001: 44–45) and acceptable levels of disrespect, dishonour, and discourtesy are negotiated and renegotiated in the light of few enforceable formal parameters of behaviour in an environment whose very existence as a commercial zone of liminality promotes transgression (Hobbs et al., 2000).

The habitus of bouncers (see Chapter 7) functions as a primary resource for the incorporation of the night-time population into the night-time economy, and violence is constantly hovering in the background of much of the social interaction forced upon bouncers as part of their working duties and working personas (Lister, 2002). Asking a person to move slightly to one side in order to regulate a queuing system can provoke an outbreak of disorder, as can waking them up and asking them to leave the premises, asking them to get down off a bar stool, or denying them entry to a bar. The structures of normative social interaction modify significantly to accommodate the inundation of drunken comportment, and seemingly innocuous situations can become tinged with threat and potential danger. Some bouncers undoubtedly respond to this constant threat by accentuating aspects of their own aggression and forcing it back onto the policed populous of a bar or night club with the hope of dissuading aggression by others, or by displaying a desire to meet any threat head-on. Indeed, such conflict serves to confirm the bouncer's view that they are important, both as individuals, and as members of a 'necessary occupation' (Van Maanen, 1978a:234).

Aside from the constant threat of violence breaking out at any time, the bouncer must be ready to deal with any number of unusual situations. Adaptation is essential, being able to change from polite to threatening, from understanding to enraged, in response to any given set of problems, is fundamental to the job. From finding a couple copulating in a toilet, to having to step swiftly between a group of brawling men, to denying entrance to potential customers, dealing with a drug dealer threatening retribution, to dealing with someone who is about to puke on you. Bouncing is a career in adaptability, tact, violent potential, and cultural knowledge. An evening at work can swing from utter boredom to extreme violence and adrenalin in a matter of seconds, and expecting the unexpected is all part of the job.

The moral mandate of bouncing

The strength of the lenses may be weaker or stronger depending on certain conditions, but they are ground on a similar axis (Skolnick, 1966:42).

Despite the informal nature of door rules and protocols, it is clear that doorstaff have developed a finely tuned occupational culture that, given the virtual lack of institutional or bureaucratic restraint, maintains personal authority (Skolnick, 1966:231). This informs the practice of bouncers, and creates a 'moral mandate' (Van Maanen, 1978a:227) for justifying and legitimizing occupational action in very personal terms. For bouncers learn their trade via their experience and the experiences of their peers and colleagues. What may seem 'capricious, random, or unnecessary behaviour... is, in fact governed by certain rather pervasive interpretative rules which lie close enough to the surface such that they can be made visible' (Van Maanen, 1978a:234).

The bouncer standing outside a venue is symbolic of the pervasive character of commercial control in the new quasi-liminal zones, and is the most visible representation of the potential of capital to impose its will upon citizens venturing into the night-time economy. The very fact of their physical obtrusiveness in the doorways and on the pavements of our cities at night, assures that the bouncer's role in establishing the protocols of this profit-driven liminal marketplace is 'as much representational or symbolic as it is one centering on instrumental action' (Rock, 1973:174). This presence highlights the dramaturgical sideshow of their function as purveyors of commercial control, set aside from the bureaucratic formalism of the quasi-militaristic state police, they are able to select for public view, symbolic and traditional images of easily interpreted symbols of unambiguous masculine social control.

Yet like the public police they mediate between economic élites and citizens, locate threats to the interests of these élites, and via their role as mechanics of incorporation, 'mark the limits of the respectable segments of society, the boundaries of informal social control, and the shapes and locations of evil' (Manning, 1977:107). While the police symbolize the state (Bittner, 1970:36–51; Manning, 1977:111) the very presence of the bouncer represents the inability of the state to function on the new frontier of liminality. As we suggested in Chapter 1, the bouncer marks these new economic and social boundaries, in the same manner that the old boundaries were marked out, by the rapid development of violent potential as a response to commercial concerns (Silver, 1967; South, 1988). Yet the bouncer subculture should not be regarded merely as a malformation of the clean machine of the state police. For the violent discretion that is built into the bouncer's working personality is in itself a powerful tool, not only of personal and professional instrumentality, but also of commercial incorporation, providing a mechanism for 'transforming structural forces into individual motivations' (Shearing, 1981:362), and utilizing nothing but 'good violence' (Toch, 1993). The bouncer's occupational culture thrives in the absence of strong and enforceable laws and codes of conduct, providing a web of common practices across the night, and filling the void created by the state's own far less nocturnal habits; habits that stem from a reluctance to recognize the night-time economy, both materially and culturally, as one of the most powerful and visible manifestations of post-industrial society.

It is now last orders. I see one man take a head butt to the bridge of his nose. We grab the attacker, and his victim, now recovered, throws a fearsome punch into his attacker's face. We throw both of the men out. We are furious at the way that they treated both our personal and professional authority with impunity, and despite the fact that one of the fighters has lost his taste for combat, we go outside to watch the resumption of hostilities on the pavement.

   Punches are thrown, but they are tired, sloppy drunks. Soon they are rolling around on the floor and a spectator pours a can of lager over the pair. Another bystander, impatient for action, gets a couple of hefty kicks in to one of the fighter's shoulders. A young woman dressed in a silver mini-dress is being sick in the doorway of a discount shoe shop. As a police van leisurely pulls up, the fight-night audience dissipates and football songs fill the air. Before a police officer can put a foot on the pavement they get a call, presumably to a more pressing incident and roar away. There are no arrests.

6
Manners Maketh the Man: Licensing 'Door Supervisors' and the Discourses of Professionalism and Safety

Manipulation of social images makes it possible for members of society to believe they live not in a jungle, but in a well organized and good society (Saloman, 1955:110).

Overall, I don't know, licensing's probably a good thing if it helps clean things up—or makes it look like things are getting cleaned up. Dougie, thirty-two year old, bouncer

Introduction

In this chapter we reflect upon the relationship between bouncers and the state. Specifically, we consider the instrumental means by which the local and central state has sought to regulate the social action of bouncers, an occupation that we stress enjoys largely 'unfettered discretion' (Shearing and Stenning, 1983a:18). We locate this regulatory drive within the wider economic and political context that shapes both the structural arrangements of the bouncing business and the development of the night-time economy. In so doing, we detail the inherent difficulties encountered by the state in its attempts to introduce a greater degree of accountability to a role that is subculturally constituted, and an industry that is embedded in the informal practices of the hidden economy. Supplementing our ethnographic observations (three of the research team trained formally as bouncers), we surveyed over sixty local licensing schemes and therefore draw upon a wide range of qualitative interview data gleaned from both sides of the regulatory divide.

Over the last thirty years the UK private security industry, of which the bouncing trade is a sizeable constituent,[1] has been the

---

[1] Walker (1999) estimates the employment pool of the industry to be approximately 100,000, however certain trade characteristics create measurement difficulties.

focus of enduring political concern, particularly in relation to matters of accountability (see for example, George and Button, 1996; Johnston 1991; South, 1988). Political debate, rather than considering the legal powers bestowed upon private security agents through the transference of institutional property rights has, on the whole, simply deliberated the case for and against the introduction of state regulation in the form of external mechanisms of public accountability (see Stenning and Shearing, 1979, 1981). The requirement to introduce suitable regulatory safeguards that 'watch the watchers' (Bowden, 1978) assumes particular salience within the unique context of bouncing, where abuse of power equates all too easily with abuse of the law. The role affords, for instance, wide opportunity for acquisitive crime, ranging from the pickpocketing of a marooned handbag to the organized conspiracy to supply whole-sale a venue's drug of choice (Morris, 1998a). And then there is the use of force. As we describe, the requirement to use varying degrees of coercive force is a component part of the role, and it is the heavy-handed application of such force, whether framed as legitimate or illegitimate, which has long tarnished the reputation of the door trade. Accordingly the policy entrepreneurs, (Kingdom, 1995) who lobbied doggedly for the imposition of statutory regulation of the entire private security industry, consistently cited the bouncer sector as *prima facie* evidence of this need (see, for example, Home Affairs Select Committee, 1995).

In 2001, after years of political wrangling, the Labour Government introduced the Private Security Act, a piece of statutory legislation that repositioned the (non-interventionist) stance of the state toward the industry. The Act, which established the Security Industry Authority (SIA) as the implementation body, requires all contracted private security operatives to possess an occupational licence prior to working within the industry.[2] Pre-empting the arrival of statutory legislation, however, mounting concerns over the 'bouncer problem' led locally forged alliances of public and private bodies to bypass central state inertia and develop non-statutory regulatory

These include the trade's transient nature and partial location in the hidden economy, and an absence of centralized regulation (for a broader discussion of the problems in assessing the size of the whole private security industry see Jones and Newburn, 1998).

[2] Although the provisions of the Act exclude in-house (i.e. directly employed) private security operatives from the licensing requirement, this exemption from the scope of the regulation does not extend to doorstaff'.

licensing systems, known as 'door supervisor registration schemes'. These local licensing initiatives, which began to appear in the late 1980s, spread quickly and over 200 presently operate across the UK. The SIA-administered national licensing scheme, however, is set to supersede these regulatory structures, thus rendering local door registration schemes redundant. Nonetheless, we argue that by discussing the development and operation of such schemes we are able to demonstrate how municipal entrepreneurship has colluded with the interests of both the state and private enterprise to create a template which will continue to shape and direct the potential impact of future regulatory development.

Context: situating the registration agenda

Command and control regulation has a tendency to focus on the symptoms rather than causes (Osborne and Gaebler, 1992:301).

Door registration schemes are one of a number of situational 'support structures' implemented in order to underpin notions of 'safety' within the night-time economy. Attempts by local authorities and other stakeholders to stretch the 'vitality' and 'viability' of urban centres into the evening and night, through the deregulation of planning and licensing controls, environmental improvements, place marketing, and other forms of investment facilitation have, out of commercial necessity, prompted a renewed focus on public safety (Hadfield et al., 2001). In this context, a range of crime prevention initiatives, which correspondingly seek to increase control over the behaviour of the most 'troublesome' of operators and consumers, developed priority status. To this end, a wide range of 'managerial' interventions are now routinely employed such as Pub and Club Watch schemes, by-laws prohibiting the consumption of alcohol in public places, exclusion orders, public and private CCTV surveillance and radio-link systems, and high profile policing. Within this evolving regulatory posture, the poor reputation of those private agents tasked with policing the licensed premises of the night-time economy inevitably received close scrutiny. In particular, concerns arose within the context of a series of violent and intimidation incidents involving civic administrators, corporate manpower, and members of the public, 'the very people door supervisors were there to protect' (Home Affairs Committee, 1995:101).

Such incidents, which often received both local and national media and indeed political scrutiny, did little to enhance this reputation. In this climate a crime control mandate evolved in which 'crime prevention' became the political justification for regulation: an aspiration transparently couched within 'public interest' discourses (Hutter, 1997).

Licensing schemes should be regarded as political acts that are both expressive in form and instrumental in nature (Himmelstrand, 1960). The instrumental function aims to counter both the steadfastly negative profile of the target group and the type of behaviour generating that profile.[3] Simultaneously licensing schemes perform an expressive function, which seeks to 'sell safety' to the wider public audience (Shapland, 1999). Within this placatory exercise registration schemes become a widely publicized expression of political activity, the aim of which is to promote public reassurance through the symbolism of action. Indeed it is within this context that the rising political capital invested within *forms* of 'partnership work' led to an acceleration in the spread of registration schemes, as their implementation became viewed as a demonstrative touchstone of local (crime prevention) partnership activity.

Yet, within the context of neo-liberal governance, securing a safe environment for the night-time city centre populous has, in large part, been a function of securing risk free conditions for capital investment (Hobbs et al., 2000). Central to our story are the massive tensions that underlie this endeavour; the irony therein being that the local state's unremitting courtship of corporate leisure capital has led to urban centres that are anything but safe. The ensuing regulation, aimed at mollifying this tension is, therefore, weighted heavily in favour of situational initiatives, which—crucially—do not impinge overly upon the commercial fertility of city centre leisure zones.[4] Viewed from this perspective, the increasing regulatory emphasis placed upon licensed premises, their customers, *and* security provision should be understood as a narrow response to the wider processes of deregulation, which are facilitating and encouraging the

---

[3] Given that these two interconnected goals are not mutually exclusive, the extent to which their outcomes collapse is central to the analysis offered herein.

[4] Although as we proceed to discuss (see Chapter 8), the metropolitan borough of Westminister, which is struggling to cope with the criminogenic and environmental impacts of the night-time economy, is now actively seeking to put the 'genie back in the lamp' and stem the current tide of corporate leisure investment.

expansion of the night-time economy (Chatterton and Hollands, 2002; Lister et al., 2001a). This apparently contradictory position demonstrates the ironies that emerge when public bodies seek to regulate a political economy they have cosseted, and upon which they are financially and politically reliant (Manning, 1987). Hence the extant conditions of local municipal regulation have largely been restricted in scope by a functional need not to bite the hand that feeds it. This observation carries analytical resonance because it lays emphasis toward the broader political context within which door regulation occurs, and by implication this influences the qualitative dynamics of the form, content, and outcome of the regulatory endeavour (ibid.).

Registration as a regulatory mechanism

The regulation of bouncers, as many other areas of economic life in which the state seeks to intervene and apply controls, represents an attempt to influence the structure and composition of the market-place through the application of the law (Manning, 1987:293; Stigler, 1975). This posture acknowledges that the aim of the state is merely to *regulate* rather than *repress* the function of the activity in question (Hawkins, 1984:10). In order to achieve this goal a discretionary 'policing' model is required, one which not only differentiates within the activity regulated but also establishes regulatory mechanisms that serve as indices to this requirement. The state has sought to administrate this command by introducing a mode of occupational licensing which imposes a binary classification model upon the supply side of the labour market (i.e. licensed and un-licensed); thereafter, the law is invoked to constrain market demand to state-sanctioned labour only. In this manner, the outcomes of door regulation rely upon the capacity of the state to restructure market demand: in other words, the aim is to apply '... public leverage to shape private decisions to achieve collective goals...' (Osborne and Gaebler, 1992:284).

Greene narrowly defines the collective goals of occupational licensing as an attempt 'to protect the public from incompetent and unscrupulous practitioners and to promote high performance standards' (Greene, 1969:1). Specifically, door registration schemes seek to achieve these outcomes by effecting change within the labour supply market through the introduction of criminal records vetting and occupational training as endpoint requirements of the licensing process. In addition, by shoring up preventative deterrents, licensing seeks to evoke greater individual accountability. In this process, two separate though interconnected modes of accountability are intended to function. First, enhanced processes of *legal* accountability may proliferate because licensing databases equip the authorities with a *modus operandi* for knowing who the people in the door trade actually are, thus potentially raising the certitude of detection and prosecution for wrongdoing. Secondly, sharpened processes of *public* accountability may result because, the threat of licence revocation, intrinsic to a licensing system, is a threat against one's livelihood. This is the operational intent of licensing and, in part, the ensuing analysis aims to tease out the blurred detail of implementation, which enables regulators to herald, not to say dramatize the positive outcomes attributed to licensing initiatives (see for example Walker, 1999).

Nationally, registration schemes developed *ad hoc* under local authority jurisdiction, and therefore each possesses clearly defined geographical parameters and independent autonomy. This serves to reduce greatly the holistic coverage, such that persons denied or stripped of a licence in one area are able to transfer their labour to a neighbouring, registration-free area. Images of spatially displaced armies of 'illegitimate' bouncers therefore cultivated local demands for regulation. A Midlands police officer voiced the following concern:

They might not get registered in Leicester or Nottingham . . . [so] they come here and they are assaulting people, they are being obnoxious. We know why they wouldn't get registered up there 'cos they come in and work here, and that's why we need to get a scheme in place to get rid of those sort. We've got a couple of them going to court at the moment for Section 18 woundings, and this wouldn't have happened if they were registered.

The fragmented regulatory structure led to (scheme-specific) non-portable licences and, therefore, (re-)registration is a requirement within each scheme, causing considerable frustration among those forced to repeat the process and pay for multiple badges. Such process duplication is, of course, highly bureaucratic, giving rise to inconsistencies and loopholes that loosen the net and reduce coverage. Furthermore, the general lack of co-ordination and standardization of procedure runs contrary to concepts of uniform, pragmatic regulation (see Better Regulation Task Force, 1998b), and although schemes function in a similar manner, wide differences across policy and process typify the haphazard nature of the implementation schedule.[5] For example, licensing periods and charges, training requirements, vetting criteria, licence revocation, and renewal protocols, as well as short-term registration policies all vary considerably.

The main 'interest groups' (Stigler, 1971) involved in promoting the registration agenda were local authorities, police divisions, entertainment corporations, and a number of commercially progressive door agencies. Ownership and authority to license doorstaff usually rests with local authorities, though nearly all rely upon some degree of (police) partnership activity for implementation. For example, police officers access past conviction data, which enables criminal record checks, and in some areas more than others, the police input resources for training and enforcement purposes. As previous research indicates, the match of organizational ethos between inter-agency 'partners' is often far from seamless (Crawford, 1997), and, unsurprisingly, implementation tensions can sometimes afflict the licensing process. When tensions surface, it is usually in relation to licence application, renewal, and revocation outcomes, insofar as local authorities at times discount police recommendations. Unremarkably, police personnel often perceive that political sensibilities severely constrain crime control agendas, as one officer vehemently described, 'it's having no impact at all. We feel very frustrated; it's basically had no effect at all. Basically it's politics—being seen to do something. But they're not backing the PEL (Public Entertainment Licence) holders, the whole thing is a teeth-less bloody sham, they have created a free-for-all'. This viewpoint suggests that, in Himmelstrand's terms (1960), the crime prevention benefits expected by the instrumental dimension of regulation have given way to the expressive dimension, the sum ambition of which is to reassure the audience through symbolic forms of action.

In contrast to local authority 'owned' schemes, a small minority are administered entirely by local police divisions, and thus represent the 'politically undiluted' attempts of the public police to regulate the private. These initiatives are of some significance because they

---

[5] Although the distribution of Home Office Circular 60/95, 'Registration Schemes for Door Supervisors', did provide administrators with a broad template for the establishment and operation of registration schemes.

pre-empt the accreditation, if not the co-ordination role that Home Office and senior UK police personnel envisage for the public police within 'the extended police family' (Blair, 1998, 2002; Home Office, 2001c). Comparatively speaking, police licensing regimes appear to be more strictly administered than local authority schemes both in relation to vetting policy and enforcement process, with less apparent remoteness between regulators and regulated. Importantly, police ownership of a registration or *accreditation* scheme levers a bureaucratic rationale for police divisions to formally assign an officer to a 'watching' role over the local doorstaff community—dubbed 'the bouncer liaison officer' by one such force. In contrast, most police divisions tend to leave this specialist task to float on the goodwill of frequently over-stretched licensing officers. Therefore, by the very nature of the administrative process, police-owned licensing schemes appear to foster closer links between the two policing providers. Although 'closer links' may not always necessarily equate to 'publicly beneficial links', we would argue that, for the most part, the increased level of routine interaction between police personnel and licensees, agency managers, and doorstaff, facilitates more effective monitoring practices, which in turn appear to fashion more proficient avenues of public accountability.

As policing provision edges toward competitive market conditions, the regulation of one policing agency by another raises some broad ethical issues relating to who is accountable to whom and for what (Loader, 2000; Scott, 2000; Shearing and Stenning, 1981). Indeed, in the absence of democratic balances, we heard a number of stinging criticisms upon the extent to which principles of 'natural justice' were transparently adhered to within these prescriptive arrangements: a sobering reminder of 'the old and thorny issue of controlling police discretion' (Loader, 2000:336). One of our informants expressed resentment at the role of police discretion, which resulted in a failed licence application:

I know the police have got it in for me, they are trying to say that I'm a bad man and that I can't do the door, that I'm not suitable to do the door. They have stopped me having a badge and my name gets mentioned all the time and they make out that I'm such a bad man. Fine, if that is the case, get my record out and if I'm such a bad man that I've beat everybody up where are all the charges? Surely if you are a criminal and you are a bad criminal and you've been done for it all, it would all be there on your record, and it isn't! So as far as I'm concerned it's hearsay—what people say. You cannot charge someone and do someone if you haven't got the proof, and a lot of things get said about me. It's a lie, but they use those things against me. Paul

Gaining control over the means of door security registration places police influence over the marketplace within a more formal framework. Traditionally, through a variety of informal methods, the police *have* been able to assert some degree of influence over market demand for licensed premises security, both in relation to specific agencies and individuals. At the less coercive end of the spectrum this involves a quiet 'advisory' word with the licensee or respective area manager, at the other end, it involves the police utilizing their capacity to oppose necessary operational licences (usually the Public Entertainment Licence). Thus, in the event that the police wish to see a security agent or agency actively removed from a door then, by threatening commercial imperatives, they are able to negotiate outcomes 'in the shadow of the law' (Manning, 1987:296). In this manner, Paul described how the local police were, he believed, striving to drive him out of town.

The police now I know are trying to stop me doing any doors at all and I can prove that. They've stopped me having a badge because they don't think I'm suitable, so I put doormen on the door for breweries, doormen who have got badges that they say are okay to work on the door; they've approved 'em—not me—the council, the police. Now they are trying to threaten landlords, blackmail landlords because they have a certain security on the door. I'm not mentioning names of the security because at the end of the day it is mine. But they are basically saying get rid of that security because you are coming up for a late licence, now why?

The 'calculated exercise' (Shearing et al., 1980) of police discretion within security markets cuts both ways, some security agencies are ordained, and others are stigmatized. Later in this chapter we discuss the nature of relations between the two policing agencies in greater depth, suffice it to say here that if 'active partnerships' with the state are to emerge more fully (Stenning, 1989), then the public police may become increasingly involved in 'ordering the market'. For example, a number of our police informants indicated that in order to facilitate the development of effective processes of 'co-operation', police divisions will increasingly need to give consideration to the optimal number of door agencies operating within their area of jurisdiction. As the police contemplate this, other state institutions might wish to consider how best to rein in the role of police discretion within this commercially sentient regulatory process.

Legal powers to regulate and the coverage shortfall

In the absence of statutory legislation the registration requirement was 'bolted-on' to the Public Entertainment Licence (PEL) of a venue—as a 'term and condition' imposed by local authority licensing departments. The London Local Authorities Act 1995 did establish specific powers to license doorstaff, though this legislation applied only within the Greater London area. Across the rest of the UK regulatory powers continued to derive from the flexibility prescribed by local authorities to PEL terms and conditions. This supposition has been a quarrelsome legal issue, only recently settled—in favour of the legality to register but not to charge a fee—at the Court of Appeal (*R. v. Liverpool City Council* [2001]). Essentially, legal ambiguity surrounded the validity of PEL powers to anchor the operational requirements of a licensing system; powers which asserted the right to demand a fee, insist upon a vetting and training obligation, and, most contentiously, deny someone their livelihood (see Licensing Review, 1998). In addition, the absence of statutory recourse to the courts, as an independent appeal mechanism, muddied the legal waters still further (Button, 1998). This legal uncertainty had an important bearing upon the uniform operation and impact of licensing systems, bringing further inconsistency to an already patchwork regulatory landscape. For example, some local authorities deemed it prudent neither to charge for registration nor insist upon training. Others decided not to refuse licence applications and many developed an extreme shyness toward revoking licences.

As well as adversely impacting upon the 'blueprint' design of licensing, this non-statutory status created wider fault lines in the operational effectiveness of the model. First, for instance, because not all types of licensed premises require a PEL, a two-tier, premises-specific pattern of licensed and unlicensed labour emerged, which reduces regulation coverage by enabling unlicensed labour to remain active within certain sectors of the marketplace.[6] Thus, a significant

---

[6] Under current law, a licensed premise must apply for a PEL prior to (a) 'music and dancing' occurring at the site and (b) a late liquor licence application; thereby, a crude distinction may be formed between nightclubs, concert venues, and late licensed bars, and 'ordinary' pubs, bars, and private members clubs.

proportion of the bar and pub market remains exempt from the licensing condition; a shortcoming of some significance, particularly within small town and semi-rural areas where pubs, rather than late licensed bars or nightclubs, frequently dominate the local night-time economy. In response, a small number of local licensing benches were persuaded to assign the registration condition to all new justices' on-licences, thus broadening the scope of the regulation. This occurred, for example, within one area after three doormen, recorded on CCTV committing serious acts of violence, were suspended from the local registration scheme only to be discovered working legitimately at a pub directly across the road from where the offences occurred.

Secondly, PEL conditions cannot define a new criminal offence: 'person working without the required licence'. Rather, in breaking PEL conditions, the offence is in the act *of employing* such a person, thus, the purchaser (the licensee), not the provider (the security), bears vicarious liability for the licensing requirement, a diversion of legal liability which places the licensee at the forefront of the enforcement process. Although this may hold some appeal as a self-regulating mechanism, the danger is that the efficient imposition of social order is the licensee's priority, with the regulatory status of those maintaining that order relegated to a distant second. Viewed within this context, the functionality of the end may outweigh the legality of the means. Importantly, this additional regulatory responsibility also fell upon licensees at a time when the licensed trade increasingly began to shed employment responsibility for security on to door agencies. The transition of employment mode from 'in-house' to 'agency', which is grounded in commercial and legal rationales (Button and George, 1998; Shearing and Stenning, 1981), has the potential to blur managerial lines of responsibility between security staff and licensees. This sometimes leads to detached relations that can serve to slacken the bond of commercial accountability. At best, a degree of managerial control is relinquished, at worst, the relationship is unfamiliar, remote, and sometimes adversarial (see Chapter 4). Furthermore, the onset of 'contracted' security arrangements led to the subsequent development of 'sub-contracted' arrangements, which, we were informed, blur accountability lines further still. One agency manager summarized the concern:

I prefer not to shed the responsibility on to somebody else, I prefer to know what's going on. How can you know what's going on at that door if you're contracting it out to another firm and they're dealing with it? How do you know what's going on at that door? How do you know what kind of people you're employing? Paul

Thirdly, registration does not stretch to cover either the licensing of agencies that supply door security, their directors, or managers.[7] Although, as discussed, local police divisions possess some capability to assert informal influence upon the purchasers of security, this remains a significant shortfall in registration coverage, not least because casual business practices adopted at the rump end of the sector erode generic processes of accountability. For instance, some agencies might be called 'Black Securities' one day and 'White Securities' the next, routinely paying cash-in-hand wages, 'forgetting' to register for VAT or tax purposes, avoiding formally documented contracts and appropriate insurance cover, and generally going about their business without leaving footprints in the sand. One senior police officer explained the desire to license such companies:

We were very worried that the smaller boys could change names and still work from a kitchen table, which a lot of them do, and just supply people without any registered office and without VAT and tax registration. And what we don't want is the cowboy who's working from home on a mobile phone, where nothing can be attributed to him, so we want to make sure we have bona fide companies.

Police officers also expressed serious alarm that directors of companies were exempt from the licensing requirement. This is because a number of agencies are managed and owned by individuals of dubious probity, including some with revoked licences, some with serious criminal histories, and some who at the time of the research were residing for lengthy periods at Her Majesty's pleasure. One senior police officer expressed the concern:

When you have a door registration scheme, it almost makes it impossible for people with substantial criminal convictions to get registered, so what you find is the criminal enterprise will tend to put people up front. So you'll find your well known criminal takes a back seat in terms of handling the door, but a front seat in terms of getting them work on doors and collecting the money, and by the backdoor you've got criminal control over the front door. So your registration scheme actually pushes the problem a little bit

---

[7] Significantly, the SIA is to endeavour to license (visible) company directors though not the actual companies.

further down... they're criminal conspiracies because two steps back the money behind it is in the drugs business or protection.

In addition to illegal acquisitive gain, such 'criminal conspiracies' potentially impact negatively upon a door agency's organizational culture, and therefore, the dispensation of policing and justice mechanisms within these 'private governments' (Shearing, 2001:211). Further, as we discuss in Chapter 7, the presence of criminally-minded operators within the marketplace routinely exposes the business dynamics of the door world to the 'regulatory' principles of the criminal world, not least because a trade that utilizes threat and muscle as a commercial resource is inherently well placed to apply that resource to (coercive) business practice. During our research we were informed about door agencies covertly and overtly sending (door)men into licensed premises to cause violent affray in order to demonstrate the 'inadequacies' of rival providers; industrial disputes settled by so-called 'door wars', which ranged from organized, bare-knuckle fights to summary beatings, gang rumbles and execution-style shootings (see Chapter 3); contracts of work secured either by bribery or intimidation against rival door firms and licensed trade managers. As one doorman succinctly stated, 'if someone else is given your door then that someone is going to send people down there to cause that much trouble that they give it straight back to you'.

The vetting requirement

You've got to have lads who know how to handle themselves on the door because that's what it's about. You can't say 'no violence' to bouncers because of the shit they have to deal with. Violence is part of it: it's why they got the jobs in the first place. Why have bouncers if there isn't going to be any bother? Dave

Within each registration scheme all applicants are screened for a criminal history, the aim of which is to ensure that only those persons deemed 'fit and proper' gain licences. Implicit within this process is an assumption that past offences serve as objective indicators of future offending risks. Fundamentally this labelling exercise, which bifurcates applicants into 'safe' and 'unsafe' categories, is premissed upon a strictly recidivist view of offending behaviour, one which—legal requirements apart—rejects outright appeals to rehabilitation. However, the extent to which previous offences serve as an accurate signpost for future offending remains debatable. While criminal vetting may exclude patently unfit persons, even the strictest policy cannot prevent licences falling into the 'clean' hands of those that will prove unfit through future (mis)conduct. Without wishing to dismiss the crime prevention value of criminal screening, a caveat should be offered to the aggrandizing proclamations of regulators, which typically herald the arrival of vetting procedures as 'a way of *ensuring* the safety of people visiting licensed premises' (Leeds City Council, 1997; our emphasis). The symbolic potency of this oversimplification would be well recognized by political theorists, whom in charting the mass response of the public to the continuing tensions between threat and reassurance, observe that 'the more dramatic and publicized features of the political process convey reassurance, but they can do so only because people are ambivalent and anxious for reassurance' (Edelman, 1964:189). In such a climate, the sentiment of the means replaces that of the end: past offending is intimately connected with future offending and, moreover, an absence of past offending foreshadows *no* offending. In acknowledgement that criminal record checks may become over-relied upon as 'indicators of safety' the Home Office issued a warning that vetting checks '... can lead to complacency and a misguided assumption by employers and managers that staff are "safe". This can lead to other recruitment safeguard failures such as checking references and providing supervision on training' (Home Office, 1993: 9).

As we discussed in Chapter 4, many of our interviewees perceived greater role experience as the principal safeguard against an 'over-the-top' physical response to work demands and, therefore, contested the recidivist rationale that underpins the crime prevention reasoning of vetting requirements (Winlow et al., 2001). Furthermore, the (inverse) perception that 'safe' bouncers were those with criminal records behind them, rather then in front of them, held some currency. Within this preventative logic age and experience serve as *the* key factors, and as Australian researchers surmise, 'unfortunately... bouncers may be leaving this sort of work just as they are beginning to acquire the sort of experience and work maturity that their job requires' (Homel and Tomsen, 1993:60). Bernie, a doorman of fourteen years' experience, articulated the concern:

Just because you haven't got any convictions doesn't mean you're all right to be a doorman. You can get young lads coming into it smacking people all over the place and just because they haven't been in any trouble they get the licence. Some of the older lads might have a bit of a history, but just because of that you can't say it's them that's going to be going daft, knocking the fucking shit out of people. You can have security firms, and that, stuck for a couple of blokes for a job, and just because you can't get the lads you might want, you take whoever's got the licence. And I'll tell you another thing; it's them that's going to be going in causing bother. They might be nervous or whatever, or trying to prove to the other lads that they are up to the job or they might be trying to get a bit of a name and that.

In keeping with other aspects of implementation, the absence of effective centralized co-ordination has led to the development of vetting policies and practices that vary widely between licensing jurisdictions, as determined by local administrative custom. The vetting criteria applied in definition of the 'fit and proper persons' assessment typically include type, severity, age, and relevance of uncovered convictions, though moral subjectivity permeates decision-making processes. The resultant ambiguities and inconsistencies are particularly apparent in prevailing attitudes toward the relevance of so-called 'grey' offences such as domestic violence, theft, criminal damage, fraud, and public drunkenness. Drug offences, which were viewed largely in isolation of context, universally debarred registration. This contrasted with a more flexible approach to violent offences, the situational circumstances of which administrators sometimes take into consideration. For example, one officer indicated that domestic violence should debar registration status because 'a violent assault is a violent assault no matter where it takes place'. In contrast, this officer's counterpart in an adjacent area offered that 'if he's had a domestic, or a grievance with his neighbour and he's involved in an assault, well that's nothing to do with his work as a doorman, so it's only something relevant to how he will work on the door'. Similar irregularities surround the application of spent offences and police intelligence reports such as pending court dates, bind-overs, and cautions. With the exception of one local authority scheme, which aimed to exclude applicants suspected of 'habitual association with criminals', all others claimed that applied vetting processes were transparent and complied with natural justice principles. The following two quotations illustrate the manner in which 'political constraints' were sometimes seen to impinge upon crime control ambitions:

Quite often police officers will see someone working on the door and they'll say 'how the hell did he get a licence?'. And they'll say 'he might just be okay but he associates with him, him, him and him, who are just really bloody villains, and we don't want that sort on the door', but they can't give us that information—their police intelligence if you like. And they might know an awful lot about him, and they don't see him as suitable, but on paper he is suitable until he does something wrong. Local authority officer

Quite honestly, there are some doormen in the scheme now, with convictions, which we wouldn't really want there; but the local authority have made the decision that they still want to condone them on the scheme, and it's their scheme. All we do is voice our concerns about a particular individual. But there are people, there are a lot of people, with convictions, some for violence and some with things for firearms, who are registered doormen. So the scheme isn't perfect, you know, they make the decision, all we do is flag them up. Police Sergeant

It soon became clear to us that despite the establishment of a *provisional* moral order, a pragmatic and malleable mode of operational decision-making tends to function, which enables persons with relatively serious convictions to gain licences. On the one hand this points to the reflexivity of administrators with regard to the uncertain legal terrain of registration schemes, on the other hand it reflects a broad characteristic of the 'compliance' (law enforcement) system to which registration functions. Under this compliance system each case is 'judged on its own merits' (often scripted as pertaining to the laws of natural justice), thereby levering a degree of interpersonal bargaining and negotiation space for the emergence of graduated outcomes[8] (Eisenberg, 1976; Hawkins, 1984; Hutter, 1997). For example, licences may be granted subject to the applicant agreeing to some form of scrutiny, (whether formal or informal), or gaining a conditional guarantee from the management of the employing door agency or licensed premises. Therefore vetting outcomes *within* schemes vary inasmuch that 'no single moral standard determines the vicissitudes of the licensing process' (Manning, 1987:313). Undeniably vetting serves to prevent many criminals from gaining licences, but not entirely in the catch-all manner that regulators commonly claim.

[8] Internal local authority appeal tribunals facilitate this compliance process.

The presence of an implementation gap between vetting rhetoric and reality reflects the practical difficulties of harmonizing a strict, formulaic criminal screening policy with the incongruent social and economic realities of the labour market.[9] This point is emphasized by the fact that on launch, and without publicizing the matter, several large city-wide schemes granted an 'amnesty' on all previous offences to all registration applicants, no matter how eventful their recent criminal history. One police manager explained the pragmatics behind this uneasy compromise, suggesting that without an amnesty 'the town would have had no doormen left, so we had to start them all on a clean slate'. Research indicates that within England and Wales almost one-third of males under the age of forty possess a criminal record (Prime et al., 2001),[10] a ratio that we would suggest is undoubtedly higher among door security. Despite the scarcity of relevant quantitative data, that which does exist is revealing, particularly in relation to serious offences. For example, police evidence presented to the 1994 Home Affairs Committee, indicated that of 476 doormen operating in one force area, five had convictions or charges pending for murder or manslaughter, twenty-five had weapons convictions, eighteen had drug convictions and more than 100 had assault convictions.

This evidence, which broadly illustrates the extent to which persons holding convictions had successfully infiltrated the trade, reinforces South's observation that 'threat and physical force *are* resources in the world of security' (1988:99). Controlling and regulating an intoxicated customer base is not for the faint-hearted and this is why the licensed trade purchases the services of bouncers and their violent potential as a 'security commodity' (Spitzer, 1979). Therein lies the paradoxical problem of the registration agenda: convictions for bouncers may be something of an occupational hazard, for successfully dealing with trouble can all-to-easily lead to unwanted police attention. The tensions between the physical demands of the role and criminal screening were not lost on our informants, many of whom reflected upon the deterrence value of a

---

[9] Given that the SIA intends to subject the door industry to an 'enhanced criminal record check', a vetting option that considers the relevance of both spent and unspent offences, and local police intelligence reports, this tension is set to increase.

[10] This research does not indicate what proportion of this conviction figure would be classified as live under the Rehabilitation of Offenders Act 1974.

tall reputation earned through actions. Paul, a northern agency manager, offered the following view:

> As I say to you again, you need streetwise kids on the doors, 'cos if you were to put Joe Bloggs, who's never had a criminal record, never had this, never had that, no blemishes, no nothing, on the door, then I tell you something now, they're putting people at risk there, 'cos it'll be like 'who's he', 'bang', know what I mean? They'll steam in there and they'll wreck young kids or young men; 'cos it's all right looking the part, but basically you have to be knowing what's going on, 'cos you've got to be wary of people glassing you, shooting you, fucking anything can happen.

Many of our informants viewed vetting requirements as an attempt to fit square pegs into round holes, a perception that many vetting outcomes reflect.

The training requirement

Alex: D'you want to interview me? I worked here last night; I'm a bouncer now.

Q: What instructions were you given?

Alex: If anyone official comes, you're not working; if you have to hit anyone, take 'em outside.

In addition to a criminal history check, the attendance of a 'recognized' training course is, for the vast majority of schemes, a prerequisite to licence acquisition. Initially, in keeping with other aspects of registration, local piecemeal developments led to courses that varied widely in form and content and which tended to be recognized, and thus accepted, only within the jurisdiction of each discrete scheme—consequently multiple registration applicants were contentiously forced to 're-train', time and time again. Across courses, the extent of any police contribution varies considerably, and as we proceed to discuss, this has important bearing upon the manner in which training aims to develop the 'door role', principally by promoting closer working practices with the public police. Obligations to undertake refresher training also vary: sometimes stipulated as a condition of licence renewal, for the most part, it remains conspicuous by its absence. Similarly, whereas some courses entail a multiple-choice exam, the majority simply require attendance; as one doorman observed bluntly, 'it's impossible to fail, I could send my dog on it and it would pass'.

State imposition of compulsory training has created a sizeable emergent marketplace within which an array of different providers fiercely competes. Courses are delivered through a variety of mechanisms; hence some municipal authorities opt 'to steer' and others 'to row' (Osborne and Gaebler, 1992). For instance, some local authorities organize their own training facility in partnership with local emergency services; others outsource to a training body, while the majority set up an internal market by way of an 'approval list' of sanctioned trainers, usually comprising of local colleges and private companies. Local authority administrators then purportedly monitor delivery standards, although some 'approved' trainers, seemingly eager to decry competitors, disputed this claim. Over the last decade, however, the market has consolidated and standardized, and thus the extent to which licence applicants are forced to re-train has considerably reduced. Currently three organizations, the Security Industry Training Organization (SITO), the British Institute of Innkeepers, and the Northern College for Further Education, widely franchise discrete courses through accredited trainers, which are—to all intents and purposes—nationally recognized.

Training regimes should be viewed within the context of labour market dynamics, which in large part serve to constrain market development. The casual and part-time nature of the work, coupled with the dominance of agency employment relations, customarily leads to labour rather than capital financing courses. Furthermore, training is widely perceived as a mandatory obligation *to* market entry, rather than as an instrument to secure competitive advantage *within* the market. It is unsurprising, then, that the least costly and time-consuming courses are usually selected. This is indicative of training provisions that are widely regarded as a means to an end (i.e. training to obtain a licence), rather than as possessing any intrinsic value in itself (i.e. training as investment). This economic constraint has prevented trainers, particularly those operating within the virtual 'perfect competition' environs of an approval list, from developing more expensive and substantive courses. This is a reconfiguration of the point argued by South, who in discussing the dynamics of the wider security market, argues that when markets evolve with a generically *accepted* standard of service delivery, demand is often tied to least cost and, by implication, quality thresholds. Consequently, although far more comprehensive qualifications are presently available (for example, one course arranges five days' training at a cost upward of £350), the established paradigm, which imparts in the region of 12–16 hours' training at a cost of between £80 and £120, remains dominant.[11]

Training courses, universally delivered in a classroom-type environment, seldom attempt to replicate workplace tasks and scenarios. Most trainers, eager to maintain the commercial leverage granted by this more passive and familiar arrangement, questioned the practical value of 'role-playing' and laid scorn upon their (in)ability to recreate the recalcitrance of real-life situations (see also Fielding, 1988:63). In many respects this mode of delivery is 'teacher-centred', as opposed to 'student-centred', which enables courses to focus, seemingly, on providing knowledge rather than attitudinal or skill-based forms of learning (ibid.:230). This factor generates some degree of tension within the trade. One experienced trainer suggesting that courses instead of being directed towards 'what makes doormen good at their job', instead focus upon the 'job's-worth necessities', adding that 'they're not necessarily as important as people like to make out'. These 'job's-worth necessities' that courses focus upon, usually reduce down to the core components of basic fire-fighting and emergency procedures, first aid, social conduct, criminal law and procedure, as well as civil and licensing law. Although some courses cover more occupation-specific areas such as drug recognition, equal opportunities protocol, search procedures and, significantly, control and restraint techniques, the majority appear indicative of top-down, externally-imposed directives that fail to appreciate the inherent dangers of the role and, therefore, the need for some form of contextually-refined risk management tuition (see Monaghan, 2002b). While knowledge of emergency procedures is important, many of our informants failed to appreciate the manner in which training promotes greater occupational competence, as they perceive it to be. Some applauded training because it appeared to denote that the authorities had begun to attach some

[11] We have argued elsewhere (Lister et al., 2001a) that current mandatory training provisions are insufficient in relation to the demands of the role. Whilst recognizing that there is no maximum threshold for training, a suitable minimum one is appropriate. For example, Australian researchers found that over 50% of security industry respondents (n=1189) believed the minimum training period for the trade of 24 hours (as stipulated by legislation) was of inadequate duration (Prenzer et al., 1998).

value to the role. Others welcomed the legal advice upon how best to avoid the punitive intrusions of the criminal justice system, but most castigated formal training as an obligatory chore that was, at best, marginal to the routine demands of the role and, at worst, simply an income-generation exercise.

All it is, is three sessions of two hours, you've got to be there and then you get your badge. I think that they should have what you call social skills training as in how to talk; they don't do that, they just skim through it, believe me. It was just like a load of lads all sat down and basically talking about a few fire hazards and looking for this and looking for that and how not to do things and all that kind of stupid things and that were it. At the end of the day it didn't teach you anything about how to approach somebody, how to say no, how to be firm but fair, 'cos I think there should be courses like how to deal with a situation . . . okay it's going to be abusive, it's going to be this it's going to be that, but at end of the day there's no training for that—you could just see everybody was bored. It's basically all about getting it out of the way; you know what I'm talking about? At the end of the day it's a hindrance to them 'cos they know they ain't going to get their card. We were just sat there, if someone asked us a question there was about, on my course, two people answering questions, and that were it, everyone else were just sat down there, time came, 'great stuff', can get ready to go to work now and that were it. I think there should have been a psychiatrist or someone who is a professional in communication and how to read body language and so on. What I teach my guys is an extension from my [services] career, discipline, man-management and how to talk to people and how to be organized. It's not all about how tough you are, but if you've got to do the job, you've got to do the job—you've got to be up for it. Liam

Of course any job of work with a tightly honed occupational subculture might be expected to demonstrate broad resistance to externally imposed reforms. However, the criticisms that we heard contained a revealing degree of consensus and, as described above, were evidently focused upon the generic nature and lack of transferability of courses. To some extent these tensions appear to evolve from a mismatch of expectations between the subject group and training administrators with regard to what training actually aspires to achieve. In this schism, the latter adopt a broad view of doorwork, which encompasses the wider, public interest concerns of the 'security role'. Teaching knowledge of (seldom required) emergency procedures, notably, fire hazards and basic first-aid situations, contrasts sharply with the bouncers' narrower view of 'security', which is moulded by the routine tasks and problematic demands of order-maintenance. Consequently, our interviewees lamented the over-emphasis on general health and safety advice at the expense of the real core issues that are of most concern to the public, the leisure trade, the police, and most importantly of course, the doorstaff themselves. These concerns gather around issues of threat and violence, and as we were informed, the bulk of courses fail to recognize sufficiently the violent social context that surrounds the role. Specifically, courses were collectively criticized for a lack of tuition in relation to conflict and risk management; coping with abusive, drunken or threatening personalities; diplomatic ejections and the appropriate use of discreet—physical or otherwise—interventions: in other words, the situational circumstances that frequently lead to trouble. One trainer robustly criticized established practice in the following manner:

Basically a lot of what is happening is wrong. The local council does the course; now the majority of the things they teach on there just don't comply with the doormen, it just does not make any sense. The doormen are sat there saying 'what are you teaching us this for, why are you telling us this?' They have to change the way they're doing it, change what they're teaching. . . I mean, I sent one on the last course a couple a weeks ago, he came back and was like 'yeah, thanks for that', he says, 'I can't believe what they were teaching, it's nothing like what we're supposed to be doing here'. I mean, why is everyone going on about doormen?: 'cause in the past people have been injured, there's been thugs on doors. The public will say a lot of them are rude, these are the things people have complained about, these need to be put straight, that's where the priority lies. Mike

Previous research with other tightly-knit occupational groups suggests that 'the expectations about what work involves and about the value of skilled work are part of a culture which exists relatively autonomously of any managerial framing' (Roberts, 1997:156; see Chapter 5). In this fashion, formal training is perceived as abstruse and, in a similar manner to public police training, offers little to equip students with the social adeptness that the policing role requires (Brogden et al., 1988; Fielding, 1988). Indeed, parallels with public police training are striking, and as Rubinstein suggests, 'things a policeman must know are mainly informal and some of them are illegal; there is no way to include them in the teaching plan' (1973:104). Nor is there a teaching plan to train individuals to throw themselves instinctively and without hesitation into the throng of a violent mêlée. As one doorman explained, 'it's like I said before, doing a bit of a course and knowing what to do on paper is a different ball game to getting someone in a pub who's had eight pints of beer, who wants to fight you when you ask him to leave'. The only aptitude training applicable to such situations emanates from biography, not the classroom (Winlow et al., 2001). Perhaps unsurprisingly therefore, what is offered is a 'culturally cleansed' perspective (Strangleman and Roberts, 1999), which in seeking to emphasize wider public interest concerns bypasses the awkward, and at times the messy reality of the role, thereby asserting what Roberts calls 'a managerially defined package of competencies' (Roberts, 1997:167). One agency manager implicitly drew reference to the deficit between managerial competencies and trade-defined occupational competencies:

What do we want, doormen who're still capable of doing a job or do we want people that have got qualifications who think they can do the job? 'Cause at the end of the day it's a violent job—or it can be. And no matter how much training people have, they can have every qualification you can give them, but they can still be in a situation and back down and run. So even though we don't want thugs working on the door you still want the right people who can handle a situation. Pete

The ability to make trouble their business is the bottom line for bouncers, and as our informants viewed it, no amount of 'paper qualifications' could circumvent the visceral realities of the role. Viewed from this perspective, it is unsurprising that training packages focus upon delivering a series of contextual outputs, which among other things, establish the normative parameters of the role, abandoning the pragmatic actualities of occupational learning, physical or otherwise, to the vagaries of the wider socialization process.

Training in the ways of the law: 'justice', culture, and commercial confidences

Q: Do you co-operate with the police when you're working the doors?

The only thing that the police will do for me is jail me, that's all that they'd do with me, so at the end of the day you don't ring the police. Just say we ring the police if there's been an incident at the door, and the police have been and come to your nightclub—you only get three chances and then they'll claim against your [liquor] licence, so you don't want the police. If they've been brought to this club for trouble three times in a particular year, they'll object for your licence at court. They want fewer nightclubs 'cause they can't handle it, the police. Stevie North

Previous research emphasizes that private security agents resolve conflict primarily within the more immediate and proximal framework of private justice systems rather than through recourse to the state's criminal justice system (Henry, 1987; Reichman, 1987; Shearing and Stenning, 1983b; Stenning and Shearing 1984).[12] Given this context, a striking feature of door training is the nomothetic components, which impart knowledge of criminal law and procedure, as well as civil and licensing law. According to police trainers and ex-police officers operating privately, these components aim to encourage doorstaff to engage with formal processes of law enforcement in a more efficient manner through greater co-operation with the public police. For example, criminal law and procedure training usually provides knowledge of 'reasonable force thresholds', 'drugs recognition', 'police powers of entry', 'scene preservation', and, significantly, 'powers and processes of arrest'. The latter provision is of particular interest because in some sense, whether implicit or explicit, it contains an appeal for doorstaff to apprehend suspected (criminal) offenders and summon police intervention.

The extent, however, to which trainers share, and thus communicate, this ambition is less clear. Dependent variables, for example, the precise nature and extent of police contributions (whether steering or rowing) and the interpretative discretion of trainers, commonly influence the tone of any appeals for closer 'partnership' relations. For instance, significant numbers of private training companies comprise of former licensed premises security. These training providers are less inclined to inculcate the partnership message, not least because such actions stand in sharp contrast to culturally embedded peer group custom—perhaps the main arterial vein through which accountability flows to the bouncer (Stenning, 1995:5). Training courses may arrange a basic education in relevant aspects of criminal law and procedure, though the extent to which

---

[12] Following on from Jones and Newburn (1998), we view the private–public justice segregation in terms of a continuum, the axis of which moves through degrees of organization and formality, from (private) informal forms to (public) formal forms. In this conjecture, the fundamental principle to understand is that private justice refers to non-state forms of behavioural regulation (ibid.:184).

doorstaff initiate this law into action is less certain. If bouncers are to resolve disputes through such formal means as the public justice system then this will be an outcome of highly discretionary individual *and* peer group decisions that are informed by a combination of situational, cultural, and commercial factors.

Bouncing is a form of 'client-directed' policing that serves the narrow interests of private employers (Shearing and Stenning, 1983b:502). This is the (unspoken) backdrop to training mandates and also the reason why 'public interest tuition' should be viewed as optional guidance rather than compulsory instruction. If public interest goals are to be actively pursued by private operatives, such as bouncers, then first they must tally with *confidential* commercial confidences (Shapland, 1999:29). This points toward the scope for divergence between 'what police managers want' and 'what club managers want' in relation to the content of what door security are supposed to do in any given (public-interest) situation. Wide scope for tension abounds state requests (by means of training or otherwise) for doorstaff to evolve closer working practices with the public police, not least because the crime control mandate of the latter can severely threaten the 'loss prevention' function of the former (Shearing and Stenning, 1980). As a result, the outcomes of any emerging collaborative work are entirely commercially conditioned. The veracity of this observation can be illustrated by reference to recent legal edicts, which among other things reveal the tensions that overlay the juxtaposition of 'commercial accountability' and 'public interest'.

Broadly speaking recent regulatory legislation, which has tightened the operating conditions of licensed premises, places a greater burden of responsibility onto security. For example, the Public Entertainments (Drugs Misuse) Act 1997 threatens a licensed premises' PEL status if serious drug use is evidenced. Given this regulatory context, local police directives for doorstaff to maintain a 'drugs box' of discovered illegal substances (thereafter the contents of which are scrutinized by the police), require particularly 'prudent' implementation strategies. In the same manner, police requests for bouncers to apprehend drug offenders are viewed through the lens of loss prevention. Consequently, some premises that perceive no immediate coercive threat from the state are more willing to instruct security to co-operate with police 'partnership' requests and directives; others that are less secure instruct security to be discerning in the manner that they 'deal with the law'. Similarly, the Criminal

Justice and Police Act 2001, which contains new police powers to order the immediate closure of licensed premises in the event of disorder, generates pressure for licensees to instruct their doorstaff to adopt and maintain an informal, 'self-help' approach to managing violent incidents and offenders.[13] Although of course, other situational variables such as whom, why, and what, also exert a strong influence, these commercial pressures are, in a ubiquitous sense, the primary contextual backdrop to decisions regarding the extent to which bouncers will invoke police attention. In the absence of legal obligation these structurally induced pressures, passed down to private security agents through legal edicts, training provisions, or otherwise are always strictly commercially filtered.

As mentioned, aside from the role taken by commercial account-ability, workplace custom also influences the nature and extent to which bouncers co-operate with the police. As we established in our discussion of occupational culture (see Chapter 5), suspicion of the state's formal apparatus engenders a strongly demarcated sense of self, the sentiment of which, on one occasion, was bluntly described to us as 'we don't do a policeman's job'. Consequently, state appeals for the two policing agencies to be 'partners in order-maintenance' (Shearing and Stenning, 1981:220) often fall on deaf ears. As Reiss suggests, 'where moral commitment is lost subcultural practices take over' (1971:138), an observation which amplifies with resonance when policing practices are commercially rather than legally or morally codified. Furthermore, our observations lead us to suspect that within the classroom environs of formal training a parallel socialization process is taking place, for training classes also bring opportunities for the uninitiated to collectively rub shoulders with more experienced colleagues and to learn the group norms, and the accepted occupational custom (see also Fielding, 1988:51 ff). To the amassed group of 'students' official directives on emergency procedures and legislative mandates appear remote and abstract, and thus generate a consensus of impassivity that informally socializes group members into the detached stance of the occupational culture. The perceived irrelevance of formal training serves to reinforce group understandings of difference and isolation. If attendees are at all

---

[13] In pragmatic custom, bouncers sometimes falsely suggest that the police have been summoned as a 'scare tactic' to disperse members of the public involved in conflictual situations either with each other or with the security team.

unsure of the occupation's cultural stance toward the state and its allies, then mock, not to say belligerent, group responses to training programmes place them firmly in the picture.

The bouncer's preference for informal methods of dispute resolution is not only symptomatic of suspicion toward the state's apparatus of control, but is also born of pragmatism grounded within the workplace. For example, apprehending criminal offenders has considerable potential to amplify conflict between detainee and doorstaff. This threatens any residual ambitions to practise 'policing by consent' and simultaneously increases the individual bouncer's situational exposure to risk—an important reason why, as with public police management of public order incidents, the occupational culture steers individuals toward informal outcomes (Stenning, 2000). One of our informants placed this issue in the following, rather vivid perspective:

> We don't involve the police. Every single time the police say, 'if you get a drug dealer, doesn't matter how small it is, you must phone us up, tell us, nick him.' They wanted us to hold them and phone them. I say 'that's fine for you, that's fantastic for you, but what about me?' Know what I mean? You'd be shot dead; you wouldn't last two minutes in the job. I park my car here and this is a black alley, I could be shot, stabbed, I mean, I've been threatened six or seven times by people with guns. So you're living on a knife-edge and the police don't understand that. So then they say, 'can you not put him out of a certain door?' But if we've got to walk a potential drug dealer from one end of a club to the other, it's not safe for us inside, especially if he's with forty or fifty lads which is the case sometimes. If you go into that situation you can create more trouble than what the situation deserves really. Marcus

Of course within the flexible realms of private policing a wide range of 'toolbox' options are available, as viable informal alternatives to arrest, perhaps primary among which is exclusion (whether through denial of entry or ejection from premises) (Shearing and Stenning, 1981; see also Chapter 5). Of particular significance to the regulatory endeavour, a further informal alternative is the application of physical pain. Although we stress that the bouncer's use of force is overwhelmingly instrumental in nature (i.e. a pragmatic, future-ordering tool of commercial governance), the moral element (i.e. a 'backward-looking', retributive punishment of a wrongful act), cannot be entirely discounted (Shearing, 2001). Hess implicitly expounds the moral dimension of the distribution of violence, suggesting that 'criminal actions, measured by the criterion of the formal law, are better understood as sanctions of an informal legal system if one realizes the general problem of subcultural peculiarities and the need for self-help within the subcultural social system' (1998:147). In a similar manner, the remote isolation of doorstaff expedites the application of retributive justice upon the occasional, overstepping, unfortunate. Training provisions aim to prevent the dispensation of this form of 'justice' by reducing the remoteness between door security and state agencies. Yet, as we imply, the distribution of violence by bouncers is, for the most part, best understood not as a form of 'justice' *per se*, but rather as a valued mechanism in the governance of commercial security (see Rigakos, 2002). If training regimes are able to persuade bouncers to manage conflict in a more formal manner, then certainly in respect of the moral formulation of force, harm reduction benefits should follow. This applies far less equally, however, to the bouncers' use of instrumental force, the situational expediency of which clearly cannot be matched by distal and uncertain threats from the state's criminal justice system.

Let's get physical: training to be (like) Steven Seagal

A small minority of courses incorporate practical demonstrations of 'control and restraint' techniques, giving rise to a significant degree of ambiguity and contention. The teaching of controlled methods of physical application does, though, raise some awkward questions in relation to the legitimate use of force, particularly when, within this context, it involves politically accountable bodies steering the training of commercially accountable agents. Police trainers in particular, fearful of both legal considerations and moral perceptions of promoting 'state-sanctioned' violence, are normally unwilling to supply or endorse such training. One police officer outlined the concerns of his local force:

There was no way the bosses would allow us to be seen to be training doormen in self-defence techniques, because by doing so, you would be giving them an inferred message that we were endorsing the behaviour of people who weren't police officers. So if somebody used extreme violence they could legitimately say, 'well I was trained to do this by Browside police'. The victim would then have an opportunity to have a go at Browside police for actually training someone for what turned out to be a criminal act, so we had to decide what we were and weren't prepared to do.

This reservation implies that if licensing broadly represents the state leasing policing responsibility to others, then the dilemmas to be confronted centre around where, in terms of political sanction, the limitations to that lease should be drawn and with what conditions attached. The legitimate use of coercive force is a fundamental characteristic of the public police (Manning, 1977), the institutional sources of which underpin the state's very claims to legitimacy (Cohen, 1985). Consequently, these wider political concerns overhang the role of controlled force training and its potential import upon harm reduction outcomes. Indicative of these concerns, material gathered from one course detailed the instruction of 'light strikes to immobilize the aggressor' and the 'application of pressure to nerve areas for restraint'. The practical application of such instructions, however, must be viewed against the legal threshold of 'reasonable force' which bouncers may lawfully use when removing customers from licensed premises under section 3(1) of the Criminal Law Act 1967. Consequently, through the embodiment of private property rights, the bouncer's use of physical force can be objectively determined as legitimate, though the nebulous term 'reasonable force' is always subjectively tied to situational contingency. The legitimacy of the bouncer's use of force, then, is conditional and bounded, and of key concern is the extent to which relevant training succeeds in shifting wider perceptions thereof. The obvious danger is that some licensed bouncers might appropriate, extend, and contort the meaning of legitimate or reasonable (minimum) 'physical contact', and therefore the state, having coalesced in this arrangement, will have facilitated a blurring of the demarcation thresholds of legitimate force.[14] In this scenario, training and by association licensing, become less a process of regulation and more a mechanism of empowerment (South, 1988).

This matter flags one of the central conundrums of licensing debates: the extent to which regulatory provisions are seen to enable or constrain power. Given that abuses of power, manifest through assault, were routinely cited as a principal motive to regulate the trade, this question gains some urgency when considered within the

---

[14] One local authority officer, who oversees controlled force training, told us that he had twice appeared in court to successfully defend bouncers accused of assault offences. On both occasions he testified that the levels of force applied by the bouncers had been consistent with those taught by the local state.

context of physical training techniques. South (ibid.:132) suggests that in order to navigate the pitfalls of this dichotomy the process of regulation requires balancing between, on the one hand, the pro-scriptive approach that limits legitimate action, and on the other, the prescriptive approach that permits legitimate action. Whilst trainers undoubtedly vary in approach, one local authority trainer we spoke with echoed the sentiment contained within South's analysis:

The reason we've got it [controlled force training] is because every night doormen have to lay hands on people and we spend a lot of time talking to them about reasonable force—what is reasonable force, what you can and you can't do in legal terms. And they say to us 'well what can I do?' So what we try to do in the restraint technique is really to show them two or three safe methods of laying hands on individuals that, probably, if they used them, they would be able to demonstrate that they've used reasonable force in the circumstances.

Training courses that adopt this approach intrinsically acknowledge that the main function of doorstaff is the maintenance of a commer-cially defined, social order. Unsurprisingly therefore, our informants overwhelmingly supported the teaching of control and restraint techniques, perceiving it to be an area of skill-based learning that is of central importance to the security function. Although we argue in Chapter 5 that once violence reaches certain boundaries then polite physical force is largely rhetorical, harm reduction benefits may be derived from attempting to refine the non-combative 'physical' aspects of the job such as routine ejections (see Lister et al., 2001b). Even if, as suggested, training sessions simply demonstrate 'what not to do', then some value, in terms of reducing injuries both to customers and bouncers, should be forthcoming. However, in the light of current training provisions, a caveat must be offered: if techniques of restrained violence are to be appropriately communi-cated and implemented, then a rolling programme of tuition may be necessary, rather than 'one-off' demonstrations. The time afforded to teaching physical control techniques is, we argue, insufficient to affect seriously the raw techniques acquired in the workplace (see Chapter 5).[15] Moreover, as one of our informants explained, the

[15] The approximate average time duration donated to this aspect of training is three hours; similar courses for mental health unit personnel average five days (Lynch, 2002).

intention to practise controlled force techniques may unravel at just those times when it is most required:

The police, I've seen them in Marseilles how they've been dealing with their minimum restraint techniques, and the truth of the matter is: when the shit goes down you've got to get it sorted. We like to get in there quick and effective, get them down if it warrants that. The last thing you want to be doing is kicking off with some guy and you're fighting rolling around the floor of a unit like at school. You've got to get in there and be quick and effective and deal with it. And what they've taught us or shown us is quite effective I suppose. But if you're a doorman and you've got ten years' experience, then you will have come up with your own way of dealing with things. I mean, it's not all the time you can take somebody and get their wrist and loop their arm working on the hinge joint applying pressure—it's very difficult to use minimum force when someone is shoving a blade in your face or if someone is coming at you with a bar stool, then what you going to do? You know we're not all Steven Seagal, sweep his legs and then [does karate chop]. It doesn't work like that. Bernie

The teaching of control and restraint techniques betrays an all- too-rare acceptance, particularly among state administrators with a training steering role, that bouncing takes place within a high risk and routinely threatening social context. The neglect of context within overall training schedules invites criticism that a symbolic notion of training is being delivered, one which leaves 'students' querying its relevance and applicability to the lived reality of the role. This is, in part, because training is a managerial exercise that seeks to buy an element of political and commercial respectability for this much-maligned occupation. Bouncers with qualifications make for great media copy, but in many ways this is politically expedient training, which is widely cited and makes a virtue out of a necessity. As implied, the introduction of some form of training should be applauded, though we would argue that given their limited duration, the courses are perhaps best viewed as short, awareness raising programmes rather than comprehensive forms of occupational training. In this respect, the assertive manner in which interest groups promote 'their' bouncers as 'fully trained' exposes the political, commercial, and rhetorical slants of the exercise.

If licensing represents an initiative that aspires to affect behavioural change by sharpening external processes of accountability, then training *ought* to aim to 'personalize processes of behaviour change *within* the individual' (Lightfoot, 1988:14). This would seem a central task in the process of professionalization, though perhaps more importantly training regimes must engage effectively with the occupational culture that shapes working custom. Training developments represent a tentative, if largely symbolic, first step towards this ambition. However, the extent to which current arrangements aspire to instil 'processes of change' by stimulating an occupational ethos supported by 'professional' attributes and based on personal or moral commitment, is questionable. Where concepts such as procedural fairness, non-arbitrary use of power, equitable treatment, and legitimate use of force are discussed—albeit rarely—within training manuscripts, then in all probability such talk isn't reinforced by the 'war stories' or the biographical experiences that shape individual and collective responses to occupational work demands (Van Mannen, 1978b:268). We discuss more fully the valourization of individualized violence in Chapter 5; suffice it to say here that current training regimes bear minimal impact on this barrier to 'professionalization'. The emergence of a more 'professionalized bouncer' is a product of commercial tuning not moral leaning; the attainment of training qualifications is little more than emblematic of this outcome.

Watching the watchers: enforcement, revocation, and accountability

How are you going to enforce it? The Council might have one enforcement officer, he might not be able to check everything up, he might not be able to do all the work required. It's all very well having a system, and having it on the PEL, but if you haven't got any form of enforcement, then you might as well not have it to start with. Mark

Despite local variation in enforcement policy and practice, a range of broad commonalities were apparent across registration schemes. Markedly, because local authorities rather than the police own the vast majority of schemes, primarily, (state) enforcement responsibility rests with the former not the latter. Yet, given that police officers—however few in number—rather than local authority officers routinely patrol city centre streets on weekend evenings, we argue they are structurally better placed proactively to enforce registration. The overlapping of roles, in time and space, between door-staff and police officers establishes a symbiotic relationship (whether positively or negatively slanted), which—comparatively speaking—

is operationally conducive to achieving enforcement goals. Within some city centre divisions, police officers *are* explicitly directed to consider licence enforcement, but without direct ownership of the schemes, this is more the exception rather than the rule. Yet, in such cases, the extent to which enforcement processes are systematically implemented may be called into question by the fire-fighting nature of night-time, city centre police work. Viewed in this context, the implementation of enforcement duties may acquire a low priority status.

Local authority enforcement practice tends to occur within the broad scope of multi-agency inspections, which include fire and general health and safety checks. These enforcement skirmishes are relatively bureaucratic in procedure and, our informants insisted, are seldom in evidence on the streets—an impression perhaps fostered by the fact that some city centres have over 500 licensed premises policed by over 2,000 doorstaff. One local authority licensing officer suggested that, within the context of multi-agency inspections, bureaucratic constraints severely limit the extent of reactive, intelligence-based enforcement, and so consequently a more methodical, systematic approach is usually preferred. Another, casting doubt upon the effectiveness of this latter detection strategy, suggested that enforcement teams rarely manage to inspect more than four premises per (bi-monthly) excursion, and that 'once you are out on the streets it takes about twenty seconds for every night-club to know about it—I think the phones start going berserk'. Enforcement practices across the majority of schemes appear at best patchy and at worst non-existent; an empirical finding replicated within other emerging studies, either implicitly (Hughes et al., 2002) or explicitly (Maguire and Nettleton, 2003). One agency manager, who runs doors nationwide, shared the following view:

Which local authority wants to pay somebody overtime to walk round from seven o'clock till half eleven at night checking licences on doors? Not many: it's not cost effective. Councils are very keen to take money from the registration schemes, but not so keen to enforce them. They say they do, but they don't. I've never seen them; my men have never seen them. And the licensees, it's a low priority for them isn't it? As long as their pubs are safe, are they bothered? What are they going to do, send them away and have no door cover for the evening? I don't think so. Ricky, agency manager.

This view advocates that licensees relegate the priority of enforcement responsibilities to more pressing, functional concerns. The extent to which licensees strictly enforce the registration requirement is unclear. It is true to say, however, that if purchasers *do* insist that providers are licensed, then the dominance of contract, as opposed to in-house, employment arrangements can, on occasion, surreptitiously undermine this ambition. Confronted with an often intimidating and remote security presence, discretion sometimes transcends the better part of valour.

Across the sixty local authorities surveyed only two licensees had faced prosecution proceedings for employing unregistered labour. While this might suggest that adherence to the registration requirement is high, we interpret this as indicative of an enforcement process that seeks to encourage compliance rather than impose legal sanction (Hawkins, 1984; Hutter, 1997). This strategy exposes the moral dimensions of door regulation, wherein the absence of a tangible 'victim', the formulation of 'the offence' is 'morally problematic' (Hawkins, 1997:10) and, thus, compliance rather than penalty imposition becomes the administrator's goal. Hence if rule-breaking is uncovered, conforming outcomes are negotiated whereby a series of conventional or discretionary warnings flow between administrators and licensees. In this process, suitable space is provided for licensees to 'right the wrong' and resolve the tension between economy and state; consequently prosecution is rare or *in extremis* (ibid.:191 ff), and the immediate threat of coercive, legal deterrents some way relieved (Cook, 1989).

Notwithstanding the strategy of regulators, deviant practices further undermine effective enforcement. As Friedman (1962:155) suggests, 'whenever you establish a block to entry into any field, you establish an incentive to find ways of getting around it'. Indeed, badge swapping practices,[16] false licence applications, and black-markets in registration badges and training certificates were not uncommon. Moreover, even if public enforcement agents are able to 'penetrate the private domains' (Manning, 1987:306) of the night-time economy, their ability to detect unregistered bouncers is hampered by the 'low visibility' of private security (Shearing and Stenning, 1981:218). Within doorwork this characteristic enables a

---

[16] Perhaps surprisingly, a number of licence badges bear neither a name nor a photograph.

cat and mouse game to be played with regulators, as one doorman described:

They've got too much work on their hands to pass around every single club and check who is and isn't badged. There's so many pubs and clubs and people who want private security, it doesn't work, they haven't got the time—the police are understaffed as it is, poor blighters. Even if the police turn up and there's checks from the entertainment licence officer then, you're talking about: 'just take your jacket off and start dancing', know what I'm talking about? Paul

Evidently, a problematic definitional issue encumbers the enforcement process, whereby 'ghost bouncers' appear as anything but paid security agents, be that sizeable 'glass collectors', 'friends' of the licensee merely 'helping out', or just ordinary punters. This observation evokes consideration of the role of non-security specialists, and of course, particularly within smaller licensed premises, general bar staff, pub regulars, and not least licensees are frequently involved in managing conflict and dealing with disorder. Hence, although designated the specific responsibility of door security, the necessity to impose a commercially-tuned social order is a rudimentary feature of securing profitable private enterprise. On occasion this commercial imperative requires an 'all hands on deck' approach, a characteristic of commercial control that door regulation per se, let alone enforcement agents, cannot address.

We were also informed of more organized conspiracies whereby registration instigates an advanced 'moral division of labour' (Harris, 1978:273) within the security function of some licensed premises. In this approach, unlicensed labour is employed to protect the registered status and commercial credibility of licensed colleagues. This involves two teams of door personnel working at a premises, one overtly and one covertly, the latter hold licences and act accordingly, the former blend into the background until the need for 'dirty work' (ibid.) arises. A police officer described the typical scenario:

Clubs now will employ a group of four unregistered guys who are the real bouncers. And what happens is that if there's trouble, these unregistered guys in plain clothes go in and sort it out, and [then] the registered bouncers do the official ejection. And when they say 'I was assaulted by a group of men in the club', the official bouncers turn round and say 'yeah we saw them, can't really describe them to you, it was a group of strangers, we have no knowledge of them'. They keep their reputation intact, 'cause they split them up and got them out, and the problem's solved. And the illicit bouncers get whatever payment per night, but it's the only way that they feel they can work and protect the legitimate bouncers' occupation and reputation so they can maintain the licensing and doorstaff reputation, and it is known about and surreptitiously accepted.

These organized conspiracies are a 'perverse outcome' (Osborne and Gaebler, 1992:290) of the registration agenda, and evidence the extent to which commercial practices are potentially propelled further out of view by state regulation that intends the opposite effect. Thus, at some premises, the forms of accountability that registration most intends to sharpen acquire instead a troubling bluntness. Furthermore, the social organization of this dual system of policing, like the role of bouncing itself, should be viewed as a situational response to the commercial exigencies of the external environment. In other words, such conspiracies re-emphasize the fact that whilst licensing aims to change the behavioural comportment of bouncers, it has little if any bearing upon the fixed (physical) demands of the role.

Symptomatic of wider enforcement problems, a perceptively small number of licence revocations occur across schemes. Admittedly a difficult area in which to gather reliable systematic data (designated officers move jobs and records are rarely kept), it appears that this necessary threat is a relatively lame one. More than twenty schemes contacted indicated that no licence revocations had occurred, and many administrators could be no more accurate beyond 'one or two' or 'very few indeed' (see Jacobs, 1983, for similar findings with regard to US security regulators). There are several interrelated reasons for this finding, which, significantly, are located widely within interest group reactions to regulation *per se* rather then narrowly within the compliance model of administrative enforcement.[17] Public complaint procedures, intended to facilitate revocations, operate across the majority of schemes. Interestingly, however, this negative feature of licensing tends to receive little if any publicity, certainly in comparison to the positive features,

---

[17] Compliance enforcement systems tend to involve victims in an aggregated sense, as opposed to the presence of a direct victim or complainant (Reiss and Biderman, 1980:298). In contrast, revocation procedures intrinsically involve a tangible complainant.

namely, training and vetting aspects. This lays bare the political dimension of door regulation, whereby within the context of 'selling city-centre safety', the negative though necessary operational requirements of licensing (e.g. matters of enforcement and revocation), are demoted to the shadows of the regulatory exercise. Within this context, publicizing (uncovered) evidence of ongoing problems is not on the registration agenda. Therein, the public face of law enforcement assumes precedence within politically expedient action that is geared towards providing symbolic reassurance. This is a salient political phenomena, of which Edelman observes, 'Some of the most widely publicized administrative activities can most confidently be expected to convey a sense of well-being to the onlooker because they suggest vigorous activity while in actual fact signifying inactivity...' (1964:38).

To some extent the lack of publicity that surrounds revocation procedures loads the dice against one of the main interest groups, namely the public, from taking up their full stake in regulation. Certainly, the administrators whom we spoke with stated that public complaints were simply not forthcoming in any great numbers. This may also be because only the most aggrieved (and courageous) complainant would embark on such a process and, moreover, the police, rather than the administrators of a licensing scheme, are most likely to be the first, and the only, port of call for an aggrieved member of the public. If this is true, then public accountability wanes further because an underlying cultural acceptance of night-time city centre violence suppresses the reporting of incidents to state agencies (see Lister et al., 2000). As one doorman suggested of assaults involving colleagues:

Even if they [the police] do find the lad, most of the time he's not even going to want to talk about it, especially not to a copper. If a bouncer gives you a dig, you're going to wake up the next day and think fuck it. Most people don't want to get involved in that kind of thing. You've got to remember it's normally the lad's fault, he's not going to get a dig for nothing. Stevie North

Significantly, local authorities, mindful of the legal fragility of the schemes, and attempting to adhere to the laws of natural justice, collectively indicate a strict unwillingness to revoke licences without a relevant court conviction. The problem therein is that the trade is relatively unaccountable to the criminal law, particularly in relation to assault offences. Assaults are not only hugely under-reported, but also relatively difficult to prove in court (Clarkson et al., 1994). Moreover, gaining an assault conviction against a bouncer can be particularly problematic. We interrogated the Crime Information System of one city centre police division and found that, over a three-year period, forty-two incidents of assault, involving bouncers as alleged assailants, were recorded. Of these assault allegations, which were reported with sufficient vigour for an investigation to be initiated, only one resulted in a successful conviction at court, and even this case did not result in a licence revocation.[18] Further analysis of the forty-one 'closed files' suggested that the occupational culture of bouncers gives rise to the adoption of strategies and devices that are successfully employed as defensive mechanisms designed to frustrate police assault investigations (Lister et al., 2000). While police files are merely *allegations* of assault, this ratio of convictions indicates that accountability to the criminal law and, by extension, local licensing systems is relatively low. Moreover, these findings would suggest that the implementation of the latter yield minimal impact upon the processes of the former.

Even when relevant court convictions are gained, revocations do not automatically follow. There is, commonly, no formal mechanism or efficient system of relay to communicate court outcomes to scheme administrators. Police IT systems do not 'flag' doorstaff or cross-reference convicted offenders with registration databases. Furthermore, the construction of operational silos stifles the efficiency of inter-agency communication. One local authority officer observed that 'even if there's no conviction, we're relying on the police saying, "look this person's been involved in too many incidents, we would like him hauled up in front of committee". But no one's coming back to us on anything'. Consequently some administrators only hear of relevant convictions through reading the local press. Effective communication between police divisions and forces is also far from a given. The only standardized means of communicating offences is through the Police National Computer checks, which are conducted typically only once every three years, on licence renewal. Most

---

[18] Though the force involved professed to employ *prima facie* recording practices (which allows crime allegations to be more readily recorded than under the *evidential* model), we would argue that, at the time of the research, the discretion of individual officers remained the prevailing and dominant factor within police recording practices.

schemes, therefore, rely upon a licensing policy of non-renewal, rather then revocation, to exclude 'rogue' bouncers.[19]

In light of the above discussion we are hesitant toward the effectiveness of enforcement regimes, both in relation to licensees and to doorstaff, not least because deterrents against non-compliance are seemingly neither stringent in application nor robust in procedure. Furthermore, we would argue that the deterrence function of licensing bears most impact upon individuals who retain a longer-term view of their position within the trade. Although we encountered many bouncers that had worked the doors for a number of years, transient labour is an identifiable feature, not to say a resource of the business. This is problematic to developing and maintaining effective channels of public accountability, a point not lost on Stenning and Shearing who saliently observe that 'attempts to impose sophisticated regulatory controls over industries with such a high turnover of personnel are almost inevitably doomed to failure' (1981:234).

The number of doorstaff consistently working without a licence is unclear, yet so is the extent to which public monitoring teams penetrate effectively the private 'bubbles of governance' (Shearing, 2001) that function within licensed premises. Furthermore, bouncers working within venues that experience high(er) rates of disorder are, we found, required to practise a more coercive style of policing, which in turn leads to a greater degree of regulatory avoidance behaviour. Moreover, the extent to which a public licensing system can be enforced *with effect* upon organized crime groups is, we were extensively informed, limited (see Chapters 3 and 7). These outcomes suggest that the enforcement agenda is least effective where it is most needed—a re-emergence of the old criminological truism that those communities most in need of crime prevention treatment are frequently the most difficult in which to successfully intervene (Skogan, 1988).

Market development, market diversification, and the division of labour

As mentioned at the outset to this chapter, redeeming the poor reputation of licensed premises security has been a function of

---

[19] A handful of police-run schemes are able to buck this trend because (a) they are less inclined to adhere to the rules of natural justice, namely, revocation procedures and (b) police officers learn of doorstaff incidents more frequently than do local authority officers, be that through word of mouth, administrative processes, or access to the PNC.

sustaining capital investment within the night-time economy, and an attempt to create an aura of 'professionalism' around the trade has been central to this exercise. Licensing systems which, we argue, aim to bestow such professionalism through the expression of state-sanctioned legitimacy, have clearly played a key role within this process. Indeed, the expressive function of licensing is intimately entwined with this re-branding exercise. Thus in the same manner that British Nuclear Fuels changed overnight the name of 'Windscale' to 'Sellafield', both the state and commerce have made significant efforts to re-brand the bouncer as a new and thoroughly domesticated breed, the 'door supervisor'. This turn in political language is part of a wider process that bids to stimulate and ensconce more robust mechanisms of commercially compatible, self-regulation. This process has, in large part, been enabled by changes occurring within the door security marketplace simultaneously to the recent implementation of local licensing initiatives. In this, the provision of licensed premises security has developed and expanded in a responsive manner to the growth of the night-time economy. This market development should be understood as a process of market diversification, whereby across parts of the trade more stringent, professional practices are slowly evolving to replace indigenous, casual practices. To appreciate fully the significance of this process, it is necessary to briefly consider the historical and economic context of the trade.

As we stress, the roots of door security are firmly entrenched within the informal economy, the key feature of which is the absence of organized, external regulation (Mattera, 1985). Within this context, the labour market has traditionally been characterized by a relatively transient and casually (dis)organized supply side and a demand side that largely views security as a non-profit-making cost. Consequently, purchasers held—and to some extent still hold—a deprecating view of security, which inevitably tied security arrangements to least cost thresholds. This commercially expedient approach, complemented by purchasers failing to differentiate (economically, if not literally) between service standards, blended with the fiercely competitive nature of the security market to hamper the emergence of more professional standards of service delivery (South, 1988). Subsequently, in large part, the 'bad money drove out the good' because 'dishonest dealings tend to drive honest dealings out of the market' (Akerlof, 1970:495). A number of the agency managers whom we interviewed broadly suggested that this informality, and the local nature of the business, led to the market being dominated by a multitude of small-scale, low level operators all-too-keen to take flight from official forms of external regulation and of accountability (see Chapter 4). Moreover, within this context, the same informants suggested the existence of a correlative connection between casual wages and casual violence. However, these generic economic conditions, which operated upon the trade when registration first emerged, no longer hold true upon the industry as a *whole*.

Over the last decade, the enormous surges of capital flowing into the night-time economy have led security purchasers to consider greatly the nature, form, and content of the 'door services' hired to protect the commercial sovereignty of sizeable financial investments. However, as implied, the extent to which door security actually has the potential to impact adversely upon profits began to be fully realized by the licensed trade. In this manner, the loss prevention function of door security became increasingly apparent to a range of commercially exposed corporate clients, many of whom modified their economically frugal approach to demand thereafter. Furthermore, the increased regulatory emphasis placed on the operation of licensed premises, for example, The Public Entertainments Licences (Drugs Misuse Act) 1997, also cast a weighty burden of responsibility onto security and, importantly, upon the purchasers of their services. At the same time, the quantitative expansion of the night-time economy has generated a qualitative diversification in the operating style and targeted consumer profile of venues (see Chapter 1). Increasingly, therefore, sections of the licensed trade began to demonstrate heightened discernment with regard to the type and quality of the individuals and agencies employed to protect their premises. Consequently, in addition to investing far more heavily in security than previously, some leisure and brewery corporations are beginning to formalize the nature of their security relations, for example, insisting that employed security agencies hold suitable insurance and VAT registration forms; some are even introducing formal contracts into purchaser arrangements. And, of course, some purchasers attempt to utilize only the services of registered doorstaff.

In response to these changes in demand, a number of security agencies began to offer an increasingly client-sensitive, commercially-tuned form of service delivery, and subsequently a greater range of client-orientated services are now available to purchasers.

Crudely put, market development has progressed in this manner because the sheer weight of money fanning around the door trade has led to the increased commercialization of the trade: an industry that originated out of a want to earn 'beer money' is now big business. Inevitably this has led to some upgrade in processes of commercial accountability and professionalism among *some* companies contesting the marketplace (i.e. companies with more stringent, transparent and accountable management structures). In consolidation of this change some doorstaff have adopted a less coercive demeanour than was traditionally on view. In addition to the malleability of this core concern, the emergence of greater bureaucratic organization within the larger national and regional door agencies is producing a greater degree of standardization of working practice. These dimensions of professionalization involve manipulation of the presentation of self, in terms of body type, hairstyle, standards of dress, and also general comportment and communicative protocols. In order to underline their distinction as 'professionals', the staff employed by such agencies are deliberately selected and groomed to work in a manner which emphasizes impressions of cultural distance from traditional images of the menacing bouncer.

These changes should be understood as commercially driven processes of economic specialization. This process not only creates a division of labour *between* but also, importantly, *within* security providers. Importantly, this has led to a sizeable increase in pay differentials and, significantly in some quarters (particularly the late-night sector), the employment of women, which has begun to challenge elements of the previously male-dominated occupational culture (see Chapter 9). Accordingly, commercially progressive agency managers were quick to offer that the role of female doorstaff facilitated the appearance of a more consensual approach to the security task, which at times returned significant dividends in terms of diffusing potentially problematic situations. Yet many of our male interviewees, seemingly informed by a stoically traditional view of gender protocols, failed to see their practical 'policing' value beyond the obviously gendered tasks of 'working the women's toilets and searching handbags and bodies at the entrance'. This perspective is confirmation that, for the vast majority of male bouncers, the physical, coercive side of the role was the *raison d'être* of the job, and in this respect many appeared to believe that females could donate little to the cause.

The recent diversification of licensed spaces within the night-time economy has led to a reciprocal diversification in the marketplace for door security, around which processes of professionalism are tied. Yet as we stress, fundamentally the function of the role remains the same—the provision of commercial security. In much the same manner, and as we proceed to emphasize (see Chapter 8), the diversification of the licensed environment itself offers limited nuance because the vast majority of venues remain essentially alcohol-dominated leisure spaces in which strangers, acquaintances, and sometimes antagonists take 'time out' in close proximity both to each other. We are also cautious not to overstate the resonance and impact of these commercial self-regulatory processes across the industry as a whole. Large swathes of the licensed trade retain a traditionally narrow and deprecating view of the security function, and therefore much of the door trade remains untouched by commercial pressures to 'professionalize'. Moreover, as we detail above, the division of labour enables the more 'professional face' of bouncing to stand in the regulatory spotlight of revisionists, whilst those tasked with the 'dirty work' continue to loiter in the shadows.

Licensing badges: symbols of safety, symptoms of threat

If the regulatory process is examined in terms of the divergence between political and legal promises on the one hand and resource allocations and group reactions on the other hand, the largely symbolic nature of the entire process becomes apparent (Edelman, 1964:23).

You look at the bouncers in this town, they are not employed to be diplomatic, they are boys, know what I mean? That is why they are there, it is ridiculous to pretend otherwise. Mark

A large number of social and political theorists have considered the extent to which state regulations successfully resolve the tensions between economy and state (for summaries see Edelman, 1964: Chapter 2; Hutter, 1997: Chapter 1; Lowi, 1969; Ogus, 1994: Chapter 1). Murray Edelman's writings point toward the symbolic function of much governmental regulation, which although designed to protect the public, actually produces little in the way of conciliatory outcomes beyond conveying the appearance of control (1964, 1977). Central to Edelman's argument is the role of spectator reassurance, which is generated by an over-simplistic response to remote political symbols within the public policy arena. This perspective connects with our analysis of door registration schemes principally because state-issued licences, intended to connote 'safety' or the suppression of threats through the symbol of a badge, actually resolve little in the tension level between economy and state out of which threat emerges. Licence badges appear to the public as a distant 'parade of abstractions' (Edelman, 1964:10), the common meaning of which is interpreted either as a symbol of reassurance or a symptom of threat; for badges received as symbols of safety, betoken figures of coercion. The antipathetic nature of the registration agenda resurfaces but cannot be dissipated inasmuch that the 'tension between threat and reassurance inevitably continues for all concerned; but role-taking assures that a viable pattern of private and public action will emerge: that both private and public actors will survive and that the former can continue to exert what sanctions they possess' (ibid.:189). 'Role-taking' within the registration process concerns the manner in which administrators, tasked with implementation, assimilate the perspective of the regulated group, the politico-economic needs of the state, the commercial interests of capital, and the inherent tensions of the bouncer role which surface through the registration agenda. This agenda grants public *licence* to private practices, it legitimizes and empowers, and whether threatening or reassuring, the shine of the licence badge reflects an expressive purpose inasmuch as 'political symbolization has its catharsis function' (Lasswell, 1960:195).

Other 'group reactions' to door regulation are less ambiguous. Leisure corporations 'capture' (Bernstein, 1955) the registration agenda, and thereby promote it as a means to blur and confuse the wider safety issues of the night-time leisure environment. Yet given the rigours of social ordering within pubs and clubs, public accountability defaults to commercial accountability. Shapland acknowledges the inevitability of this outcome, suggesting that 'if service standards are seen as a commercial, and hence a commercially confidential matter, then it is very difficult to develop effective measures, or create codes of practice about how third parties (such as the public) should be treated' (1999:29). In this manner, public police agencies, summoned by licensees and security on a 'when it suits' basis, will face a continuous struggle to harness private interests in furtherance of wider public interests. The jeopardy is that if the two policing providers *do* become closer 'partners in order-maintenance' then some (role-taking) police officers, demonstrating symmetrical understandings and an empathetic appreciation of the harsh demands of the policing role, may more readily collude with their private 'colleagues' over 'difficult incidents' (Lister et al., 2000).

Local authorities, wishing to present positive 'action on safety', offer little by way of enforcement resources and plenty by way of political acquiescence to the wider overtures of the market. Discarding the specific uncertainties of implementation, regulators are able to cite registration within their robust claims for a safe, night-time, trading environment. Put another way, registration is a means of legitimizing and *accommodating* this much-vilified trade, thus bestowing (state-sanctioned) professionalism upon an occupation increasingly central to the commercial viability of the night-time economy. The analysis offered hitherto exposes the accountability shortcomings contained within this accommodation exercise, suggesting that regulating agencies offer little more than a chimera of control because 'government measures, ostensibly designed to protect the public, yield more in symbolic reassurance and mystification than in protection' (Edelman, 1977:148). State attempts to make virtuous this private policing form will inevitably founder because the liminal zones of the night-time economy are places where recourse to coercion is a primary resource of commercial control.

If the violence and intimidation distributed by bouncers is conceptualized as a commercial resource, then we begin to uncover why registration can yield only limited impact upon its allocation (Lister, 2002). For it should be recognized that the physical side of the bouncer's role is largely a response to the demands of the violent environment that the licensed trade hires bouncers to police, and in this respect the aggressive potentiality of bouncers is merely a reflection of the propensity for aggression in the night-time populous. Although training and licensing aims to influence the dynamics of this response, the problem remains that those demands, generated by the commercial facilitation of drunken comportment, stand outside the loop of occupational licensing. This observation was, for our informants, an unremarkable one:

I'm not saying it's right to hit people because it's not, but in this line of work it's going to come up and there's fuck all you can do about it. And there's no point in taking someone's licence away. The next bloke's going to be just the same isn't he? It goes for everyone I think. We aren't thugs, we're paid to do a job, and sometimes things happen. Mark

This quotation suggests that a tightly implemented occupational licensing scheme cannot withstand the demands of the 'dirty work' which corporate capital places upon bouncers. Yet, even if current licensing arrangements are viewed as little more than 'superficial systems of public accountability' (Flavel, 1973:15), the publicity that surrounds their implementation has, to some extent, succeeded in placing the 'door role' under a temporary spotlight of regulatory scrutiny. At the same time a re-branding exercise has been apparent, to the extent that in some market sectors 'door supervisors' now wear pastel blazers, are forced to cover up tattoos and stand without slouching; unfortunately broken noses are difficult to rehabilitate and, for instrumental purposes, many clearly refuse to lose the crew cut. Regulatory attention, in conjunction with commercial self-regulating mechanisms, may contribute in *some* premises to improving outcomes of inter-personnel behaviour; although the concern remains that this may not trickle down to those individuals and premises where it is most required. Whilst the licensing of bouncers may reduce some degree of violence instigated or caused by the trade, it remains a narrow response that seeks merely to ease a symptom of the violent social context within which bouncers ply their trade. For it is apparent that as long as Britain's youth-orientated and alcohol-fuelled night-time economy continues to grow unabated, the aggregate number of hired private policing hands will continue to rise significantly and, with it, aggregate levels of violence and disorder *involving* door security.

7

Market Force: Class, Violence, and Liminal Business on the Night-time Frontier

The same forces that have organized the factory and the office have organized leisure as well, reducing it to an appendage of industry (Lasch, 1979:123).

In this chapter, we will consider the cultural capital that bouncers bring with them to the night-time economy (Winlow et al, 2002), and discuss the occupational culture of bouncers as being significantly informed by contemporary masculine working-class habitus, and the commercialization of this habitus. We then proceed to consider the emergence of liminal business and its status as a mutant form of enterprise, and discuss the role of violence in both organized crime and in doorwork. Finally we will consider the long term implications for governance that result from the state encouraging and facilitating this expanded night-time economy, while simultaneously surrendering its monopoly over the means of violence to the commercial sector.

Class, commerce, and violent competence

What time is it?—Macho Time. Hector 'Macho Man' Camacho, WBC Lightweight Champion

The unleashing of market forces into the night has created an environment within which its clientele, disproportionately the young, are at risk (Hutchinson et al., 1998). However, the danger of such an analysis is that it can easily be interpreted as fuelling a moral panic concerning 'violent youth' (Hollands, 2000), and it is hoped that readers are clear that our purpose is not to further demonize the usual suspects, but rather to highlight the dangers of accepting the relentless reorganization of society 'according to so-called "free market" principles... and without much reflection on the human costs' (Currie, 1997a:147). Further, a combination of hypocrisy and incompetence on behalf of liberal society has ensured that the night-time economy has been permitted to undercut and overwhelm those functions of the state that profess to protect both individuals and communities.

Although we have highlighted both here and elsewhere (see for example Hobbs et. al., 2002) the scant resources available to the public police in dealing with this newly expanded economy, we concede of course that even in market society, déjà vu shakes hands with amnesia. For whenever British capitalism has been found wanting in dealing with a threat to profitability it has consistently turned to unregulated muscle in the guise of various forms of private policing (Hobbs, 1988:20–26). Further, this historical 'commercial compromise' (South, 1988) has also created opportunities for sub-governmental control agencies to exploit criminal opportunities (Dilnot, 1929:18–21; Tobias, 1979:48–49).

As mentioned in Chapter 6 we found teams of bouncers being organized from prison cells, and security firms run by convicted criminals working under a respectable corporate front, using violence to spread their operations from city centre pubs and clubs to impoverished communities. Local licensees were intimidated and their premises taken over, whilst local shopkeepers and householders were forced to pay a weekly premium to 'protect' themselves from burglary and criminal damage.

Pauline's story: where security meets protection

Pauline is in her early thirties and stands about five feet and six inches tall. She lives above the Long Mile pub where she has been the licensee for the last eleven months—but not for much longer. The pub sits next to a row of shops close to the centre of Dogtown. The pub is all fruit machines, fake wooden beams, ash-scarred seats, and dysfunctional carpets; recent corporate investment appears to have bypassed the Long Mile—but for prominence of security cameras. Of average size, the pub has an open plan layout with spacious alcoves and surround seating, there's also an off-room that the staff call a conservatory. Pauline took over the running of the pub eleven months ago, the procession of managers through the door should have deterred her from taking it on:

I was at a pub about a mile up the road and I was approached to take on this pub because it'd had about eight landlords in three years, and with it being only a mile between the two pubs I honestly thought it couldn't have been that much different—and with the people that I was used to having in my own pub—so I agreed to take it. Things didn't happen immediately, I was allowed to settle in for about six or eight weeks, and then it started. When you've been doing this for a while you tend to get a sense if there's trouble, you've like a sixth sense and you can feel the change of atmosphere and you know there's trouble brewing and I just kept missing it. There was just fights kicking off and I didn't feel it brewing.

Christmas was an absolute nightmare. It was just fights, fights, fights, fights all the time. At first it tended to be nineteen–twenty year olds that were fighting: groups of lads.... it was just fighting all the time, people were beginning to not start coming in because of the fighting and eventually—after Christmas—we got approached in January. We had a bloke come in, and he walked in the door, he walked through the door with six men and the first thing one of them did was reach up behind the bar—we've got a covert camera—and took the camera out, and as he's taking the camera out he's saying, 'don't fucking look at me, don't fucking look at me' and he's ripped the camera out of the bar, then he went over to the other camera and sprayed something on that so it couldn't be used. And then he started abusing the staff; we had these big heavy pots: ashtrays, he started throwing them at staff, throwing drip trays, throwing the spirit optics, and his parting shot as he walked out was 'bit of a trouble pub, you need doorstaff in here'.

A week later it was followed up by somebody walking in saying 'I believe you're looking for doorstaff,' left me his card. Well it's a front really for a protection firm. And he told me the price that it would cost me, quoting me the price, which was eight hundred pounds a week, for a Thursday night, a Friday night, a Saturday night and a Sunday night. He said probably have two on the door and one inside. I just stood there and let him do the talking, and he's promising me there would be 'no more trouble but it doesn't come cheap, but you can't carry on the way you're going 'cos you can't handle it yourself'. He did say 'you've got two young kids,' and straight away I said 'well like what's it got to do with them' and he said 'oh nothing, I'm just saying you've got to take care of yourself 'cause you've got two young kids.' And I declined. And then, we had one or two more incidents—fights in the pub. And it took the form of, there was like six men and they'd attack another one and they'd kick him until he was unconscious, they'd really knock him out, and then just pick him up and walk out with him, not leave him there, just straight out with him.

It was someone who was with them, it was all set up, but they'd seriously beat him unconscious—on two or three occasions. But then they'd take him out so there's nobody there if you phoned the police. And then it all accumulated. It came to a head in April, when I was confronted by three of them in the pub—three men and three women. They'd rolled a joint and were smoking it, and I don't have it at all, and I asked them to put it out. Immediately the three women stood up and literally backed me into a corner, I could see what was happening and the three women went for me and one of the barmaids came and helped me. And we were doing quite well against the three, but they were pushed out of the way, and the three lads were joined by another two and they started on me, a barmaid, assistant manager and another barman. We were leathered—I had a broken nose, split lip, black eyes, cracked ribs. And as they were leaving a customer turned round and said 'come on now lads, the police have been called'. So two of the blokes held him down and another one—glass straight in his face. He had to have micro-surgery. That was on the Saturday, so my area manager came to see me on the Sunday and we decided to shut down for a couple of days because my face was just, this eye was closed and I was just black, I really was, I couldn't see out of this eye, big black eye here, and my nose, they'd split my nose right down the middle. So I shut down for a couple of days and got the police in.

I'd been liaising with the police right along. They obviously wanted it to stop but the only way they could get it to stop was for me to set up cameras and set up audio equipment, and actually get the threats on tape. I had the cameras put in, the audio equipment was waiting to go in, the only thing is they do not say, 'we want protection money off you'. It's very legal wording they use, you know, 'you need doorstaff, here's our card', and that. So unless they are actually threatening and use a threatening tone there's nothing they can do. But it's totally illegal what they are doing 'cause it's just a front for a protection racket. The person who fronted it was never in when the violence went on, but it was made known. The people who were doing it never actually said 'this is a warning of so and so', but you knew, you knew—it was so staged it was unbelievable. It wasn't just a scuffle between two people who'd had too much to drink, these were sober people sat in a corner and all of a sudden off it would go, they'd leather somebody or turn on a customer, or go for a barstaff and then they'd be gone. So it was very unnatural, so you knew it was a set-up.

We had very regular uniformed visits [from the police], we were issued with a Home Office alarm which has a ninety-second response time, an emergency alarm if ever we hit it, and we've hit it about five times and they were here within minutes mob-handed. They issued myself and my two children, 'cause at one point they mentioned the children and the school the children went to. I wasn't even in the pub at the time, I was in the newsagents and one of them came up to me and said, 'kids back at school, not a bad school that St. Peter's', which it isn't even in this area, it's where I'm from originally and I just didn't move the schools. So I just looked at him and thought nothing of it, anyway I got a phone call off the Head Teacher to say somebody had called in to say they were picking up the kids to take them home early because I'd been ill and she rung up to check. And I said 'no, no-one should be picking them up.' So after that I told the police and, on the police's advice, I moved them to about seventeen miles away from here. But, again, we don't know who it was, someone must have followed us—pretty regular thing going to school at half past eight in the morning five days a week.

They can't go out on the streets, well I won't let them out. And also, I won't let them in the pub, at all, on an evening. And when it was going off, in April, they heard all this commotion going on downstairs so they just walked in the office and switched the video [link of the pub] on and just watched it, sat in here, on video which wasn't very pleasant. They saw me getting clobbered, and the youngest one's seven, Alison's eight, she's like me: she's a tough cookie; but Daniel was hysterical, and he was like that for weeks. He had to go and see the paediatric psychologist at the hospital 'cause he was so disturbed by it, he started wetting the bed and all sorts.

We've got no assistant manager here now, 'cause the assistant manager left just after Christmas, he couldn't take it, he was beaten up and it wasn't in here it was outside. He didn't know if it was connected with here, but he left anyway. We had a supervisor called Tom, and I was asking some lads— I don't know if it's connected—to put out a joint and I was called away to the phone and Nick was stood behind me at the time, and they said to him 'why you backing her?' And he said 'I'm not backing her, I'm doing me job', and they said 'June Elliot', which is his mum, 'registration blah, blah, blah, Campbell's tomorrow, one o'clock'. They quoted the car registration, name, where she worked and what time she was working the following day. He resigned on the spot. Another two staff, when they came in and started throwing ashtrays and smashing the optics, resigned on the spot. So we've got a high turnover of staff. In April, when we were beaten up, one of the barmen that was beaten up was literally knocked from the fireplace to the conservatory. He quit on the spot, so it's not just me. I know Bruce and Alison, who I took over from, left with a police escort and they had their kids threatened going to school. And Alison had been threatened, and they'd had the same: approach for protection, and they got out before it went any further. But I don't know if I was just stupid and hung on, I'm just so glad I'm out before Christmas 'cause I know it's just going to start all over again.

It's a nightmare, very high turnover of staff. There's one girl who's been here, in the day, for two years but she won't do any evenings. But the

216 Violence and Governance in the Night-time Economy

evening staff, since I've been here, has turned over two or three times. The longest serving in the evening has been Michelle and she's been here five months, they won't stay. I mean we had an incident last week—it was nothing to do with the situation—but it just goes to show you the type of area. A guy walked in at ten to twelve, and one of the barstaff told him we're shut, and he's got a knife like this [machete size], 'I'm having the tills', it's just the area. He could see the panic alarms under the counter so he wouldn't let her go near the counter. So she said she was going in the vault and went in, buzzed me. She's whispering on the phone 'you better get down here' 'cause it was my night off and I was fuming. I said 'what's the problem?', he said 'I'm having the tills', I went 'GO ON THEN YOU BASTARD', I went ballistic, I shouldn't have done it, shouldn't have done it at all. But no he didn't get the tills. I've been issued with a tracker and I hit the panic alarm button, and six huge coppers turned up and used his head to go through the front door.

I'm just totally disgusted with the way I've been treated here, no support whatsoever, it's just a case of 'aw, bang another camera in', and it's just been nightmare after nightmare. It's not just the assaults, it's the break-ins as well. That's been done three times, assaulted twice, there's been, I don't know how many fights, three and a half incident books full, must 'ave been over a hundred fights, and I'm not just talking a little scuffle, we're talking where somebody's been injured, damage to property. Nobody gets prosecuted though, 'cause—I don't know if you know Dogtown—but for some reason they grow up absolutely hating the police, nobody will speak to the police. I used to regularly get 'police grass' sprayed on the outside of the pub, because I will have them in, I want the uniforms to be in the pub and for people to see that I do speak to the police and I get on with the police. And I think that's why I've had a lot of back-up from the police, 'cause no-one co-operates with the police.

You can't relax downstairs you can never ever relax downstairs ever. You can never have your back to a door, you can never take your eyes of the door, you've always got to be walking around watching. I can never serve behind the bar on an evening 'cause I always have to be out watching what's going on—it's a horrible way to live. The only way I can relax is to go away, get away from the pub, go and stay at my Mum and Dad's 'cause you can't do it here. 'Cause even when you're upstairs you're wondering if it's going off downstairs, are the staff okay, and then at night, you know, they're trying to get in.

My area manager said 'do whatever it needs'. I mean we were talking to the police at the time, and we said 'what is best?' They said there's one of two things you can do, you can bring in legitimate, outside door agencies, but you might as well just cut their throats now, or you can use a local door firm which is just a front for this protection racket anyway. There's only two door firms in Dogtown and they're both fronted for the same man so you're paying them anyway. And once you start paying them...I've got a friend who runs a pub in Dogtown Basin, now he's got the security firm who came to me, and his fees have just gone like that, and that, and that [arm moves upwards] and you cannot get rid of them once they are in, you know, you can't get rid of them. But he uses them purely because when he went into the pub they was already there and he was warned against getting rid. So they're tied to him basically. So we decided no, not to have them. That was after an earlier incident, but after the big one in April I said 'right I'm not doing this anymore, I'm not taking this anymore, I'm not hard enough to keep taking this, I want doorstaff' and the District and General manager said 'no, won't fund it' and that's when I said to him 'right you get me a move, I want to move' and he said, 'oh yes, I'll do everything in my power to get you moved, you've taken a lot, you've done a lot for this company' and he's done sod all basically.

The takings are down about twenty-five, thirty per cent from last year. They set us this totally ludicrous budget [target] and it was already behind when I took over and you can actually see as an incident happens the takings dip and then slowly climb back up again. So average-wise, it's down about twenty-five per cent on last year, so it is struggling. The pub over the road, Willy was in there: a fifty-five-year-old man beaten senseless so he had enough—left three weeks ago. So they've put a women in there. The pub a hundred yards away, the Black Swan: he left last Saturday—they've put a women in there—he's had enough, he was sick of getting beaten and everything. And the second night in that pub she was there, they've had some lads come in trying it on, as they do, went outside smashed the benches up, put them through every window in the pub, when she went out to try and stop it she got a good hammering so she quit after two days, so they're looking for a new manager up there. This one over the road's a new manager, I've been here eleven months and Mark next door has been there eight months, so I'm the longest serving but they are just running us off the turf.

The businesses are all the same. There's a road down at the back called Westcliffe Road and that goes right into the heart of Dogtown and every shop on that road is paying protection money. We're talking building sites, pubs, alarms, everything. My brother has a house just off Chestnut Road, he bought it seven years ago for £23,000, you would have thought with inflation it'd be mid-thirties now. He wants to move and he's just had it valued at £12,000—because of the area. He's absolutely gutted. A couple of months ago he got a leaflet through his door, and it was for security: 'We'll protect your homes while you're at work for only a pound a week'. And it went to every single house, now, of course, he's paying that 'cause if he doesn't then his house is going to get done anyway isn't it? and they call for it every week, and all the other houses pay and it's all the same firm. You know, it's a pound at the moment, but after Christmas, what's it going to go up too? They're bleeding the place dry, they really are; and they go in and destroy a pub and it shuts down and they pick it up for next to nothing and open it themselves. I can name you four pubs that this guy owns in this area already, and he's probably after this one 'cause it's the second largest taking pub in the area so I wouldn't be surprised if this is on his list.

Yes, the assault, I'm going to court for that. That's another reason I'm bailing out 'cause at the moment I'm on a witness support scheme and it's going to be upgraded to witness protection as soon as we get a court date. But, as I say, I was assaulted, Grace was assaulted, Keith was assaulted, Carol was assaulted. Colin wouldn't make a statement, Keith wouldn't make a statement, Grace made a statement and withdrew it, the customer who was glassed made a statement and withdrew it three or four days later. They have to live round here. The police think probably the guy that got glassed: somebody visited him in hospital because they asked the nurse and he did have a visitor on the afternoon of the night he retracted his statement.

They're killing this area, 'cause it's not just businesses they're getting it off, it's the residents as well, so they've got the whole area in their pocket. The police's hands are tied; unless someone makes a complaint, to say they are being intimidated into taking the protection or security, there's not much they can do. Everybody's got the right to have security on their house or business, it's just the way it's done. As I say, my brother felt a pound was a small price to pay for not having his house burgled. He pays an insurance company as well.

I don't know how many doorstaff you've spoken to but most of the doorstaff in Dogtown are connected with organized crime in some way. It's just a front, it's easy money really isn't it, just put a big monkey on the door and pay 'em a hundred quid a night. It's racketeering 'cause nine times out of ten they're coming in a couple of weeks before to kick it off.

It's had a massive effect on me; I don't like what I've become. I've become this really hard tough... it's quite funny really people here they call me 'the Dyke' cause, since I've been in here—many years ago I used to do kick boxing—I've took it up again, I do it six days a week. I used to have hair down here, I had long hair and it's got shorter and shorter and shorter, until now I'm having it shaved. But, yeah, it's had a massive effect on me, I'm this real tough cookie now and I'm not really like that, but you've got to be, you cannot afford to show an ounce of weakness.

Pauline's story of life on the front line of the night-time economy is drained of all the pseudo-glamour of the neon-lit city centre night strips. The state's inability to provide adequate security, despite the undoubted dedication of street level police officers, has made these once proud working-class neighbourhoods vulnerable to predatory criminal colonization. This colonization requires a level of organization parallel to that of the state police, yet remaining unfettered by both bureaucratic regimes and the reins of democratic accountability.

The muscle market

Criminal door firms and individual 'security consultants' were also involved in a form of labour-leasing, controlling the provision of bouncers and acting as intermediaries between doorstaff and venue management (Neff, 1989). Legitimate security companies, brewers, and leisure corporations, 'faced with the constant threat of cut-throat competition are subject to easy temptation to pay gangsters for protection against competitors' (Lippman, 1962:61), and were not adverse to contacting local crime groups to 'iron out' the situation before they commenced work on a contract. As the New York State Organized Crime Task force explained with reference to the construction industry, organized crime can utilize its extensive network of relationships to reduce uncertainties and promote, indeed enforce, stability. 'In this role organized crime serves the same functions, albeit by criminal means, as a highly effective, legitimate labor consultant' (1988:66).

However, alliances between legitimate businesses and criminal firms can lead to commercial disaster. Major security companies were forced out of lucrative regional market places as a result of their unwillingness to sub-contract to organized crime. For instance, when a nationally known nightspot reopened after a spell of closure, the security company contracted to control the door, in an attempt to avoid any friction, contacted the local criminal firms to inform them that they were taking over. The head of this company told us that this was vital, and communications were put out to the effect that 'you are welcome, but please play by the rules, and control your henchmen and hangers-on'. All seemed well, and the pre-eminent local crime group was obliging. But problems soon developed. The head of the company explained that the problem was that the city's other gangs were not as well structured, and control, therefore, 'not as tight'. After two weeks, a doorman attempted to search someone who was not normally searched at the entrance to the club. Fifteen minutes later a car with black windows pulled up and a man wearing a black balaclava and waving a hand gun at the doormen uttered, 'do you know where you are?, don't fuck about here'. The company stopped working at the club and the venue is now closed.

We discovered numerous cases of doorstaff informally sub-contracting their violence (see for example Winlow, 2001:155–159), sometimes on behalf of the firm, and sometimes on a freelance basis. This violent entrepreneurship had spread to restaurants, take-aways, and boutiques and to venues beyond the bright lights of the city centre. Its influence was as extensive as an individual's or group's reputation, sometimes requiring periodic visits or demonstrations of power, but often word of mouth sufficed. As this licensee of an out-of-town pub explains:

I already knew Jimmy for a few years and he's a mate of mine. I knew he did the doors over at some of the pubs in town so I just asked him to call in. I just picked a time when I knew some of the local lads would be in and he comes in and has a coke. We talk for about five minutes and you can hear them go quiet then start talking about him. After a few minutes he just walked over and said 'all right' to them, and that he was working there now, they didn't say a fucking word. They knew who he was obviously, everyone knows Jimmy don't they? It's not like you can miss him. And that's it. I gave him twenty quid for that first time, and fifteen quid a week after that. He gave me his mobile number to 'phone if there's any bother' and he comes in every now and then, just has a quick drink and leaves. With someone like Jimmy doing that I don't need a bouncer on at all really. I'm still here all the time and I keep a pickaxe handle behind the bar.

The business of bouncing constitutes but one point on the 'spectrum of legitimacy' (Smith, 1980) that pervades post-industrial enterprise. Most importantly, it shares with organized crime, violent potential-ity as an essentially pragmatic resource (Gambetta, 1993:2). Such a resource has proved to be highly adaptable for generations of organ-ized criminals in the establishment of illegal enterprise, the market-ing of violence as a commodity, as a tool to deal with competition, and the resolution of personal disputes within the organized crime community (Hobbs, 2003).

Despite the undoubted sophistication and market orientation of contemporary organized crime (Coles, 2001), the cultural inherit-ance of traditional visceral practices (Hall, 1997) remains central to the establishment, marketing, regulation, and culture of illegal markets. Indeed, we would argue that the shared cultural collateral upon which both criminal entrepreneurship and doorwork is grounded, ensures that violence often becomes an obligation (Hobbs, 1995:122) accumulated in social networks that are not exclusively criminal, but are based upon an urban ethic of market and personal exploitation that differs little from purely legitimate enterprise. This violent obligation can clearly be a creative or destructive force; creating identities and reinforcing networks which, along with commercially sanctioned tendencies, combine to form the portfolios of both licit and illicit authorities (Moore, 1987).

By encouraging the night-time economy without taking full responsibility for its regulation, the state, both local and central, has ensured that the liberal conceit that violence is a subordinate element in society is exposed. Violence is of course a crucial element, embedded in the dominant socio-economic structure (Arlacchi, 1986:115). Further, although the 'systems of accumulated expertise' (Giddens, 1991:3) that constitute both contemporary organized crime, and the bouncing community, are malleable and not located in the fixed terrain (Chaney, 1994:149) of the formal institutional order, they feature the cultural inheritance of traditional criminogenic locales (Arlacchi, 1986:227). Consequently, they inject a branded assurance of consistency (Hobbs, 2001) impacting upon indigenous trust networks (Evans et al., 1996) that enable both the criminal firm and the security firm to establish a 'protected enclave' (Arlacchi, 1986:195), within and across markets that are fluid and transitory.

As a consequence of the state's inability to maintain a monopoly over the use of force in the night-time economy, and in the absence of a sufficiently competent and effective agent of state-sanctioned violence, state interventions, when they are made, are seen as particularistic and *ad hoc*, resulting in a shortfall in legitimacy (Pierson, 1991; see Chapter 6). Consequently, 'if they couldn't connect with the forces of law and order, it was on to the forces of law and disorder' (Wilson, 2002:223) and night-time economy entrepreneurs, seeking to protect and consolidate their interests whilst bereft of any effective recourse to the monopoly of violence which orthodoxy insists is central to state sovereignty (Elias, 1994), turned to local 'Men of Respect', (Catanzarro, 1992). Further, 'what earned these men "respect" was, first their capacity to coerce with physical violence and thus invoke fear in others' (Blok, 1974:62).

Thus violence becomes located within the ambit of market exchange, and we are introduced here to the notion of violence, as both a private and commercial resource. Consequently, to understand the cultural and ultimately commercial emergence of these 'men of respect', we need to recognize the ideal of embodied masculinity that we referred to in Chapter 5, for such an ideal emanates from social conditions where 'aggressiveness and violence were positively endorsed' (Arlacchi, 1986:12).

Bouncing as class work

Most bouncers have emerged from a social environment that embraces the potential benefits and rewards of violent conduct.[1] In our view they do not represent a cross section of society, but are generally men with similar class backgrounds, similar goals, beliefs and concerns, and bouncing provides both a practical and esoteric function within their lives (Ford, 1985; Winlow, 2001).[2] Recruits to the profession bring with them baggage in the form of cultural capital, that reflects their socialization as contemporary working-class men acutely conscious of their physicality, and drawing on violence and its negotiation in their everyday social interactions. Clearly, their working environment, their relationships with colleagues and the occupational pragmatics of doorwork all help to shape the overall occupational culture of bouncers. However, their class experiences, in the form of a habitus closely linked to a modified working class culture, in which violence is not some alien threat, but a frame of action brimming with meaning, provides much of the cultural framework upon which occupational mores are based. The durable, transposable dispositions (Bourdieu, 1977:72) that constitute the habitus of the bouncer are cultural manifestations of mutating traditional industrial working-class masculinities (Winlow, 2001), and although the resultant practices are clearly grounded in

[1] Since the outset of this study, it was clear that social class and class-based masculinities would be a crucial analytical devices in explaining the social organization of bouncers. These issues are specifically addressed in Winlow, 2001 and Winlow et al., 2002.

[2] Our stance on the class orientation of doorstaff is derived from our interviews and ethnography. Walker's research for the Home Office (1999) is largely inconclusive on this issue. However, although we were constantly informed, often forcibly, by representatives of the security industry, that their particular organization had a large number of students, teachers, nurses, etc. on their payroll, we found them to be conspicuous by their rarity within the enacted environment of the night-time economy. The same research found that 7% of doorstaff were female (Walker 1999).

something so apparently archaic and regulated, the outcome of these practices is, as we have stressed, not entirely an instrumental package and is far from being a product of pure 'strategic intention' (Bourdieu 1977:73).

Physical resilience and competence in relation to male-on-male violence (see Connell, 1995) have long been considered crucial concerns and ideals within working-class masculinities (see Miller, 1958; Wacquant, 1995b; Willis, 1977). In addition, historically it is the lower classes who have always felt the forces of violence most discernibly (Elias, 1994; Hall, 1997), and class is a key tool in understanding both the social and cultural determinants of violence, and its meanings to participants (see Jones, 2000). Violence possesses a multiplicity of meanings within working-class cultures that elevate its importance in everyday life. Working-class men are more likely to be socialized within a framework of cultural capital that places violence central to concepts of the male self (Robins and Cohen, 1978), and as a consequence it is often treated as a personal resource, informing and advising social interaction and performance.

Violence is regarded as a social function to be treated with a degree of esteem, solemnity, and gravitas and whilst of course violent action is not adopted as a strategy by all members of the working classes, and aspects of violence may well blight their everyday lives, we suggest that violence, especially for working-class males, is often an aspect of their cultural environment and inheritance that has a major influence upon their social and cultural understanding of everyday life (see Winlow, 2001). Indeed, the violent potential, and instrumental physicality that is the flotsam and jetsam of industrial employment cultures, once divested of the potential for communal action in both the workplace, and in the workplace-dependent neighbourhood, has provided an ideal pool of apprentices to the ranks of both bouncing and organized crime (Hobbs, 1995; Winlow, 2001). Further, as we shall explain, it is an ideal vehicle for the transformation of cultural capital into economic capital (Bourdieu, 1977:183–184).

Our research located a range of men to whom violence was important for a variety of reasons, who had established reputations as successfully violent men, who had engaged in combat sports, and even those who had rarely experienced violence at first hand, but had long looked on and acknowledged both the physical and cultural consequences of violence. Cumulatively this knowledge of where and how violence was situated in relation to both culture and the self, provided the primary skills, and indeed the essential and prerequisite cultural triggers for the choice of bouncing as an occupation (see Winlow et al., 2001).

The practicalities of many bouncers' working environments, in conjunction with their gendered and class-specific cultural socialization, leads to a heightened *sense* of violence. As we have seen in Chapter 5, violence is a continuous concern for bouncers, constituting a primary form of social interaction in which they specialize. Indeed, they are engaged in doorwork not merely because they regard themselves as competent, or because they possess certain fighting skills, but also because they are knowledgeable about the micro-intricacies and choreography of contemporary urban violence. For bouncers are required to understand the complex interactive preludes and precursors of violence, to assess who is most likely to be involved and devise strategies to manage and resolve potentially violent situations.

As bouncers become increasingly conversant with their working environment they formulate new strategies geared towards coping with the proximal threat of violence (see Chapter 5). It is these intensely practical occupational considerations, when amalgamated with violence as an inherent class and gender-specific focal concern, which forces actual and potential violence to the very core of both the occupational culture of door work and the individual bouncer's sense of self.

Similarly, the practicalities of the occupation reinforce the importance of violence, setting in motion occupational strategies that bolster the ideal of a robust and dominant masculinity (Yllo, 1993). This form of hyper-masculinity, with its defining characteristics of toughness, autonomy, vitality, power, dominance, respect, honour, pride, and of course violence, is certainly not restricted to those who engage in doorwork, but when transformed from cultural competence to cultural and economic capital, is embodied by bouncers (Monaghan, 2002b).

Violence provides a contextual framework for concepts of respect, pride, and honour (Neff et al., 1991), and cultures with a powerful emphasis upon honour typically flourish, 'where the state is weak or its rationalizing minions are held in contempt' (Courtwright, 1996: 29). This is clearly the case in the habitas of bouncers where many have already inculcated violence into their own self-identity, and when faced with conflict, violence is confirmed and underlined as both an obligation and expectation (Tedeschi and Felson, 1994). In the environments in which bouncers move, pride, honour, and respect remain bound up with concepts of 'maintaining face' (Goffman, 1967, 1971) which constitutes a powerful motivation in all forms of interaction. As Bourdieu (1979:115) suggests, perceptions of honour are strongest in those who see themselves through the eyes of others, and given both their prominent profile in the night-time economy, and their concerns regarding the presentation of a reflexive and robust masculinity (Kimmel, 1987; Mac an Ghaill, 1996) this is particularly relevant to bouncers. This occupational self-consciousness is manifested in a number of forms. Body size and shape are accentuated, and stance, clothing, facial expression and general demeanour are often tailored to display the mental and physical toughness deemed to be required of a pragmatic gatekeeper and arbiter. However, the rewards that emerge from this prized gatekeeper role are more than merely cultural, as much of the rich plethora of market possibilities that open up at night are channelled via the door, for the night-time economy is also a zone that offers multi-layered pecuniary opportunities.

Market force

Pubs and clubs have always been associated with the hidden economy, and doorstaff are ideally situated within this consumer market. Not only are there opportunities to make money from drug dealing, whether by handling or by proxy, but, given that pubs and clubs are frequently the hub of local, illicit trading networks, a plethora of other criminal opportunities also avail, not least those presented by the inelastic demand for, for instance, counterfeit and stolen goods. Further, many punters were happy to engage in commercial discourse and curry favour with individuals possessing such cultural power. Which is how one can find oneself combining the cultural clout of an exclusive logo, with the moisture retaining qualities of polyester. From fake roses at a pound a pop, to 'snide' bottles of *Möet et Chandon* (weak cider—wholesaled at £10 per magnum, immaculately packaged and particularly effective in Indian or Mexican restaurants after ten bottles of premium lager), from cocaine to baking powder, the night-time economy is a bizarre bazaar of sharpened, distorted senses.

Bouncers can be 'pitched' with various money-making schemes, sometimes by professional criminals and sometimes by sycophants keen to be a part of the bouncer's circle. There were cigarette and beer importation scams, fake designer clothes, handbags, perfume, jewellery, currency, drugs, anabolic steroids. Stolen 'everything', from videos to razor blades, goods bought on hire purchase which would never be paid, the produce of credit card scams, shoplifting and commercial burglary. Whatever commodity was on offer, bouncers were the ideal conduits (Winlow, 2001:115–117).

We note that official politico-crime control discourses retain a narrow view that focuses almost entirely upon the involvement of bouncers with the drugs trade (Morris, 1998a; Morris, 1998b). However, we suggest that the business of drugs should be understood as but one contested, potentially violent segment of a political economy sold as a sequin-studded, liberating force of transcendence, yet grounded in the dull and grinding inevitability of business: of measured subservience to market forces and the cause of profit. Consequently, drugs should be regarded merely as part of the myriad of consumables available in the night-time economy. However, due to the prevalence of the drug trade and its necessary co-ordination within multi-faceted urban networks, a focus upon it does permit the unpacking of the dense commercial core of the bouncing business.

The conception of the night-time economy as a 'community', is a powerful slice of rhetoric for night-time entrepreneurs and city boosters alike (Chatterton and Hollands, 2001). However, beyond the rhetoric, 'the locality relevance' (Warren, 1973:9) of the functions of both bouncer subcultures and organized crime groups are their distinct proximity to the client community's primary access points to the world of leisure, and their demand for the provision of specific commodities that are accessories to the notion of competent leisure attainment (see, Parker et al., 1998). By conceptualizing this quasi-community in terms of the organization and control of these access points and the activities that they generate, it is possible to understand the night-time economy in terms of its production-distribution-consumption function (Warren, 1973) in relation to key commodities, rather than as a phenomenon encased within the physical parameters of a specific cityscape.

As we have already stressed, alcohol is the drug of choice within the night-time economy (see Parker et al., 1998; Chapter 3). Further, it is the role of doorstaff to provide appropriate levels of commercially-tuned social control within alcohol outlets, and increasingly to other related premises such as fast-food restaurants. However, not all of the drugs of choice are legal; illicit drugs are, for a section of the night-time community, an essential part of a good night out, either as a condiment or main course, as an isolated stimulant or part of a cocktail, the use of drugs by youth in contemporary British society has come to be normalized (Parker et al., 1998; South 1999). Illegal drugs are then a central dynamic of the contemporary night-time economy with cultural products being moulded to complement their use, and the commercial viability of some dance-oriented venues being dependent upon their chemically induced ambiance (Collin, 1997; Haslam, 1999; Malbon, 1999). For example, as Silcott (2000:185–6) has noted:

> What Superclub companies peddle is their vibe and their vibe simply wouldn't be there if countless thousands weren't taking E every weekend . . . every Superclub experienced one huge, glaring problem in the legitimacy department . . . at the centre of their shining corporate empires, in the middle of their Saturday night, lay Ecstasy. Not just E the idea, but E the chemical. An illegal drug, a Class A.

To this extent, dance clubs can be seen to tread a fine line between the licit and illicit marketplace in that an 'atmosphere' induced by the consumption of an illegal drug forms a core component of their commercial appeal. In such contexts, any attempt to totally eradicate drug use would be futile and would serve to undermine not only the venue's competitive advantage within the marketplace, but also the very rationale of its business project. As Silcott goes on to ask, somewhat rhetorically, 'could a club designed around the pleasures of Ecstasy—the sounds, the lights, the podiums, survive without people actually experiencing the effects of the drug within its confines?' (ibid.). Within such contexts, the role of doorstaff is to regulate protocols regarding not only the behaviour of consumers, but also the very organization of the drug trade at the point of consumption.

However, in most of the pubs and clubs that we encountered, alcohol was the sole or dominant substance, and the principal commodity consumed by those participating in violence. As Mark, a bouncer intimately aware of the perils of alcohol noted:

> See people react different to beer. . . it's all down to beer and the individual. Like they say do drugs do that?, do drugs do this? . . . What about

beer?...There is more crime committed through beer than anything through drugs. Well obviously not hard drugs...they send you mental, you don't wanna overdo it, but beer, let's face it: people get murdered, people get stabbed, people get shot, people fight, people wreck places, cause criminal damage, kill people through drink driving, all caused through beer.

As we suggest above, this enacted reality is seldom indicated in accounts of doorwork, nor in popular media accounts in the aftermath of highly publicized drug deaths, which are always seen as more tragic, heartrending, and somehow avoidable than their alcohol-inspired equivalent. Yet despite this myopic stance, from the point of view of doorstaff it is violence and not drugs that constitutes their major problem and obstacle to a quiet night's work:

More rubbish [is] talked about drugs than anything. It's not going away, people want it and in most places that are not your average Bert and Doris venues, you can get what you want. If it's controlled, well that's all you can do anyway because it is everywhere. They get sick, oh yeah, and it's part of our job to look after them but it isn't as dangerous as in the drinker's places where they are fighting all the time. Course there's drugs and drugs, and anybody can over egg it a bit. What it must be doing to some of their brains I don't want to think about it, but in terms of the way punters behave it's really easy to work with. It's the business that will damage you; It's the business that makes me wary. Charlie

An orthodox take on the relationship between drugs and bouncers designates doorstaff as 'gatekeepers' for the drug trade (Hobbs, 1995; O'Mahoney, 1997). This version is relatively simplistic and regards control of the door as going hand in hand with control of the drug market within particular premises (see Morris, 1998a). However, Charlie explains both the inevitability, but also the complexity that is often intrinsic to such arrangements:

If you got a door which is very, very lucrative then it will be a drug-driven thing. People are either buyers or sellers, and you can't work such a door without being involved. You make your mind up whose market it is, and you keep out the opposition. Money? If I am working five nights a week and putting myself on offer for whoever is placing their dealers inside, then it's hard to think of me not getting £750 a week. With sub-contracting, which does work if you are shrewd, then many times that...A couple of us will have one of our own inside and make out it's one of the official firm whose got the place...If I take too much of the trade then people are gonna get mightily pissed off, and I will be confronted with a degree of grief... Oh yes Professor, you know, violence. First you get taken off the door as a bit of notice that you have been sussed by the head doorman, who is responsible for keeping everybody sweet, but if you are still in business for yourself, well they are not going to slap somebody like me 'cause I might slap back. It is serious or it's nothing...

Venues featuring a significant drug market are often regarded as less problematic than venues fuelled by the consumption of alcohol. Charlie explains:

All in all I get paid a lot of money to keep things sweet, and there is a lot less actual fighting than in the usual old places with pissed punters wanting to whack you.

However, although the risk of customers engaging in violence may be reduced in these venues, the violent potential that is unleashed when commercial rivalries come to a head can be very serious. Charlie again:

But if it ever goes off on a door like ours, it's usually away from the door. And it has to be said [it's] a bit more serious than dealing with some crying Doris whose boyfriend has been defending her honour and thrown up on your *Patrick Cox's*. Know what I mean?

Consequently, the protocols of commercial competition are extremely delicate, and require doorstaff to, yet again, exhibit qualities that defy the boneheaded stereotype:

Other firms' dealers we always treat well, and just don't let them in. [But] if you take a backhander and let them in, well you will politely be asked not to come back. It's a mistake and it's polite. But you might get a firm work itself up between a little group of security who are running their own thing. Then the proper firm with the contract have to deal with it, and you might get most of the firm sacked. But if they come back the next night and say 'we are the new door', then management just might have to swallow it and sack the remains of the old firm. Or at a push you might get two firms running the door letting their own people [dealers] in and keeping the others out. Or the other thing is that the door breaks down and everybody has got their own dealer in and it's chaos, nobody can control it so the gaff gets battles and the scream goes up and gets shut down. That's no good, its dangerous and nobody makes any money. That's why controlling the door is so important.

Monopolies, mergers, and cartels therefore rely heavily upon doorstaff, but only a minority are making money from the trade. We interviewed many bouncers who were working in a purely alcohol-based environment and for whom the drug trade was largely an irrelevancy. We spoke to others who were not benefiting commercially from drugs, and indeed were vehemently opposed to the trade. But they were above all else pragmatic. Frank North, who had spent a number of years working at a venue where drug use was prominent, explained why he did not take a harder line on drugs:

Why not kick the dealers out? That is a fucking stupid thing. I have seen people throw up, taken in to have their stomach pumped, fight anybody and try to kill each other, all through drink. The pills just make people stupid but nobody makes them do it. And it's not those people who want to fight, they're not the people standing on the pavement with a chisel offering out the bouncers. So let 'em sell the pills, if they weren't [selling] my job would be war. Well, I wouldn't do it, you would need the army.

Such pragmatism extends to the choices doorstaff make in where to work, and stresses again the inevitability of drugs as an aspect of significant sectors of the night-time economy:

For instance, let's say I run four legitimate pubs and one ropey, old pub, and the ropey old drug runners come along and say to me, 'Oh, you do so and so and so, we're coming in there. If you don't let us in there you're going to suffer on this and your other pubs, and your staff are going to suffer—they are going to get it'. So what do I do, do I put my staff in danger? If I go to the police are the police going to give me full protection twenty-four hours a day on the staff, their families, their wives, their children, the rest of my business? They can't do it, it's not possible. Ninety-nine per cent is intimidation, one per cent of it is probably carried out, but there's always intimidation there, so that's why I'm selective. Alan

The management of liminality requires doorstaff to acknowledge the realities of the choices made by customers who include illegal substances among their drugs of choice. However, the management of these liminal choices places doorstaff in a highly ambiguous situation, for to abide by the letter of the law in relation to drugs can be dangerous, and requires careful and sensitive negotiations involving heightened local knowledge. Frank North is a pragmatist:

I used to say on the rave scene, 'look I know your situation, I know the clubs have got to be run with a certain amount of drugs etc., the only thing that we're going to do is control it, in other words I don't want your gang present. If you've got a runner in here and he's selling, I can guarantee he won't get beaten up by my doormen or have stuff taken off him by my doormen. If we find him, he's out and he doesn't get back in. So if we do throw them out don't let them tell you that we've taken the drugs of them 'cos we wouldn't have, they're just telling you fucking lies'. I've had them turn up...outside my clubs; five or six...with shooters and everything. They've told us that 'you've took the gear', 'ain't took no gear, get the little shit in here now'. So they bring him in, 'Right who's took the fucking gear, me?', 'no it weren't you', 'well who was it? I'll bring me doormen down, this was all who was working that night. If I was you I'd take this fucking cunt and throw him under a bus'...So you don't nick-'em, you don't take the drugs off them, you certainly don't take the drugs of them. A lot of people make mistakes by taking the drugs off them and then they get repercussions because they want their money back, they've laid out say five thousand pounds and that's a fifteen thousand pounds profit. You just don't know who you're dealing with.

Bouncing as police work

Although relationships between the police and doorstaff vary enormously, liaison is common over the issue of drugs. If a venue is not reliant upon a drug-orientated clientele, doorstaff resist drugs being brought in and sold on 'their' premises. Larry, who worked in a corporately-owned high street nightclub, explains:

In some ways we work very closely with the police, we are quite strict on drugs. I have been known to ring up the police and give them information on certain individuals who I have observed in the course of my job. I don't want them in my venue, so I would rather they were picked up outside...Yeah, I have quite a good relationship with the local police, they will come up here and have a coffee and a chat when it is quiet for them. They will tell me if they are looking for anyone in particular, pass on a description to me of some pretty dangerous characters. It's like an exchange really, we help them, they help us.

When there is close agreement between public and private control agencies regarding the parameters of both comportment and commercial activity in the night-time economy, relationships, based on common interest tend to prosper. However, ambiguity, both moral and economic, abounds (see Chapter 5), for in containing the violence that is generated by the drug trade, extremely complex arrangements often involving both police and doorstaff are developed. However, regardless of the complexity of these tactics, at their core lies violent potential.

George describes being employed by a nightclub owner whose club was threatened with closure by the police. In order to clean the place up he had to rid the club of the doormen who were overseeing the drug dealing taking place inside. This example clearly stresses one of the methods by which doorstaff often carry out what most citizens would regard as the job of the police:

I turned up one night with five doormen and said to them 'right fellers unfortunately we don't know the situation what's going on (obviously we do), but we've just been told to turn up tonight'. So he says 'no, no, get on the phone and tell him [the club owner] that there's already doormen here'. I said 'no, you're not working here anymore, the management don't want you working here and we're taking over the door, don't get yourselves in lumber. Tell your boss to phone me up or to come and see me anytime he wants, but it's impossible for you to work here anymore, the police are going to shut it down'. So they've lost face, they've got to go. So they go back to their top man and he arranges a meeting for the next night with all his doorstaff and possibly a few more of his friends. So when forty or fifty of them turn up the next night, and they're all big fellers, absolute lunatics, the police were waiting. Just a little skirmish at the door... and the police arrested about ten or twelve of them.

However collaborating with the police can be risky.

Recently there was two guys got shot... there's no need for you to call the police. Just tell them to go away and that's it. But they were holding people and calling the police and letting police pick them up and everything. That's doing overtime, you're doing a policeman's job when you're just supposed to be doing a doormen's job... you're going beyond your job. That's the police's job, know what I mean, that's what they're there for, but when you start grassing people up and grabbing people in and holding them for the police to nick-'em... and that's why the two guys got shot. Marcus

The decision to retain a monopoly of alcohol in a premises demands that doorstaff not only have to be particularly vigilant on the door, but have to utilize innovative strategies inside the premises:

I used to get two kids, give them a few quid each and say 'go and get me an E. They used to go and buy me an E; 'who'd you get it off, him?' Okay let's sit back, let's watch him, let's see who he's with and then as soon as we've got the whole gang that's it, they don't get back in. Simple, a few quid we've got two dealers... But if they're a gang you don't hit them that night, you sit back and wait. Someone will be carrying the drugs, someone else will be holding the money, so for security to actually find them you've got to sit back a couple of weeks; it's like the police with their observations on drug dealers themselves, they don't go in straight away, they sit back and wait and that's how they do it. So you wait till next time and get the whole gang. That's when you say to the management 'look we've got the gangs that are selling in here and we're going to come down on them this week, but will you employ an extra five doormen for this particular night'. Now if there's enough of us we'll go in and just take them out and they've all got to go at once. Nobody gets hurt, no drugs get stolen but their times up. All good things come to an end: 'sorry boys you're not coming back in, okay, out you go.' Frank North

The potential profit to be gleaned from dealing in drugs is particularly enticing to doormen who observe at first hand the dealers that they arrest/protect/extort or generally coexist with in the night-time economy. The opportunity to make large sums of money from an activity that involves utilizing the same qualities as it takes to earn £40 per night is an overwhelming temptation. Further, niche dealing within the huge drug economy that spreads across the night can prove to be a window opening upon new horizons that emphasize nightlife's global appeal, an appeal that is acknowledged by legal and illegal entrepreneurs alike. Doorwork can then proffer significant benefits, and the potent forms of bodily and cultural capital embodied by bouncers carries with it a significant amount of status. These men possess power, and within the night-time economy and the class context of that economic sphere, such power impacts upon the entire orbit of commercial and cultural life. Yet as we have seen, occupying such a crucial location within the liminal cultural and economic territories that constitute the night-time economy carries with it not only opportunities, but also responsibilities that are riven with ambiguities. At the core of this ambiguous profession lies the commercial enactment of hedonistic rituals, rituals that are not dominated by legal restraints, but by the limitations imposed by economic assessments of a specific venue's strategic position within the liminal market.

Consequently, standing on the door of a popular pub, bar, or nightclub, the bouncer embodies a variation on traditional masculine authority far exceeding the simple ability to refuse admittance. For his is a proficiency that 'incorporates the practical transference of incorporated, quasi-postural schemes' (Bourdieu, 1977:116), and constitutes a special competence whose lineage stretches beyond the magic kingdom of bright lights and lager.

The monopoly of muscle

Most people think of violence as an abstraction. It never is. It's always ugly, it always demeans and dehumanizes...it's meant to... (James Lee Burke)

Given the impotence of public authorities in the night-time economy, this special competence emerges as a response to an, 'expression of a need for order' (Falcone, 1993:56), and the response is made by 'persons who had a reputation for violence and who eschewed recourse to public authorities [who] commanded respect [while] others less skilled in the realm of violence turned to them for protection' (Blok, 1974:211). As we have indicated in Chapter 5, such men command deference, and the emergent pattern of interdependencies that constitute the control culture in the night-time economy relies heavily upon men skilled in the practice and threat of violence.

This relationship between bouncers and organized crime therefore goes beyond the stock drug/gatekeeping role that has tended to dominate official discourse on doorstaff (e.g. Morris, 1998a). Whether or not a bouncer is criminal, or works for a reputable company, the night-time economy's reliance upon entrenched local systems of traditional male violent potential as a commercial resource, stands in contrast to the state's inability to impose order in a realm that it has fostered and encouraged under the convenient flag of 'regeneration' and economic advancement. For as Collin (1997:183) has noted, 'optimistic free-market boosterism about the "night-time economy" [has] tended to gloss over the fact that, all over the country, it was underpinned by criminality, something not so easily integrated with civic renaissance'.

In traditional organized crime, 'violence functioned to keep restive peasants in submission, and created opportunities for upwardly mobile entrepreneurs of violence, and was therefore essentially conservative in its use as a mechanism of social and economic control' (Falcone, 1993:62–65; Hobbs, 2003; Ruggiero, 1993). So, within both doorwork and contemporary organized crime, the mode of violence imposed in support of the indigenous order is not the blunt instrument of an army of strangers, but is harmonious with local culture, 'an aberrant version of the traditional...way of life' (Falcone, 1993:52).

In both bouncing and organized crime, authority is based upon violence and violent potential, and once violent reputation is secured, a brokerage of power can be instituted that is both congruent with local cultural precedent, and functional to the needs of the state whose ability to both utilize violence, and regulate private security and the environment within which it thrives is limited. As Wilson explains of his decision to collaborate with organized crime groups at the world famous, but doomed, Hacienda, 'The door was connected—had to be—a matter of survival' (Wilson, 2002:238; see Chapter 3). In many towns and cities, bouncers, like the early Mafia in Sicily, are the most prominent form of social control apparent within their respective environments, and become, in effect, unofficial instruments of the state (Blok, 1974; Hobsbawn, 1959:30–56), buttressing the dominant economic system through the use of private violence (Blok 1974:102; Catanzaro, 1992).

However, the hiring of men with violent reputations to protect property tells only part of the story, for in the absence of any adequate state regulation, locally phrased power domains also become markets for extortion. Non-existent threats to property can be created, and if ignored the threat can become reality (Blok, 1974:151; Catanzaro, 1992:21–23). For instance, Eric, a bodybuilder and businessman explained how his close friend, a successful bouncer and security consultant, drummed up trade in a similar manner to that experienced by Pauline, mentioned earlier in this chapter:

How he got his clients is pure entrepreneurial businessmanship. It worked like this. Jackie would walk in a pub, any pub, and speak to the owner saying words to the effect of 'this is a rough pub that looks like it needs doormen to keep out the wankers.' If the owner who invariably knew who he was, if not literally, then certainly by reputation, refused this generous offer, then coincidentally, some of these 'wankers' would fight in the pub that very night. The next day Jackie would survey the damage, which was always high, because graphic detail sells, and once again offer his services. The ratio of closed deals he got on the second visit was very high (see also McLean, 1978:75).

Together with 'non-interference' pacts with other bouncer firms or organized crime groups (Reuter, 1987), such practices succeed in creating a virtual monopoly of instrumental violence and a degree of social order that cannot be guaranteed by the state. Eric continues:

Jackie played a pivotal role of peacekeeper in the town, both from the point that if the 'Smiths', 'Jones' or 'Browns' [organized crime families] or whoever wanted to do business, he had to approve it first...The 'Smiths' were moving in on a number of doors...One of these doors was *Roxy's*...The reason to get into this club was so they could control the amount of drugs and hence monitor profit by the use of bouncers on their payroll. The club was held [the door was run] by a sole entrepreneur who would not let the Smiths take control of the club, so they hired Jackie to teach him a lesson...the lesson consisted of Jackie beating him to within an inch of his life...The Smiths got the club and Jackie's service fee was 15% which reliable estimates put at around £20k a year. This is only one of the thirty or so clubs and pubs that Jackie had an interest in.

Where the state is weak, and unable to enforce the distinction between private and public force, the market for violence broadens (Blok, 1974:68), resulting in the penetration of civil society by both private security and organized crime. In our research, both national and local élites, particularly brewers and leisure companies, conspired, often knowingly, with local organized crime groups to provide levels of security commensurate with commercial good health. This could vary from extortionate pay-offs, to the employment, either at the front of the house, or in the back regions, of established crime figures.

Informally, police officers in some forces acknowledged this problem and found themselves engaged in colloquial agreements with known crime figures in order to cope. For instance when an associate of a notorious drug importer showed an interest in reopening a large nightspot in the North of England, an informal agreement was reached with the local police that he would not apply to operate licensed premises for a period of three years. This man is a renowned member of the criminal fraternity but has few convictions and would therefore ostensibly pass the criterion of being a 'fit and proper person' to hold a drinks licence.

It needs to be stressed that in relation to licensed premises, the police are primarily concerned with maintaining public order and may therefore choose to turn a blind eye to entertainment premises operated by criminals, or financed by dirty money. For some sections of the police, if there is no 'trouble' in the form of public disorder, then there is 'no problem'. A Sergeant commented, 'they are well run premises, they don't bother us, we don't bother them...it's all the pissed-up kids we need to worry about'.

Trevor's security company is a pragmatic going concern:

At the end of the day there's certain areas and there's certain gangs, and for me to run my doors in certain areas, you cannot just put some person in there who's a doorman. . . . you're going to have to get a member of a gang, . . . who people recognize and they know who he belongs to, right . . . So what I would do in that area, I would put in the doormen from that gang . . . in that area. That way they'll have a bit of respect and I can do my job.

Such dangerous practices when situated alongside the vulnerable impotence of central state policing and local state licensing and regulation regimes (Chapter 6) have 'created the preconditions for the failed affirmation of the state's monopoly of violence . . . and thus the essential circumstances for the social affirmation of [organized crime]' (Catanzaro, 1992:70). Indeed, it should be noted that when the Sicilian Mafia originally established their monopoly of violence via their management of estates, and extracted profit from peasant and landowner alike, thus creating an environment where the commercialization of traditional respect rooted in violence became a vehicle for serious wealth accumulation, they were then able to proceed to broker electoral support. Further, as within early twenty first century Britain, such activity was not contrary to the mores of a society that valued violence as a resource, and accepted that highly competent practitioners should be rewarded (Catanzaro, 1992:31). As a further warning for the imminent future of the night-time economy we should glance back at the early years of the USA's twentieth century, when organized crime recruited violent labour from the same working-class communities as the legitimate work force. Organized crime utilized this violent base for the penetration of municipal politics via the corruption of politicians and law enforcement personnel. The result was a powerful urban coalition of police, organized crime, business, and politicians founded on violence (Block, 1983:163–199). The vulnerability of brittle local democracies in the face of a familiar alliance of big men and big money should not be ignored.

Frontier business

Out of the maw of competitive capitalism and possessive individualism marched the extortionists—the entrepreneurs of violence whose function was to mediate this state of greed while they skimmed as much as they could for themselves (Block, 1983:239).

There is some element of truth to Melbin's description of the interchange between day-time to night-time as a switch 'from

co-ordinated actions (day-time) to unconnected ones (night-time)'
(1978:9). For as he goes on to explain, like the frontier of the
American West, the night-time frontier is somewhat removed from
conventional power structures. In the West, this was due to the
physical distance between Eastern-based governmental and legal
agencies (ibid.:9–10), while the primary administrators of contemporary cities '... are generally on duty only during the day-time. At
night they go to sleep and a similar decentralization of power
follows' (Melbin, 1978:10). Yet, while the night-time frontier may
lack formal administrative hierarchies, it would be wrong to suggest
that the night-time economy lacks co-ordination. For in the night-
time economy, as in the West, the function of co-ordination is
provided by 'the frontiersmen [who] not only enforced their own
law, they chose which laws should be enforced and which should be
ignored' (Melbin, 1978:10). Like the Western frontier, both the
problems and solutions of incorporation (Trachtenberg, 1982) in
the night-time economy are often manifested in lawlessness and
violence.

 If we regard the night-time economy as a commercial frontier,
some of the glitter begins to peel away to reveal the bars, pubs, and
clubs of early twenty-first century British towns and cities at the
vanguard of trajectories which expose the instrumental venom of
capitalism. Like the night-time economy, the American frontier was
also mythologized as a special place of freedom and adventure (Hine
and Faragher, 2000:472–511), despite, and partly because of the role
of violence in an era of exploration, pacification, incorporation, and
institutional legitimation on behalf of the forces of capital (Robbins,
1994; Tyler, 1962:44–45). Indeed, the symbol of the heroic bouncer
policing the frontiers of the night (Thompson, 1994) has clear and
distinct parallels with the American West, where violent criminals
were harnessed by the 'conservative, consolidating authority of
capital' (Brown, 1991:40) to exploit the absence of the rule of law
to incorporate the frontier and its vast natural resources, 'into an
America dominated by new forms of commerce, industry and
finance' (Brown, 1991:56).

 As Bell points out, 'the early settlers and founding fathers, as well
as those who "won the west"... often did so by shady speculations
and not an inconsiderable amount of violence' (Bell, 1953:152). So
with the night-time economy, where the bouncers and the security
firms that employ them are made up of 'good guys' and 'bad guys'

employing various levels of force to enable this new frontier to prosper despite the threat of marauding bands of young men wearing inappropriate footwear.

Criminals have traditionally been paid off by entrepreneurs operating in highly competitive markets (Block and Chambliss, 1981; Potter and Jenkins, 1985) and Alan Block clearly illustrates the historical trajectory of organized crime's awesome ability to adapt to new markets (Block, 1994:51), a trajectory that continues to arc through capitalism's various manifestations which happen to be currently cloaked in the man-made fibre of the night-time economy. By using violence or the threat of violence to strategically position itself, organized crime and security 'consultants' dictate contract protocols and police trade agreements designed to restrict competition. As Reuter et al., (1983:11) indicate, such activity may not involve actual physical violence but, 'it seems reasonable to infer that the racketeers provide a credible continuing threat of violence that ensures compliance.' While both the reality and threat of violence remains a constant, mutations of legitimate business are enabled, before the circle is completed by organized crime's penetration of legal trade and commerce (Anderson, 1979; Moore, 1987; Reuter, 1987), which in turn creates additional business opportunities, as 'legitimate' security firms are created, and pubs, clubs, restaurants, and taxi firms are purchased, creating an expanded economy, policed by recourse to violence and the threat of such recourse (Block and Scarpetti, 1985; Hess, 1998; Kwitny, 1979).

As Ian Taylor has highlighted, protection is a growth industry, 'in insecure and competitive market societies' (1999:169) and the ability of organized crime groups to adapt rapidly to the feebly regulated night-time economy, while liberals, marketeers, and city boosters turn the other cheek, highlights the currency afforded to the reputations of organized crime groups that 'guarantee that individuals and firms yield to their demands' (Jacobs, 1999:118). Such reputations clearly constitute economic power, and in particular, afford access to financial resources (Arlacchi, 1986:91–92), imbuing the criminal entrepreneur with an eternal essence of malevolent authority that informs the way he is received in the realms of both licit and illicit enterprise. This authority and its related obligations and expectations forge the essential essences of both bouncers and organized crime personnel. Their complementary qualities exist independent of observable behaviour (Katz, 1975:1371), and feature violent potential and proficiency as a common inherent factor. Both operate with a moral licence that relieves them of normative obligations of physical restraint, and both make claims to possessing a special competence (Katz, 1975:1381).

Consequently violence impacts upon the entire 'spectrum of enterprise' (Reuter, 1983; Smith, 1980), a view that underlines the role of violence in assisting us to question the prurient assumption that crime and business are distinct categories of human endeavour (Ruggiero, 2000:64–74). Indeed, the clear logic of competition within this 'durable violent habitus' (Hall, 1997:462), can only be located within violent essences common to the often illusory distinction between 'legal' and 'illegal' enterprise in the night-time economy. However, as Arlacchi notes, when two entrepreneurial criminal firms who both enjoy the competitive advantages discussed above find themselves in direct competition, coercive power, or the threat of it, can be the only deciding factor (1986:157).

Door war

Police bid to contain violence as struggle for club security contracts escalates...When Tony Lawler was shot dead last Thursday, he became the latest victim of a bloodthirsty gang war that police believe is linked to the fight to control Merseyside's lucrative club security business (Thompson, 2001:3).

Within the night-time economy, both legitimate security companies and organized criminals emerge as entrepreneurs of trust via the threat and utility of violence. However, the protection on offer to venues is often protection against other extortionists seeking to gain a monopoly over the protection business (Buchanan, 1973). Consequently the protection procured is based upon a perception of the extorter as more violent than his rivals in the securing of trust (see McLean, 1998:75). Indeed, if '... one of the structural... features of protection is the toughness of the supplier, then it is part of the logic of the commodity itself to invite toughness comparisons... who hits harder can be expected to be a far more reliable protector. The most credible proof he can offer, in fact, consists in eliminating his competitors altogether' (Gambetta, 1988:140).

Mickey, a bouncer in a prominent Northern club, offered this example of his boss's physical, and therefore commercial prowess:

In the doorway of *Sadies* I was talking to Binman and Lee was there. Two large gentlemen with Dogtown accents appeared and asked where they could find Lee Cash. Unfortunately for them they asked Lee himself. When Lee replied, 'what do you want him for?,' they said that a well known Dogtown businessman was interested in taking over the doors in Lagerville. At that point Lee introduced himself, and they just attacked him. It did not last long . . . Both were hospitalized by Lee . . . one of the men had bitten Lee, drawing blood, so Lee went to the same hospital for a tetanus injection. While he was there the paramedics stretchered his attackers in. Lee kicked them off the stretchers and beat them again in the emergency room.

And so 'door wars' commence (see Chapter 3): 'in the last two months there's been about six machete attacks in Portville and we're talking arms hanging off, one guy even lost his leg. So it's really open warfare at the moment' (Fred, a licensee). As Falcone indicates (1993:116), extortion is a highly effective vehicle for consolidating control over territory, for territorial monopoly parallels success in the protection market in a way that is not apparent in commodity markets, either legal or illegal (Behan, 1996:110–112). While the majority of commodities are traded in terms of continuous, if negotiated, quantities and prices, protection is contingent upon violence, which as Gambetta points out is a 'dichotomous variable, i.e. if not you, then me' (1988:141). Violent force, not price, is the key, and especially visceral levels of competence that will attract the entire market within a given territory, 'he who beats hardest not only does away with the beaten competitors, but advertises himself as an adequate protector' (ibid.:140).

Of course, the role of protector/extortionist relies upon the provider of security being more violent than his clients. Frank North offered a hypothetical example of the process that occurs when organized crime firms want to take over a door, and then recites an actual example of how one nightclub manager has dealt with the threat:

Say the *Archers* from Burnchester come into this town and they want to start off in this town because they've been chased out of Burnchester, they can't operate there because of police pressure. So the Archers come in and they bring thirty or forty lads and they kick off and the doormen get beaten up, seriously beaten. Then one of them will go up to the manager and say I run a door firm in Burnchester and that would never happen to us. Then it's up to the manager and him to agree a price because all he wants is a peaceful club, he doesn't want it smashing to bits every night of the week. And if they don't reach an agreement they'll keep coming back and keep coming back, until there's no customers...

There's a Melchester firm in the Keynote area and town centre, run by a guy called Ditton, who's basically a protection racket. They've asked for five hundred pound a week from Arthur at *Trafalgar* nightclub which holds three thousand people. He says no chance and he's brought in an ex-SAS feller... and there's now fifteen ex-SAS doormen there. And they've said to Ditton basically, 'if you want to shoot people, if you want to cause trouble here, we'll wake you up in your own bed'. You know what I mean, these guys are experts, they're through your house and you don't even know till you've got a knife at your throat.

However, in the night-time economy extortion is often accepted as an informal tax (Winlow, 2001:147–153), and the careers of many notable organized crime figures were initially propelled by their successful involvement in extorting money from bars, and clubs (Pearson, 1973). Our research confirms that the exponential increase in public disorder generated by the boom in the night-time economy has produced a demand for security that cannot be met by the state, which in turn has severely damaged the credibility of neo-liberal institutions tasked with the provision of incorporation and market coherence in settings beyond the night-time economy (Evans et al., 1996:379). Further, extortion via protection is a difficult crime to police as it tends to occur behind closed doors and often leaves victims feeling aggrieved, but too afraid and intimidated to involve the police. Often the power of local community-based crime networks is such that 'grassing' is not a viable option for those who wish to live and/or conduct a business in the area (Evans et al., 1996).

Conclusion: class, capital, and trajectories of force

As an enduring expert system based upon 'local contextualities' (Giddens, 1991:22), the door-minding community operates within multiple cross-cutting networks of both criminal and legitimate opportunity. Bouncers are bonded by a powerful urban ethic constituting hubs of action and information, linking networks that feature webs of diversified coherence.

The potency of bouncer activity relies upon the degree of connectivity between urban élites, and it is this connectedness rather than the corporate identity of commercial leisure institutions, that creates powerful systems of commercial control across the city at night.

These connections have multi-dimensional faces connected by hubs (Gould, 1991:25; Johnson, 1983), and doorstaff constitute hubs who by virtue of their interconnectedness with these multidimensional sets of urban élites, combine flexibility and mobility with crucial qualities of relationality: family, pub, club, neighbourhood, and gym, combine with takeaways and cab firms, dealers and customers, buyers, and sellers.

The bouncing fraternity constitutes a local social system, '... patterns of relationship among individuals... which can be changed only by drastic... action' (Ianni, 1971:35). In locales where the material base for traditional communities has been obliterated, both crime and the muscle, so central to the provision of security, becomes located within loose collectivities of *ad hoc* groupings, for, 'the same processes that destroy autonomy are now creating new kinds of locality and identity' (Wilk, 1995:130).

The night-time economy as a locale, constitutes, as we claim in Chapter 1, a liminal zone, and the emergence of powerful forms of social control, bolstered by innovative variations on traditional pro-letarian male identities, offers both real and imagined segues into the contemporary urban aesthetic via the iconography of gangster chic, and a glimpse at the fiscal vicissitudes of contemporary urban entre-preneurship, largely devoid of normative (day-time) restraint. This lack of restraint in the liminal market, 'represents... an extension of a legitimate market spectrum (in this case the alcohol-based leisure industry) into areas normally proscribed' (Smith, 1974:164). Our analysis has documented that the prime concern of doorstaff is the management of liminality in a manner that maximizes profit, and it is clear that a spectrum of control has been established that flexes according to the specific requirements of designated venues. The management of liminality, as we stress in Chapter 5, enables informal methodologies of locally-based control to emerge that are above all pragmatic and responsive to the demands of the consumer market of the night-time economy, sharing the pragmatics of control regardless of the legal status of a venue's internal commerce. Consequently, for both legitimate and illegitimate entrepreneurs in the night-time econ-omy, muscle and money become interconnected with systems, subcul-tures, firms, chains, and corporations of mutual reciprocity in which, 'their separate strengths derive from the same fundamental consider-ations that govern entrepreneurship in the legitimate market place: a necessity to maintain and extend one's share of the market' (ibid.).

8

Night Futures: The Marketization of License and Control

Plunder and pollution were component parts of the frontier economy, attributable to the desire for rapid exploitation of an economic system that awarded the highest premium to the fiercest competitor, and a laissez faire government thoughtless of the common good (Hine and Faragher, 2000:438–39).

Throughout our story, intoxicants and fashions may have changed, but the passionate, chaotic, allure of the urban night remains constant as people continue to seek 'time out' from their daily lives by sharing in liminal communion. What has changed is not only the economic status of the liminal zones, but the manner in which transgression in the night-time economy is regarded by governing élites, and the concurrent ways in which such activities are regulated and policed. This chapter explores contemporary trends in the control, regulation, and policing of the night-time economy. We identify a series of profound and dynamic shifts in governmental arenas as diverse as alcohol licensing, planning law, public and private policing, and town centre management, all of which impact significantly upon the nature of the night-time urban environment. These mostly incremental, but sometimes radical, transformations are, we argue, driven by one underlying process: marketization. The marriage of leisure and commerce within after-dark post-industrial urban centres is a union consummated by deregulatory pragmatism and ordained via implicit governmental sanction and an expectation of righteous consumption. The increasing willingness to 'grant licences to trade' reflects the contemporary ascendancy of a political economy which upholds the 'licence to sell and consume an intoxicating leisure experience' as a valued marker of individual and collective freedom. Yet, as this chapter describes, the ascendance of market freedom is being accompanied by the corresponding decline of local democratic accountability and individual and collective opportunity.

Development, diversification, and homogeneity

As described in our case study of Manchester (Chapter 3), although many local governmental strategies seeking to facilitate the night-time economy have been economically successful, they have often failed to meet the social needs and aspirations of local communities. We would suggest that the gulf between the initial visions of a vibrant, urbane, and inclusive marriage of culture and commerce inherent in the much-lauded concept of the '24-hour city' (Heath and Stickland, 1997; Jones et al., 1999) and the subsequent reality of almost exclusively alcohol- and youth-centred 'leisure zones' is so great that such strategies now face something of a credibility crisis. Whilst the prophets of 'cultural regeneration' foresaw post-modern 'playgrounds,' the market forces unleashed by deregulation have contributed to the creation of scenes more akin to a pre-modern battleground. Jane Jacobs' (1961) famous arguments regarding the social and economic benefits of the populous after-dark street have been important theoretical cornerstones of the '24-hour city' concept, and also of official crime prevention policy guidance (DoE, 1994). However, the market-led monoculture of theme bars, branded pub, and fast-food outlets emerging from the strategies of deregulation pursued in the name of this concept are a corruption of Jacobs' vision. Although many night-time leisure venues may be responsibly run and of benefit to local economies, all too often the 'entertainment offer' is targeted at a socially narrow, youth and drink-based segment of the market. Jacobs specifically warned against what she called this 'duplication of the most profitable of use' (1961:259). Yet, *alcohol*-based leisure pursuits now dominate the nightlife of our urban centres, and the ability of towns and cities to attract investment from the purveyors of this commodity has become a central gauge of post-industrial prosperity.

We have found that once drinking circuits are established around clusters of licensed premises, such areas often become city-wide or even regional attractions for revellers, and the increased activity levels begin to place a chronic drain, not only upon local policing, but also upon the resources of the NHS, local authorities, and the criminal justice system. Relatively little violence may occur within licensed premises themselves, rather problems tend to flare on the street and around taxi ranks and fast-food outlets as people compete for scarce resources and antagonistically inclined groups connect.

Many of the problems are more 'low-level quality of life' issues, the cumulative effects of which should not be underestimated. In particular, current development trends impact adversely upon the lives of the residents of central urban areas. In addition to bearing witness to violence and disorder and experiencing the fear and anxiety of crime, residents may face an almost intolerable range of problems, including late-night noise, vandalism of property, litter, and the fouling of pavements and doorsteps. These unpleasant experiences sit uneasily with the vision of 'urban renaissance' contained in the recent Urban White Paper (DETR, 2000b), which calls upon local government to encourage residential communities to return to the 'compact' core of our urban centres.

Furthermore, the concentration of night-time entertainment uses in an area can often encourage rental levels to be set by reference to the profitability of such venues, which within city centre drinking circuits can be very high. The market pressures placed upon less profitable, non-alcohol-based businesses such as high street cinemas, theatres, live music venues, and restaurants, then ensure that they can no longer afford to operate in the area, being displaced by additional alcohol-led businesses. This loss of diversity can have the effect of discouraging wider community participation in night-life, an important issue given that the very presence of socially and culturally diverse crowds can serve to 'normalize' the on-street environment and enhance informal controls (Jacobs, 1961). Young and not-so-young drinkers now 'own' many town and city centres at night. When such ownership is established, these areas become even more attractive to people seeking a permissive leisure environment free from the supervision or censure of the other citizens with whom they share these spaces at other times. This 'honey-pot' effect facilitates the creation of social environments in which aggressive hedonism and disorder become the norm. In such ways, the market-led destruction of diversity serves to fuel the gradual atrophy of 'democratically accessible' night-time public space.

For example, were one asked to deliberately devise a way of exacerbating problems of violence and disorder in a small English market town one would be hard pushed to better a proposal to replace the only cinema with a 700-capacity bar/nightclub sitting cheek and jowl next to several other high capacity licensed premises and adjacent to a late-night kebab shop in an area with no late-night public transport and assault and disorder rates already four times higher than those of any other location in the county. Yet, *in the night-time economy, locations that are 'bad' for crime and disorder are invariably 'good' for business* and the ambitious national 'roll-out' plans of the licensed trade ensure that proposals of this kind are commonplace. As the deregulation of municipal control continues apace, there is now an urgent need to reconcile the competing interests of businesses, residents, consumers, the police, local authorities, and other stakeholders. As the state attempts to keep pace with the whirlwind of post-industrial alcohol-based redevelopment, legislative and regulatory innovations designed to impact upon the night-time economy are multiplying.

Contemporary controls

At the time of writing (September, 2002), alcohol licensing in England and Wales remains governed by the Licensing Act 1964 (as amended by subsequent legislation), which imposes a set of universally prescribed trading hours. Normal licensing hours for pubs and registered clubs run from 11 a.m. to 11 p.m. Monday–Saturday, and from 12 noon to 10.30 p.m. on Sundays. However, Section 77 of the Licensing Act also provides for Special Hours Certificates which licensing justices may grant to venues providing 'substantial refreshment' (food) and holding a Public Entertainment Licence (PEL) which permits music and dancing. Special Hours Certificates permit alcohol to be sold as an ancillary to the music, dancing and refreshment beyond the normal licensing hours up to 2 a.m. (3 a.m. in central London). Unlike liquor licences (which have traditionally been granted by magistrates), PELs fall within the jurisdiction of local authorities who, using powers conferred in the Local Government (Miscellaneous Provisions) Act 1982 and the London Government Act 1963, exercise complete discretion with regard to their duration.

A profound transformation has recently occurred in the way in which the magistrates consider new liquor licensing applications. Following publication of the Justices' Clerks Society's *Good Practice Guide* (1999), justices have been issued with new guidelines recommending the abolition of need/demand as a criterion relevant to the granting of licences. Considerations of how many licensed premises already exist in an area and the resultant 'need' for further outlets had traditionally been used as a means of exerting control over the number of licences permitted within popular localities. The recent abandonment of the 'need' criterion (see Light, 2000), has played a key role in facilitating the recent growth of city centre drinking circuits. The *Guide* states that the test of need is now 'out of date and unnecessary' (para. 3.25), thereby endorsing laissez-faire opinion that within a competitive market, economic pressures alone will serve to regulate the number of licensed premises in an area. A police licensing officer alluded to the policing implications of this shift from municipal regulation to market regulation:

The government view is that if two pubs want to open up next door to each other then one will survive and one will go to the wall if there's not enough custom. Now it's all right for them to say that because they don't have to mop-up afterwards when they're selling it for fifty pence a pint or reducing the price of vodka like they did in Sunderland for ten pence a shot. It's all right saying just let the licensed premises fight it out for themselves because as well as the trade wars it also means they'll let people in that they wouldn't normally; they are not bothered if they are under age, they are not bothered if they are too drunk already, as long as they get some money off them to stay in business.

The *Guide* does not, however, entirely abandon the principle of imposing artificial market restrictions. Committees are required to be primarily concerned 'with issues of public safety and the protection of the public against nuisance and disorder' by ensuring that the 'licensed premises in an area do not become so numerous as to produce problems of noise and disorder' (para. 3.28). In such circumstances it is expected that the police will make a formal objection to each new licence application and also produce evidence that the risk to public order is 'real rather than fanciful' (para. 3.28).[1] The deregulation of alcohol licensing is also proceeding in a number of other ways. The Sunday Licensing De-regulation Order, passed by the House of Lords in March 2001, has amended the Licensing Act to permit Special Hours Certificates to be granted for late-night Sunday opening. More importantly, the most radical reform of the alcohol licensing laws for almost a century is now in prospect. Shelved in 2001, the new laws will be based on proposals contained in a now over two year old White Paper entitled *Time for Reform: Proposals for the Modernization of our Licensing Laws* (Home Office, 2000a).

---

[1] A full discussion of the difficulties police and other objectors can face in meeting this test can be found in Hadfield (forthcoming a).

The White Paper reveals plans to remove responsibility for liquor licensing from the magistracy and to transfer licensing powers to local authorities. *Time for Reform* ... also proposes that existing statutory trading hours be abolished and replaced by a more flexible and discretionary system which would, in principle, permit licensed premises to remain open twenty-four hours a day, seven days a week. The new legislation looks likely to be introduced as the Licensing and Entertainment Bill in the November 2002 Queen's Speech. If the Bill is selected for inclusion it will probably receive Royal Assent in the summer of 2003 and take effect some time in 2004. *Time for Reform* ... attempts to balance its deregulatory stance by proposing a range of measures to counter any criminogenic 'side effects' arising in the new era of market-led 'flexibility' and 'consumer choice'. These controls include specified 'tough new powers for the police', a more graduated and 'flexible range of sanctions',[2] the introduction of personal licences for licensees which could be endorsed and eventually forfeited (after three endorsements), and the greater use of exclusion orders with regard to troublesome customers (Home Office, 2000a:14). Despite the absence of any substantial evidence base (Hadfield, 2002), the White Paper also supports claims that the introduction of more 'flexible' trading hours will, in itself, serve to reduce violence and disorder by removing the incentive to 'binge drink' before 'last orders', whilst promoting a more relaxed 'continental' atmosphere in which people drink the same amount, but over a longer period of time. It is also suggested that revellers will disperse more gradually, thus reducing crowding and tension at taxi ranks, fast food outlets and other flashpoints (ibid.: para. 64:32; Marsh and Fox-Kibby, 1992).

Surprisingly, given the current government emphasis upon evidence-led policy-making, very little is known about whether this approach actually works. Whilst *Time for Reform* ... confidently predicts that the removal of statutory hours will reduce violence and disorder, the only research presented in support of this argument is funded and published by the drinks industry, contains serious flaws, and is now over ten years old (see Marsh and Fox-Kibby, 1992). More recently, the Department of Culture, Media and Sport (DCMS), (the government department presently responsible for

---

[2] Proposed sanctions include temporarily or permanently reduced trading hours for premises in breach of the conditions attached to their licence (para. 96, pp. 40–41).

alcohol licensing reforms), has expounded the predicted benefits of relaxed licensing hours by highlighting apparently falling violent crime statistics in the rather atypical Isle of Man, which abolished set closing times in July 2001. The Chief Constable's *Annual Report 2001–2002* for the Isle of Man Constabulary, however, contains a rather more cautious evaluation:

...the changes in the law have altered the shape of demand faced by us. On the positive side the old closing time rush no longer seems to happen, but on the negative side, more incidents now take place well into the night and on Sundays.... the percentage of calls to the police in relation to alcohol-related matters has not altered as a result of de-regulation. What has changed is the time at which these incidents occur. There is now a more gradual call on police resources. I would sound some warnings, however: calls now extend well into the night and weekends, as people appear to be out much later than before. This has an effect on police staffing levels. Secondly, Sunday is fast becoming a day on which many drink-related incidents occur. Again this has resource implications for the police (p. 12).

According to the report, in 2001 there were on the whole of the Isle of Man, 268 on-licensed premises, including restaurant and residential licences, eighty off-licences and forty-six registered clubs. The figures for Douglas are 155 on-licences, thirty-three off-licences and thirteen registered clubs. Clearly, the DCMS is less familiar than the Home Office with the importance of context when attempting to transfer crime reduction lessons (see Pawson and Tilley, 1997). Major British cities attract thousands upon thousands of revellers from across regional conurbations every weekend and the number of outlets in Douglas is far smaller than to be found in these locations. For example, Norwich has 876 on- and off-licences and 106 registered clubs; Southampton 821 on- and off-licences and 156 registered clubs. Birmingham has 1,527 on- and off-licences and 273 registered clubs. Notwithstanding the annual pilgrimage to the Isle of Man of hordes of leather-clad motorcyclists, such unsophisticated attempts at meaningful comparison are, we would argue, plainly spurious.

One reason why the evidence on the proposed reforms remains inconclusive is due to the difficulty of isolating the 'cause and effect' of longer drinking hours when wider structural changes are occurring simultaneously, significantly for example, the exponential growth in the number of drinking venues. Other salient issues, such as the concentration of venues in small areas and the availability of transport in the early hours, also exert considerable influence over people's activities and behaviour, and the potential impact of later hours should be considered within this wider context. Although the notion that more 'flexible' licensing hours will encourage the stretching of drinking patterns across longer periods of time does seem plausible, evidence emerging from cities that have experienced deregulation under current licensing laws, suggests that this may not always be the case.

As the Bar Entertainment and Dance Association (BEDA, 2000) point out, in areas where some venues are open longer than others, many operators will seek to trade late in order to remain commercially competitive. To some extent this has already occurred in places such as Liverpool city centre and the West End of London where a large proportion of premises now sell alcohol until the very latest currently permitted time (2 a.m. and 3 a.m. respectively). Equally, operators can sometimes be reluctant to remain open later than the locally prevailing trading hour due to a combination of diminished takings and undiminished costs (LGA, 2002). Thus, whilst it might be argued that extending closing times up to a pre-set legal limit (as has occurred under the current licensing system) could realize different effects from abolishing closing times altogether, evidence would suggest that market pressures encourage businesses to close at similar times (BEDA, 2000). Therefore, even though premises might not remain completely full until their terminal hour, the orderly and staggered dispersal of crowds that liberals envisage is, in many contexts, improbable. The mass exodus may simply be delayed, rather than avoided. In addition, it is less than certain that customers will simply drink the same amount over a longer period of time. It seems equally probable, given the current emphasis upon the youth market and drinking to intoxication, that increasingly the availability of alcohol might also increase aggregate levels of consumption. If the state thereby unintentionally encourages rather than discourages 'binge drinking', as appears to have been the case in the Scottish and Irish post-deregulation experience, elected officials may find the adverse criminological and environmental impacts of the new legislation rather more difficult to swallow.

Whilst the Association of Chief Police Officers (ACPO) generally supports deregulation, many of the police officers that we encountered took a more critical stance, suggesting that the potential negative impact upon operational policing resources should be more fully explored prior to legislative change. We have already witnessed many UK police forces restructuring shift patterns in order to time-match peak resources to peak demand. This inevitably requires reactive overlay shifts to operate on Friday and Saturday nights, which thereby squeeze operational resources from other places and times of the week at the expense of other 'virtual' or 'real' communities. If the majority of city centre venues are to trade further into the night, the pattern of violence and disorder is likely to correspondingly shift, with incidents peaking at later hours. This outcome would stretch police manpower still further across time, and heighten the skew that the night-time economy already places on police resources.

So, you think you're tough?

A number of the 'tough new powers for the police' proposed in *Time for Reform* . . . have already been enacted within the Criminal Justice and Police Act, which came into force on 1 December 2001. The Act gives the police new powers to issue 'on the spot' penalties for disorderly behaviour (section 1), and also, as detailed in Chapter 6, to serve immediate closure orders on licensed premises for initial periods of up to twenty-four hours (section 17). Local authorities are afforded the power to designate areas within which drinking in public is prohibited (sections 12 and 13), licensees and bar staff are required to take 'all reasonable steps' to verify the age of their younger customers (section 30), and the offence of permitting drunkenness and disorderly behaviour within licensed premises is extended to all staff, rather than simply the licensee (section 32).

Although, baldly stated, such powers may sound draconian, it should be noted that there are a number of sub-sections within the Act that might well serve to restrict its utility as an instrument of regulation. Moreover, if the general failure to apply other recent 'strong' legislation can be used as an indicator, it would seem that within the current regulatory context, which favours compliance, dialogue, and partnership, rather than 'conflict' between police, local authorities and 'the trade', many of the Act's provisions could well remain largely unused. For example, the Public Entertainment Licences (Drugs Misuse) Act [1997] gave local authorities the power to immediately revoke the PELs of premises identified by police as having a serious and ongoing 'drugs problem'. The Act sought primarily to target late-night venues whose operators were found to be either 'unable or unwilling' to resolve effectively their venue's drug-related problems. BEDA and other trade associations expressed their concern about the potential scope and implications of this legislation, 'forcefully reminding senior government, council, and police figures that the Act should not be used lightly and that communication and partnership should always come first' (Night, 2001:14). To this end, BEDA secured an offer from the Home Office to serve on a working party to help develop operational guidance to accompany the Act. The subsequent guidelines (BEDA, 1997) sought to minimize the possibility of nightclub operators being wrongly prosecuted and indeed, notwithstanding its application in a few high profile cases (most notably the closure of the Home nightclub in central London[3]), the full provisions of the Act have rarely been invoked.

Deregulation of the night-time economy has also been accompanied by new forms of control at the local level. As noted in Chapter 6, an array of spatially and temporally targeted 'multi-agency' initiatives seeking to reduce criminal opportunities, increase formal controls, detect crime, and reassure the public have been implemented including CCTV and radio-link initiatives, door registration schemes, and restrictive by-laws.[4] However, in many towns and cities there remains a distinct reluctance among municipal regulators to arrest the phenomenal growth of the licensed trade infrastructure and to thereby restrict the availability of alcohol. As the Town Centre Manager of a Northern city commented, 'we won't restrict, the market will decide whether expansion continues'. In response to our questions regarding the public safety implications of such continued expansion, he had this to say:

There is an argument, in the main from the police, that you can't go on opening up more pubs and clubs without the infrastructure being in place to support, contain and control all of that. But our view is that we'll handle it, we'll deal with it, by putting in place a range of security initiatives. There are a number of ways things can be improved.

[3] Home cost its operators Big Beat £10 million to develop. The City of Westminster revoked the venue's PEL after an undercover police operation revealed extensive evidence of drug dealing. Although a subsequent hearing reinstated the club's licence, the subsequent loss of cash flow forced Big Beat into receivership.

[4] For a detailed summary of recent measures employed in the prevention of alcohol-related violence and disorder see Hadfield (forthcoming b).

The 'ways things can be improved' should be understood as attempts to set rules and impose a degree of order within what can often be an essentially 'lawless' environment. However, we would argue that many of these initiatives are having a limited impact upon crime reduction outcomes. First, they have done little to enhance the scarce resources available to the police and other agencies for enforcement purposes. Secondly, alcohol-related crime and disorder is by nature spontaneous and expressive rather than premeditated and acquisitive, participants often being oblivious to the presence of CCTV for example.[5] Thirdly, in many towns and cities, late-night transport services continue to be minimal or non-existent resulting in large numbers of people, some in a particularly vulnerable state, competing for taxis (Morleo, 2002). Fourthly, those who fall outside the night-time economy's 'target consumer group', particularly older people and women, often regard these leisure zones as threatening and therefore seek to avoid them (Bromley et al., 2000; Thomas and Bromley, 2000). The absence of these groups not only undermines informal processes of social control but also raises issues of social exclusion, as does the plight of central area residents, the poorer of whom are denied even the option of avoidance, the seductions of fashionable 'loft living' having somehow passed them by. Most importantly however, although many of the initiatives seek to crack down on licensed trade 'bad apples', they do little to improve the problems in public space, thus leaving a 'rotten barrel' on the streets.

More radically, attempts have recently been made to encourage and develop arrangements under which licensed businesses make a financial contribution to the policing and crime prevention costs generated by their commercial activities. Using powers contained in the Police and Magistrates' Courts Act 1994, which permits police authorities to seek additional income equivalent to one per cent of

[5] A recent Home Office-funded summary of evaluation studies found that in the city centre setting 'CCTV led to a negligible reduction in crime of about two per cent *in* experimental areas compared with control areas' (Welsh and Farringdon, 2002:vi). Similarly, Armitage notes that CCTV is most effective in reducing property crime and least effective in preventing public order offences involving alcohol, 'where "rationality" is often lost' and deterrent effects are thereby weakened (2002:3; see also Brown, 1998). By contrast, Farringdon and Welsh (2002) found that in some circumstances improved street lighting *did* appear to have crime preventative utility in central urban locations.

their annual budgets by charging for extra services, a number of police forces have introduced innovative schemes in which city centre operators are asked to 'club together' to purchase additional public policing provision on the basis of a standard overtime levy (see Lister, 2001). This 'polluter pays' approach, which has already been piloted in a number of areas, including Manchester, Leeds, and London, received government endorsement in the policing reform White Paper (Home Office, 2001d:97). As part of the government's wide-ranging review of public policing services, such schemes are seen to encourage businesses to take 'responsibility themselves for the public order implications of their activities' (ibid.).

Within this context, however, the penetration of the public police by private finance has the capacity to create significant conflicts of interest. Within these contractual arrangements Johnston queries the extent to which the 'customer is always right' maxim may impact upon the police's 'judicious use of discretion' (1992:69). Clearly, insofar as the police retain a key discretionary role within the processes of granting, renewing, and revoking operational liquor licences, there exists cause for concern. Unsurprisingly, we have discovered that leisure corporations, which contribute financially to discrete policing schemes, are not slow to cite these 'philanthropic' gestures when making court applications for new liquor licences.

New methods of gaining access to sustainable private sector funding streams are also being explored under proposals to introduce Business Improvement Districts (BIDS) schemes into the UK. BIDS are a North American model of urban management which promote the establishment of public–private sector partnership funding, typically in support of a range of service interventions which seek to enhance the 'cleanliness and safety' of urban public space. BIDS operate within distinct spatial boundaries usually determined by an identifiable community of interest or requirement of need. At the time of writing, it appears that BIDS schemes are soon to be supported by new enabling legislation to allow a supplementary tax to be added to local business rates thus permitting their widespread facilitation by local authorities. Recent proposals by the Central London Partnership (GLA, 2002) include the creation of BIDs in nightlife areas such as the West End, in which local businesses would be encouraged to purchase additional refuse and cleansing services and also, importantly, to fund additional levels of policing, whether civilian 'street wardens', such as those currently operational in Leicester Square, or public police officers in the format described above. Such innovative schemes aim to create a 'safer trading and investment environment' by inserting 'extra' policing agents into the public spaces of the night-time city, yet the normative implications of these arrangements may be far-reaching.

As Norris and Johnson note, 'town centre management could in future be delivered by a fully business-led partnership' (2002:7), yet the danger remains that 'not surprisingly, the economic and market strength of an area influences the willingness of businesses to contribute. It is clearly easier to extract money from businesses in already thriving places where they can see a real prospect of return' (ibid.:6). Thus it seems likely that achieving private sector support might, from the outset, involve prioritizing the needs of business (ATCM, 2002). Yet, in the context of the night-time economy at least, the basic needs of business seem already to have been met. As the public spaces of our urban centres become apparently ever more dirty, noisy, and dangerous, the alcohol-based attractions which draw in their narrowly constituted, but voluminous, congregations continue to prosper. The concern must be that commerce is able to co-opt the activities of the state in pursuit of private interests at the expense of the wider public good. Potentially this may occur if privately funded wardens, acting as extra 'eyes and ears' for the police, are able to lay greater claim to scarce operational police resources. More generally the concern must arise that the gradual transfer of responsibility from public to private sector will involve a corresponding transference of operational control. This shift could create opportunities for 'self-regulation' in which business, rather than democratically accountable local government, has the ability to define managerial priorities within the night-time city.

Such attempts to foster corporate responsibility provide the key to contemporary governmentality's essential pragmatism with regard to the night-time economy, opening the door to a future that is deregulated, privatized, and largely dependent upon the market's willingness, at best in collaboration with state control agencies, to engage with public order problematics. Notwithstanding any deep-seated normative concerns, recent managerial initiatives should, from an operational perspective, be understood as attempts to ease the symptoms of the problems now facing the night-time economy, whilst offering little by way of a cure.

At the heart of the problem lies the fact that since city centre drinking circuits now attract unprecedented numbers of consumers they have also become highly attractive locations for further licensed trade investment. Yet concurrently, a number of local authorities, responding to rising levels of night-time crime and disorder, are now attempting to *restrict* further colonization of their city centres by the licensed trade. For example, and significantly, The City of Westminster, the UK's flagship council in terms of the number and density of licensed premises, has recently identified a number of 'stress' areas in the West End of London. Within these designated 'stress' areas, the council has acknowledged that civic amenities such as policing, transport, environmental services and residential quality of life are being placed under chronic strain by existing levels of development and that the infrastructure can no longer cope with further incremental growth in the number of licensed premises. Thus the uncomfortable reality is that the night-time economy is a fiercely contested arena, and our experiences indicate that the public order problematics which surround it are continually rendered ever more ambiguous by the leisure chains' highly resourced legal teams who descend upon courtrooms across the land to contest with democratic institutions and their agencies the imposition of yet another 1,500 plus capacity youth-orientated theme pub (Hadfield, forthcoming a). If the leisure industry win, the shareholders are happy. If, as is often the case, the local state loses, this has both immediate and ongoing resource implications inasmuch as the public purse, which funds schooling, welfare, and a host of other municipal services, can be significantly depleted. It is not an equal contest.

Going with the flow

Although '24-hour city' strategies in Britain have generally failed to deliver the 'public goods' (Hadfield et al., 2001) many officials of the local state continue to cling to their initial visions of an inclusive and 'civilized' night-time economy. The plea that 'this is not what we intended' now echoes around more than a few council offices, strategy meetings, and conference tables. When faced with questions of what is to be done to reduce problems of violence and disorder, the typical refrain is to call for the promotion of a more diversified leisure provision, supported *this time* by, for example, an improved late-night transport system, better street lighting, or a consideration of the needs of residents. Although reducing the current monopoly of youth-orientated bars and clubs in favour of attractions for different age groups such as theatres, cinemas, and shops appears to be a welcome discovery of what a cynic might call common sense, such a seemingly noble stance requires some qualification. The stance, in our experience, is usually adopted after several years of rapid and unco-ordinated expansion and a concomitant rocketing of street violence and disorder. Thus new regulatory controls often come to be developed in response to problems that the planners and policy-makers themselves helped initially to create (see Chapter 6). Further, it is now proving to be very difficult, retrospectively, to insert commercial diversity into a marketplace that is, as we have consistently stressed, driven primarily by cold commercial, rather than social, considerations. For instance, in accordance with the requirements of section 77 of the Licensing Act, it has long been necessary for operators of late-night bars to display their credentials as the providers of services as diverse as food and dancing. In many cases, the preparation of glossy menus is little more than a cynical exercise in 'window dressing' to parade before the more gullible of magistrates, Local Authority Licensing Committees and police officers. One police officer provided the benefit of his experience on the matter:

Whenever you get an application they never say this pub is going to be for drunken young people who are just out of school, still chewing gum, while drinking from the neck of a bottle and talking about school; they never come to the court and say that. They always say 'well this is a different pub now, it's a different image to all the others which you've granted. This is for the more mature, more discerning drinker and look at our wonderful menu'; and it's a load of bollocks basically and I know that it is at the time. I've been doing this long enough to know it's the same application done by a different solicitor every time, you know, same keywords, same trigger words and nothing changes.

However, we have also noted some small shifts toward diversity that are driven not by the concerns of local regulators, but purely by the recognition by corporate forces that not all potential alcohol revenue is to be gleaned from youthful consumers. A small number of corporate branded venues together with a range of smaller independent operations, currently target a market segment referred to as the 'virtual 30s', that is, affluent consumers in their 30s and 40s who still enjoy nightlife, but who wish to conduct it within attractive premises where they can drink, dance, and eat in an environment which is not dominated by boisterous 18–25 year olds. The central problems preventing the further commercial exploitation of this market appear to surround the continued development of such premises within city centre leisure zones. Even the most 'enlightened' of operators are loath to take the additional financial risks inherent in investing in off-circuit or unfashionable locations. When contemplating development costs of rarely less than £1 million, long-term accumulation strategies which seek to tap 'new markets' will often be subordinated to the hard-headed managerial pursuit of the 'bottom line': guaranteed short-term returns.

Once a new operator enters a city centre leisure zone they must, out of commercial necessity, be prepared to accommodate the needs and wishes of the area's existing clientele. Moreover, although investing in existing nightlife areas may make sound economic sense in terms of projected profitability, such locations almost invariably come with a certain amount of 'baggage' in terms of negative local perceptions among the very consumer groups one's diversified product might hope to attract. In view of such problems, some commentators suggest that, at least in the short term, existing drinking circuits might be considered 'a lost cause' and that the development of new spatially and functionally distinct leisure zones appealing to the more mature or discerning consumer should be encouraged (Bromley et al., 2000). Whilst in a number of larger cities and conurbations it is indeed possible to identify what might be termed 'branded specialist enclaves', such as Manchester's Northern Quarter, Leeds' Exchange Quarter, and Newcastle's Osborne Road, such areas appear mostly to provide market niches rather than any more radical form of functional diversity. Put more simply, such enclaves remain firmly alcohol-based. Whilst independently operated bars may offer their customers a degree of distinction from the 'masses', they remain in essence *bars*. As our discussion of contemporary Manchester attests, the night-time leisure market is a fickle one in which perceptions of 'safety', 'exclusivity', and 'credibility' carry considerable market premium. Thus, areas move in and out of fashion, what is a 'safe haven' or 'mild zone' one year can become the 'main strip' by the next. Hence the mutant profile of Manchester's 'Gay Village', the meteoric rise of Peter Street/Quay Street (referred to in Chapter 3) and the distinct consumer switch within Newcastle upon Tyne away from the traditional Bigg Market drinking circuit, toward the 'upmarket' attractions of the Quayside (see Chatterton and Hollands, 2001).

Fashions in entertainment also promise change. In 1998 when we began the research for this book, 'superclubs' such as *Cream* in Liverpool, Sheffield's *Gatecrasher* and London's *Ministry of Sound* were still at the height of their popularity. Five years on these infamous weekly events, once the flagships of their respective city's night-time economies have now either closed due to diminished takings or have drastically scaled down their events calendar. Late-night bars, outdoor festivals, and specialist club nights such as those organized by promotions company *School Disco.com* 'where nostalgia rules and lager is the drug of choice' (Petridis, 2002:2) are now in the ascendancy.

Thus, we would argue that within the current regulatory context at least, attempts to create differentiated 'mild zones' will gain limited success due to the fluidity and instrumental venom of the market. In the long term we would suggest that only diversification of the night-time economy as a whole can offer real opportunities for the development of safer and more sustainable urban environments. Many barriers exist to the realization of this vision, perhaps the most important of which are actively created by the nature of contemporary regulatory structures themselves. Licensed premises are subject to three main forms of municipal control: planning, public entertainment licensing, and liquor licensing. A brief description of planning issues in particular is essential to an understanding of the recent development trends we describe.

(De)regulating the night-time city

Owing to processes of decentralization and rationalization, many provincial urban centres have experienced a loss of retail and financial service investment. This has had a profound effect upon the distribution of land uses, as successful applications to convert empty shops and offices into leisure-related businesses have begun to transform the commercial character of many central areas. Despite the existence of contrary government planning policy guidance (DoE, 1996), planning permission for new 'food and drink' developments continues to be granted in areas where the major activity, particularly at night, has already become drinking alcohol and eating fast food. Other problems surround the issue of land use planning law.

The Town and Country Planning (Use Classes) Order 1987 (UCO) allocated a standard (A3) land use classification to all types of business selling food or drink for consumption on the premises, or hot food for consumption off the premises. This has had a considerable deregulatory impact, as changes of use to other purposes within this category are no longer taken to involve development. Thus cafés and takeaways can turn into restaurants and then into bars and pubs (which subsequently may seek to obtain PELs and Special Hours Certificates), without requiring further planning consent.

Special conditions with regard to issues such as 'trading hours' and 'the adverse effects of concentration' can currently be imposed upon the Use Class as a whole in the form of supplementary planning guidance or through changes to the Local or Unitary Development Plan. Yet although such measures provide a degree of flexibility, given the breadth of class A3 and also that of class D2 (which incorporates nightclubs), planners are still left with a very blunt instrument with which to control the environmental impact and cumulative effects of a market-led 'destruction of diversity'.

In response to such problems, a number of local authorities have long urged a review of the UCO (see Delafons, 1996) involving revised wording to control changes of use within the A3 and D2 categories. Planning research published by the Department of Transport, Local Government and the Regions (DTLR), found that 85 per cent of local authorities responding to a survey on the issue reported concerns related to 'the breadth of the activities included within the A3 Use Class and hence with the opportunity for change to take place without planning control' (Baker Associates, 2001:35). The recommendations of the Baker Associates study have subsequently formed the basis of a consultation paper outlining a number of options for change to the UCO (ODPM, 2002) emerging in the context of a wider consultation exercise relating to the publication of *Planning: Delivering a Fundamental Change* (DTLR, 2001), a Green Paper proposing major reform of the planning system. At the time of writing, the results of this consultation process have yet to be announced and there appears to be no specific timetable for confirming and implementing any changes. However, interestingly, the principal option outlined in the consultation document proposes the creation of a 'Mixed Retail Use Class' which would have the effect of *further* deregulating planning controls with regard to smaller licensed premises (up to 100 sq.m). Clearly the likely impact of increasing the concentration of smaller licensed premises, as has occurred in London's Soho, has not been anticipated.

The proposed reform of the UCO should also be viewed within the context of the wide-reaching changes to the planning system envisaged in the Green Paper. The document proposes to replace the existing Unitary Development Plans and Local Plans used by local authorities to outline their land use policies with a new system based around more 'flexible' Local Development Frameworks (LDFs). Whilst permitting local authorities to make 'statements of core policy', the LDF system effectively abolishes the ability of planners to incorporate specific geographical designations such as 'entertainment stress area' or 'primary retail frontage' within their policies, thereby removing the ability to specify the maximum thresholds for different types of use within different localities. Such strategic approaches are currently the mainstay of urban planning policies intended to maintain and facilitate mixed use, and their abolition is likely to undermine the ability of local authorities to resist the over-concentration of licensed premises of any size.

The key objectives of the Green Paper are to increase the speed and efficiency of a planning system which 'is too often perceived to be a set of rules aimed at preventing development' and which business finds 'frustrating and potentially damaging to their competitiveness' (DTLR, 2001:3). Whilst 'an emphasis on supporting business and competitiveness is evident throughout the Green Paper' (Elson, 2002:31), issues relating to sustainable development and the environment are afforded somewhat lesser priority. A recent report by MPs on the Transport, Local Government and the Regions Select Committee concluded that a 'business agenda is running through much of the Green Paper. It largely ignores the environment while supporting business development' (Urban Environment Today, 2002:3).

A principle extolled by Government is that licensing and planning should not duplicate each other (Home Office, 2000a:para. 46) and indeed, as previously noted, traditional tests of 'need' have largely been removed from existing alcohol licensing deliberations. Thus, although magistrates still retain the right to refuse a licence when presented with 'real, rather than fanciful' police evidence that the density of licensed premises is causing problems of public nuisance and disorder, in the current context, 'planning provides not so much the key, as the only form of control over the number of outlets in a locality (McNeill, 2002:22). For the night-time economy, the crucial issues arising from the current reviews of planning law therefore relate to a potential undermining of the ability of municipal regulators to prevent the market-led spatial intensification of monocultural development. More specifically what is at stake is the power of local government to 'plan in diversity' and 'plan out crime'. The potential impact of the proposed changes to planning law thus relate closely to the most contentious and divisive issue in the regulation of contemporary nightlife: cumulative effect (Hadfield, forthcoming a). Issues of cumulative effect, explained below, are also central to the debate surrounding the proposed changes to alcohol licensing law.

One of the principal defects of *Time for Reform*..., the aforementioned alcohol licensing White Paper (Home Office, 2000a), is that it seeks to tackle issues of violence and disorder solely at the level of individual premises whilst failing to acknowledge the cumulative effects of concentrations of outlets in particular localities. Under the *Time for Reform*...proposals, which now form the basis of a draft Licensing Bill, each local authority will be given powers to develop a comprehensive licensing policy for its area, thus providing a framework within which the licensing committee's decisions on individual applications can be assessed. Applicants will be required to submit a proposed operating plan, setting out how the premises would be run, with applications considered on their individual merit.

The main emergent issues, which at the time of writing still remain unclear, relate to the status of these new licensing policies. For example, it is not known whether such policies will carry legal force or the extent to which the new licensing authorities will gain sufficient powers to protect the public interest, with regard for example, to the two major and inter-related issues of outlet density and hours of trading. In particular, it remains unclear whether the licensing authorities of the future will retain the right to refuse licences on the basis of evidence that, regardless of the quality of service provided by individual operators, the number or density of premises in an area is such as to generate significant levels of violence, disorder, and nuisance in surrounding public space. Representations on the need to acknowledge issues of cumulative effect are still being made by various bodies, but are likely to meet fierce opposition from sections of the leisure industry. The government's present position on the issue has been expressed in a letter from Kim Howells MP to Chris Smith MP dated 4 September 2002:

Local authorities would not have the discretion they currently enjoy to refuse a licence or impose any condition unless a reasonable objection to the licensee's operating plan had been raised by the police, an environmental health officer, the fire authority or local residents. In granting or refusing licences, or imposing any conditions, the local councils would be legally bound to take into account the guidance issued by the Secretary of State. Departure from this guidance, without a good and justifiable reason, would provide grounds for an appeal to the courts.

At least one prominent licensing lawyer is of the opinion that the government's intention with regard to cumulative effect concerns is nothing less than:

The abolition of all such criteria so that planning and market forces are the only regulators. The new licensing system will be able to consider noise nuisance and disorder emanating from the premises or directly outside it if it can be attributed to the one particular set of premises. Conditions could be attached for dealing with sound proofing or external CCTV for example. The major departure from the current system will be that the licensing authority will not be able to refuse to grant a licence simply because of its location within a hot spot... under the new law the cumulative effect of people on the street would not be taken into account. The licensing authority would have no choice but to grant the licence (Allen, 2002:48).

Thus it seems that, first, in the absence of any formal objection to a proposed operating plan, a licence must be granted and that, secondly, licensing authorities will be placed under a statutory obligation to have regard to any guidance accompanying the Act to be issued by the Secretary of State. The Association of Chief Police Officers have also expressed concern:

We would like to see the Bill specifically allow for consideration of the cumulative impact of a number of licensed premises within certain locations. There comes a point where saturation is reached and additional premises, however well run, can exacerbate problems of crime, disorder and nuisance in the locality. We do not feel that the demand for premises should be just a matter of commercial concern (ACPO, 2002:1).

Thus it seems that the future ability of local government to control the cumulative impact of growth within the night-time economy now depends entirely upon the, as yet unknown, wording of such guidelines. At the time of writing, discussions of the National Guidance Sub-Group of the Licensing Bill Advisory Group indicate that the question has yet to be finally decided. If market forces are allowed to prevail, such concerns, which have informed alcohol licensing policy for over 500 years, and which arguably form the key mechanism of public protection, will be lost. As discussed, in this radically deregulated future there may be little recourse to planning law. Yet interestingly, this is not an approach which finds favour in many of the places which British '24-hour city' initiatives purport to emulate. The Parisian licensing code for example, states that new licences will not be granted to a venue within 75 metres of an existing licensed premises; similar regulation exists in New York where the licensing code imposes a minimum of 152 metres between venues (Town Centres Ltd, 2001:54).

If, as seems likely, alcohol licensing powers are indeed transferred to local authorities, councils will gain jurisdiction over all the main forms of control regarding the night-time economy, allowing, in principle, much greater scope for 'joined-up' thinking and integrated policy. Yet, whilst it might optimistically be concluded that the proposed shift to local authority control might finally create new opportunities in the realm of strategic municipal regulation, the as yet unknown outcomes of Central Government's current review of both planning and licensing law suggest that the future remains highly uncertain. It would appear that, as in other arenas of economic life, commerce is attempting to gain the assistance of neo-liberal government in veraciously seeking to 'minimize costs and remove themselves from, or exert control over, external constraints' (Pearce and Tombs, 1997:82). In this contemporary context, the market is king, and the mechanisms which evolved to regulate the excesses of economic activity in the industrial city are gradually being recast as 'damaging restrictions', 'red tape', and 'political interference'. These shifts in the nature of urban governance relations indicate that, within the next five years, the total de-deregulation of municipal controls over the development of the night-time economy, may gravitate from leisure corporation fantasy to laissez-faire reality.

As this book has described, within the recent past deregulatory tendencies have already had a quite profound impact upon the nature and quality of night-time public space. Concurrently of course, in towns and cities throughout the UK, leisure investment has created a plethora of new employment opportunities and played a key role in the regeneration of the built environment. However, as the government's own planning policy guidance and Urban White Paper (op. cit.) indicate, economic development is only one of many material considerations which should be taken into account by planners and other municipal regulators. If the '24-hour city' vision of a high-density, mixed-use urban core featuring both a varied and economically prosperous nightlife and excellent residential amenities is ever to become a reality, a much more integrated and interventionist approach to municipal regulation will need to be adopted.

9

Big People, Dirty Work:
A Conclusion

You will see that there are two orders of questions. One set concerns the good people who did not themselves do this work. The other concerns those who did do it. But the two sets are not really separate; for the crucial question concerning the good people is their relation to the people who did the dirty work . . . (Hughes, 1971:89).

We have written this book at a time of intense social and economic change, but also during an era when the central British state has not only retreated from engagement with a particularly pugnacious manifestation of capitalism, but also entered into partnership with it. It is clear that regeneration of the derelict citadels of Fordism will reproduce neither the communities that fed the production process, nor the order or regulation (Lipietz, 1996) that was so essential to its continuity. Lives now organized around consumption 'must do without norms' and be 'guided by seduction, ever rising desires and volatile wishes—no longer by normative regulation' (Bauman, 2001:76). As we have stressed throughout this book, the quasi-liminal zones that have developed in our urban centres are essentially non-conducive to normative comportment. The consequences of mass consumption, not of cars, clothes, or washing machines, but of alcohol and liminal experience itself, are especially profound when matched by the vulnerability of the target age group, and the promotion of transgression which lies at the commercial core of the night-time economy.

As discussed in Chapters 6 and 8, such developments have not gone entirely unchallenged. At the level of both the national and local state, skirmishes are being fought, and major battles planned. We have detected a gradual dawning among local government officials and police managers that the free market requires resisting, or at least moulding into directions more congruent with the public interest. As we have shown, in order to understand this partial shift, one must first acknowledge the intensely contested nature of the night (Hadfield, forthcoming a), a struggle conducted between the power of the alcohol and leisure industries in their attempt to colonize the night-time city, and the fragmented, disorganized, often opportunist and sometimes cynical agencies of liberal democratic government. Such contests are a day-time sport, fought within planning departments, redevelopment agencies, council chambers, and most importantly court rooms: those layers of neo-liberal governance most conveniently connected by the valorization of enterprise as an ideal type of commercial and civic activity (Rose, 1992).

Win or lose we are on the booze: a moral contradiction

The profitability of such commerce made it inexpedient to have too much law and order... it was intended to minimize both taxpayer expense and ancillary violence, though its inconsistencies—one is tempted to call them the cultural contradictions of capitalism—made control of violence difficult (Courtwright, 1996:98).

In the real world of powerful vested interests, harsh commercial pragmatism and legal contestation, the likely scenario is that our courts will continue to be clogged by a multitude of appeals, and that business imperatives will often be fettered only by the forms of compromise that we recently encountered involving property developers promising shops (not schools, day care centres, or nurseries) in exchange for planning permission for several uber boozers. We should expect no reversal of the night-time economy's continued expansion. Consequently, the demand for private security, buttressed by the soft words of liberal critics, and rather harsher noises from security entrepreneurs, will inevitably carry beyond the private to the public space, a move that is clearly flagged by our discussion of BIDS schemes in Chapter 8 and the introduction of private sector funded street wardens (see also Home Office, 2001c:77).

As we discuss in Chapter 6, although we acknowledge that registration schemes have to some extent helped to 'professionalize' the door trade, attempts to regulate bouncers have been largely symbolic, patently failing to transform deeply embedded attitudes and expectations regarding the use of force held by many within the industry. Indeed, most attempts at occupational licensing have been less than stringent, and are characterized by chaotic implementation, poor enforcement, and insufficient resources (Lister et al., 2001a). The remoteness and impotence of regulatory enforcement permits transgressive doorstaff to maintain a low visibility, whilst pristine operators, who are themselves constantly treading the line between legal and illegal definitions of reasonable force, place themselves in the regulatory firing line via regimes of training and registration. The physical force used by doorstaff is often a response to the disorderly situations they are tasked to resolve, and like so much of the disorder encountered by the state police, the enacted experience of these situations is largely removed from the edicts and regulatory codes emanating from the licensing and training regimes of administrative bureaucracies.

As we stress in Chapter 5, just like any other 'dirty work professional' for whom violence is both a primary concern and resource, bouncers must devise pragmatic methodologies which prioritize self-preservation within a hostile working environment. Central to the construction and understanding of these methodologies, as we emphasize in Chapter 7, are the powerful masculinist traditions which have found fresh utility within this particular post-industrial labour market. Further, as commercial forces swarm to fill the emerging void of control within our night-time cities, we should not be too shocked to find that some segments of this new policing order prove to be criminally inclined. For as we indicated in Chapter 7, the commercial viability of the criminal firm as well as that of the most pristine, orderly, and commercially correct security company, is ultimately grounded upon the same core resource. However, whilst liberal, democratic orthodoxy is compelled to stress the inevitable superiority of state-sponsored agencies via the controls through which the sovereign rhetorics of accountability to governmental structures are threaded, the reality remains that whether utilized by a representative of the state or by an agent of commerce, in its enacted application this resource remains unrelentingly brutal.

It is of course difficult to see the state ever being able to provide adequate public order policing of the enormous and potentially transgressive crowds who fill Britain's pubs, clubs, and high streets at night. But public police accountability, although flawed in practice, does provide for the possibility of some restraint and a measure of recourse in the event of perceived malpractice. Moreover, for the state not to apply the full professionalism of the police service to the management of the night-time economy and all accompanying aspects of licensing and regulation, is to submit *ad hoc* and hypocritical regimes of local governance and its ambivalent town hall entrepreneurship to the full uncompromisingly predatory forces of the alcohol industry. The market is a democratically unaccountable sphere.

Leisure development is now commonly regarded as the 'future' and the very commercial lifeblood of our central cities. Yet, as we have consistently stressed, it is the logic of the market rather than the utopianism of the liberal democratic project that has created, maintained, and nourished the night-time economy. The current inability of the state to impact effectively upon this economy does not, as so many cultural commentators claim, lead to freedom of expression and intellectual creativity. For as Bauman explains, 'a new protector-cum-censor fills the vacuum left by the withdrawal of the state: the market' (1992:100). Which is why the night-time economy in Britain is not awash with galleries and museums, and that safe spaces only remain safe as long as the logic of the market is able to maintain appropriate boundaries in the form of designated market niches (see Chapter 3). Certainly, a genuinely diverse night-time economy, with venues and cultural and commercial attractions catering for a wide range of the population, could only be achieved by local and central government suddenly, and against all historical precedent, resisting rather than colluding with market forces. Further, such a shift would require regimes of regulation from the urban planning stage upwards that are unlikely to meet with the approval of even the most enlightened champions of market diversity. For their critique of the marketplace remains locked in the liberal democratic orthodoxy that seeks to resist state intervention on the grounds that the state always aids 'the development of particular types of consumption pattern to match and stabilize production' (Chatterton and Hollands, 2001:114).

Indeed, as our discussion of Manchester in Chapter 2 attests, with the exception of the leisure industry itself, the interests of capital in the industrial city were generally ill-served by the promotion of night-time distractions, thus prompting the insertion of often draconian regulation and policing. However, this conception of the relationship between production and consumption, based as it is upon the outdated assumptions of Fordism, becomes redundant when applied to the contemporary night-time economy, for *now* the intervention of the state would not only interfere with patterns of consumption but also *curtail* capital accumulation. This is due to the specific nature of cultural and material consumption apparent within the night-time economy, and the highly particularistic systems of social control that have emerged within its ever-expanding boundaries. In short, even if it were possible to apply systems of regulation and policing that might ensure day-time levels of order and public safety, this outcome would be likely to have a severe economic impact within commercial frontier zones founded upon the allure of transgression, danger, and hedonism.

Consequently, the night-time economy has created for the state a maelstrom of control dilemmas that cannot be resolved by reference to the stock liberal critiques of class and governance applied within the context of the industrial era. Further, the liminal marketplace of the night-time economy poses problems for conventional liberal takes on the seduction/repression domination thesis. This is primarily due to the reliance of liberals upon assumptions of consumption based upon patterns established in Fordism: patterns that equate consumption with the acquisition of material goods and private property. For contrary, for instance, to Bauman's romantic underdog assertion that it is non-consumers, those who have resisted the seduction of the market or been bypassed by it, who will be targeted by the police (Bauman, 1992:105), within the night-time economy, troublesome individuals are *more* likely to have succumbed to the seduction of the market. Indeed, it is those most thoroughly seduced of consumers, to the tune of a dozen lagers, who are most inclined to be targeted by swarming police units, teams of bouncers, and couplets of street wardens.

The actual, rather than preferred control patterns that are operational within the night-time economy can best be understood by observing the reactions of agents of social control when they interface with comportment which during the daylight hours would inspire quick and effective reaction from the state police. Further, as we have stressed throughout this book, to understand the interactional motivations of control agents in the night-time economy we must first understand the political economy of de-industrialization and how it has shaped cityscapes, the workforce, and dimensions of gender and class. Because the state is historically unable to undermine capital, particularly given the potency of huge capital insertions applied during an era in which the industrial landscapes of Britain are in a process of ossification, the signature nudges, pushes, punches, and poses of violent professionals are permitted to reign. Capital requires them to pacify and colonize this new market frontier effectively and efficiently. Thus, the numerous well meaning, but essentially piecemeal responses of the public police and local authorities are unlikely to result in any real opposition to the ultimate affirmation of commercial security as the dominant provider of order within the night-time economy.

Within our neo-liberal and post-industrial era, the competencies of the remnants of modernity, particularly in the form of municipal government, state policing, and the multiplicity of regulatory mechanisms that cling to the central state to construct viable techniques of governance, are increasingly called into question. Further, liberal assumptions concerning the role of leisure are deeply embedded in the rigid yet raucous politics and protocols of Friday and Saturday nights in the shadow of the factory. Patterns of consumption are now clearly inclusive of intense and compacted markets whose liminal character promotes comportment that is not, as in the industrial era, contrary to the established productive order, but integral to it. The state's response has been filtered through control and regulatory agencies often barely able to acknowledge, let alone confront, the vast challenges posed by this newly expanded marketplace. As a consequence any notion of the state suddenly willing itself to assert its sovereign power to ensure the safety and quality of life of its citizens to the detriment of what are now primary economic interests, is both unrealistic and historically naive. The dawn of a fully marketized night-time economy is now a bleak but real prospect, not only for those who wish to control nightlife, *but also for those who love it* and wish to explore its full possibilities.

As can be seen from our discussion of the regulation of bouncers and of the introduction of various hybrid forms of policing, the state has proved highly adaptable and has maintained a tentative monopoly over the legitimate use of force (Weber, 1978). For as Ryan and Ward explain, 'the monopoly claimed by the state... is over the power to define the legitimate use of force... This power does not necessarily depend on the state owning the means of force or employing the individuals who use it' (1989:69). This crucial nuance upon the orthodoxy of the relationship between the state and the utilization of violence, in effect the licensing of force, seems to us to indicate the future of bouncers. Increased professionalism in the form of nationally recognized training and improvements in vetting will enable what South has expertly dubbed a 'mixed social control economy of informal and formal, private and public' (2001:261). Regulatory visions of this mixed economy invoke valorized notions of an 'extended police family', a metaphor that in a similar manner to 'community' bristles with rhetorical appeal (Cohen, 1985; Crawford, 1997). Yet, as we emphasize, the different mandates pinned to distinct policing forms beg questions of putative mutual shared interests and goals. The danger is that as the public police grapple to reign-in narrow private interests in the furtherance of the wider public good, then the spectre of the 'dysfunctional police family' may move closer into view (Crawford and Lister, 2003).

As state-sanctioned private force is operationalized, specialisms will emerge. For instance, as mentioned in Chapter 6, the growth in the employment of female doorstaff sees the security industry mimicking the public police in their employment of women as gender specialists (Westmarland, 2001) tasked with, for example, the body searching of females and entering female toilets in an attempt to prohibit drug use. Certainly our interviews with female doorstaff indicate that it is the specific control demands of the venue that will define how women are used. As Debbie explains, 'there's a blonde there about a size eight and about five foot nothing, and she doesn't get involved in fights... some clubs tend to have a female as like a glamour thing'. However, the general consensus among the female doorstaff that we interviewed was that apart from the gendered demands of the job, women on the door, are faced with the same levels of violence as their male colleagues. 'It's a fight, it happens in a split second, they don't notice anyone let alone a woman. I mean, I've had loads of lads, I have took out [ejected] haven't known I've been a woman until they've got outside... they're just concentrating on whoever they're fighting' (Helen).

Whilst we continue to maintain that doorstaff provide the dominant form of social control in the night-time economy, the emergence of a fully trained, fashionably diverse, professional, and vetted workforce (which will be the first UK University to offer a Masters degree in bouncing or door management?) would enable the move from pub doorway to pavement, from private to public. Further, once bouncing (now formally re-named as 'door supervision') has shed its back street, steroid popping, drug dealing, public image, those corporate purveyors of uniformed security at shopping malls will feel sufficiently confident to bid for night-time as well as day-time monopoly of the policing of zones of consumption. The role of bouncers as icons of the free liminal market will give way to that of state-sponsored agents, dispensing legitimate force on behalf of interlocking commercial and governmental interests.

Night moves

...there was a distinct need for a body of men who could provide a measure of security at the disturbed edge of the frontier where the writ of the federal or local law-enforcement did not reach (Bowden, 1978:241).

The state and the market appear destined to continue their many entanglements. Within the context of the urban night, suspicion of further state incursion into civil society now seems little more than self indulgent, and we would welcome a warm wind of enlightenment that would impose an economic plan to ensure that further night-time development placed safety above profit. In actuality, the particular political and economic sphere within which both violence and the private regulation of violence are generated is conveniently ignored, and the usual suspects are wheeled out. As Ritzer points out, 'to point the finger at the consumer is in modern terms to "blame the victim"' (2001:235), but for as long as the causes of night-time violence are pathologized into neatly labelled packages such as 'violent youth', or 'violent bouncer', the mighty will prevail and the criminogenic dynamics of the night-time economy will remain shrouded in a cloak of corporately-controlled good times. Consumerism and its accompanying processes of 'pseudo-individualization' (Horkheimer and Adorno, 1973) dominate the night-time economy, and despite the delights of the 'experiential commodities' (Lee, 1993:135–136) on offer, all too often the result is frustration, disorder and violence. For reality in these 'obscene sites of consumption' (Ritzer, 2001:235), seldom lives up to the uniquely spectacular 'commodity aesthetics' (Haug, 1986) so expertly put on display. At two-thirty am on a Saturday morning in a British town or city, it is difficult to regard the night-time economy as much more than a promissory note written on discarded fast-food wrapping, and for too many night-time revellers, 'the paradise offered by the culture industry is the same old drudgery' (Horkheimer and Adorno, 1973:141–2).

Whilst the legal interventions mentioned above will impose themselves in as yet unknown ways upon the future of the night-time economy, it will be business as usual in the pubs and clubs, and on the high streets of Britain after dark. Britain's youth will still queue in the rain without their coats while under surveillance for belligerent comportment, or deviant footwear. They will drink alcohol, use drugs, and have a good time. They will urinate in public, for despite the vast quantities of liquids consumed at night, public toilets are as rare as a night bus. They will dodge the fights that simmer, boil and break outside of the 'two ambulance pubs' and in taxi queues and fast-food outlets, and somehow wake up in the morning safe. For others the night will continue to hold darker promises, of punches, kicks and stabbings, of drunken sprints down wet cul-de-sacs, of desperate leaps over blind railings, of blue flashing lights and Dantesque Accident and Emergency departments.

The heady cocktail of allures and dangers served up by the night-time economy have spawned an ambiguous series of control devices designed above all to ensure commercial prosperity. Current economic trajectories have created a need for social order that the liberal state is loath to adequately address, and the subsequent 'mandate by default' (Hughes, 1971:95) that has fallen into the hands of private security should be understood as a historically consistent utilization of physical force in the interests of capital.

In analysing the dilemmas of governance that the night-time economy poses to the state, we have offered a socio-economic snapshot of contemporary Britain at work and play. The role of commercial leisure in framing this picture is crucial, as is the impact of free market policies upon the urban environment, and the safety and well-being of the youthful consumers who populate its congested foreground. It would only contribute further to the night's illusory qualities if by ignoring the relationship between violence and the forces that now dominate the night-time economy we merely demonize those professionals of violence who do its dirty work.

The queue for the last kebab

It's twenty to one and I'm desperate to get out of here. My legs are sore, my eyes are stinging, my clothes and hair stink of cigarette smoke, and I'm thoroughly exhausted. It's been one of those nights;

busy, frustrating, and completely devoid of the humour and enjoyment that occasionally visit during our working hours. The lights are
now up and as I consider sneaking out early, I survey the devastation
of the night. The fake smoke has faded and the magic migraine disco
lights are off. A few groups linger on as the bouncers make one last
attempt to move the stragglers out of the bar. The classic, 'can you
see your drinks off now please!', is shouted at high volume and at no-
one in particular, seemingly by each of the bouncers in rotation,
while some also employ the more personal, 'If you're going to finish
your drink, can you do it now? We're waiting to lock up'. Even the
DJ sparks back into life and the speakers crackle with the legend,
delivered with faux American accent, 'You don't have to go home,
but you can't stay here!'

The people who remain only vaguely resemble the lively, fashion-
conscious hedonists who populated the bar a few short hours previously. Everyone looks tired and drained in a precursor to the fearful
predictability of the hangover that will soon intrude. Those with the
energy have already left for the local nightclubs, kebab shops, and
taxi ranks, whilst the remainder seem desperate to prolong their final
drink. Make-up and speech is slurred and smeared, and I can make
out a footprint on the back of the white shirt of a patron I am now
asking to leave. Across the dance floor a couple are locked in a
passionate embrace, and I'm not particularly keen to interrupt
them. They haven't come up for air in the last ten minutes, and
two of the barmen are having a laugh at them as they scan the floor
of the bar area in the hope of picking up money dropped during hasty
purchases when the bar was packed to its fake wooden rafters.

Some of the glass collectors and bar staff are steering wheelie bins
around the bar, filling them with the masses of empty bottles that lie
strewn around the floor and balanced on every available even surface. Others are attempting to clear up the broken glass with impro-
vized tools and tentative hands as the bar manager mops up the
liquid oozing underneath the toilet door and onto the carpet. In
time, the remaining patrons are hustled out, the ashtrays are emp-
tied; the industrial-sized refrigerators are re-stoked with bottled
lager and alcopops. The head doorman hands me thirty quid and
asks me if I'm going clubbing. I'm not.

As I unlock the door and ease myself out onto the street I'm met by
a number of couples crowded into the doorway clinging to each
other to protect against the biting cold. As they move to let me out,

I brush past two men and two women furiously dialling for taxis, but they appear to be having about as much success as those at the kerbside attempting to flag down speeding private hire drivers seemingly locked in a city centre 0 to 60 test. The walk back to my car should take me no more than five minutes if I hurry.

The street is now populated by a hungry assortment of young men, grouped mostly around the entrances to pizza and kebab shops. Some stare at me as I pass, others attempt to flag down passing motorists, others talk in groups and some give their undivided attention to their takeaway food. As I turn the corner I can see two men having a piss in a shop doorway as they shout encouragement to a group of friends chatting up some young women seated on a nearby bench. Small queues have developed at a group of telephone boxes and at a cashpoint that is adjacent to the boarded up shell of what was once a popular local grocery store. A police van is parked on the pedestrianized section of the street and the officer in the shotgun seat engages a group of young women in conversation. The street life picks up a little as I pass a local nightclub. Music once again fills the air as I acknowledge the doormen, but keep moving past the long queue littered with talkative and still hopeful groups of young men and women, and the occasional couple. I cheer up a little as I pass a young man trying to persuade a young women to give him her phone number, but the moment quickly passes as I almost step in a freshly laid pile of puke, and pass a group of angry young men talking loudly of vengeance against an unseen enemy who has wounded one of their number. The man with the bleeding face doesn't seem keen. I keep my eyes away from theirs and carry on my way. My brisk pace is tempered somewhat as I have to circumnavigate a flock of warring seagulls, the size of small dogs, fighting over discarded takeaway food, the raucous cries of which have now replaced the repetitive beats of dance music that recently dominated the area.

A man with the well-developed physique of a bodybuilder has cunningly removed his shirt in order to have his friend appraise a tattoo as a group of young women walk by. A couple kiss in a doorway, and more young people file in and out of take-aways and head in the general direction of the taxi rank at the bottom of the street. When I arrive at the junction it's possible to see perhaps a couple of hundred young people queuing for taxis, some clutching food, others clutching the new found love of their life. There's shouting and staggering, but I can see no violence as I hurry past.

As I approach the car park I pass a small street cleaning vehicle. Its presence on the street strikes me as slightly peculiar, but nobody else appears to be paying much attention. Its insistent drone and the mask of concentration on the face of driver is a stark reminder, as if I needed it, that the night is a workplace as well as a play space. Its motorized brushes strike empty bottles left in the gutter sending them spinning across the pavement as I make my way past more pissing young men, relieving themselves away from the biting wind in the relatively cosy ambience of the concrete car park.

I drive home past a blur of faces distorted with drink, laughter, and the cold. Fingers grasp at kebabs, pizzas, and warm bodies. Jellied legs do the lateral tango homewards. Whether the next night or next week, we will all be back for more.

References

Abrams, M. (1959) *The Teenage Consumer*, London: London Press Exchange.

ACPO (Association of Chief Police Officers) (2002) Association of Chief Police Officers: Briefing for Licensing Bill, ACPO.

Akerlof, G. A. (1970) 'The Market For "Lemons": Quality Uncertainty And The Market Mechanism', *Quarterly Journal of Economics*, 84/3:488–500.

Allen, J. (2002) 'On the Case: Licensing Reform', *Night*, August:48.

Allen, R. (1998) 'Liquor Licensing, England and Wales, July 1997–June 1998', *Home Office Statistical Bulletin* Issue 27/98, Research Development and Statistics Directorate: London.

Amin, A. (ed.) (1994) *Post-Fordism: A Reader*, Oxford: Blackwell.

Anderson, A. (1979) *The Business of Organized Crime*, Stanford, Calif.: Hoover Institute Press.

Anderson, K. (1998) *Night Dogs*, London: Arrow.

Anthony, W. (1998) *Class of 88: The True Acid House Experience*, London: Virgin Publishing.

Arantes, A. A. (1996) 'The War of Places: Symbolic Boundaries and Liminalities in Urban Space', *Theory, Culture and Society*, 13/4: 81–92.

Archer, J., Holloway, R., and McLoughlin, K. (1995) 'Self-Reported Physical Aggression Among Young Men', *Aggressive Behaviour*, 21:325–342.

Arlacchi, P. (1986) *Mafia Business: The Mafia Ethic and the Spirit of Capitalism*, London: Verso.

Armitage, R. (2002) *To CCTV or not to CCTV?* London: NACRO.

Armstrong, G. (1998) *Football Hooligans: Knowing the Score*, Oxford: Berg.

Aspland, A. (1868) *Criminal Manchester*, Manchester.

ATCM (Association of Town Centre Management), (2002) *Sustainable Funding for Town Centre Management*, London: ATCM.

Baggott, R. (1986) 'The Politics of Alcohol: Two Periods Compared', *Institute of Alcohol Studies*, Occasional Paper No. 8, London: IAS.

——(1990) *Alcohol, Politics and Social Policy*, Aldershot: Avebury.

Bailey, P. (1978) *Leisure and Class in Victorian England*, London: Routledge & Kegan Paul.

——(ed.) (1986) *Music Hall: The Business of Pleasure*, Mil⌐ Open University Press.

Baker Associates (2001) *Review of the Use Classes Order and Part 4 of the GPDO (Temporary Uses)*, London: DTLR (Department for Transport, Local Government and the Regions).

Bakhtin, M. (1984) *Rabelais and His World*, Bloomington: Indiana University Press.

Baldwin, R. and Kinsey, R. (1982) *Police Powers and Politics*, London: Quartet Books.

Ballham, A. (2002) Witness Statement by AED Consultant in Hereford General Hospital in *Hereford Community Safety Partnership v. J. D. Wetherspoon plc*, Hereford Magistrates Court, 31 May 2002.

Barnes, T. (2000) *Mean Streets: A Journey Through the Northern Underworld*, Bury: Milo Books.

Bassett, K. (1993) 'Urban Cultural Strategies and Urban Regeneration: A Case Study and Critique', *Environment and Planning A*, 25:1773–1788.

—— (1996) 'Partnerships, Business Elites and Urban Politics: New Forms of Governance in an English City?' *Urban Studies*, 33/3:539–555.

Baudrillard, J. (1968) *Le Systeme des Objects: la Consommation des Signes*, Editions Gallimard: Paris.

Bauman, Z. (1991) *Modernity and Ambivalence*, Cambridge: Polity.

—— (1992) *Intimations of Postmodernity*, London: Routledge.

—— (2001) *Liquid Modernity*, Cambridge: Polity Press.

Beattie, G. (1986) *Survivors of Steel City, A Portrait of Sheffield*, London: Chatto & Windus Limited.

Beck, U. (1992) *Risk Society: Towards a New Modernity*, London: Sage.

BEDA (Bar, Entertainment and Dance Association, formerly, British Entertainment and Discotheque Association) (1997) *Good Practice Guide on the Implementation of the Public Entertainment Licences (Drugs Misuse) Act 1997*, Stockport: BEDA.

—— (2000) *Time for Reform: Proposals for the Modernisation of our Licensing Laws: A Response by the British Entertainment and Discotheque Association*, Stockport: BEDA.

Bee, M. (1984) *Industrial Revolution and Social Reform in the Manchester Region*, Manchester: Neil Richardson.

Begg, I. (1999) 'Cities and Competitiveness', *Urban Studies*, 36(5–6): 795–809.

Behan, T. (1996) *The Camorra*, London: Routledge.

Bell, D. (1953) 'Crime as an American Way of Life', *The Antioch Review*, 13:131–54.

—— (1961) *The End of Ideology*, London: Free Press/Collier-Macmillan.

Benny, M. (1936[1981]) *Low Company*, Facsimile edn. Caliban Books: Sussex.

Berkowitz, L. (1986) 'Some Varieties of Human Aggression: Criminal Violence as Coercion, Rule-Following, Impression Management and Impulsive Behavior', in A. Campbell and J. J. Gibbs (eds.) *Violent*

Transactions. The Limits of Personality, Oxford: Basil Blackwell, 87–103.

Bernstein, M. (1955) *Regulating Business by Independent Commission*, Princeton: Princeton University Press.

Better Regulation Task Force, (1998a) *Review of Licensing Legislation*, London: Central Office of Information.

—— (1998b) *Principles of Good Regulation*, London: Central Office of Information.

Bez (1998) *Freaky Dancin'*, London: Pan Books.

Bianchini, F. (1990) 'The Crisis of Urban Public Social Life in Britain: Origins of the Problem and Possible Responses', *Planning, Practice and Research*, 5(3):4–8.

—— (1993) 'Remaking European Cities: The Role of Cultural Policies', in F. Bianchini and M. Parkinson (eds.) *Cultural Policy and Urban Regeneration*, Manchester: Manchester University Press.

—— (1995) 'Night Cultures, Night Economies', *Planning Practice and Research*, 10/2:121–126.

—— Fisher, M., Montgomery, J., and Worpole, K. (1988) *City Centres, City Cultures: The Role of the Arts in Urban Revitalization*, Manchester: CLES.

—— and Parkinson, M. (eds.) (1993) *Cultural Policy and Urban Regeneration*, Manchester: Manchester University Press.

Bittner, E. (1970) *The Functions of the Police in Modern Society*, Chevy Chase, Md: National Institute of Mental Health.

Black, D. (1968) *Police Encounters and Social Organization: An Observational Study*, Unpublished PhD Dissertation, University of Michigan.

Blair, I. (1998) *Where do the Police Fit into Policing?* Speech to the Association of Chief Police Officers' Annual Conference, July.

—— (2002) *Surprise News: Policing Works*. Speech to the British Society of Criminology Conference, Keele University, July.

Block, A. (1983), *East Side-West Side: Organizing Crime in New York, 1930–1950*, Newark, NJ: Transaction.

—— (1994) *Space Time and Organized Crime*, New Brunswick: Transaction.

—— and Chambliss, W. (1981) *Organizing Crime*, New York: Elsevier.

—— and Scarpitti, F. (1985) *Poisoning for Profit: The Mafia and Toxic Waste*, New York: William Morrow.

Blok, A. (1974) *The Mafia of a Sicilian Village*, New York: Harper.

BLRA (Brewers and Licensed Retailers Association) (1998) *Statistical Handbook*, London: BLRA.

Bolton Town Centre Partnership, (1998) *For a Night on the Town*, Bolton: BTCP.

Bottoms, A. E. (1994) 'Environmental Criminology', in M. Maguire, R. Morgan and R. Reiner (eds.) *The Oxford Handbook of Criminology*, (1st edn.), Oxford: Clarendon Press.

Bottoms, A. E. and Wiles, P. (1996) 'Understanding Crime Prevention in Late-Modern Societies', in T. H. Bennett (ed.) *Preventing Crime and Disorder: Targeting Strategies and Responsibilities*, Cambridge: Institute of Criminology.

Bourdieu, P. (1977) *Outline of a Theory of Practice*, Cambridge: Cambridge University Press.

—— (1979) *Algeria 1960*, Cambridge: Cambridge University Press.

—— (1984) *Distinction: A Social Critique of the Judgement of Taste*, London: Routledge and Kegan Paul.

Bowden, T. (1978) *Beyond The Limits of the Law*, Harmondsworth: Penguin Books.

Brain, K. J. (2000) *Youth, Alcohol and the Emergence of the Postmodern Alcohol Order*, Occasional Paper No. 1, London: IAS.

Branigan, T. (1999) 'The Making of Manchester, 1961–1970: The End of Cottonopolis', *Manchester Evening News*, (September 8):8.

Briggs, A. (1996) *Victorian Cities*, Bury St. Edmunds: Folio Society.

Brogden, M., Jefferson, T. and Walklate, S. (1988) *Introducing Police Work*, London: Unwin Hyman.

Bromley, R., Thomas, C. and Millie, A. (2000) 'Exploring Safety Concerns in the Night-time City', *Town Planning Review*, 71:71–96.

—— and Nelson, A., (2002) 'Alcohol-Related Crime and Disorder Across Urban Space and Time: Evidence from a British City', *Geoforum*, 33:239–254.

Brown, A., O'Connor, J. and Cohen, S. (2000) 'Local Music Policies within a Global Music Industry: Cultural Quarters in Manchester and Sheffield', *Geoforum*, 31/4:437–451.

Brown, R. M. (1991) *No Duty to Retreat*, New York: Oxford University Press.

Brown, S. (1998) 'What's the Problem, Girls? CCTV and the Gendering of Public Safety', in C. Norris, J. Moran, and G. Armstrong (eds.) *Surveillance, Closed Circuit Television and Social Control*, Aldershot: Ashgate, pp. 207–220.

Browne, J. R. (1871) *Adventures in the Apache Country*, New York: Harper.

Brumhead, D. (1988) *Castlefield: Britain's First Heritage Park*, Manchester: MCC.

Buchanan, J. (1973) 'In Defence of Organized Crime', in S. Rottenburg (ed.) *The Economics of Crime and Punishment*, Washington DC: American Enterprise Institute.

Burns, T. F. (1980) 'Getting Rowdy With the Boys', *Journal of Drug Issues*, 10:273–286.

Burton, N. (1987) 'Leisure in the City: The Entertainment Sector in the Manchester Central Business District, 1770–1930', *The Manchester Geographer*, 8:15–32.

Bushman, B. J. (1997) 'Effects of Alcohol on Human Aggression: Validity of Proposed Mechanisms', in M. Galanter (ed.) *Recent Developments in Alcoholism*, New York: Plenum Press, 13:227–244.

Button, J. (1998) 'Door Staff Registration Outside Greater London', *Noter Up: The Journal of the Local Government Group of the Law Society*, (19) July.

Button, M. and George, B. (1998) 'Why Some Companies Prefer Contract to In-house Security Staff', in M. Gill (ed.) *Crime at Work, Volume II*, Leicester: Perpetuity Press.

Callois, R. (1959) *Man and the Sacred*, Glencoe: Free Press.

Castells, M. (1983) *The City and the Grass Roots*, Berkeley: University of California Press.

Catanzaro, R. (1992) *Men of Respect*, New York: Free Press.

Cavan, S. (1966) *Liquor License: An Ethnography of a Bar*, Chicago: Aldine.

Champion, S. (1990) *And God Created Manchester*, Manchester: Wordsworth.

Chaney, D. (1994) *The Cultural Turn: Scene-setting Essays in Contemporary Cultural History*, London: Routledge.

——(1998) 'The New Materialism?: The Challenge of Consumption', *Work Employment and Society*, 12:533–44.

Chatterton, M. (1983) 'Police Work and Assault Charges', in M. Punch (ed.) *Control in the Police Organization*, Cambridge, Mass.: MIT Press

Chatterton, P. and Hollands, R. (2001) 'Changing Our "Toon"': Youth, Nightlife and Urban Change in Newcastle, Newcastle upon Tyne: University of Newcastle upon Tyne.

—— and ——(2002) 'Theorising Urban Playscapes: Producing, Regulating and Consuming Youthful Nightlife City Spaces', *Urban Studies*, 39/ 1:95–116.

City Life (2000) *City Life Guide to Manchester*, 3rd edn., Manchester: Diverse Media Ltd.

Clarkson, C., Cretney, A., Davis, G., and Shepherd, J. P. (1994), 'Assaults: the Relationship Between Seriousness, Criminalization and Punishment', *Criminal Law Review*, January, 4–20.

Clift, S. and Forrest, S. (1999) 'Gay Men and Tourism: Destinations and Holiday Motivations', *Tourism Management*, 20:615–625.

Cochrane, A., Peck, J. A., and Tickell, A. (1995) 'Manchester Plays Games: Exploring the Local Politics of Globalization', *Urban Studies*, 33 (8):1319–1336.

Cohen, L. E. and Felson, M. (1979) 'Social Change and Crime Rate Trends: A Routine Activity Approach', *American Sociological Review*, 44/4:588–608.

Cohen, P. (1979) 'Policing the Working Class City', in B. Fine et al., (eds.) *Capitalism and the Rule of Law*, London: Hutchinson.

Cohen, (1985) *Visions of Social Control*, Cambridge: Polity Press.
—— (1991) 'Popular Music and Urban Regeneration: The Music Industries of Merseyside', *Cultural Studies*, 5(3):332–346.
—— (1994) 'Identity, Place and the Liverpool Sound', in M. Stokes (ed.) *Ethnicity, Identity and Music*, Oxford: Berg.
Coleman, C. and Moynihan, J. (1996) *Understanding Crime Data: Haunted by the Dark Figure*, Buckingham: Open University Press.
Coles, N. (2001) 'It's Not What You Know—It's Who You Know That Counts: Analysing Serious Crime Groups as Social Networks', *British Journal of Criminology*, 41:4:580–594.
Collin, M. with contributions by Godfrey, J. (1997) *Altered State: The Story of Ecstasy Culture and Acid House*, London: Serpent's Tail.
Collins, J. (ed.) (1982) *Drinking and Crime: Perspectives on the Relationship Between Alcohol Consumption and Criminal Behaviour*, New York: Tavistock.
Comedia, (1991) *Out of Hours: A Study of Economic, Social and Cultural Life in Twelve Town Centres in the UK*, London: Comedia.
Connell, R. W. (1995), *Masculinities*, Oxford: Blackwell.
Cook, D. (1989) *Rich Law, Poor Law: Different Responses to Tax and Supplementary Benefit Fraud*, Milton Keynes: Open University Press.
Corner, L. (2000) 'They're Only Here For The Queers', *The Independent*, The Thursday Review, (6 April): 7.
Coulson, P. (1994) 'Licensing and the Law: An Overview', in A. Lovatt, J. O'Connor, J. Montgomery and P. Owens (eds.) *The 24-Hour City: Selected Papers from the First National Conference on the Night-time Economy*, Manchester: Manchester Metropolitan University.
Countryside Agency (2001) *The Pub is the Hub: A Good Practice Guide*, Wetherby: The Countryside Agency.
Courtwright, D. (1996) *Violent Land: Single Men and Social Disorder from the Frontier to the Inner City*, Cambridge, Mass.: Harvard University Press.
Crawford, A. (1997) *The Local Governance of Crime: Appeals to Community and Partnership*, Oxford: Clarendon Press.
—— and Lister, S. (2003) *Plural Policing: Policing beyond the Police in England*, paper presented to the Law Commission of Canada, In Search of Security Conference, Montreal, February.
Cruse, D. and Rubin, J. (1973) *Determinants of Police Behaviour: A Summary*, National Institute of Law Enforcement and Criminal Justice, Washington DC: United States Government Printing Office.
Cunningham, H. (1980) *Leisure in the Industrial Revolution*, London: Croom Helm.
Currie, E. (1997) 'Market, Crime and Community: Toward a Mid-range Theory of Post-Industrial Violence', *Theoretical Criminology*, 1/2: 147–172.

Currie, R. R. (1997) 'A Pleasure-Tourism Behaviours Framework', *Annals of Tourism Research*, 24/4:884–897.

Cuthbert, M. (1990) 'Investigation of the Incidence and Analysis of Cases of Alleged Violence reporting to St. Vincent's Hospital', in D. Chappell, P. Grabosky and H. Strang (eds.) *Australian Violence: Contemporary Perspectives*, Canberra: Australian Institute of Criminology.

Damer, S. (1976) 'Wine Alley: The Sociology of a Dreadful Enclosure', in P. Wiles (ed.) *The Sociology of Crime and Delinquency in Britain*, Vol. 2, London: Martin Robinson.

Davies, A. (1992) *Leisure, Gender and Poverty: Working-class Culture in Salford and Manchester, 1900–1939*, Buckingham: Open University Press.

——(1998) 'Youth Gangs, Masculinity and Violence in Late Victorian Manchester and Salford', *Journal of Social History*, 32/2:349–69.

——(1999) 'These Viragoes are no Less Cruel than the Lads: Young Women, Gangs and Violence in Late Victorian Manchester and Salford', *British Journal of Criminology*, 39/1:72–89.

Davies, J. (1988) 'From Municipal Socialism to ... Municipal Capitalism?', *Local Government Studies*, 14:19–22.

Davies, R. T. (1999) *Queer As Folk: The Scripts*, London: Channel 4 Books.

Davies, S. J. (1985) 'Classes and Police in Manchester 1829–1880', in A. J. Kidd and K. W. Roberts (eds.) *City, Class and Culture, Studies of Social Policy and Cultural Production in Victorian Manchester*, Manchester: Manchester University Press.

de Tocqueville, A. (1958) *Journeys to England and Ireland*, J. P. Mayer (ed.), London: Faber and Faber Limited.

DETR (Department of the Environment, Transport and the Regions) (1999) *Personal Security Issues in Pedestrian Journeys*, http://www.mobility-unit.detr.gov.uk/psi/psi02.htm.

——(2000a) *White Paper: A Fair Deal for Rural Communities*, London: DETR/The Stationery Office.

——(2000b) *Our Towns and Cities: The Future. Delivering an Urban Renaissance*, Cm 4911, Urban White Paper, November, London: DETR/The Stationery Office.

Delafons, J. (1996) 'Too Many Pubs?' *Town and Country Planning*, 65 (December): 346–347.

DiGaento, A. and Klemanski, J. S. (1993) 'Urban Regimes in Comparative Perspective—The Politics of Urban Development in Britain', *Urban Affairs Quarterly*, 29:54–83.

Dillon, M. (2000) 'Time to Ban This Horror Pub Weapon', *Manchester Evening News*, 19 May, p.1 and p.3.

Dilnot, G. (1929) *Scotland Yard*, London: Geoffrey Bles.

DoE (Department of the Environment and Welsh Office), (1994) *Planning Out Crime*, Circular 1994/5, London: HMSO.

DoE (1996) *Town Centres and Retail Development: Revised Planning Policy Guidance 6*, London: HMSO.

Dorn, N. (1983) *Alcohol, Youth and the State*, London: Croom Helm.

DTLR (Department for Transport, Local Government and the Regions) (2001) *Planning: Delivering a Fundamental Change*, London: The Stationery Office.

Dunkerley, C. (2001) 'Regeneration Game', *Hotline*, 16:46–49.

Dyck, N. (1980) 'Booze, Barrooms and Scrapping: Masculinity and Violence in a Western Canadian Town', *Canadian Journal of Anthropology*, 1:191–8.

Dziembowska-Kowalska, J. and Funck, R. H. (1999) 'Cultural Activities: Source of Competitiveness and Prosperity in Urban Regions', *Urban Studies*, 36(8): 1381–1398.

Edelman, M. (1964) *The Symbolic Uses of Politics*, Urbana, Ill.: University of Illinois Press.

—— (1977) *Political Language: Words That Succeed and Policies That Fail*, New York: Academic Press.

Eisenberg, M. A. (1976) 'Private Ordering Through Negotiation: Dispute Settlement and Rule-Making', *Harvard Law Review*, 89:637:81.

Ekblom, P. and Heal, K. (1982) *The Police Response to Calls from the Public*, Research and Planning Unit, Paper 9, London: Home Office.

Elias, N. (1994) *The Civilizing Process: The History of Manners, Vol. 1*, translated by E. Jephcott, Oxford: Blackwell.

Elkin, S. (1987) *City and Regime in the American Republic*, Chicago: University of Chicago Press.

Elson, M. (2002) 'The Frictionless World of the Planning Green Paper', *Town and Country Planning*, 71/2 (February): 31.

Engels, F. (1987) [1845] *The Condition of the Working Class in England*, Edited with a Foreword by V. Kiernan, London: Penguin.

Esser, J. and Hirsch, J. (1989) 'The Crisis of Fordism and the Dimensions of a "Post-Fordist" Regional and Urban Structure', *International Journal of Urban and Regional Research*, 13/3:417–437.

Evans, K. and Fraser, P. (1993) *Difference in the City: Locating Marginal Use of Public Space*, Paper presented to the British Sociological Association's Conference on 'Research Imaginations', University of Essex, April.

—— —— and Walklate, S. (1996) 'Whom Can You Trust? The Politics of "Grassing" on an Inner City Housing Estate', *The Sociological Review*, 44/3:361–380.

Falcone, G. (1993) *Men of Honour*, London: Warner.

Farrington, D. P. and Welsh, B. C. (2002) *Effects of Improved Street Lighting on Crime: A Systematic Review*, Home Office Research Study 251, London: RDSD.

Featherstone, M. (1991) *Consumer Culture and Postmodernism*, London: Sage.

Felson, R. B. (1982) 'Impression Management and the Escalation of Aggression and Violence', *Social Psychology*, 45:245–254.

—— (1997) 'Routine Activities and Involvement in Violence as Actor, Witness, or Target', *Violence and Victims*, 12/3:209–221.

Fenn, D. (ed.) (1999) *Public Houses 1999 Market Report Plus*, Keynote.

Fielding, N. (1984) 'Police Socialization and Police Competence', *British Journal of Sociology*, 35/4.

—— (1988) *Joining Forces: Police Training, Socialization, and Occupational Competence*, London and New York: Routledge.

Finch, J. (1999) 'Death Dance of the Disco: The Chameleon Pub is Changing the Business Behind a Big Night Out', Finance, *Guardian*, 23 January:3–5.

Flavel, W. (1973) *Research into Security Organizations*, Unpublished Paper, Second Bristol Seminar on the Sociology of the Police, April.

Foote, J. (1990) 'Madchester: Britain's Feel-good Music Scene', *Newsweek*, (July 23): 1 and 5–6.

Ford, A. (1985) *Men*, London: Weidenfeld & Nicolson.

Fraser, P. (1996) 'Social and Spatial Relationships and the "Problem" Inner City: Moss Side in Manchester', *Critical Social Policy*, 16:43–65.

Friedman, M. (1962) *Capitalism and Freedom*, Chicago: University of Chicago Press.

Frisby, D. (1985) *Fragments of Modernity*, Cambridge: Polity.

Frith, S. (1993) 'Popular Music and the Local State', in T. Bennett and S. Frith (eds.) *Rock and Popular Music*, London: Routledge.

Gambetta, D. (1988) 'Fragments of an Economic Theory of the Mafia', *Archives Europeennes de Sociologie*, 29:127–45.

—— (1993) *The Sicilian Mafia: The Business of Private Protection*, Cambridge, Mass.: Harvard University Press.

Garland, D. (1985) *Punishment and Welfare*, Aldershot: Gower.

Garratt, S. (1998) *Adventures in Wonderland: A Decade of Club Culture*, London: Headline.

Garreau, J. (1991) *The Edge City: Life on the New Frontier*, New York: Doubleday.

Gaskell, E. (1970) *Mary Barton*, Harmondsworth: Penguin.

Gatrell, V. (1980) 'The Decline of Theft and Violence in Victorian and Edwardian England', in V. Gatrell, B. Lenman and G. Parker (eds.) *Crime and the Law*, London: Europa.

Geddes, M. (1994) 'Public Services and Local Economic Regeneration in a Post-Fordist Economy', in R. Burrows and B. Loader (eds.) *Towards a Post-Fordist Welfare State?* London: Routledge.

George, B. and Button, M. (1996) 'The Case for Regulation', *International Journal of Risk, Security and Crime Prevention*, 1:53–7.

Gibbs, J. J. (1986) 'Alcohol Consumption, Cognition and Context, Examining Tavern Violence', in A. Campbell and J. J. Gibbs (eds.) *Violent Transactions: The Limits of Personality*, Oxford: Blackwell.

Giddens, A. (1984) *The Constitution of Society*, Cambridge: Polity.
—— (1991) *Modernity and Self-Identity*, Cambridge: Polity.
Godfrey, B. (2002) 'Rough Girls, 1880–1930: The "Recent" History of Violent Young Women', in C. Alder and A. Worrall (eds.) *Criminal Girls*, Albany: State University of New York Press.
Goffman, E. (1959) *The Presentation of Self in Everyday Life*, Harmondworth: Penguin.
—— (1967) *Interaction Ritual*, Chicago: Aldine.
—— (1971) *Relations in Public*, London: Allen Lane The Penguin Press.
Gofton, L. (1990) 'On the Town: Drink and the "New Lawlessness"', *Youth and Policy*, 29, (April): 33–39.
Goodwin, M. and Painter, J. (1996) 'Local Governance, the Crises of Fordism and the Changing Geographies of Regulation', *Transactions of the Institute of British Geographers*, 21/4:635–648.
Gottdiener, M. (2000) 'The Consumption of Space and the Spaces of Consumption', in M. Gottdiener (ed.) *New forms of Consumption: Consumers, Culture, and Commodification*, Rowman and Littlefield: Maryland, 265–285.
Gould, P. (1991) 'Dynamic Structures of Geographic Space', in S. D. Brunn and T. R. Leinbach (eds.) *Collapsing Space and Time*, London: Harper Collins.
Graham, K., LaRocque, L., Yetman, R., Ross, T. J., and Guistra, E. (1980) 'Aggression and Bar Room Environments', *Journal of Studies on Alcohol*, 41:277–292.
—— West, P., and Wells, S. (2000) 'Evaluating Theories of Alcohol-related Aggression Using Observations of Young Adults in Bars', *Addiction*, 95/6:847–863.
—— and West, P. (2001) 'Alcohol and Crime: Examining the Link', in N. Heather, T. J. Peters, and T. Stockwell (eds.) *International Handbook of Alcohol Dependence and Problems*, Sussex: John Wiley and Sons, 439–470.
Graham, P. and Clarke, J. (1996) 'Dangerous Places: Crime and the City', in J. Muncie and E. McLaughlin (eds.) *The Problem of Crime*, London: Sage.
GLA (Greater London Authority), (2002) *Minutes: Culture, Sport and Tourism Committee 2*, July 2002, Unpublished, GLA.
Greene, K. (1969) 'Occupational Licensing and the Supply of Non-Professional Manpower', *Manpower Research Monograph No. 11*. Washington: Department of Labor.
Gregson, N., Simonsen, K., and Vaiou, D. (1999) 'The Meaning of Work', *European Urban and Regional Studies*, 6/3:197–214.
Griffin, C. (1993) *Representations of Youth: The Study of Youth and Adolescence in Britain and America*, Cambridge: Polity Press.
Guftanson, R. (1993) 'Alcohol-Related Expected Effects and the Desirability of these Effects for Swedish College Students Measured with the

Alcohol Expectancy Questionnaire (AEQ)', *Alcohol and Alcoholism*, 28:469–475.

Gurr, T. (1989) *History of Violent Crime*, California: Sage.

Gurr, T. R. and King, D. S. (1987) *The State and the City*, Basingstoke: Macmillan.

Gutzke, D. W. (1989) *Protecting the Pub: Brewers and Publicans against Temperance*, Woodbridge: Boydell Press.

Hadfield, P. (2002) 'Open All Hours?', *Police Review*, 16 August: 110/ 5686:21.

—— (forthcoming, a) *Night as Contested Timespace*, Unpublished PhD thesis, University of Durham.

—— (forthcoming, b) 'The Prevention of Public Disorder' in J. Philips and P. Kolvin (eds.) *Licensed Premises: Law and Practice*, London: Butter-worths.

—— Lister, S., Hobbs, D. and Winlow, S. (2001) 'The "24-Hour City"— Condition Critical?', *Town and Country Planning*, 70/11, November: 300–302.

—— —— and —— (2002) 'Location, Location, Location: Preventing Alcohol-related Crime and Disorder via Development Controls', *Criminal Justice Matters, Special Issue on Drugs*, 47, Spring:34–35.

Hall, S. (1997) 'Visceral Cultures and Criminal Practices', *Theoretical Criminology*, 1/4:453–478.

—— (2000) 'Paths to Anelpis: 1: Dimorphic Violence and the Pseudo-Pacification Process', *Parallax: A Journal of Metadiscursive Theory and Cultural Practices*, 6/2:36–53.

Hall, T. and Hubbard, P. (1996) 'The Entrepreneurial City: New Urban Politics, New Urban Geographies?', *Progress in Human Geography*, 20/2:53–174.

—— and —— (1998) 'The Entrepreneurial City and the "New Urban Politics"', in T. Hall and P. Hubbard (eds.) *The Entrepreneurial City: Geographies Of Politics, Regime and Representation*, Chichester: John Wiley & Sons Ltd.

Hannigan, J. (1998) *Fantasy City: Pleasure and Profit in the Postmodern Metropolis*, London and New York: Routledge.

Harding, A. (1995) 'Elite Theory and Growth Machines', in D. Judge, G. Stoker, and H. Wolman (eds.) *Theories of Urban Politics*, London: Sage.

Harris, R. N. (1978) 'The Police Academy and the Professional Self-Image', in P. K. Manning and J. Van Mannen (eds.) *Policing: A View from the Streets*, California: Goodyear.

Harrison, B. (1967) 'Religion and Recreation in Nineteenth-Century England', *Past and Present*, 38:98–125.

—— (1994) *Drink and the Victorians: The Temperance Question in England 1815–1872*, Keele: Keele University Press.

Harvey, D. (1989a) 'From Managerialism to Entrepreneurialism: The Transformation in Urban Governance in Late Capitalism', *Geografiska Annaler*, 71/1:3–17.

——(1989b) *The Condition of Postmodernity*, Cambridge: Polity Press.

Haslam, D. (1999) *Manchester England: The Story of the Pop Cult City*, London: Fourth Estate.

Haug, W. F. (1986) *Critique of Commodity Aesthetics: Appearance, Sexuality and Advertising*, Cambridge: Polity Press.

Hawkins, K. (1984) *Environment and Enforcement*, Oxford: Clarendon Press.

Healey, P., Davoudi, S., O'Toole, M., Tavsanoglu, S., and Usher, D. (eds.) (1992) *Rebuilding The City: Property-led Urban Regeneration*, London: Spon.

Heath, T. and Stickland, R. (1997) 'The Twenty-Four Hour City Concept', in T. Oc and S. Tiesdell (eds.) *Safer City Centres: Reviving the Public Realm*, London: Paul Chapman Publishing.

Henry, S. (1987) 'Private Justice and the Policing of Labor: the Dialectics of Industrial Discipline', in C. D. Shearing and P. C. Stenning (eds.) *Private Policing*, California: Sage.

Hess, H. (1998) *Mafia and Mafiosi: Origin, Power and Myth*, 4th edn., (translated by Ewald Osers), London: Hurst and Co. Ltd.

Hewitt, E. J. (1979) *A History of Policing in Manchester*, Manchester: Morten.

Himmelstrand, U. (1960) *Social Pressures, Attitudes and Democratic Processes*, Stockholm: Almqvist and Wiksell.

Hindle, P. (1994) 'Gay Communities and Gay Space in the City', in S. Whittle (ed.) *The Margins of the City: Gay Men's Urban Lives*, Aldershot: Arena.

Hine, R. V. and Faragher, J. M. (2000) *The American West*, New Haven: Yale University Press.

Hobbs, D. (1988) *Doing the Business*, Oxford: Clarendon.

——(1995) *Bad Business: Professional Crime in Modern Britain*, Oxford: Oxford University Press.

——(1998) 'Going Down the Glocal: The Local Context of Organized Crime', *The Howard Journal*, 37/4:407–422.

——(2001) 'The Firm: Organizational Logic and Criminal Culture on a Shifting Terrain', *British Journal of Criminology*, 41/4:549–560.

——(2003) 'Violence and Organized Crime', in J. Hagen (ed.) *The Handbook of Violence*, Boulder: Westview Press.

——Lister, S., Hadfield, P., Winlow, S., and Hall, S. (2000) 'Receiving Shadows: Governance and Liminality in the Night-time Economy', *British Journal of Sociology*, 51/4:701–717.

——Hadfield, P., Lister, S., and Winlow, S. (2002) 'Door Lore: The Art and Economics of Intimidation', *British Journal of Criminology*, 42/2:352–370.

Hobsbawn, E. (1959) *Social Bandits and Primitive Rebels*, Glencoe, Ill.: Free Press.

Hobsbawn, E. J. (1969) *Industry and Empire*, Harmondsworth: Penguin.

Holdaway, S. (1983) *Inside The British Police*, Oxford: Basil Blackwell.

Holgate, G. (1999) 'Reform of the Liquor Licensing Legislation', *The Police Journal*, 72/2:117–130.

Hollands, R. (2000) 'Lager Louts, Tarts, and Hooligans': The Criminalization of Young Adults in a Study of Newcastle Nightlife', in V. Jupp, P. Davies and P. Francis (eds.) *Doing Criminological Research*, London: Sage.

Holt, R. (1989) *Sport and the British*, Oxford: Oxford University Press.

Home Affairs Select Committee (1995) *The Private Security Industry, Volumes 1 and 2*, London: HMSO.

Home Office (1993) *Disclosure of Criminal Records for Employment Vetting Purposes*, Cm. 2319, London: HMSO.

—— (1995) *Circular 60/95 Registration Schemes for Door Supervisors*, London: HMSO.

—— (2000a) *Time For Reform: Proposals for the Modernization of Our Licensing Laws*, London: HMSO.

—— (2000b) *Recorded Crime Statistics England and Wales, April 1999 to March 2000*, at homeoffice.gov.uk/new.htm.

—— (2001a) *Assessing Local Alcohol-Related Crime: A Demonstration Project in Crime and Disorder Partnerships: Tender Document*, London: Home Office Research, Development and Statistics Directorate.

—— (2001b) *Fighting Violent Crime Together: An Action Plan*, London: Home Office.

—— (2001c) *Criminal Justice: The Way Ahead*, London: Home Office.

—— (2001d) *Policing a New Century: A Blueprint For Reform*, London: Home Office.

—— (2002) *Liquor Licensing, England and Wales, July 2000–June 2001*, London: Home Office.

Homel, R. and Clark, J. (1994) 'The Prediction and Prevention of Violence in Pubs and Clubs', in R. V. Clarke (ed.) *Crime Prevention Studies, Volume 3*, Monsey, New York: Criminal Justice Press.

—— and Tomsen, S. (1993) 'Hot Spots for Violence: The Environment of Pubs and Clubs', *Homicide: Patterns, Prevention and Control*, Canberra: Australian Institute of Criminology.

—— Tomsen, S., and Thommeny, J. L. (1991) 'The Problem of Violence in Licensed Premises: The Sydney Study', in T. Stockwell, E. Lang, and P. Rydon (eds.) *The Licensed Drinking Environment: Current Research in Australia and New Zealand*, Melbourne: National Centre for Research into the Prevention of Drug Abuse.

—————— and —— (1992) 'Public Drinking and Violence: Not Just an Alcohol Problem', *Journal of Drug Issues*, 22/3:679–697.

Hope, T. (1985) 'Drinking and Disorder in the City Centre: A Policy Analysis,' in *Implementing Crime Prevention Measures*, Home Office Research Study No. 86, London: HMSO.

Horkheimer, M. and Adorno, T. (1973) *Dialectic of Enlightenment*, London: Allen Lane.

Horne, R. and Hall, S. (1995) 'Anelpis: A Preliminary Expedition into a World Without Hope or Potential', *Parallex*: 1:81–92.

Hughes, E. (1971) *The Sociological Eye: Selected Papers*, Chicago: Aldine Atherton.

Hughes, G., Fergusson, R., and Toon, I. (2002) *The 'New' and the 'Old' in the Governance of Safety and Pleasure: A Case-Study of Policing and Regulation of the Night-Time Economy in Milton Keynes*, Paper presented to the British Society of Criminology Conference, Keele University, July.

Humphries, S. (1981) *Hooligans or Rebels?: An Oral History of Working-Class Childhood and Youth 1889–1939*, Oxford: Basil Blackwell.

Hunt, G., Mellor, J. and Turner J. (1989) 'Wretched, Hatless and Miserably Clad: Women and the Inebriate Reformatories 1900–1913', *British Journal of Sociology*, 40/2:244–70.

Hutchinson, I. L., Magennis, P. Shepherd, J. P., and Brown, A. E. (1998) 'B.A.O.M.S United Kingdom Survey of Facial Injuries, Pt 1: Aetiology and the Association with Alcohol Consumption', *British Journal of Maxillofacial Surgery*, 36:3–13.

Hutter, B. M. (1997) *Compliance: Regulation and Environment*, Oxford: Clarendon Press.

Ianni, F. (1971) 'Formal and Social Organization in an Organized Crime "Family": A Case Study', *University of Florida Law Review*, 24:31–41.

Ingram, G. B., Bouthillette, A. M. and Retter, Y. (eds.) (1997) *Queers in Space: Communities, Public Places, Sites of Resistance*, Washington: Bay Press.

Isle of Man Constabulary, (2002) *Annual Report 2001–2002*, Douglas: Isle of Man Constabulary.

Jackson, P. (1989) *Maps of Meaning*, London: Unwin Hyman.

Jacobs, J. (1961) *The Death and Life of Great American Cities*, Harmondsworth: Penguin.

Jacobs, J. (1983) 'Police: Private Police and Security Forces', in S. H. Kadish (ed.) *Encyclopedia of Crime and Justice*, New York: MacMillan.

Jacobs, J. B. (1999) *Gotham Unbound*, New York: New York University Press.

Jacobson, J. (1999) *Policing Drug Hot-spots*, Police Research Series Paper 109, London: Home Office.

Jenkins, R. (1997) 'Clubland Acts to Curb Violence', *The Times*, (11 October): 3.

Jessop, B. (1994) 'The Transition to Post-Fordism and the Schumpeterian Workfare State', in R. Burrows and B. Loader (eds.) *Towards a Post-Fordist Welfare State?*, London: Routledge.

—— (1998) 'The Narrative of Enterprise and the Enterprise of Narrative: Place Marketing and the Entrepreneurial City', in T. Hall and P. Hubbard (eds.) *The Entrepreneurial City: Geographies of Politics, Regime and Representation*, Chichester: John Wiley & Sons Ltd.

Johnson, R. (1983) *On Human Geography*, Oxford: Blackwell.

Johnston, L. (1992) *The Rebirth of Private Policing*, London: Routledge.

—— (1996) 'Policing Diversity: The Impact of the Public-Private Complex in Policing,' in F. Leishman, B. Loveday, and S. P. Savage (eds.) *Core Issues in Policing*, London: Longman.

—— (2000) *Policing Britain: Risk, Security and Governance*, London: Longman.

Johnstone, G. (1996) 'From Vice to Disease? The Concepts of Dipsomania and Inebriety, 1860–1908', *Social and Legal Studies*, 5/1:7–56.

Jones, A. and Kantonen, J. (1999) *Saturday Night Forever: The Story of Disco*, Edinburgh: Mainstream Publishing.

Jones, D. (1982) *Crime, Protest, Community and Police in Nineteenth-Century Britain*, London: Routledge & Kegan Paul.

Jones, P. (1996) 'Enter the Superpub', *Town and Country Planning*, April: 110–112.

—— Hillier, D., and Turner, D. (1999) 'Towards the 24-Hour City', *Town and Country Planning*, 68, May: 164–165.

Jones, S. (1999) 'Leeds Café Society: Emerging from the Shadows of the City's Industrial Past', *Financial Times*, (5 July):6.

Jones, S. (2000) *Understanding Violent Crime*, Buckingham: Open University Press.

Jones, T. and Newburn, T. (1998) *Private Security and Public Policing*, Oxford: Clarendon Press.

Jowitt, J. (1999) 'Birmingham at Crossroads as Clubs pull it into a New Groove', *Financial Times*, (21 April): 8.

Justices' Clerks Society, (1999) *Good Practice Guide: Licensing*, London: JCS.

Katz, J. (1975) 'Essences as Moral Identities', *American Journal of Sociology*, 80/6.

—— (1988) *Seductions of Crime: The Moral and Sensual Attractions of Doing Evil*, New York: Basic Books.

Kay, J. P. (1832) *The Moral and Physical Condition of the Working Classes Employed in the Cotton Manufacture in Manchester*, Manchester.

Kearns, G. and Philo, C. (eds.) (1993) *Selling Places: The City as Cultural Capital, Past and Present*, Oxford: Pergamon.

Keat, R. (1991) 'Starship Britain or Universal Enterprise?' in R. Keat and N. Abercrombie (eds.) *Enterprise Culture*, London and New York: Routledge.

Kidd, A. (1993) *Manchester*, Keele: Keele University Press.

Kimmel, M. S. (1987) 'Rethinking Masculinity', in M. S. Kimmel (ed.) *Changing Men: New Directions in Research on Men and Masculinity*, London: Sage.

King, R. (1999a) 'Restoring the Glory of a Tarnished City Jewel', *Manchester Evening News*, (20 October): 24–25.

——(1999b) 'City Crime Toll Fury', *Manchester Evening News*, (2 December): 1–2.

Kingdom, J. (1995) *Agendas: Alternative and Public Policies*, 2nd edn., New York: Harper Collins.

Kowinski, W. S. (1985) *The Malling of America*, New York: Morrow.

Kreitzman, L. (1999) *The 24-Hour Society*, London: Profile Books Limited.

Kwitny, J. (1979) *Vicious Circles: The Mafia in the Marketplace*, New York: Norton

Lang E., Stockwell, T., Ryan, P. and Lockwood, A. (1995) 'Drinking Settings and Problems of Intoxication', *Addiction Research*, 3:141–149.

Langley, J., Chalmers, D., and Fanslow, J. (1996) 'Incidence of Death and Hospitalization from Assault Occurring in and around Licensed Premises: A Comparative Analysis', *Addiction*, 91:985–993.

Lasch, C. (1979) *The Culture of Narcissism*, New York: Norton.

Lash, S. and Urry, J. (1987) *The End of Organized Capitalism*, Cambridge: Polity.

——and——(1994) *Economies of Signs and Space*, London: Sage.

Lasswell, H. (1960) *Psychopathology and Politics*, New York: Viking Press, Compass Books.

Lauria, M. and Knopp, L. (1985) 'Towards an Analysis of the Role of Gay Communities in Urban Renaissance', *Urban Geography*, 6:152–169.

Law, C. M. (1986) 'The Uncertain Future for the City Centre: The Case of Manchester', *The Manchester Geographer*, 7:26–43.

——(1992) 'Property-led Urban Regeneration in Inner Manchester', in P. Healey et al., *Rebuilding the City: Property-led Urban Regeneration*, London: Spon.

——(1993a) *Urban Tourism: Attracting Visitors to Large Cities*, London: Mansell.

——(1993b) 'Tourism in Greater Manchester', *The Manchester Geographer*, 14: 38–53.

Lawson, A. (1992) *It Happened in Manchester: The True Story of Manchester's Music 1958–1965*, Bury: Multimedia.

Lee, C. P. (1995) 'And Then There Were None: Government Legislation and Manchester Beat clubs, 1965', paper given at the first Critical Musicology Conference, Salford.

—— (1996) 'Popular Music Making in Manchester (1950–1995)', Unpublished Ph.D. dissertation, Manchester Institute of Popular Culture at Manchester Metropolitan University.

Lee, M. J. (1993) *Consumer Culture Reborn: The Cultural Politics of Consumption*, London: Routledge.

Leeds City Council (1997) *Number of Registered Door Staff in Leeds Passes 1000 Mark*, Press Release.

Lefebvre, H. (1976) *The Survival of Capitalism*, London: Allen & Unwin.

LGA (Local Government Association) (2002) *All Day and All of the Night?: An LGA Discussion Paper*, London: LGA.

Licensing Review (1998) 'Door Staff Schemes May Be "Ultra Vires"', (32) January.

Light, R. (2000) 'Liberalizing Liquor Licensing Law: Order Into Chaos?', *New Law Journal*, 150/6941 (23 June): 926–929.

Lightfoot, M. (1988) 'Community and Race Relations Training', in P. Southgate (ed.), *New Directions in Police Training*, London: Home Office.

Lipietz, A. (1996) 'The Next Transformation', in M. Cangiani (ed.) *The Milano Papers: Essays in Societal Alternatives*, Montreal: Black Rose Books.

Lippman, W. (1962) 'The Underworld as Servant', in G. Tyler (ed.) *Organized Crime in America*, Ann Arbor: University of Michigan Press. Article originally published in 1931.

Lipsey, M. W., Wilson, D. B., Cohen, M. A. and Derzon, J. H. (1997) 'Is there a Causal Relationship Between Alcohol and Violence?', in M. Galanter (ed.) *Recent Developments in Alcoholism*, New York: Plenum Press, 13:245–282.

Lister, S. (2001) 'Closing Time for Crime and Disorder', *Police Review*, 30 November, 109ii/5650:20–21.

—— (2002) 'Violence as a Commercial Resource: Situating Bouncers and the Use of Force in Context', *Journal of Forensic Psychiatry*, 12/2: 245–249.

—— Hobbs, D., Hall, S., and Winlow, S. (2000) 'Violence in the Night time Economy; Bouncers: The Reporting, Recording and Prosecution of Assaults', *Policing and Society*, 10:383:402.

—— Hadfield, P., Hobbs D., and Winlow, S. (2001a) 'Be Nice: The Training of Bouncers', *Criminal Justice Matters, Special Issue on Training*, 45, Autumn: 20–21.

—— —— and —— (2001b) 'Accounting for Bouncers: Occupational Licensing as a Mechanism for Regulation', *Criminal Justice*, 1/4:363–384.

Lloyd, P. E. and Mason, C. M. (1978) 'Manufacturing in the Inner-City: A Case Study of Greater Manchester', *Transactions of the Institute of British Geographers*, NS.3: 66–90.

Loader, I. (1999) 'Consumer Culture and the Commodification of Policing and Security', *Sociology*, 33/2:373–392.

Loader, I. (2000) 'Plural Policing and Democratic Governance', *Social and Legal Studies*, 9/3:323–346.

Lofland, L. H. (1973) *A World of Strangers*, New York: Basic Books.

Loftman, P. and Nevin, B. (1996) 'Going for Growth: Prestige Projects in Three British Cities', *Urban Studies*, 33/6:991–1019.

Logan, J. R. and Molotch, H. (1987) *Urban Fortunes: The Political Economy of Place*, Berkeley: University of California Press.

Lovatt, A. (1994a) 'The More the Merrier', *Policing*, 10/4:268–275.

——(1994b) 'The Economy of the City at Night: A Research Note', in A. Lovatt, J. O'Connor, J. Montgomery, and P. Owens (eds.) *The 24-Hour City: Selected Papers from the First National Conference on the Nighttime Economy*, Manchester: Manchester Metropolitan University.

——(1996) 'The Ecstasy of Urban Regeneration: Regulation of the Night-time Economy in the Transition to a Post-Fordist City', in J. O'Connor and D. Wynne (eds.) *From the Margins to the Centre: Cultural Production and Consumption in the Post-industrial City*, Aldershot: Arena.

——(1997) 'Turning up the Lights in the Cities of the Night', *Planning*, 1224 (27 June): 20–21.

——(1999) 'The City and the Night-time Economy: Strategies of Regulation and Regeneration', Unpublished Ph.D. dissertation, Manchester Institute of Popular Culture at Manchester Metropolitan University.

——(forthcoming) 'Dance Culture and the City: An Order Without Law?' in H. Reitveld (ed.) *Dancing in a Global Matrix*, London: Garland.

——and O'Connor, J. (1995) 'Cities and the Night-time Economy', *Planning Practice and Research*, 10/2:127–135.

Lowi, T. J. (1969), *The End of Liberalism: Ideology, Policy, and the Crisis of Public Authority*, New York: W. W. Norton and Company.

Lunt, P. and Livingstone, S. (1992) *Mass Consumption and Personal Identity*, Buckingham: Open University Press.

Lury, C. (1996) *Consumer Culture*, Cambridge: Polity.

Lyman, J. L. and Scott, M. (1970) *Sociology of the Absurd*, New York: Appleton Century Crofts.

Lynch, J. E. (2002) 'Getting What They Pay For?', *Criminal Justice Matters*, Spring, 47:42–43.

McClelland, D. C., Davis, W. N., Kalin, R., and Wanner, E. (1972) '*The Drinking Man: Alcohol and Human Motivation*', Toronto: Collier-Macmillan.

McClintock, F. H. and Wikström, P-O. H. (1992) 'The Comparative Study of Urban Violence: Criminal Violence in Edinburgh and Stockholm', *British Journal of Criminology*, 32/4:505–520.

McCracken, G. (1990) *Culture and Consumption*, Bloomington, Ind.: Indiana University Press.

McIntosh, A. J. and Prentice, R. C. (1999) 'Affirming Authenticity: Consuming Cultural Heritage', *Annals of Tourism Research*, 26/3:589–612.

McKenna, P. (1996) *Nightshift*, Argyll: S. T. Publishing.

McLean, L. (1998) *Guv'nor*, London: Blake Publishing.

McMurran, M. and Hollin, C. R. (1989) 'Drinking and Delinquency: Another Look at Young Offenders and Alcohol', *British Journal of Criminology*, 29/4:386–394.

McNeill, A. (2002) 'Open All Hours? Literature Review', Unpublished: IAS and The Civic Trust Steering Committee.

McVeigh, A. (1997) 'Screening for Straights: Aspects of Entrance Policy at a Gay Disco', *Irish Journal of Sociology*, 7:77–98.

McWilliams, T. (2002) An analysis of crime and disorder trends in Newcastle city centre 31.12.1997–31.12.2001, personal correspondence with the authors.

MacAndrew, C. and Edgerton, R. B. (1969) *Drunken Comportment: A Social Explanation*, London: Thomas Nelson and Sons Ltd.

Mac an Ghaill, M. (1996) *Understanding Masculinities*, Buckingham: Open University Press.

Maffesoli, M. (1995) *The Time of the Tribes: The Decline of Individualism in Mass Society*, London: Sage.

Maguire, M. and Nettleton, H. (2003) *Reducing Alcohol-related Violence and Disorder: an Evaluation of the 'TASC' Project*, London: Home Office.

Malbon, B. (1998) 'The Club, Clubbing: Consumption, Identity and the Spatial Practices of Every-Night Life', in T. Skelton and G. Valentine (eds.) *Cool Places: Geographies of Youth Cultures*, London: Routledge.

——(1999) *Clubbing: Dancing, Ecstasy and Vitality*, London: Routledge.

Manning, P. K. (1977) *Police Work: The Social Organization of Policing*, Cambridge Mass. and London: MIT Press.

——(1987) 'Ironies of Compliance', in C. D. Shearing and P. C. Stenning, (eds.) *Private Policing*, California: Sage.

——and Van Maanen, J. V. (1978) 'Practice of Policing' in P. K. Manning and J. A. Van Maanen (eds.) *Policing: A View From the Street*, Santa Monica: Goodyear Publishing.

MCC (Manchester City Council) (1994) *Manchester 2002*, Manchester: MCC.

——(1998) *Crime and Disorder: An Audit of Problems and Priorities for Manchester, November 1998*, Manchester: MCC.

——(2000) *Crime and Disorder Audit for Manchester, March 2000*, Manchester: MCC.

——(2001) *Crime and Disorder: Working in Partnership for a Safer Manchester. Audit March 2001*, Manchester: MCC.

MEN (*Manchester Evening News*) (1998a) 'I Think The Gay Scene Will Move Out', Go Entertainment Guide, (10 April): 21.

——(1998b) 'Karney Defies Threat Thugs', (6 May): 2.

——(2001) 'Non-stop Julia Unveils World's Biggest Gay Hotel', Village Life, Go Entertainment Guide, (29 June): 16–17.

Manchester Training and Enterprise Council, (1998) *Economic Assessment 1998*, Manchester: Manchester TEC.

Marsh, P. and Fox-Kibby, K. (1992) *Drinking and Public Disorder*, London: The Portman Group.

Marshall, M. (1979) '*Weekend Warriors*': Alcohol in a Micronesian Culture, Palo Alto, Calif.: Mayfield.

Martin, J., Nada-Raja, S., Langley, J., Feehan, M., McGee, R., Clarke, J., Begg, D., Hutchinson-Cervantes, M., Moffit, T., and Rivara, F. (1998) 'Physical Assault in New Zealand: The Experience of 21 Year Old Men and Women in a Community Sample', *New Zealand Medical Journal*, 111:158–160.

Martin, P. (1999) 'The British Economy: High-tech Industries and Coffee Bars offer up a Revolution', *Financial Times*, (15 September): 1.

Martin, R. (1988) 'Industrial Capitalism in Transition: the Contemporary Reorganization of the British Space-Economy', in D. Massey and J. Allen (eds.) *Uneven Re-Development*, London: Hodder & Stoughton.

Mattera, P. (1985) *Off the Books, The Rise of the Underground Economy*, London: Pluto Press Limited.

Meakin, R. (1999) 'Gay Tourism Drive "Is Good Business Sense"', *Manchester Evening News*, (23 July): 1 and 4.

Measham, F., Newcombe, R., and Parker, H. (1994) 'The Normalization of Recreational Drug Use Amongst Young People in North-West England', *British Journal of Sociology*, 45/2:287–312.

Mehigan, S. and Phillips, J. with contributions from Collins, D. and Farrelly, E. (2001) *Paterson's Licensing Acts 2001*, 109th edn., London: Butterworths.

Melbin, M. (1978) 'Night as Frontier', *American Sociological Review*, 43/1:3–22.

Messinger, G. S. (1985) *Manchester In The Victorian Age: The Half-Known City*, Manchester: Manchester University Press.

Milestone, K. (1996) 'Regional Variations: Northernness and New Urban Economies of Hedonism', in J. O'Connor and D. Wynne (eds.) *From the Margins to the Centre: Cultural Production and Consumption in the Post-Industrial City*, Aldershot: Arena.

—— (1998) 'Love Factory: The Sites, Practices and Media Relationships of Northern Soul', in S. Redhead, D. Wynne, and J. O'Connor (eds.) *The Clubcultures Reader: Readings in Popular Cultural Studies*, Oxford: Blackwell.

Miles, S. (1998) *Consumerism as a Way of Life*, London: Sage.

Miller, W. (1977) *Cops and Bobbies*, Chicago: Chicago University Press.

Miller, W. B. (1958) 'Lower Class Culture as a Generating Milieu of Gang Delinquency', *Journal of Social Issues*, 15.

Mingione, E. (1991) *Fragmented Societies*, Oxford: Basil Blackwell.

Mintel Leisure Intelligence, (1998) *Nightclubs and Discotheques*, Mintel International Group.

——(2001) *Late Licensing*, July, London: Mintel International Group.

——(2002) *High Street Pubs and Bars*, February, London: Mintel International Group.

Mole, P. (1996) 'Fordism, Post-Fordism and the Contemporary City', in J. O'Connor and D. Wynne (eds.) *From the Margins to the Centre: Cultural Production and Consumption in the Post-Industrial City*, Aldershot: Arena.

Molotoch, H. (1976) 'The City as a Growth Machine: Toward a Political Economy of Place', *American Journal of Sociology*, 82/2:309–330.

——(1996) 'L. A. as a Design Product: How Design Works in a Regional Economy', in A. J. Scott and E. Soja (eds.) *The City: Los Angeles and Urban Theory at the end of the Twentieth Century*, Berkeley and Los Angeles: University of California Press.

Monaghan, L. F. (2002a) 'Regulating "Unruly" Bodies: Work Tasks, Conflict and Violence in Britain's Night-Time Economy', *The British Journal of Sociology*, 53/3:403–29.

——(2002b) 'Hard Men, Shop Boys and Others: Embodying Competence in a Masculinist Occupation', *The Sociological Review*, 50/3:334–55.

——(forthcoming) 'Danger on the Doors: Bodily Risk in a Demonized Occupation', *Health, Risk & Society*, 5/1.

Montgomery, J. R. (1990) 'Cities and the Art of Cultural Planning', *Planning Practice and Research*, 5/3:17–24.

——(1994) 'The Evening Economy of Cities', *Town and Country Planning*, 63/11:302–307.

——(1995a) 'Urban Vitality and the Culture of Cities', *Planning Practice and Research*, 10/2:101–109.

——(1995b) 'The Story of Temple Bar: Creating Dublin's Cultural Quarter', *Planning Practice and Research*, 10/2:135–172.

——(1998) Quoted by B. Walsh in 'The 24-Hour City—Do We Really Want It?', *Urban Environment Today*, 26 November:7–8.

Moore, M. (1987) 'Organized Crime as a Business Enterprise', in *Major Issues in Organized Crime Control*, H. Edelhertz (ed.) Washington, DC: Government Printing Office, 51–64.

Morleo, M. (2002) *Public Transport in the Night-time Economy: A Case Study of Durham City*, Unpublished M.A. Dissertation, Department of Sociology and Social Policy: University of Durham.

Morris, S. (1998a) *Clubs, Drugs and Doormen*, Crime Detection and Prevention Series Paper 86, London: Home Office Police Research Group.

——(1998b) 'Drugs and Doors: Improving Door Security and Tackling Drug Dealing in Clubs and Pubs', in M. Gill (ed.) *Crime at Work: Increasing the Risk for Offenders, Volume II*, Leicester: Perpetuity Press.

Morton, J. (1993) *Gangland: London's Underworld*, London: Warner.
—— (1994) *Gangland Volume 2: The Underworld in Britain and Ireland*, London: Little, Brown and Company.
Muir, Jr., J. W. (1977) *Police: Streetcorner Politicians*, Chicago: Chicago University Press.
Narain, J. and Scheerhout, J. (1998) 'Tale of Two Swinging Cities', *Manchester Evening News*, (16 March): 1–3.
Naylor, T. and Morrison, S. (1998) 'Cruising for a Boozing? Publand's Threat to Clubland', *Ministry*, (July):28–30.
Neale, W. B. (1840) *Juvenile Delinquency in Manchester*, Manchester.
Neff, J. (1989) *Mobbed Up*, New York: Atlantic Monthly Press.
Neff, J. A., Prichoda, T. J., and Hoppe, S. K. (1991) 'Machismo, Self Esteem, Educational and High Maximum Drinking Among Anglo, Black and Mexican American Male Drinkers', *Journal of Studies on Alcohol*, 52:458–463.
Negus, K. (1996) *Popular Music in Theory: An Introduction*, Cambridge: Polity.
Neiderhoffer, A. (1967) *Behind The Shield: The Police in Urban Society*, New York: Doubleday.
Nelson, A., Bromley, R., and Thomas, C. (2001) 'Identifying Micro-spatial and Temporal Patterns of Violent Crime and Disorder in a British City Centre', *Applied Geography*, 21:249–274.
New Scientist, (1999) *Alcohol: The Inside Story*, (December), London: New Science Publications.
New York State Organized Crime Force (1988) *Corruption and Racketeering in the New York City Construction Industry*, Ithaca, NY: Cornell University School of Labor and Industrial Relations.
Night, (2001) 'BEDA Builds Bridges With Home Office', *Night*, December: 14.
Norris, S. and Johnson, T. (2002) 'New Town Centre Management Styles Needed to Unlock Private Funding', *Urban Environment Today*, 154, 22 August: 6–7.
Nott, A. and Taylor, P. (1997) 'Tragic Heroes', *Manchester Evening News*, (6 October), p. 1.
Oc, T. and Tiesdell, S. (eds.) (1997) *Safer City Centres: Reviving the Public Realm*, London: Paul Chapman Publishing Ltd.
O'Connor, J. and Wynne, D. (1992) 'The Uses and Abuses of Popular Culture: Cultural Policy and Popular Culture', *Loisir et Societe*, 14/2:465–483.
—— (1996a) 'Introduction' in J. O'Connor and D. Wynne (eds.) *From the Margins to the Centre: Cultural Production and Consumption in the Post-Industrial City*, Aldershot: Arena.
—— (1996b) 'Left Loafing: City Cultures and Postmodern Lifestyles,' in J. O'Connor and D. Wynne (eds.) *From the Margins to the Centre:*

Cultural Production and Consumption in the Post-Industrial City, Aldershot: Arena.

O'Connor, J. (1998) 'Popular Culture, Cultural Intermediaries and Urban Regeneration', in T. Hall and P. Hubbard (eds.) *The Entrepreneurial City: Geographies of Politics, Regime and Representation*, Chichester: John Wiley & Sons Ltd.

ODPM (Office of the Deputy Prime Minister) (2002) *Consultation on Possible Changes to the Use Classes Order and Temporary Uses Provisions*, London: OPDM.

Ogus, A. L. (1994) *Regulation: Legal Form and Economic Theory*, Oxford: Clarendon Press.

O'Mahoney, B. (1997) *So This Is Ecstasy?* Edinburgh: Mainstream Publishing.

Osborne, D. and Gaebler, T. (1992) *Reinventing Government*, Reading, Mass.: Addison-Wesley.

Osborne, T. and Rose, N. (1999) 'Governing Cities: Notes on the Spatialization of Virtue', *Environment and Planning D: Society and Space*, 17:737–760.

Pacione, M. (ed.) (1997) *British Cities*, London: Routledge.

Pakulski, J. and Walters, M. (1996) *The Death of Class*. London: Sage.

Panter, S. and King, R. (1998) 'Mob Victim: Clubs Demand New Police Crackdown/after Fifth Killing', *Manchester Evening News* (6 April): 1.

—— and Watson, J. (1998) 'Rampant Lawlessness: Council Boss's Astonishing Outburst on Police Tactics', *Manchester Evening News*, (12 March): 1.

Park, R. E. (1969) [1916] 'The City: Suggestions for Investigations of Human Behaviour in the Urban Environment', in R. Sennett (ed.) *Classic Essays on the Culture of Cities*, New York: Appleton Century-Crofts.

Parker, H., Aldridge, J., and Measham, F. (1998) *Illegal Leisure: The Normalization of Adolescent Recreational Drug Use*, London: Routledge.

Pawson, R. and Tilley, N. (1997) *Realistic Evaluation*, London: Sage.

Pearce, F. and Tombs, S. (1997) 'Hazards, Law and Class: Contextualizing the Regulation of Corporate Crime', *Social & Legal Studies*, 6/1:79–107.

Pearson, G. (1983) *Hooligan: A History of Respectable Fears*, London: Macmillan.

Pearson. J. (1973) *The Profession of Violence*, London: Granada.

Peck, J. A. (1995) 'Moving and Shaking: Business Elites, State Localism and Urban Privatism,' *Progress in Human Geography*, 19/1:16–46.

—— and Emmerich, M. (1992a) *Recession, Restructuring and the Greater Manchester Labour Market: An Empirical Overview*, Spatial Policy Analysis working paper No. 17, School of Geography, University of Manchester.

Peck, J. A. and Emmerich, M. (1992b) 'Recession, Restructuring...and Recession Again: The Transformation of the Greater Manchester Labour Market', *Manchester Geographer*, 13:9–46.

—— and Tickell, A. (1995) 'Business Goes Local: Dissecting the Business Agenda in Manchester', *International Journal of Urban and Regional Research*, 19/1:55–78.

—— and —— (1997) 'Manchester's Job Gap', New Deal Monitoring Group School of Geography Working Paper, University of Manchester.

Pernanem, K. (1976) 'Alcohol and Crimes of Violence', in B. Kissin and H. Begleiter (eds.) *The Biology of Alcoholism*, New York: Plenum Press, 351–444.

Petridis, A. (2002) 'Boys and Girls Come Out to Play', *The Guardian Friday Review*, 5 July: 2–5.

Phillips, T. and Smith, P. (2000) 'Police Violence Occasioning Police Complaint: An Empirical Analysis of Time-Space Dynamics', *British Journal of Criminology*, 40:480–496.

Pierson, C. (1991) *Beyond the Welfare State?* Cambridge: Polity Press.

Pileggi, N. (1987) *Wise Guy*, London: Corgi.

Poole, R. (1982) *Popular Leisure and the Music Hall in Nineteenth Century Bolton*, Lancaster: University of Lancaster Press.

Porter, M. E. (1996) 'Competitive Advantage, Agglomeration Economies and Regional Policy', *International Regional Science Review*, 19/1–2:85–94.

Potter, G. and Jenkins, P. (1985) *The City and the Syndicate*, Lexington Mass.: Ginn Press.

Prenzer, T., Hayes, H., and Wortley, R. (1998) *An Evaluation of the Queensland Security Providers Act: Implications for National Regulation*, Report to the Criminology Research Council Commonwealth Attorney General's Department. School of Justice Administration, Griffin University, Brisbane.

Presdee, M. (2000) *Cultural Criminology and the Carnival of Crime*, London: Routledge.

Prime, J., White, S., Liriano, S., and Kinnari, P. (2001) *Criminal Careers of those Born between 1953 and 1978*, England and Wales, Home Office Statistical Bulletin, 4/01. London: HMSO.

Prince, M. (1988) *God's Cop: The Biography of James Anderton*, London: Frederick Muller.

Punch, M. (1979) *Policing the Inner City*, London: Macmillan.

Punter, J. V. (1990) 'The Privatization of the Public Realm', *Planning, Practice and Research*, 5/3:9–16.

Push, and Silcott, M. (2000) *The Book of E: All About Ecstasy*, London: Omnibus Press.

Quilley, S. (1995) 'Manchester's "Village in the City": The Gay Vernacular in a Post-Industrial Landscape of Power', *Transgressions*, 1/1:36–50.

—— (1997) 'Constructing Manchester's "New Urban Village": Gay Space in the Entrepreneurial City', in G. B. Ingram, A. M. Bouthillette and Y. Retter (eds.) *Queers in Space: Communities, Public Places, Sites of Resistance*, Washington: Bay Press.

—— (1999) 'Entrepreneurial Manchester: The Genesis of Elite Consensus,' *Antipode*, 31/2:185–211.

Raban, J. (1974) *Soft City*, London: Harper Collins.

Ramsay, M. (1989) *Downtown Drinkers: The Perceptions and Fears of the Public in a City Centre*, Crime Prevention Unit Paper 19, London: HMSO.

—— (1990) *Lagerland Lost?, An Experiment in Keeping Drinkers off the Streets in Central Coventry and Elsewhere*, Crime Prevention Unit Paper 22, London: HMSO.

Randall, S. (1995) 'City Pride—From "Municipal Socialism" to "Municipal Capitalism?" ', *Critical Social Policy*, 43:40–59.

Redhead, S. (1990) *The End of the Century Party: Youth and Pop Towards 2000*, Manchester: Manchester University Press.

—— (ed.) (1993) *Rave Off: Politics and Deviance in Contemporary Youth Culture*, Aldershot: Avebury.

—— (1997) *Subculture to Clubcultures*, Oxford: Blackwell.

—— Wynne, D., and O'Connor, J. (eds.) (1998) *The Clubcultures Reader: Readings in Popular Cultural Studies*, Oxford: Blackwell.

Reeves, G. (1993) *Communications and the 'Third World'*, London: Routledge.

Reichman, N. (1987) 'The Widening Webs of Surveillance: Private Police Unravelling Deceptive Claims', in C. D. Shearing and P. C. Stenning (eds.) *Private Policing*, California: Sage.

Reiner, R. (1985) *The Politics of the Police*, 1st edn., Brighton: Wheatsheaf Books.

Reiss, Jr., A. J. (1965) 'Police Brutality—Answers to Key Questions', *Transactions*, 5/8: 10–19.

—— (1971) *The Police and the Public*, New Haven: Yale University Press.

—— and Biderman, A. D. (1980) *Data Sources on White-Collar Crime Law-Breaking*, Washington, DC: National Institute of Justice.

Reuter, P. (1987) *Racketeering in Legitimate Industries: A Study in the Economics of Intimidation*, Santa Monica: Rand Corporation.

—— Rubinstein, J., and Wynn, S. (1983) *Racketeering in Legitimate Industries*, Washington, DC: US Government Printing Office.

Rigakos, G. S. (2002) *The New Parapolice: Risk Markets and Commodified Social Control*, Toronto: University of Toronto Press.

Ritzer, G. (2001) *Explorations in the Sociology of Consumerism*, California: Sage.

Robb, J. (1997) *The Stone Roses and The Resurrection of British Pop*, London: Ebury Press.

Robb, J. (1999) *The Nineties: What The F**K Was That All About?* London: Ebury Press.

Robbins, W. G. (1994) *Colony and Empire: the Capitalist Transformation of the American West*, Lawrence, Kan.: University Press of Kansas.

Roberts, I. (1997) 'The Culture of Ownership and the Ownership of Culture', in R. K. Brown (ed.) *The Changing Shape of Work*, Basingstoke: Macmillan.

Roberts, R. (1973) *The Classic Slum: Salford Life in the First Quarter of the Century*, Harmondsworth: Penguin.

Robertson, R. (1992) *Globalization: Social Theory and Global Culture*, London: Sage.

—— (1995) 'Glocalization: Time-Space and Homogeneity-Heterogeneity', in M. Featherstone, S. Lash, and R. Robertson (eds.) *Global Modernities*, London: Sage.

Robins, D. and Cohen, P. (1978) *Knuckle Sandwich*, Harmondsworth: Penguin.

Robins, K. (1991) 'Tradition and Translation: National Culture in its Global Context', in J. Corner and S. Harvey (eds.) *Enterprise and Heritage: Crosscurrents of National Culture*, London: Routledge.

Rock, P. (1973) *Deviant Behaviour*, London: Hutchinson.

Rojek, C. (1985) *Capitalism and Leisure Theory*, London: Tavistock.

—— (1993) *Ways of Escape*, London: Macmillan.

—— (2000) 'Mass Tourism or the Re-Enchantment of the World?', in M. Gottdiener (ed.) *New forms of Consumption: Consumers, Culture, and Commodification*, Maryland: Rowman and Littlefield, 51–70.

Roncek, D. W. and Maier, P. A. (1991) 'Bars, Blocks, and Crimes Revisited: Linking the Theory of Routine Activities to the Empiricism of "Hot Spots"', *Criminology*, 29/4:725–753.

Room, R. and Collins, G. (eds.) (1983) *Alcohol and Disinhibition: Nature and Meaning of the Link*, Research Monograph No. 12, Rockville, Md.: National Institute of Alcohol Abuse and Alcoholism.

Rose, N. (1992) 'Governing the Enterprising Self', in P. Heelas and P. Morris (eds.) *The Values of the Enterprise Culture*, London: Routledge, 141–164.

Rubinstein, W. (1973) *City Police*, New York: Ballantine.

Ruggiero, V. (1993) 'Brixton, London: A Drug Culture without a Drug Economy?' *International Journal of Drug Policy*, 4/2:83–90.

—— (2000) *Crime and Markets: Essays in Anti-Criminology*, Oxford: Oxford University Press.

Russell, G. (1999) 'Toast of the Town: The Bars that Helped to Cheer Up the City', *Manchester Evening News*, Weekend Supplement, (3 July): 22.

Ryan, J. and Fitzpatrick, H. (1996) 'The Space that Difference Makes: Negotiation and Urban Identities through Consumption Practices', in J. O'Connor and D. Wynne (eds.) *From the Margins to the Centre: Cultural Production and Consumption in the Post-Industrial City*, Aldershot: Arena.

Ryan, M. and Ward, T. (1989) *Privatization and the Penal System*, Milton Keynes: Open University Press.

Sacks, H. (1972) 'Notes on Police Assessment of Moral Character', in D. Sudnow (ed.) *Studies in Social Interaction*, New York: The Free Press.

Saloman, A. (1955) 'Symbols and Images in the Constitution of Society', in L. Bryson, H. Finkelstein, H. Hoagland and R. M. MacIver (eds.) *Symbols and Society*, New York: Harper Collins.

Samuel, R. (1981) *East End Underworld: The Life and Times of Arthur Harding*, London: Routledge and Kegan Paul.

Savage, M. and Warde, A. (1993) *Urban Sociology, Capitalism and Modernity*, Basingstoke: Macmillan.

Sayette, M. A., Wilson, T., and Elias, M. J. (1993) 'Alcohol and Aggression: A Social Information Processing Analysis', *Journal of Studies on Alcohol*, 54:399–407.

Schechner, R. (1993) *The Future of Ritual*, London: Routledge.

Scott, A. J. (1997) 'The Cultural Economy of Cities', *International Journal of Urban and Regional Research*, 21/2:323–339.

Scott, C. (2000) 'Accountability in the Regulatory State', *Journal of Law and Society*, 27/1:38–60.

Sebald, W. S. (1993) *The Emigrants*, London: The Harvill Press.

Sennett, R. (1990) *The Conscience of the Eye*, London: Faber and Faber.

Shapely, P. (1998) 'Charity, Status and Leadership: Charitable Image and the Manchester Man', *Journal of Social History*, 32/1:157–177.

Shapland, J. (1999) 'Selling Safety: Police and Social Control', in J. Shapland and L. Van Outrive (eds.) *Policing and the Public/Private Divide*, Paris: L'Harmattan, 17–32.

Shaw, C. R. and McKay, H. D. (1942) *Juvenile Delinquency in Urban Areas*, Chicago: Chicago University Press.

Shearing, C. D. (1981) 'Subterranean Processes in the Maintenance of Power', *Canadian Review of Sociology and Anthropology*, 18/3:283–98.

——(2001) 'Punishment and the Changing Face of Governance', *Punishment and Society*, 3/2:203–220.

——Farnell, M., and Stenning, P. C. (eds.) (1980) *Contract Security*, Toronto: University of Toronto Press.

——and Stenning, P. C. (1981) 'Modern Private Security: Its Growth and Implications', in M. Tonry and N. Morris (eds.) *Crime and Justice: An Annual Review of Research, Vol.3*, Chicago: University of Chicago Press, 193–245.

——and——(1983a) 'Powers of Private Security Personnel', in A. Rees (ed.) *Policing and Private Security*, Canberra: Australian Institute of Criminology, 22–32.

——and——(1983b), 'Private Security: Implications for Social Control', *Social Problems*, 30/5:493–505.

Shepherd, J. (1990) 'Violent Crime in Bristol: An Accident and Emergency Perspective', *British Journal of Criminology*, 30/3:289–305.
—— and Lisles, C. (1998) 'Towards Multi-Agency Violence Prevention and Victim Support', *British Journal of Criminology*, 38/3:351–370.
Shepherd, J. P., Shapland, M., and Scully, C. (1989) 'Recording of Violent Offences by the Police: An Accident and Emergency Department Perspective', *Medicine, Science and the Law*, 29:251–257.
Shercliff, W. H. (1983) *Manchester: A Short History of its Development*, 6th edn., Manchester: Revell & George Limited.
Sherman, L. W., Gartin, P. R., and Buerger, M. E. (1989) 'Hot Spots of Predatory Crime: Routine Activities and the Criminology of Place', *Criminology*, 27:27–55.
Shields, R. (1991) *Places on the Margin: Alternative Geographies of Modernity*, Routledge: London.
—— (1992) 'Spaces for the Subject of Consumption', in R. Shields (ed.) *Lifestyle Shopping: The Subject of Consumption*, London: Routledge.
Shilling, C. (1993) *The Body and Social Theory*, London: Sage.
Shover, N. and Honaker, D. (1991) 'The Socially Bounded Decision Making of Persistent Property Offenders', *Howard Journal*, 31:276–93.
Silcott, M. (2000) 'Superclubs and the Mainstreaming of E Culture' in Push and M. Silcott (eds.) *The Book of E: All About Ecstasy*, London: Omnibus Press.
Silver, A. (1967) 'The Demand for Order in Civil Society', in D. Bordua (ed.) *The Police*, New York: Wiley.
Simmel, G. (1950) *The Sociology of Georg Simmel*, Glencoe: The Free Press.
—— (1978) [1900] *The Philosophy of Money*, translated by T. Bottomore and D. Frisby, London: Routledge.
—— (1995) [1903] 'The Metropolis and Mental Life', in P. Kasinitz (ed.) *Metropolis: Center and Symbol of our Times*, London: Macmillan.
Singleton, J. (1991) *Lancashire on the Scrapheap: The Cotton Industry 1945–1970*, Oxford: Oxford University Press.
Sitford, M. (1999) 'Gay for Gold as City Counts the Mardi Millions', *Manchester Evening News*, (31 August), p. 5.
Skeggs, B. (1999) 'Matter out of Place: Visibility and Sexualities in Leisure Spaces', *Leisure Studies*, 18:213–232.
Skogan, W. (1988) 'Community Organizations and Crime', in N. Morris and M. Tonry (eds.) *Crime and Justice: An Annual Review of Research*, Chicago: Chicago University Press, 39–78.
Skolnick, J. H. (1966) *Justice Without Trial*, New York: Wiley.
Slater, D. (1997) *Consumer Culture and Modernity*, Cambridge: Polity Press.
Smith, Jr., D. (1974) *The Mafia Mystique*, New York: Basic Books.
—— (1980) 'Paragons, Pariahs, and Pirates: A Spectrum-Based Theory of Enterprise', *Crime and Delinquency*, 26:58–86.

Van Maanen, J. (1978a) 'The Asshole', in P. K. Manning and J. Van Maanen (eds.) *Policing: A View from the Streets*, Santa Monica, Calif.: Goodyear.

—— (1978b) 'Socialization for Policing', in P. K. Manning and J. Van Maanen (eds.) *Policing: A View for the Streets*, Santa Monica, Calif.: Goodyear.

Veblen, T. (1994) [1899] *The Theory of the Leisure Class*, London: Constable.

Wacquant, L. (1992) 'The Social Logic of Boxing in Black Chicago: Towards a Sociology of Pugilism', *Sociology of Sport Journal*, 7/3, 221–54.

—— (1995a) 'Review Article: Why Men Desire Muscles', *Body and Society*, 1/1:163–79.

—— (1995b) 'Pugs at Work: The Self-Production of Professional Fighters', *Body and Society*, 1/1:65–93.

Walker, A. (1999) *The Safer Doors Project*, London: Home Office Policing and Reducing Crime Unit.

Waller, T. (1999) *Manchester City Council's Support for the Lesbian and Gay Village*, Manchester: Manchester City Council.

Walsh, B. (1998) 'The 24-Hour City—Do We Really Want It?' *Urban Environment Today*, 26 November: 7–8.

Warburton, A. L. and Shepherd, J. P. (2002) *An Evaluation of the Effectiveness of New Policies Designed to Prevent and Manage Violence through an Interagency Approach (a Final Report for WORD)*, Cardiff: Cardiff Violence Research Group.

Ward, S. V. (1998) *Selling Places: The Marketing and Promotion of Towns and Cities 1850–2000*, London: Spon.

Warren, R. L. (1973) *The Community in America*, New York: Rand McNally.

Weber, M. (1978) *Economy and Society* (2 vols), Berkeley: University of California Press.

Webster, N. (1999a) 'City of the Future', *Manchester Evening News*, (12 August):8–9.

—— (1999b) 'Just Manc-Tastic', *Manchester Evening News*, (19 August): 8–9.

Weir, A. (1984) 'Obsessed with Moderation: The Drinks Trade and the Drink Question (1870–1930)', *British Journal of Addiction*, 79:93–107.

Wells, S. and Graham, K. (1999) 'The Frequency of Third Party Involvement in Incidents of Barroom Aggression', *Contemporary Drugs Problems*, 26:457–480.

Welsh, B. C. and Farrington, D. P. (2002) *Crime Prevention Effects of Closed Circuit Television: A Systematic Review*, Home Office Research Study 252, London: RDSD.

South, N. (1988) *Policing for Profit*. London: Sage.

—— (1999) 'Debating Drugs and Everyday Life: Normalization, Prohibition and "Otherness"', in N. South (ed.) *Drugs: Cultures, Control and Everyday Life*, London: Sage.

—— (2001) 'Police, Security and Information: The Use of Informants and Agents in a Liberal Democracy', in S. Einstein and M. Amir (eds.) *Policing Security and Democracy: Special Aspects of Democratic Policing*, Huntsville: OICJ.

Southgate, P. (1986) *Police–Public Encounters*, London: HMSO

Spinoza, A. (1999) 'A Mancunian's home is his Castlefield', *Manchester Life*, (May/June):15–17.

Spitzer, S. (1979) 'The Rationalization of Crime Control in Capitalist Society', *Contemporary Crises*, 3:187–206.

—— (1987) 'Security and Control in Capitalist Societies: The Fetishism of Security and the Secret Thereof', in J. Lowman, R. J. Menzies, and T. S. Palys (eds.) *Transcarceration: Essays in the Sociology of Social Control*, Aldershot: Gower.

—— and Scull, A. (1977) 'Privatization and Capitalist Development: The Case of Private Police', *Social Problems*, 25/1:18–29.

Stedman-Jones, G. (1971) *Outcast London*, London: Oxford University Press.

Steedman, C. (1984) *Policing the Victorian Community*, London: Routledge & Kegan Paul.

Stenning, P. C. (1989) 'Private Police and Public Police: Toward a Redefinition of the Police Role', in D. Loree (ed.) *Future Issues in Policy: Symposium Proceedings*, Ottawa: Minister of Supply and Services Canada, 169–192.

—— (1995) 'Introduction' in P. Stenning (ed.) *Accountability for Criminal Justice*, Toronto: University of Toronto Press, 3–14.

—— (2000) 'Powers and Accountability of Private Police', *European Journal of Criminal Policy and Research*, 8/3:325–352.

—— and Shearing, C. D. (1979) 'Private Security and Private Justice', *The British Journal of Law and Society*, 12/6:261–271.

—— and —— (1984) 'Corporate Justice: Some Preliminary Thoughts', *Australian and New Zealand Journal of Criminology*, 17/2:79–86.

Stenson, K. and Watt, P. (1998) 'The Street: "It's a Bit Dodgy Around There", Safety, Danger, Ethnicity and Young People's Use of Public Space', in T. Skelton and G. Valentine (eds.) *Cool Places: Geographies of Youth Cultures*, London: Routledge.

Stigler, G. (1971) 'The Theory of Economic Regulation', *Bell Journal of Economics*, 2: 2–31.

—— (1975) *The Citizen and the State*, Chicago: University of Chicago Press.

Stoker, G. (1988) *The Politics of Local Government*, Basingstoke: Macmillan.

Storch, R. D. (1976) 'The Policeman as Domestic Missionary: Urban Discipline and Popular Culture in Northern England, 1850–1880', *Journal of Social History*, 4:481–509.

Strangleman, T. and Roberts, I. (1999) 'Looking Through the Window of Opportunity: The Cultural Cleansing of Workplace Identity', *Sociology*, 33/1:47–67.

Swanton, O. (1997) 'Gangchester/Bright Lights, Big Trouble', *Manchester Evening News*, 15 December:9 and 16 December:9.

——(1998) 'Gang Law', *Mixmag*, February (Issue 81): 68–76.

Sykes, G. M. and Matza, D. (1962) 'Techniques of Neutralization: A Theory of Delinquency', in M. E. Wolfgang, L. Savitz, and N. Johnston (eds.) *The Sociology of Crime and Delinquency*, New York: John Wiley & Sons.

Sykes, R. and Clark, J. (1975) 'A Theory of Deference Exchange in Police-Civilian Encounters', *American Journal of Sociology*, 81:587–595.

Taylor, H. (1998) 'Rationing Crime: The Political Economy of Criminal Statistics Since the 1850s', *Economic History Review*, LI (3):569–590.

——(1999) *Forging the Job: A Crisis of 'Modernization' or Redundancy for the Police in England and Wales, 1900–39, British Journal of Criminology* 39/1:113–135.

Taylor, I. (1999) *Crime in Context*, Cambridge: Polity.

——Evans, K. and Fraser, P. (1996) *A Tale of Two Cities: Global Change, Local Feeling and Everyday Life in the North of England. A Study in Manchester and Sheffield*, London: Routledge.

——and Jamieson, R. (1997) 'Proper Little Mesters: Nostalgia and Protest Masculinity in De-industrialised Sheffield' in S. Westwood, and J. Williams (eds.) *Imagining Cities, Scripts, Signs, Memory*, London: Routledge.

Tedeschi, J. T. and Felson, R. B. (1994) *Violence, Aggression and Coercive Actions*, Washington, DC: American Psychological Association.

Thom, B. (1999) *Dealing With Drink: Alcohol and Social Policy From Treatment to Management*, London: Free Association Books.

Thomas, C. J. and Bromley, R. D. F. (2000) 'City-centre Revitalisation: Problems of Fragmentation and Fear in the Evening and Night-time Economy', *Urban Studies*, 37:1403–1429.

Thompson, E. P. (1963) *The Making of the English Working Class*, Harmondsworth: Penguin.

——(1967) 'Time, Work-Discipline and Industrial Capitalism', *Past and Present*, 38:56–97.

Thompson, G. (1994) *Watch My Back: A Bouncer's Story*, Chichester: Summersdale.

Thompson, T. (1995) *Gangland Britain*, London: Hodder and Stoughton.

——(2001) 'Fear Grips Liverpool as Gang Feud Claims its Sixth Victim', *The Observer*, 14 October: 3.

Thornton, S. (1994) 'Moral Panic, the Media and British Rave Culture', in A. Ross and T. Rose (eds.) *Microphone Fiends: Youth Music and Youth Culture*, London: Routledge.

——(1995) *Club Cultures: Music, Media and Subcultural Capital*, Cambridge: Polity.

Tickell, A. and Peck, J. A. (1996) 'The Return of the Manchester Men: Men's Words and Men's Deeds in the Remaking of the Local State', *Transactions of the Institute of British Geographers*, 21/4:595–616.

Tierney, J. and Hobbs, D. (2003) *Alcohol-related Crime and Disorder Data: Guidance for Local Partnerships*, London: Home Office.

Tobias, J. J. (1979) *Crime and Police in England 1700–1900*, London: Gill and Macmillan.

Toch, H. (1993) 'Good Violence and Bad Violence: Self-Presentation of Aggressors Through Accounts and War Stories', in R. B. Felson and J. Tedeschi (eds.) *Aggression and Violence: Social Interactionist Perspectives*, Washington, DC: American Psychological Association, 193–206.

Tomsen, S. (1997) 'A Top Night: Social Protest, Masculinity and the Culture of Drinking Violence', *British Journal of Criminology*, 37/1:90–102.

——Homel, R. and Thommeny, J. (1991) 'The Causes of Public Violence: Situational "Versus" Other Factors in Drinking-Related Assaults', in D. Chappell, P. Grabosky and H. Strang (eds.) *Australian Violence: Contemporary Perspectives*, Canberra: Australian Institute of Criminology.

Town Centres Limited (2001) *West End Entertainment Impact Study: Final Report, 2001*, London: City of Westminster.

Trachtenberg, A. (1982) *The Incorporation of America*, New York: Hill and Wang.

Tuck, M. (1989) *Drinking and Disorder: A Study of Non-Metropolitan Violence*, Home Office Research Study No. 108, London: HMSO.

Tupling, G. H. (1934) 'Old Manchester: A Sketch of its Growth to the End of the Eighteenth Century', reprinted in *The Manchester Geographer*, 5, (1984): 106–115.

Turner, V. (1967) *The Forest of Symbols*, Ithaca, NY: Cornell University Press.

——(1969) *The Ritual Process*, London: Routledge and Kegan Paul.

——(1974) *Drama, Fields and Metaphors*, Ithaca, NY: Cornell University Press.

Tyler, G. (1962) (ed.) *Organized Crime in America*, Ann Arbor: University of Michigan Press.

Urban Environment Today (2002) 'MPs Condemn "Unworkable" Planning Green Paper', *Urban Environment Today*, 151, 13 July:3.

Urry, J. (1990) *The Tourist Gaze*, London: Sage.

Valverde, M. (1998) *Diseases of the Will: Alcohol and the Dilemmas of Freedom*, Cambridge: Cambridge University Press.

Westley, W. (1953) 'Violence and the Police', *American Journal of Sociology*, 59/1 (July):34–41.

—— (1970) *Violence and the Police*, Cambridge Mass.: MIT.

Westmarland, L. (2001) *Gender and Policing: Sex Power and Police Culture*, Cullompton: Willan.

White, J. (1980) *Rothschild Buildings: Life in an East End Tenement Block*, London: Routledge.

Whittle, S. (1994) 'Consuming Differences: The Collaboration of the Gay Body with the Cultural State', in S. Whittle (ed.) *The Margins of the City: Gay Men's Urban Lives*, Aldershot: Arena.

Widdicombe, S. and Wooffitt, R. (1995) *The Language of Youth Subcultures*, London: Harvester Wheatsheaf.

Wikström, P.-O. (1995) 'Preventing City Centre Street Crimes', in M. Tonry and D. P. Farrington (eds.) *Building a Safer Society: Strategic Approaches to Crime Prevention, Crime and Justice: A Review of Research, Vol. 19*, London: University of Chicago Press.

Wilk, R. (1995) 'Learning to be Local in Belize: Global Systems of Common Difference', in D. Miller (ed.) *Worlds Apart: Modernity Through the Prism of the Local*, London: Routledge.

Williams, G. P. and Brake, G. T. (1980) *Drink in Great Britain 1900–1979*, London: Edsall.

Williams, R. (2000) *Making Identity Matter: Identity, Society and Social Interaction*, Durham: Sociologypress.

Willis, P. (1977) *Learning to Labour*, London: Saxon House.

—— (1990) *Common Culture*, Milton Keynes: Open University Press.

Wilson, A. H. (2002) *24-Hour Party People: What The Sleeve Notes Never Tell You*, London: Channel 4 Books.

Wilson, E. (1991) *The Sphinx and the City*, Virago: London.

Wilson, G. B. (1940) *Alcohol and the Nation*, London: Nicholson and Watson.

Wilson, J. Q. (1968) *Varieties of Police Behaviour*, Cambridge Mass.: Harvard University Press.

Winlow, S. (2001) *Badfellas: Crime, Tradition and New Masculinities*, Oxford: Berg.

—— (forthcoming) *Night and the City: Youth Identities, Violence and the Business of Pleasure after Dark*, Oxford: Berg.

—— Hobbs, D., Lister, S., and Hadfield, P. (2001) 'Get Ready to Duck: Bouncers and the Realities of Ethnographic Research on Violent Groups', *British Journal of Criminology, Special Issue: Methodological Dilemmas of Research*, 41/3:536–548.

—— —— and —— (2002) 'Bouncers and the Social Context of Violence: Masculinity, Class and Violence in the Night-time Economy' in E. Stanko (ed.) *The Meanings of Violence: Volume 1*, London: Routledge.

Wirth, J. D. (1978) 'Introduction' in J. D. Wirth and R. L. Jones (eds.) *Manchester and Sao Paulo: Problems of Rapid Urban Growth*, Stanford Calif.: Stanford University Press.

Wirth, L. [1938] (1995) 'Urbanism as a Way of Life', in P. Kasinitz (ed.) *Metropolis: Centre and Symbol of Our Times*, London: Macmillan.

Worpole, K. (1991) 'The Age of Leisure' in J. Corner and S. Harvey (eds.) *Enterprise and Heritage: Crosscurrents of National Culture*, London: Routledge.

——(1992) *Towns for People: Transforming Urban Life*, Buckingham: Open University Press.

Wynne, D. and O'Connor, J. (with statistical analysis by Dianne Phillips), 'Consumption and the Postmodern City', *Urban Studies*, 35/5–6: 841–864.

Yllo, K. A. (1993) 'Through a Feminist Lens: Gender, Power and Violence', in R. J. Gelles and D. R. Loseke (eds.) *Current Controversies on Family Violence*, Newbury Park, Calif: Sage, 47–63.

Zukin, S. (1991) *Landscapes of Power: From Detroit to Disney World*, Berkeley: University of California Press.

——(1998) 'Urban Lifestyles: Diversity and Standardisation in Spaces of Consumption', *Urban Studies*, 35(5–6):825–839.

Cases

R. (on the application of Barry) v. Liverpool City Council [2001] EWCA 384 *The Times*, 27 March 2001.

Index

South, N. (1988) *Policing for Profit*. London: Sage.

—— (1999) 'Debating Drugs and Everyday Life: Normalization, Prohibition and "Otherness" ', in N. South (ed.) *Drugs: Cultures, Control and Everyday Life*, London: Sage.

—— (2001) 'Police, Security and Information: The Use of Informants and Agents in a Liberal Democracy', in S. Einstein and M. Amir (eds.) *Policing Security and Democracy: Special Aspects of Democratic Policing*, Huntsville: OICJ.

Southgate, P. (1986) *Police–Public Encounters*, London: HMSO

Spinoza, A. (1999) 'A Mancunian's home is his Castlefield', *Manchester Life*, (May/June):15–17.

Spitzer, S. (1979) 'The Rationalization of Crime Control in Capitalist Society', *Contemporary Crises*, 3:187–206.

—— (1987) 'Security and Control in Capitalist Societies: The Fetishism of Security and the Secret Thereof', in J. Lowman, R. J. Menzies, and T. S. Palys (eds.) *Transcarceration: Essays in the Sociology of Social Control*, Aldershot: Gower.

—— and Scull, A. (1977) 'Privatization and Capitalist Development: The Case of Private Police', *Social Problems*, 25/1:18–29.

Stedman-Jones, G. (1971) *Outcast London*, London: Oxford University Press.

Steedman, C. (1984) *Policing the Victorian Community*, London: Routledge & Kegan Paul.

Stenning, P. C. (1989) 'Private Police and Public Police: Toward a Redefinition of the Police Role', in D. Loree (ed.) *Future Issues in Policy: Symposium Proceedings*, Ottawa: Minister of Supply and Services Canada, 169–192.

—— (1995) 'Introduction' in P. Stenning (ed.) *Accountability for Criminal Justice*, Toronto: University of Toronto Press, 3–14.

—— (2000) 'Powers and Accountability of Private Police', *European Journal of Criminal Policy and Research*, 8/3:325–352.

—— and Shearing, C. D. (1979) 'Private Security and Private Justice', *The British Journal of Law and Society*, 12/6:261–271.

—— and —— (1984) 'Corporate Justice: Some Preliminary Thoughts', *Australian and New Zealand Journal of Criminology*, 17/2:79–86.

Stenson, K. and Watt, P. (1998) 'The Street: "It's a Bit Dodgy Around There", Safety, Danger, Ethnicity and Young People's Use of Public Space', in T. Skelton and G. Valentine (eds.) *Cool Places: Geographies of Youth Cultures*, London: Routledge.

Stigler, G. (1971) 'The Theory of Economic Regulation', *Bell Journal of Economics*, 2: 2–31.

—— (1975) *The Citizen and the State*, Chicago: University of Chicago Press.

Stoker, G. (1988) *The Politics of Local Government*, Basingstoke: Macmillan.

Storch, R. D. (1976) 'The Policeman as Domestic Missionary: Urban Discipline and Popular Culture in Northern England, 1850–1880', *Journal of Social History*, 4:481–509.

Strangleman, T. and Roberts, I. (1999) 'Looking Through the Window of Opportunity: The Cultural Cleansing of Workplace Identity', *Sociology*, 33/1:47–67.

Swanton, O. (1997) 'Gangchester/Bright Lights, Big Trouble', *Manchester Evening News*, 15 December:9 and 16 December:9.

——(1998) 'Gang Law', *Mixmag*, February (Issue 81): 68–76.

Sykes, G. M. and Matza, D. (1962) 'Techniques of Neutralization: A Theory of Delinquency', in M. E. Wolfgang, L. Savitz, and N. Johnston (eds.) *The Sociology of Crime and Delinquency*, New York: John Wiley & Sons.

Sykes, R. and Clark, J. (1975) 'A Theory of Deference Exchange in Police-Civilian Encounters', *American Journal of Sociology*, 81:587–595.

Taylor, H. (1998) 'Rationing Crime: The Political Economy of Criminal Statistics Since the 1850s', *Economic History Review*, LI (3):569–590.

——(1999) *Forging the Job: A Crisis of 'Modernization' or Redundancy for the Police in England and Wales, 1900–39*, British Journal of Criminology 39/1:113–135.

Taylor, I. (1999) *Crime in Context*, Cambridge: Polity.

——Evans, K. and Fraser, P. (1996) *A Tale of Two Cities: Global Change, Local Feeling and Everyday Life in the North of England. A Study in Manchester and Sheffield*, London: Routledge.

——and Jamieson, R. (1997) 'Proper Little Mesters: Nostalgia and Protest Masculinity in De-industrialised Sheffield' in S. Westwood, and J. Williams (eds.) *Imagining Cities, Scripts, Signs, Memory*, London: Routledge.

Tedeschi, J. T. and Felson, R. B. (1994) *Violence, Aggression and Coercive Actions*, Washington, DC: American Psychological Association.

Thom, B. (1999) *Dealing With Drink: Alcohol and Social Policy From Treatment to Management*, London: Free Association Books.

Thomas, C. J. and Bromley, R. D. F. (2000) 'City-centre Revitalisation: Problems of Fragmentation and Fear in the Evening and Night-time Economy', *Urban Studies*, 37:1403–1429.

Thompson, E. P. (1963) *The Making of the English Working Class*, Harmondsworth: Penguin.

——(1967) 'Time, Work-Discipline and Industrial Capitalism', *Past and Present*, 38:56–97.

Thompson, G. (1994) *Watch My Back: A Bouncer's Story*, Chichester: Summersdale.

Thompson, T. (1995) *Gangland Britain*, London: Hodder and Stoughton.

——(2001) 'Fear Grips Liverpool as Gang Feud Claims its Sixth Victim', *The Observer*, 14 October: 3.

Thornton, S. (1994) 'Moral Panic, the Media and British Rave Culture', in A. Ross and T. Rose (eds.) *Microphone Fiends: Youth Music and Youth Culture*, London: Routledge.

—— (1995) *Club Cultures: Music, Media and Subcultural Capital*, Cambridge: Polity.

Tickell, A. and Peck, J. A. (1996) 'The Return of the Manchester Men: Men's Words and Men's Deeds in the Remaking of the Local State', *Transactions of the Institute of British Geographers*, 21/4:595–616.

Tierney, J. and Hobbs, D. (2003) *Alcohol-related Crime and Disorder Data: Guidance for Local Partnerships*, London: Home Office.

Tobias, J. J. (1979) *Crime and Police in England 1700–1900*, London: Gill and Macmillan.

Toch, H. (1993) 'Good Violence and Bad Violence: Self-Presentation of Aggressors Through Accounts and War Stories', in R. B. Felson and J. Tedeschi (eds.) *Aggression and Violence: Social Interactionist Perspectives*, Washington, DC: American Psychological Association, 193–206.

Tomsen, S. (1997) 'A Top Night: Social Protest, Masculinity and the Culture of Drinking Violence', *British Journal of Criminology*, 37/1:90–102.

—— Homel, R. and Thommeny, J. (1991) 'The Causes of Public Violence: Situational "Versus" Other Factors in Drinking-Related Assaults', in D. Chappell, P. Grabosky and H. Strang (eds.) *Australian Violence: Contemporary Perspectives*, Canberra: Australian Institute of Criminology.

Town Centres Limited (2001) *West End Entertainment Impact Study: Final Report, 2001*, London: City of Westminster.

Trachtenberg, A. (1982) *The Incorporation of America*, New York: Hill and Wang.

Tuck, M. (1989) *Drinking and Disorder: A Study of Non-Metropolitan Violence*, Home Office Research Study No. 108, London: HMSO.

Tupling, G. H. (1934) 'Old Manchester: A Sketch of its Growth to the End of the Eighteenth Century', reprinted in *The Manchester Geographer*, 5, (1984): 106–115.

Turner, V. (1967) *The Forest of Symbols*, Ithaca, NY: Cornell University Press.

—— (1969) *The Ritual Process*, London: Routledge and Kegan Paul.

—— (1974) *Drama, Fields and Metaphors*, Ithaca, NY: Cornell University Press.

Tyler, G. (1962) (ed.) *Organized Crime in America*, Ann Arbor: University of Michigan Press.

Urban Environment Today (2002) 'MPs Condemn "Unworkable" Planning Green Paper', *Urban Environment Today*, 151, 13 July:3.

Urry, J. (1990) *The Tourist Gaze*, London: Sage.

Valverde, M. (1998) *Diseases of the Will: Alcohol and the Dilemmas of Freedom*, Cambridge: Cambridge University Press.

312 References

Van Maanen, J. (1978a) 'The Asshole', in P. K. Manning and J. Van Maanen (eds.) *Policing: A View from the Streets*, Santa Monica, Calif.: Goodyear.

—— (1978b) 'Socialization for Policing', in P. K. Manning and J. Van Maanen (eds.) *Policing: A View for the Streets*, Santa Monica, Calif.: Goodyear.

Veblen, T. (1994) [1899] *The Theory of the Leisure Class*, London: Constable.

Wacquant, L. (1992) 'The Social Logic of Boxing in Black Chicago: Towards a Sociology of Pugilism', *Sociology of Sport Journal*, 7/3, 221–54.

—— (1995a) 'Review Article: Why Men Desire Muscles', *Body and Society*, 1/1:163–79.

—— (1995b) 'Pugs at Work: The Self-Production of Professional Fighters', *Body and Society*, 1/1:65–93.

Walker, A. (1999) *The Safer Doors Project*, London: Home Office Policing and Reducing Crime Unit.

Waller, T. (1999) *Manchester City Council's Support for the Lesbian and Gay Village*, Manchester: Manchester City Council.

Walsh, B. (1998) 'The 24-Hour City—Do We Really Want It?' *Urban Environment Today*, 26 November: 7–8.

Warburton, A. L. and Shepherd, J. P. (2002) *An Evaluation of the Effectiveness of New Policies Designed to Prevent and Manage Violence through an Interagency Approach (a Final Report for WORD)*, Cardiff: Cardiff Violence Research Group.

Ward, S. V. (1998) *Selling Places: The Marketing and Promotion of Towns and Cities 1850–2000*, London: Spon.

Warren, R. L. (1973) *The Community in America*, New York: Rand McNally.

Weber, M. (1978) *Economy and Society* (2 vols), Berkeley: University of California Press.

Webster, N. (1999a) 'City of the Future', *Manchester Evening News*, (12 August):8–9.

—— (1999b) 'Just Manc-Tastic', *Manchester Evening News*, (19 August): 8–9.

Weir, A. (1984) 'Obsessed with Moderation: The Drinks Trade and the Drink Question (1870–1930)', *British Journal of Addiction*, 79:93–107.

Wells, S. and Graham, K. (1999) 'The Frequency of Third Party Involvement in Incidents of Barroom Aggression', *Contemporary Drugs Problems*, 26:457–480.

Welsh, B. C. and Farrington, D. P. (2002) *Crime Prevention Effects of Closed Circuit Television: A Systematic Review*, Home Office Research Study 252, London: RDSD.

Westley, W. (1953) 'Violence and the Police', *American Journal of Sociology*, 59/1 (July):34–41.
—— (1970) *Violence and the Police*, Cambridge Mass.: MIT.
Westmarland, L. (2001) *Gender and Policing: Sex Power and Police Culture*, Cullompton: Willan.
White, J. (1980) *Rothschild Buildings: Life in an East End Tenement Block*, London: Routledge.
Whittle, S. (1994) 'Consuming Differences: The Collaboration of the Gay Body with the Cultural State', in S. Whittle (ed.) *The Margins of the City: Gay Men's Urban Lives*, Aldershot: Arena.
Widdicombe, S. and Wooffitt, R. (1995) *The Language of Youth Subcultures*, London: Harvester Wheatsheaf.
Wikström, P.-O. (1995) 'Preventing City Centre Street Crimes', in M. Tonry and D. P. Farrington (eds.) *Building a Safer Society: Strategic Approaches to Crime Prevention, Crime and Justice: A Review of Research, Vol. 19*, London: University of Chicago Press.
Wilk, R. (1995) 'Learning to be Local in Belize: Global Systems of Common Difference', in D. Miller (ed.) *Worlds Apart: Modernity Through the Prism of the Local*, London: Routledge.
Williams, G. P. and Brake, G. T. (1980) *Drink in Great Britain 1900–1979*, London: Edsall.
Williams, R. (2000) *Making Identity Matter: Identity, Society and Social Interaction*, Durham: Sociologypress.
Willis, P. (1977) *Learning to Labour*, London: Saxon House.
—— (1990) *Common Culture*, Milton Keynes: Open University Press.
Wilson, A. H. (2002) *24-Hour Party People: What The Sleeve Notes Never Tell You*, London: Channel 4 Books.
Wilson, E. (1991) *The Sphinx and the City*, Virago: London.
Wilson, G. B. (1940) *Alcohol and the Nation*, London: Nicholson and Watson.
Wilson, J. Q. (1968) *Varieties of Police Behaviour*, Cambridge Mass.: Harvard University Press.
Winlow, S. (2001) *Badfellas: Crime, Tradition and New Masculinities*, Oxford: Berg.
—— (forthcoming) *Night and the City: Youth Identities, Violence and the Business of Pleasure after Dark*, Oxford: Berg.
—— Hobbs, D., Lister, S., and Hadfield, P. (2001) 'Get Ready to Duck: Bouncers and the Realities of Ethnographic Research on Violent Groups', *British Journal of Criminology, Special Issue: Methodological Dilemmas of Research*, 41/3:536–548.
—————— and —— (2002) 'Bouncers and the Social Context of Violence: Masculinity, Class and Violence in the Night-time Economy' in E. Stanko (ed.) *The Meanings of Violence: Volume 1*, London: Routledge.

Wirth, J. D. (1978) 'Introduction' in J. D. Wirth and R. L. Jones (eds.) *Manchester and Sao Paulo: Problems of Rapid Urban Growth*, Stanford Calif.: Stanford University Press.

Wirth, L. [1938] (1995) 'Urbanism as a Way of Life', in P. Kasinitz (ed.) *Metropolis: Centre and Symbol of Our Times*, London: Macmillan.

Worpole, K. (1991) 'The Age of Leisure' in J. Corner and S. Harvey (eds.) *Enterprise and Heritage: Crosscurrents of National Culture*, London: Routledge.

——(1992) *Towns for People: Transforming Urban Life*, Buckingham: Open University Press.

Wynne, D. and O'Connor, J. (with statistical analysis by Dianne Phillips), 'Consumption and the Postmodern City', *Urban Studies*, 35/5–6: 841–864.

Yllo, K. A. (1993) 'Through a Feminist Lens: Gender, Power and Violence', in R. J. Gelles and D. R. Loseke (eds.) *Current Controversies on Family Violence*, Newbury Park, Calif: Sage, 47–63.

Zukin, S. (1991) *Landscapes of Power: From Detroit to Disney World*, Berkeley: University of California Press.

——(1998) 'Urban Lifestyles: Diversity and Standardisation in Spaces of Consumption', *Urban Studies*, 35(5–6):825–839.

Cases

R. (on the application of Barry) v. *Liverpool City Council* [2001] EWCA 384 *The Times*, 27 March 2001.

Index

Printed in the United Kingdom
by Lightning Source UK Ltd.
135399UK00001BA/2/P